MW00814000

CLYMER®
MANUALS

YAMAHA
V-STAR 1300 • 2007-2010

WHAT'S IN YOUR TOOLBOX?

More information available at haynes.com
Phone: 805-498-6703

J H Haynes & Co. Ltd.
Haynes North America, Inc.

ISBN-10: 1-59969-379-8
ISBN-13: 978-1-59969-379-8
Library of Congress: 2011920349

Author: *Clymer Staff*
Technical Photography: *George Parise and Curt Jordan at Jordan Engineering, Oceanside, CA*
Technical Illustrations: *Errol and Mitzi McCarthy*
Wiring Diagrams: *Bob Meyer*
Cover: *Mark Clifford Photography at www.markclifford.com*
2009 V-Star 1300 courtesy of Bert's Mega Mall at bertsmotorcyclemall.com

© Haynes North America, Inc. 2011
With permission from J.H. Haynes & Co. Ltd.

Clymer is a registered trademark of Haynes North America, Inc.

All rights reserved. No part of this book may be reproduced or transmitted in any form or by any means, electronic or mechanical, including photocopying, recording or by any information storage or retrieval system, without permission in writing from the copyright holder.

There are risks associated with automotive repairs. The ability to make repairs depends on individual skill, experience and proper tools. Individuals should act with due care and acknowledge and assume the risk of making automotive repairs. While every attempt is made to ensure that the information in this manual is correct, no liability can be accepted by the authors or publishers for loss, damage or injury caused by any errors in, or omissions from, the information given.

Common spark plug conditions

NORMAL
Symptoms: Brown to grayish-tan color and slight electrode wear. Correct heat range for engine and operating conditions.
Recommendation: When new spark plugs are installed, replace with plugs of the same heat range.

WORN
Symptoms: Rounded electrodes with a small amount of deposits on the firing end. Normal color. Causes hard starting in damp or cold weather and poor fuel economy.
Recommendation: Plugs have been left in the engine too long. Replace with new plugs of the same heat range. Follow the recommended maintenance schedule.

TOO HOT
Symptoms: Blistered, white insulator, eroded electrode and absence of deposits. Results in shortened plug life.
Recommendation: Check for the correct plug heat range, over-advanced ignition timing, lean fuel mixture, intake manifold vacuum leaks, sticking valves and insufficient engine cooling.

CARBON DEPOSITS
Symptoms: Dry sooty deposits indicate a rich mixture or weak ignition. Causes misfiring, hard starting and hesitation.
Recommendation: Make sure the plug has the correct heat range. Check for a clogged air filter or problem in the fuel system or engine management system. Also check for ignition system problems.

PREIGNITION
Symptoms: Melted electrodes. Insulators are white, but may be dirty due to misfiring or flying debris in the combustion chamber. Can lead to engine damage.
Recommendation: Check for the correct plug heat range, over-advanced ignition timing, lean fuel mixture, insufficient engine cooling and lack of lubrication.

ASH DEPOSITS
Symptoms: Light brown deposits encrusted on the side or center electrodes or both. Derived from oil and/or fuel additives. Excessive amounts may mask the spark, causing misfiring and hesitation during acceleration.
Recommendation: If excessive deposits accumulate over a short time or low mileage, install new valve guide seals to prevent seepage of oil into the combustion chambers. Also try changing gasoline brands.

HIGH SPEED GLAZING
Symptoms: Insulator has yellowish, glazed appearance. Indicates that combustion chamber temperatures have risen suddenly during hard acceleration. Normal deposits melt to form a conductive coating. Causes misfiring at high speeds.
Recommendation: Install new plugs. Consider using a colder plug if driving habits warrant.

OIL DEPOSITS
Symptoms: Oily coating caused by poor oil control. Oil is leaking past worn valve guides or piston rings into the combustion chamber. Causes hard starting, misfiring and hesitation.
Recommendation: Correct the mechanical condition with necessary repairs and install new plugs.

DETONATION
Symptoms: Insulators may be cracked or chipped. Improper gap setting techniques can also result in a fractured insulator tip. Can lead to piston damage.
Recommendation: Make sure the fuel anti-knock values meet engine requirements. Use care when setting the gaps on new plugs. Avoid lugging the engine.

GAP BRIDGING
Symptoms: Combustion deposits lodge between the electrodes. Heavy deposits accumulate and bridge the electrode gap. The plug ceases to fire, resulting in a dead cylinder.
Recommendation: Locate the faulty plug and remove the deposits from between the electrodes.

MECHANICAL DAMAGE
Symptoms: May be caused by a foreign object in the combustion chamber or the piston striking an incorrect reach (too long) plug. Causes a dead cylinder and could result in piston damage.
Recommendation: Repair the mechanical damage. Remove the foreign object from the engine and/or install the correct reach plug.

CONTENTS

QUICK REFERENCE DATA

MOTORCYCLE INFORMATION

MODEL:_____ YEAR:_____

VIN NUMBER:_____

ENGINE SERIAL NUMBER:_____

TIRE SPECIFICATIONS

Item	Specification
Front Tire	
Type	Tubeless
Size	130/90-16M/C 67H
Model	
Dunlop	D404F X
Bridgestone	EXEDRA G721
Wear limit	1.0 mm (0.04 in.)
Rear Tire	
Type	Tubeless
Size	170/70B 16M/C 75H
Model	
Dunlop	K555
Bridgestone	EXEDRA G722 G
Wear limit	1.0 mm (0.04 in.)
Tire inflation pressure (cold)[1]	
Front	250 kPa (36 psi)
Rear	280 kPa (41 psi)
Maximum load[2]	
XVS13A models	210 kg (463 lb.)
XVS13CT models	190 kg (419 lb.)
Wheel runout limit	
Radial	1.0 mm (0.04 in.)
Lateral	0.5 mm (0.02 in.)

1. Tire inflation pressures apply to original equipment tires only. Aftermarket tires may require different pressures. Refer to the tire manufacturer's specifications.
2. Load equals the total weight of rider, passenger, accessories and all cargo.

RECOMMENDED LUBRICANTS AND FLUIDS

Brake fluid	DOT 4
Cable lubricant	Cable lubricant or engine oil
Coolant quantity	
Total system capacity	2.10 L (2.22 qt.)
Radiator capacity	0.55 L (0.58 qt.)
Reservoir capacity (to FULL level line)	0.45 L (0.48 qt.)
Coolant temperature	90-100° C (194-212° F)
Engine oil	
Classification	API SG or SH, JASO MA
Viscosity	SAE 20W40
Quantity	
Oil change only	3.20 L (3.38 qt.)
Oil and filter change	3.40 L (3.59 qt.)
When totally dry	3.70 L (3.91 qt.)
Oil temperature	70-80° C (158-176° F)

(continued)

RECOMMENDED LUBRICANTS AND FLUIDS (continued)

Fuel	Regular unleaded
Pump octane	86 (R+M) / 2 method
Research octane	91 or higher
Fuel tank capacity	
Total	18.5 L (4.89 gal.)
Reserve	3.7 L (0.98 gal.)

MAINTENANCE SPECIFICATIONS

Item	Specification
Brake lever free play (at lever end)	2-5 mm (0.08-0.20 in.)
Brake pad wear limit	0.8 mm (0.03 in.)
Clutch cable free play (at lever end)	5-10 mm (0.20-0.39 in.)
Compression pressure	
Standard pressure @ sea level	1450 kPa (210 psi) @ 400 rpm
Minimum-Maximum pressure	1200-1500 kPa (170-218 psi)
Drive belt free play	
Motorcycle on the sidestand	5.0-7.0 mm (0.20-0.28 in.)
Motorcycle on a suitable stand	4.0-6.0 mm (0.16-0.24 in.)
Engine idle speed	950-1050 rpm
Intake vacuum pressure	32.0-37.3 kPa (240-280 mm Hg)
Ignition minimum spark gap	6 mm (0.24 in.)
Ignition timing	5° B.T.D.C. @ 1000 rpm. Not adjustable.
Radiator cap opening pressure	93.3-122.7 kPa (13.5-17.8 psi)
Rim runout wear limit	
Radial	1.0 mm (0.04 in.)
Axial	0.5 mm (0.02 in.)
Shift rod installed length	255-259 mm (10.04-10.20 in.)
Shock absorber spring preload settings	
Minimum (softest)	1
Standard	4
Maximum (hardest)	9
Spark plug	
Recommended plug	NGK LMAR7A-9
Spark plug gap	0.8-0.9 mm (0.031-0.035 in.)
Throttle cable free play (at the flange)	4-6 mm (0.16-0.24 in.)
Valve clearance	
Intake	0.09-0.13 mm (0.0035-0.0051 in.)
Exhaust	0.14-0.18 mm (0.0055-0.0071 in.)

MAINTENANCE TORQUE SPECIFICATIONS

Item	N•m	in.-lb.	ft.-lb.
Alternator damper cover bolt	7	62	–
Coolant reservoir cap cover bolt	4	35	–
Cooling system			
Coolant drain bolt	2	18	–
Coolant reservoir bolt*	7	62	–
Drive belt adjuster locknut	16	–	12
Exhaust system			
Exhaust header nuts	20	–	15
Exhaust header studs	15	–	11
Exhaust pipe clamp bolts	12	106	–
Exhaust pipe guard bolts	7	62	–
Exhaust-pipe-guard clamp screws	6	53	–
Muffler bracket bolts	53	–	39
Muffler bolts	35	–	26
Muffler clamp bolts	12	106	–
Flywheel bolt plug	10	89	–
Oil check bolt	15	–	11
Oil drain bolt	43	–	32

(continued)

MAINTENANCE TORQUE SPECIFICATIONS (continued)

Item	N•m	in.-lb.	ft.-lb.
Oil filter	17	–	12.5
Rear axle nut	150	–	110
Rear brake hose guide bolt	7	62	–
Rear brake hose holder bolt	7	62	–
Rear brake pushrod adjuster locknut	16	–	12
Shift rod locknuts	8	71	–
Sidestand nut	56	–	41
Spark plugs	13	115	–
Tappet cover bolts	10	89	–
Timing inspection plug*	6	53	–
Valve adjuster locknut	14	–	10

*Refer to text.

CHAPTER ONE

GENERAL INFORMATION

This detailed and comprehensive manual covers V-Star 1300 and V-Star 1300 Tourer models from 2007-2010.

The text provides complete information on maintenance, repair and overhaul. Hundreds of photos and drawings guide the reader through every job. All procedures are in step-by-step format and designed for the reader who may be working on the motorcycle for the first time.

MANUAL ORGANIZATION

A shop manual is a reference tool and, as in all Clymer manuals, the chapters are thumb-tabbed for easy reference. Important items are indexed at the end of the manual. Frequently used specifications and capacities from individual chapters are summarized in the *Quick Reference Data* at the front of the manual.

Some steps in the procedures refer to headings in other chapters or sections of the manual. When a specific heading is called out in a step, it is italicized as it appears in the manual. If a sub-heading is indicated as being "in this section" it is located within the same main heading. For example, the sub-heading *Handling Gasoline Safely* is located within the main heading *SAFETY*.

This chapter provides general information on shop safety, tool use, service fundamentals and shop supplies. **Tables 1-5** at the end of the chapter provide general motorcycle, mechanical and shop information.

Chapter Two provides methods for quick and accurate diagnoses of problems. Troubleshooting procedures present typical symptoms and logical methods to pinpoint and repair a problem.

Chapter Three explains all routine maintenance and the recommended maintenance intervals.

Subsequent chapters describe specific systems, such as engine, clutch, transmission, fuel system, exhaust system, drive system, suspension, brakes and body components.

Specification tables, when applicable, are located at the end of each chapter.

WARNINGS, CAUTIONS AND NOTES

The terms WARNING, CAUTION and NOTE have specific meanings in this manual.

A WARNING emphasizes areas where injury or even death could result from negligence. Mechanical damage may also occur. WARNINGS *are to be taken seriously.*

A CAUTION emphasizes areas where equipment damage could result. Disregarding a CAUTION could cause permanent mechanical damage, though injury is unlikely.

A NOTE provides additional information to make a step or procedure easier or clearer. Disregarding a NOTE could cause inconvenience, but would not cause equipment damage or injury.

SAFETY

Follow these guidelines and practice common sense to safely service the motorcycle.

1. Do not operate the motorcycle in an enclosed area. The exhaust gases contain carbon monoxide, an odorless, colorless and poisonous gas. Carbon monoxide levels build quickly in small, enclosed areas and can cause unconsciousness and death in a short time. Always properly ventilate the work area or operate the motorcycle outside.

2. Never use gasoline or any extremely flammable liquid to clean parts. Refer to *Handling Gasoline Safely* and *Cleaning Parts* in this section.

3. Never smoke or use a torch in the vicinity of flammable liquids, such as gasoline or cleaning solvent.

4. If welding or brazing on the motorcycle, remove the fuel tank to a safe distance at least 50 ft. (15 m) away.

5. Use the correct size and type of tool to avoid damaging fasteners.

6. Keep tools clean and in good condition. Replace or repair worn or damaged equipment.

7. When loosening a tight fastener, be guided by what would happen if the tool slips.

8. When replacing fasteners, make sure the new fasteners are the same size and strength as the original ones.

9. Keep the work area clean and organized.

10. Wear eye protection *anytime* the safety of the eyes is in question. This includes procedures that involve drilling, grinding, hammering, compressed air and chemicals.

11. Wear the correct clothing for the job. Tie up or cover long hair so it does not get caught in moving equipment.

12. Do not carry sharp tools in clothing pockets.

13. Always have an approved fire extinguisher available. Make sure it is rated for gasoline (Class B) and electrical (Class C) fires.

14. Do not use compressed air to clean clothes, the motorcycle or the work area. Debris may be blown into eyes or skin. Never direct compressed air at anyone. Do not allow children to use or play with any compressed air equipment.

15. When using compressed air to dry rotating parts, hold the part so it does not rotate. Do not allow the force of the air to spin the part. The air jet is capable of rotating parts at extreme speeds. The part may disintegrate or become damaged, causing serious injury.

16. Do not inhale the dust created by brake pad and clutch wear. These particles may contain asbestos. In addition, some types of insulating materials and gaskets may contain asbestos. Inhaled asbestos particles are a health hazard.

17. Never work on the motorcycle while someone is working under it.

18. When placing the motorcycle on a stand, make sure it is secure before walking away.

Handling Gasoline Safely

Gasoline is a volatile, flammable liquid and is one of the most dangerous items in the shop. Because gasoline is used so often, many people forget it is hazardous. Only use gasoline as fuel for gasoline internal combustion engines. Keep in mind when working on the machine, gasoline is always present in the fuel tank, fuel line and throttle bodies. To avoid a disastrous accident when working around the fuel system, carefully observe the following precautions:

1. *Never* use gasoline to clean parts. Refer to *Cleaning Parts* in this section.

2. When working on the fuel system, work outside or in a well-ventilated area.

3. Do not add fuel to the fuel tank or service the fuel system while the motorcycle is near open flames, sparks or where someone is smoking. Gasoline vapor is heavier than air; it collects in low areas and is more easily ignited than liquid gasoline.

4. Let the engine cool completely before working on any fuel system component.

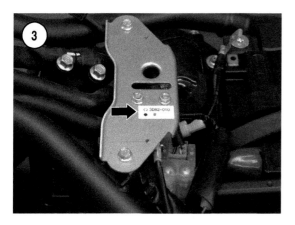

8. Keep chemical products away from children and pets.

9. Thoroughly clean all oil, grease and cleaner residue from any part that must be heated.

10. Use a nylon brush when cleaning parts. Metal brushes may cause a spark.

11. When using a parts washer, only use the solvent recommended by the manufacturer. Make sure the parts washer is equipped with a metal lid that will lower in case of fire.

Warning Labels

Most manufacturers attach information and warning labels to the motorcycle. These labels contain instructions that are important to personal safety when operating, servicing, transporting and storing the motorcycle. Refer to the owner's manual for the description and location of labels. Order replacement labels from the manufacturer if they are missing or damaged.

SERIAL NUMBERS

Serial numbers are stamped on various locations on the frame, engine, transmission and throttle body. Record these numbers in the *Quick Reference Data* section in the front of the manual. Have these numbers available when ordering parts.

The vehicle identification number is stamped into the right side of the steering head (**Figure 1**). This number also appears on a plate affixed to the gusset at the front of the frame, just beneath the steering head.

The engine serial number (**Figure 2**) is stamped onto a pad on the right side of the crankcase.

The model number label (**Figure 3**) is on the seat bracket under the rider's seat.

5. Do not store gasoline in glass containers. If the glass breaks, a serious explosion or fire may occur.

6. Immediately wipe up spilled gasoline with rags. Store the rags in a metal container with a lid until they can be properly disposed of, or place them outside in a safe place for the fuel to evaporate.

7. Do not pour water onto a gasoline fire. Water spreads the fire and makes it more difficult to put out. Use a class B, BC or ABC fire extinguisher to extinguish the fire.

8. Always turn off the engine before refueling. Do not spill fuel onto the engine or exhaust system. Do not overfill the fuel tank. Leave an air space at the top of the tank to allow room for the fuel to expand due to temperature fluctuations.

Cleaning Parts

Cleaning parts is one of the more tedious and difficult service jobs performed in the home garage. Many types of chemical cleaners and solvents are available for shop use. Most are poisonous and extremely flammable. To prevent chemical exposure, vapor buildup, fire and serious injury, observe each product warning label and note the following:

1. Read and observe the entire product label before using any chemical. Always know what type of chemical is being used and whether it is poisonous and/or flammable.

2. Do not use more than one type of cleaning solvent at a time. If mixing chemicals is required, measure the proper amounts according to the manufacturer's instructions.

3. Work in a well-ventilated area.

4. Wear chemical-resistant gloves.

5. Wear safety glasses.

6. Wear a vapor respirator if the instructions call for it.

7. Wash hands and arms thoroughly after cleaning parts.

FASTENERS

WARNING
Do not install fasteners with a strength classification lower than what was originally installed by the manufacturer. Doing so may cause equipment failure and/or damage.

Proper fastener selection and installation ensures that the motorcycle operates as designed and can be serviced efficiently. The choice of original equipment fasteners is not arrived at by chance. Make sure replacement fasteners meet the same requirements as the originals.

Threaded Fasteners

Threaded fasteners secure most of the components on the motorcycle. Most are tightened by turning them clockwise (right-hand threads). If the normal rotation of the component being tightened would loosen the fastener, it may have left-hand threads. If a left-hand threaded fastener is used, it is noted in the text.

Two dimensions are required to match the thread size of the fastener: the number of threads in a given distance and the outside diameter of the threads.

The two systems currently used to specify threaded fastener dimensions are the U.S. standard system and the metric system (**Figure 4**). Pay particular attention when working with unidentified fasteners; mismatching thread types can damage threads.

To ensure that the fastener threads are not mismatched or cross-threaded, start all fasteners by hand. If a fastener is hard to start or turn, determine the cause before tightening with a wrench.

The length (L, **Figure 5**), diameter (D) and distance between thread crests (pitch) (T) classify metric screws and bolts. A typical bolt may be identified by the numbers, 8—1.25 × 130. This indicates the bolt has a diameter of 8 mm, the distance between thread crests is 1.25 mm and the length is 130 mm. Always measure bolt length as shown in L, **Figure 5** to avoid purchasing replacements of the wrong length.

The numbers on the top of the fastener (**Figure 5**) indicate the strength, or grade, of metric screws and bolts. The higher the number, the stronger the fastener. Typically, unnumbered fasteners are the weakest.

Many screws, bolts and studs are combined with nuts to secure particular components. To indicate the size of a nut, manufacturers specify the internal diameter and the thread pitch. The measurement across two flats on a nut or bolt indicates the wrench size.

Torque Specifications

The materials used in the manufacturing of the motorcycle may be subjected to uneven stresses if the fasteners of the various subassemblies are not installed and tightened correctly. Improperly installed fasteners can work loose and cause extensive damage. Always use an accurate torque wrench to torque fasteners. Refer to *Torque Wrenches* in *Tools* in this chapter.

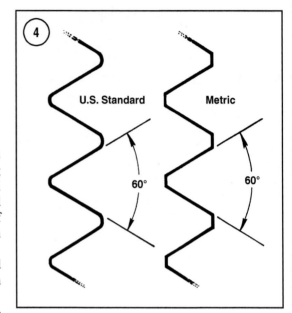

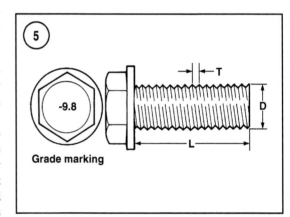

Grade marking

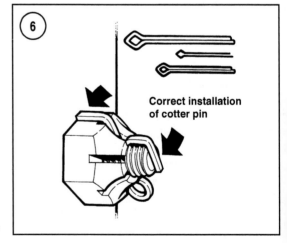

Correct installation of cotter pin

Torque specifications for specific fasteners appear at the end of each chapter. **Table 5** in this chapter lists general torque recommendations. To use **Table 5**, first measure the diameter of the fastener as described in *Threaded Fasteners* in this section.

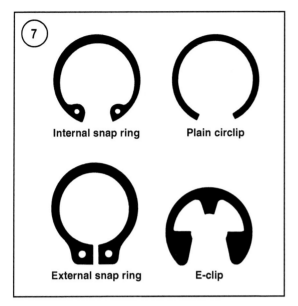

7

Internal snap ring   Plain circlip

External snap ring   E-clip

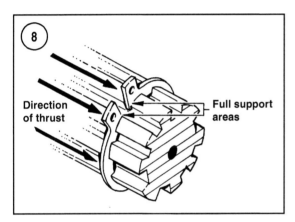

8

Direction of thrust   Full support areas

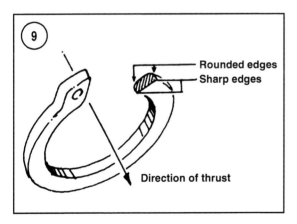

9

Rounded edges
Sharp edges

Direction of thrust

Self-Locking Fasteners

Several types of bolts, screws and nuts incorporate a system that creates interference between the two fasteners. Interference is achieved in various ways. The most common types are the nylon insert nut and a dry adhesive coating on the threads of a bolt.

Self-locking fasteners offer greater holding strength than standard fasteners, which improves their resistance to vibration. Self-locking fasteners cannot be reused. The materials used to form the lock become distorted after the initial installation and removal. Discard and replace self-locking fasteners after removing them. Do not replace self-locking fasteners with standard fasteners.

Washers

The two basic types of washers are flat washers and lockwashers. Flat washers are simple discs with a hole to fit a screw or bolt. Lockwashers are used to prevent a fastener from working loose. Washers can be used as spacers and seals, or can help distribute fastener load and prevent the fastener from damaging a component.

As with fasteners, when replacing washers make sure the replacement washers are of the same design and quality as the originals.

Cotter Pins

A cotter pin is a split metal pin inserted into a hole or slot to prevent a fastener from loosening. In certain applications, such as the rear axle on an ATV or motorcycle, the fastener must be secured in this way. For these applications, a cotter pin and castellated (slotted) nut is used.

To use a cotter pin, first make sure the diameter is correct for the hole in the fastener. After correctly tightening the fastener and aligning the holes, insert the cotter pin through the hole and bend the ends over the fastener (**Figure 6**). Unless instructed to do so, never loosen a tightened fastener to align the holes. If the holes do not align, tighten the fastener enough to achieve alignment.

Cotter pins are available in various diameters and lengths. Measure the length from the bottom of the head to the tip of the shortest pin.

Snap Rings and E-clips

Snap rings (**Figure 7**) are circular-shaped metal retaining clips. They are required to secure parts and gears in place on shafts, pins or rods. External type snap rings are used to retain items on shafts. Internal type snap rings secure parts within housing bores. In some applications, in addition to securing the component(s), snap rings of varying thicknesses also determine endplay. These are usually called selective snap rings.

The two basic types of snap rings are machined and stamped snap rings. Machined snap rings (**Figure 8**) can be installed in either direction, because both faces have sharp edges. Stamped snap rings (**Figure 9**) are manufactured with a sharp and a round edge. When installing a stamped snap ring in a thrust application, install the sharp edge facing away from the part producing the thrust.

E-clips are used when it is not practical to use a snap ring. Remove E-clips with a flat blade screwdriver by prying between the shaft and E-clip. To install an E-clip, center it over the shaft groove and push or tap it into place.

Observe the following when installing snap rings:
1. Remove and install snap rings with snap ring pliers. Refer to *Tools* in this chapter.
2. In some applications, it may be necessary to replace snap rings after removing them.
3. Compress or expand snap rings only enough to install them. If overly expanded, they lose their retaining ability.
4. After installing a snap ring, make sure it seats completely.
5. Wear eye protection when removing and installing snap rings.

SHOP SUPPLIES

Engine Oil

Engine oil for four-stroke motorcycle engine use is classified by three standards: the American Petroleum Institute (API) service classification, the Society of Automotive Engineers (SAE) viscosity rating and the Japanese Automobile Standards Organization (JASO) T 903 Standard rating.

The API and SAE information is on all oil container labels. The JASO information is found on oil containers sold by the oil manufacturer specifically for motorcycle use. Two letters indicate the API service classification. The number or sequence of numbers and letter (10W-40 for example) is the oil's viscosity rating. The API service classification and the SAE viscosity index are not indications of oil quality. The JASO certification label identifies two separate oil classifications and a registration number to ensure the oil has passed all JASO certification standards for use in four-stroke motorcycle engines.

The API service classification indicates that the oil meets specific lubrication standards. The first letter in the classification *S* indicates that the oil is for gasoline engines. The second letter indicates the standard the oil satisfies. Do not use automotive oil with an SJ or higher classification. They are designed for automotive applications and contain friction modifiers that reduce frictional losses. Oils with this classification can cause engine wear in a motorcycle.

The JASO certification label identifies two separate oil classifications and a registration number to ensure the oil has passed all JASO certification standards for use in four-stroke motorcycle engines. The classifications are: MA (high friction applications) and MB (low friction applications). Only oil that has passed JASO standards can carry the JASO certification label.

Always use oil with a classification recommended by the manufacturer. Refer to Chapter Three. Using oil with a different classification can cause engine damage.

Viscosity is an indication of the oil's thickness. Thin oils have a lower number while thick oils have a higher number. Engine oils fall into the 5- to 50-weight range for single-grade oils.

Most manufacturers recommend multi-grade oil. These oils perform efficiently across a wide range of operating conditions. Multi-grade oils are identified by a W after the first number, which indicates the low-temperature viscosity.

Engine oils are most commonly mineral (petroleum) based, but synthetic and semi-synthetic types are used more frequently. When selecting engine oil, follow the manufacturer's recommendation for type, classification and viscosity. Refer to *Engine Oil* in Chapter Three. Using other oil can cause engine damage.

Moly Oil

A 50:50 mixture of engine oil and molybdenum disulfide grease is called for during some procedures.

Grease

Grease is lubricating oil with an added thickening agent. Grease maintains its lubricating qualities better than oil on long, strenuous rides. Furthermore, water does not wash grease off parts as easily as it does oil.

The National Lubricating Grease Institute (NLGI) grades grease. Grades range from No. 000 to No. 6, with No. 6 being the thickest. Typical multipurpose grease is NLGI No. 2. For specific applications, manufacturers may recommend water-resistant type grease or one with an additive such as lithium or molybdenum disulfide (MoS_2).

Various types of greases are needed when servicing a motorcycle. Unless otherwise indicated, use lithium-soap grease when grease is called for in this manual.

Brake Fluid

WARNING
Never put a mineral-based (petroleum)
oil into the brake system. Mineral oil

causes rubber parts in the system to swell and break apart, causing complete brake failure.

Brake fluid is the hydraulic fluid used to transmit hydraulic pressure (force) to the wheel brakes. Brake fluid is classified by the Department of Transportation (DOT). Current designations for brake fluid are DOT 3, DOT 4 and DOT 5. This classification appears on the fluid container. Motorcycles in this manual use DOT 4 brake fluid.

Each type of brake fluid has its own definite characteristics. Do not mix different types of brake fluid as this may cause brake system failure. DOT 5 brake fluid is silicone-based. DOT 5 is not compatible with other brake fluids or in systems for which it was not designed. Mixing DOT 5 fluid with other fluids may cause brake system failure. When adding brake fluid, only use the fluid recommended by the manufacturer.

Brake fluid will damage any plastic, painted or plated surface it contacts. Use extreme care when working with brake fluid and wash any spills immediately with soap and water.

Hydraulic brake systems require clean and moisture free brake fluid. Never reuse brake fluid. Keep containers and reservoirs properly sealed.

Coolant

Coolant is a mixture of water and antifreeze used to dissipate engine heat. Ethylene glycol is the most common form of antifreeze. Check the motorcycle manufacturer's recommendations (Chapter Three) when selecting antifreeze. Most require one specifically designed for use in aluminum engines. These types of antifreeze have additives that inhibit corrosion.

Only mix antifreeze with distilled water. Impurities in tap water may damage internal cooling system passages.

Cleaners, Degreasers and Solvents

Many chemicals are available to remove oil, grease and other residue from a motorcycle. Before using cleaning solvents, consider how they will be used and disposed of, particularly if they are not water-soluble. Local ordinances may require special procedures for the disposal of many types of cleaning chemicals. Refer to *Safety* in this chapter.

Use brake parts cleaner to clean brake system components. Brake parts cleaner leaves no residue. Use electrical contact cleaner to clean electrical connections and components without leaving any residue. Carburetor cleaner is a powerful solvent used to remove fuel deposits and varnish from fuel system components. Use this cleaner carefully, as it may damage finishes.

Generally, degreasers are strong cleaners used to remove heavy accumulations of grease from engine and frame components.

Most solvents are designed to be used with a parts washing cabinet for individual component cleaning. For safety, use only nonflammable or high flash point solvents.

Gasket Sealant

Sealant is used in combination with a gasket or seal. In other applications, such as between crankcase halves, only a sealant is used. Follow the manufacturer's recommendation when using a sealant. Use extreme care when choosing a sealant other than the type originally recommended. Choose sealant based upon its resistance to heat, various fluids and its sealing capabilities.

Before applying any sealant, clean all old gasket residue from the mating surfaces. Remove all gasket material from blind threaded holes to avoid inaccurate bolt torque. Spray the mating surfaces with aerosol parts cleaner and then wipe the surfaces with a lint-free cloth. The area must be clean for the sealant to adhere.

The manufacturer recommends the use of Yamaha bond No. 1215 (part No. 90890-85505) or Three Bond No. 1215. Always use these sealants, or equivalent sealants, where called for in this manual.

Removing sealant

Silicone sealant is used on many engine gasket surfaces. When cleaning parts after disassembly, a razor blade or gasket scraper is required to remove the silicone residue that cannot be pulled off by hand from the gasket surfaces. To avoid damaging gasket surfaces, use Permatex Silicone Stripper (part No. 80647) to help soften the residue before scraping.

RTV sealant

Room temperature vulcanization (RTV) sealant is a common sealant that cures at room temperature over a specific time period. This allows the repositioning of components without damaging gaskets.

Moisture in the air causes the RTV sealant to cure. Always install the tube cap as soon as possible after applying RTV sealant. Keep partial tubes sealed and discard them if they have surpassed the expiration date. RTV sealant has a limited shelf life and will not cure properly if the shelf life has expired.

Manufacturers usually specify a shelf life of one year after a container is opened, though it is recommended to contact the sealant manufacturer to confirm shelf life.

Applying RTV sealant

Clean all old sealant residue from the mating surfaces. Then inspect the mating surfaces for damage. Remove all sealer material from blind threaded holes; it can cause inaccurate bolt torque. Spray the mating surfaces with aerosol parts cleaner, and then wipe with a lint-free cloth. Because gasket surfaces must be dry and oil-free for the sealant to adhere, be thorough when cleaning and drying the parts.

Apply RTV sealant in a continuous bead 2-3 mm (0.08-0.12 in.) thick. Circle all the fastener holes unless otherwise specified. Do not allow any sealant to enter these holes. Drawings in specific chapters show how to apply the sealer to specific gasket surfaces. Assemble and tighten the fasteners to the specified torque within the time frame recommended by the RTV sealant manufacturer.

Gasket Remover

Aerosol gasket remover can help remove stubborn gaskets. This product can speed up the removal process and prevent damage to the mating surface that may be caused by using a scraping tool. Most of these types of products are very caustic. Follow the gasket remover manufacturer's instructions for use.

Threadlocking Compound

CAUTION
Threadlocking compounds are anaerobic and damage most plastic components. Use caution when using these products near plastic components.

A threadlocking compound is a fluid applied to the threads of fasteners. When the fluid dries it becomes solid between the threads. This makes it difficult for the fastener to work loose from vibration or heat expansion and contraction. Some threadlocking compounds also provide a seal against fluid leaks.

Before applying a threadlocking compound, remove any old compound from both thread areas, and clean them with aerosol parts cleaner. Use the compound sparingly. Excess fluid can run into adjoining parts.

The manufacturer recommends the use of Loctite Threadlocker, which is available with various strength and temperature characteristics. Follow the

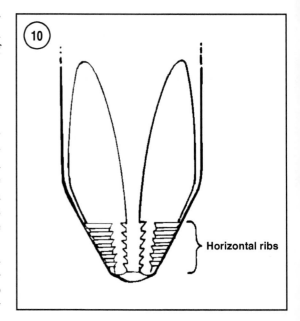

Horizontal ribs

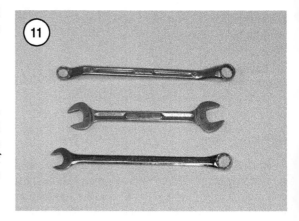

manufacturer's recommendations when selecting the appropriate Loctite for a particular fastener and application.

TOOLS

Most of the procedures in this manual can be carried out with simple hand tools and test equipment familiar to the home mechanic. Always use the correct tools for the job at hand. Keep tools organized and clean. Store them in a tool chest with related tools organized together.

Quality tools are essential. The best are constructed of high-strength alloy steel. These tools are light, easy to use and resistant to wear. Their working surface is devoid of sharp edges and carefully polished. They have an easy-to-clean finish and are comfortable to use. Quality tools are a good investment.

When purchasing tools, consider their potential frequency of use. If a tool kit is just now being started, consider purchasing a basic tool set from a quality tool supplier. These sets are available in many tool combinations and offer substantial savings when compared to individually purchased tools. As work experience grows and tasks become more complicated, specialized tools can be added.

Some of the procedures in this manual specify special tools. In many cases the tool is illustrated in use. In some cases, it may be possible to substitute a similar tool or fabricate a suitable replacement. However, in other cases, the specialized equipment or expertise may make it impractical for the home mechanic to attempt the procedure. The text identifies these operations and in many instances, recommends that the task be performed by a dealership or specialist.

Screwdrivers

The two basic types of screwdrivers are the slotted tip (flat blade) and the Phillips tip. These are available in sets that often include an assortment of tip sizes and shaft lengths.

As with all tools, use a screwdriver designed for the job. Make sure the size of the tip conforms to the size and shape of the fastener. Use them only for driving screws. Never use a screwdriver for prying or chiseling metal. Repair or replace worn or damaged screwdrivers. A worn tip may damage the fastener, making it difficult to remove.

Phillips-head screws are often damaged by incorrectly fitting screwdrivers. Quality Phillips screwdrivers are manufactured with their crosshead tip machined to Phillips Screw Company specifications. Poor quality or damaged Phillips screwdrivers can back out (camout) and round over the screw head. In addition, weak or soft screw materials can make removal difficult.

The ACR Phillips II screwdriver uses horizontal anti-camout ribs on the driving faces or flutes of the screwdriver's tip (**Figure 10**). ACR Phillips II screwdrivers were designed specifically for ACR

Phillips II screws, but they work well on all common Phillips screws and damages screws where a positive grip is difficult. Another way to prevent camout and to increase the grip of a Phillips screwdriver is to apply valve grinding compound or Permatex Screw & Socket Gripper onto the screwdriver tip. After loosening/tightening the screw, clean the screw recess to prevent contamination.

Wrenches

Box-end, open-end and combination wrenches (**Figure 11**) are available in a variety of types and sizes. The number stamped on the wrench refers to the distance between the work areas. This size must match the size of the fastener head.

The box-end wrench is an excellent tool because it grips the fastener on all sides. This reduces the chance of the tool slipping. The box-end wrench is designed with either a 6- or 12-point opening. For stubborn or damaged fasteners, the 6-point provides superior holding because it contacts the fastener across a wider area at all six edges. For general use, the 12-point works well. It allows the wrench to be removed and reinstalled without moving the handle over such a wide arc.

An open-end wrench is fast and works best in areas with limited overhead access. It contacts the fastener at only two points and is subject to slipping if under heavy force or if the tool or fastener is worn. A box-end wrench is preferred in most instances, especially when breaking loose and applying the final tightness to a fastener.

The combination wrench has a box-end on one end and an open-end on the other. This combination makes it a convenient tool.

Adjustable Wrenches

An adjustable, or Crescent, wrench (**Figure 12**) can fit nearly any nut or bolt head that has clear access around its entire perimeter. An adjustable wrench is best used as a backup wrench to keep a large nut or bolt from turning while the other end is being loosened or tightened with a box-end or socket wrench.

Adjustable wrenches contact the fastener at only two points, which makes them more subject to slipping off the fastener. Because one jaw is adjustable and may become loose, this shortcoming is aggravated. Make certain the solid jaw is the one transmitting the force.

Socket Wrenches, Ratchets and Handles

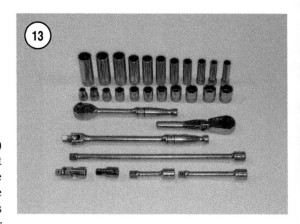

WARNING
Do not use hand sockets with air or
impact tools because they may shatter
and cause injury. Always wear eye pro-
tection when using impact or air tools.

Sockets that attach to a ratchet handle (**Figure 13**) are available with 6-point (A, **Figure 14**) or 12-point (B) openings and different drive sizes. The drive size indicates the size of the square hole that accepts the ratchet handle. The number stamped on the socket is the size of the work area and must match the fastener head.

As with wrenches, a 6-point socket provides superior-holding ability, while a 12-point socket needs to be moved only half as far to reposition it on the fastener.

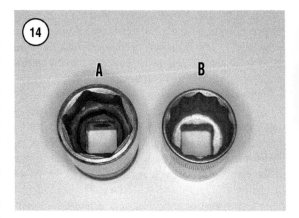

Sockets are designated for either hand or impact use. Impact sockets are made of thicker material for more durability. Compare the size and wall thickness of a 19-mm hand socket (A, **Figure 15**) and the 19-mm impact socket (B). Use impact sockets when using an impact driver or air tools. Use hand sockets with hand-driven attachments.

Various handles are available for sockets. Use the speed handle for fast operation. Flexible ratchet heads in varying lengths allow the socket to be turned with varying force and at odd angles. Extension bars allow the socket setup to reach difficult areas. The ratchet is the most versatile. It allows the user to install or remove the nut without removing the socket.

Sockets combined with any number of drivers make them undoubtedly the fastest, safest and most convenient tool for fastener removal and installation.

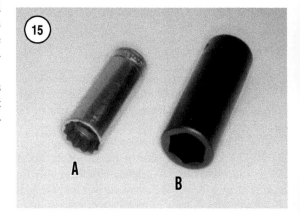

Impact Drivers

WARNING
Do not use hand sockets with air or
impact tools because they may shatter
and cause injury. Always wear eye pro-
tection when using impact or air tools.

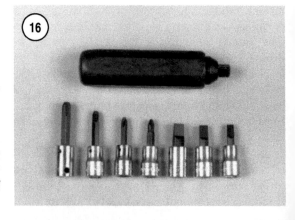

An impact driver provides extra force for removing fasteners by converting the impact of a hammer into a turning motion. This makes it possible to remove stubborn fasteners without damaging them. Impact drivers and interchangeable bits (**Figure 16**) are available from most tool suppliers. When using an impact driver, always use a socket is designed for impact use. Refer to *Socket Wrenches, Ratchets and Handles* in this section.

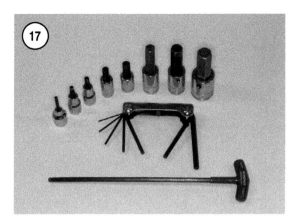

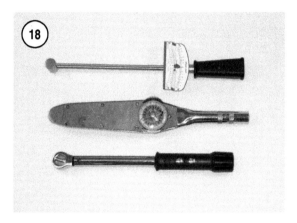

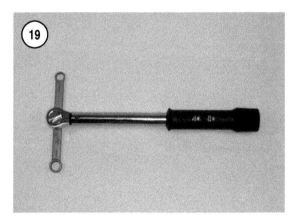

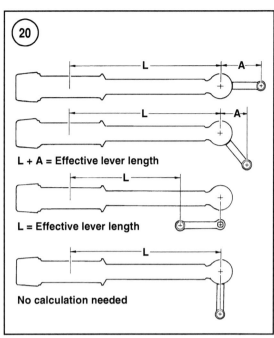

L + A = Effective lever length

L = Effective lever length

No calculation needed

tener to a measured torque. Torque wrenches come in several drive sizes (1/4, 3/8, 1/2 and 3/4) and have various methods of reading the torque value. The drive size indicates the size of the square drive that accepts the socket, adapter or extension. Common methods of reading the torque value are the deflecting beam, the dial indicator and the audible click.

When choosing a torque wrench, consider the torque range, drive size and accuracy. The torque specifications in this manual provide an indication of the range required.

A torque wrench is a precision tool that must be properly cared for to remain accurate. Store torque wrenches in cases or separate padded drawers within a toolbox. Follow the manufacturer's instructions for their care and calibration.

Torque Adapters

Torque adapters or extensions extend or reduce the reach of a torque wrench. The torque adapter shown in **Figure 19** is used to tighten a fastener that cannot be reached because of the size of the torque wrench head, drive, and socket. If a torque adapter changes the effective lever length (**Figure 20**), the torque reading on the wrench will not equal the actual torque applied to the fastener. It is necessary to recalibrate the torque setting on the wrench to compensate for the change of lever length. When using a torque adapter at a right angle to the drive head, calibration is not required, because the effective length has not changed.

Allen Wrenches

Use Allen, or setscrew, wrenches (**Figure 17**) on fasteners with hexagonal recesses in the fastener head. These wrenches are available in L-shaped bar, socket and T-handle types. A metric set is required when working on most motorcycles. Allen bolts are sometimes called socket bolts.

Torque Wrenches

Use a torque wrench (**Figure 18**) with a socket, torque adapter or similar extension to tighten a fas-

To recalculate a torque reading when using a torque adapter, use the following formula and refer to **Figure 20**:

$$TW = \frac{TA \times L}{L + A}$$

TW is the torque setting or dial reading on the wrench.

TA is the torque specification and the actual amount of torque that is applied to the fastener.

A is the amount that the adapter increases (or in some cases reduces) the effective lever length as measured along the centerline of the torque wrench.

L is the lever length of the wrench as measured from the center of the drive to the center of the grip.

The effective length is the sum of *L* and *A*.

Example:

TA = 20 ft.-lb.

A = 3 in.

L = 14 in.

$$TW = \frac{20 \times 14}{14 + 3} = \frac{280}{17} = 16.5 \text{ ft.-lb.}$$

In this example, the torque wrench should be set to the calculated torque value of 16.5 ft.-lb. Although the torque wrench is set to 16.5 ft.-lb., the applied torque is 20 ft.-lb. When using a beam-type wrench, tighten the fastener until the pointer aligns with 16.5 ft.-lb.

Pliers

Pliers come in a wide range of types and sizes. Pliers are useful for holding, cutting, bending, and crimping. Do not use them to turn fasteners. **Figure 21** and **Figure 22** show several types of useful pliers. Each design has a specialized function. Slip-joint pliers are general-purpose pliers used for gripping and bending. Diagonal cutting pliers are needed to cut wire and can be used to remove cotter pins. Use needlenose pliers to hold or bend small objects. Locking pliers (**Figure 22**), sometimes called Vise-Grips, are used to hold objects very tightly. They have many uses ranging from holding two parts together, to gripping the end of a broken stud. Use caution when using locking pliers, as the sharp jaws will damage the objects they hold.

Snap Ring Pliers

WARNING
Snap rings can slip and fly off when removing and installing them. Also, the snap ring pliers' tips may break. Always wear eye protection when using snap ring pliers.

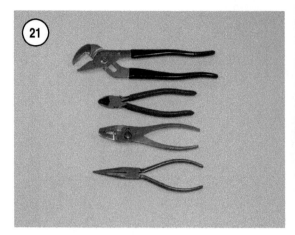

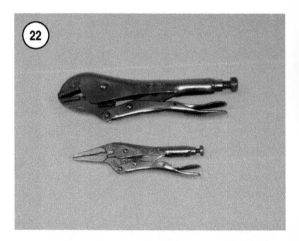

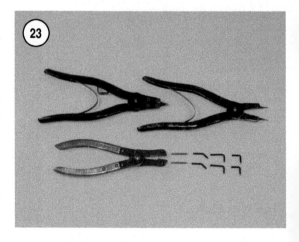

Snap ring pliers are specialized pliers with tips that fit into the ends of snap rings to remove and install them.

Snap ring pliers (**Figure 23**) are available with a fixed action (either internal or external) or convertible (one tool works on both internal and external snap rings). They may have fixed tips or interchangeable ones of various sizes and angles. For general use, select convertible type pliers with interchangeable tips (**Figure 23**).

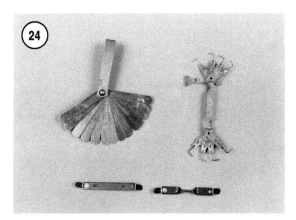

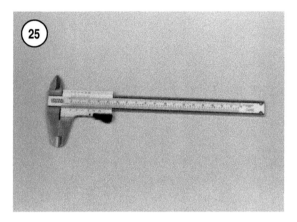

the measuring tool, make sure it is applicable to the task.

As with all tools, measuring tools provide the best results if cared for properly. Improper use can damage the tool and cause inaccurate results. If any measurement is questionable, verify the measurement using another tool. A standard gauge is usually provided with micrometers to check accuracy and calibrate the tool if necessary.

Precision measurements can vary according to the experience of the person taking the measurement. Accurate results are only possible if the mechanic possesses a feel for using the tool. Heavy-handed use of measuring tools produces inaccurate results. Hold the tool gently by the fingertips to easily feel the point at which the tool contacts the object. This feel for the equipment produces more accurate measurements and reduces the risk of damaging the tool or component. Refer to the following subsections for specific measuring tools.

Feeler Gauge

Use feeler or thickness gauges (**Figure 24**) for measuring the distance between two surfaces.

A feeler gauge set consists of an assortment of steel strips of graduated thicknesses. Each blade is marked with its thickness. Blades can be of various lengths and angles for different procedures.

A feeler gauge is commonly used to measure valve clearance. Use wire (round) type gauges to measure spark plug gap.

Calipers

Calipers (**Figure 25**) are excellent tools for obtaining inside, outside and depth measurements. Although not as precise as a micrometer, they allow reasonable precision, typically to within 0.05 mm (0.001 in.). Most calipers have a range up to 150 mm (6 in.).

Calipers are available in dial, vernier or digital versions. Dial calipers have a dial readout that provides convenient reading. Vernier calipers have marked scales that must be compared to determine the measurement. The digital caliper uses a liquid-crystal display (LCD) to show the measurement.

Properly maintain the measuring surfaces of the caliper. There must not be any dirt or burrs between the tool and the object being measured. Never force the caliper to close around an object. Close the caliper around the highest point so it can be removed with a slight drag. Some calipers require calibration. Always refer to the manufacturer's instructions when using a new or unfamiliar caliper.

Hammers

Various types of hammers are available to fit a number of applications. Use a ball-peen hammer to strike another tool, such as a punch or chisel. Use soft-faced hammers when a metal object must be struck without damaging it. Never use a metal-faced hammer on engine and suspension components because damage occurs in most cases.

Always wear eye protection when using hammers. Make sure the hammer face is in good condition and the handle is not cracked. Select the correct hammer for the job and make sure to strike the object squarely. Do not use the handle or the side of the hammer to strike an object.

MEASURING TOOLS

The ability to accurately measure components is essential to perform many of the procedures described in this manual. Equipment is manufactured to close tolerances, and obtaining consistently accurate measurements is essential to determine which components require replacement or further service.

Each type of measuring instrument is designed to measure a dimension with a certain degree of accuracy and within a certain range. When selecting

Figure 26 shows a measurement taken with a metric vernier caliper. The fixed scale is marked in 1-mm increments. Ten individual lines on the fixed scale equal 1 cm. The movable scale is marked in 0.05 mm (hundredth) increments.

The value of a measurement equals the reading on the fixed scale plus the reading on the movable scale.

To determine the reading on the fixed scale, look for the line on the fixed scale immediately to the left of the 0-line on the movable scale. In **Figure 26**, the fixed scale reading is 1 centimeter (or 10 millimeters).

To determine the reading on the movable scale, note the one line on the movable scale that precisely aligns with a line on the fixed scale. Look closely. A number of lines will seem close, but only one lines up precisely with a line on the fixed scale. In **Figure 26**, the movable scale reading is 0.50 mm.

To calculate the measurement, add the fixed scale reading (10 mm) to the movable scale reading (0.50 mm) for a value of 10.50 mm.

Micrometers

A micrometer (**Figure 27**) is an instrument designed for linear measurement using the decimal divisions of the inch or meter. While there are many types and styles of micrometers, most of the procedures in this manual call for an outside micrometer. Use an outside micrometer to measure the outside diameter of cylindrical forms and the thickness of materials.

A micrometer's size indicates the minimum and maximum size of a part that it can measure. The usual sizes are 0-25 mm (0-1 in.), 25-50 mm (1-2 in.), 50-75 mm (2-3 in.) and 75-100 mm (3-4 in.).

Micrometers that cover a wider range of measurements are available. These use a large frame with interchangeable anvils of various lengths. This type of micrometer offers a cost savings, but its overall size may make it less convenient.

Adjustment

Before using a micrometer, check its adjustment as follows:
1. Clean the anvil and spindle faces.
2A. To check a 0-1 in. or 0-25 mm micrometer:
   a. Turn the thimble until the spindle contacts the anvil. If the micrometer has a ratchet stop, use it to ensure that the proper amount of pressure is applied.
   b. If the adjustment is correct, the 0 mark on the thimble will align exactly with the 0 mark on

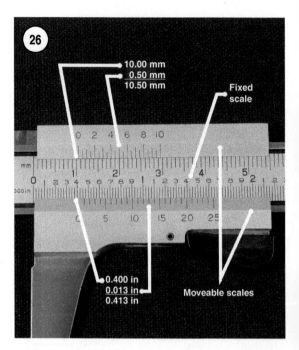

the sleeve line. If the marks do not align, the micrometer is out of adjustment.
   c. Follow the manufacturer's instructions to adjust the micrometer.
2B. To check a micrometer larger than 1 in. or 25 mm, use the standard gauge supplied by the manufacturer. A standard gauge is a steel block, disc or rod that is machined to an exact size.
   a. Place the standard gauge between the spindle and anvil, and measure its outside diameter or length. If the micrometer has a ratchet stop, use it to ensure that the proper amount of pressure is applied.
   b. If the adjustment is correct, the 0 mark on the thimble will align exactly with the 0 mark on the sleeve line. If the marks do not align, the micrometer is out of adjustment.
   c. Follow the manufacturer's instructions to adjust the micrometer.

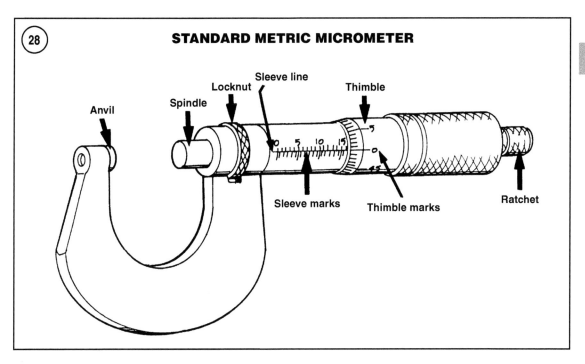

STANDARD METRIC MICROMETER

Anvil · Spindle · Locknut · Sleeve line · Thimble · Sleeve marks · Thimble marks · Ratchet

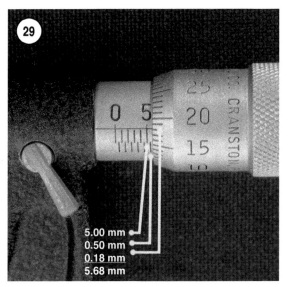

5.00 mm
0.50 mm
0.18 mm
5.68 mm

Care

Micrometers are precision instruments. They must be used and maintained with great care. Note the following:

1. Store micrometers in protective cases or separate padded drawers in a toolbox.

2. When in storage, make sure the spindle and anvil faces do not contact each other or an other object. If they do, temperature changes and corrosion may damage the contact faces.

3. Do not clean a micrometer with compressed air. Dirt forced into the tool will cause wear.

4. Lubricate micrometers to prevent corrosion.

Reading

When reading a micrometer, numbers are taken from different scales and added together. The following subsections describe how to read the measurements of various types of outside micrometers.

For accurate results, properly maintain the measuring surfaces of the micrometer. There cannot be any dirt or burrs between the tool and the measured object. Never force the micrometer to close around an object. Close the micrometer around the highest point so it can be removed with a slight drag.

The standard metric micrometer (**Figure 28**) is accurate to one one-hundredth of a millimeter (0.01 mm). The sleeve line is graduated in millimeter and half millimeter increments. The marks on the upper half of the sleeve line equal 1.00 mm. Each fifth mark above the sleeve line is identified with a number. The number sequence depends on the size of the micrometer. A 0-25 mm micrometer, for example, will have sleeve marks numbered 0 through 25 in 5 mm increments. This numbering sequence continues with larger micrometers. On all metric micrometers, each mark on the lower half of the sleeve equals 0.50 mm.

The tapered end of the thimble has 50 lines marked around it. Each mark equals 0.01 mm. One complete turn of the thimble aligns its 0 mark with the first line on the lower half of the sleeve line or 0.50 mm.

When reading a metric micrometer, add the number of millimeters and half-millimeters on the sleeve line to the number of one one-hundredth millimeters on the thimble. To read a standard metric micrometer, refer to **Figure 29** and perform the following:

1. Read the upper half of the sleeve line and count the number of lines visible. Each upper line equals 1 mm.

2. See if a half-millimeter line is visible on the lower sleeve line. If so, add 0.50 mm to the reading in Step 1.

3. Read the thimble mark that aligns with the sleeve line. Each thimble mark equals 0.01 mm.

NOTE
If a thimble mark does not align exactly with the sleeve line, estimate the amount between the lines. For accurate readings in two-thousandths of a millimeter (0.002 mm), use a metric vernier micrometer.

4. Add the readings from Steps 1-3.

Telescoping and Small Hole Gauges

Use telescoping gauges (**Figure 30**) and small hole gauges (**Figure 31**) to measure bores. Neither gauge has a scale for direct readings. Use an outside micrometer to determine the reading.

To use a telescoping gauge, select the correct size gauge for the bore. Compress the movable post and carefully insert the gauge into the bore. Carefully move the gauge in the bore to make sure it is centered. Tighten the knurled end of the gauge to hold the movable post in position. Remove the gauge and measure the length of the posts. Telescoping gauges are typically used to measure cylinder bores.

To use a small hole gauge, select the correct size gauge for the bore. Carefully insert the gauge into the bore. Tighten the knurled end of the gauge to carefully expand the gauge fingers to the limit within the bore. Do not overtighten the gauge because there is no built-in release. Excessive tightening can damage the bore surface and damage the tool. Remove the gauge and measure the outside dimension (**Figure 32**) with a micrometer. Small hole gauges are typically used to measure valve guides.

Dial Indicator

A dial indicator (A, **Figure 33**) is a gauge with a dial face and needle used to measure variations in dimensions and movements. Measuring brake rotor runout is a typical use for a dial indicator.

Dial indicators are available in various ranges and graduations and with three basic types of mounting bases: magnetic (B, **Figure 33**), clamp, or screw-in stud. When purchasing a dial indicator, select one with a continuous dial (A, **Figure 33**).

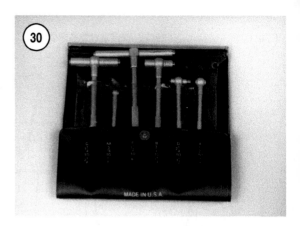

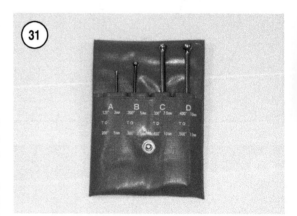

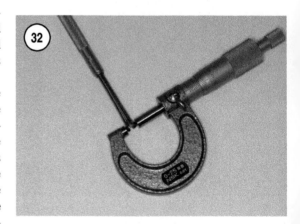

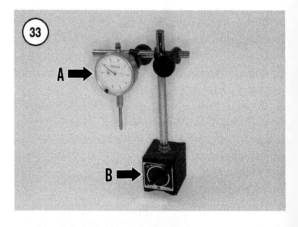

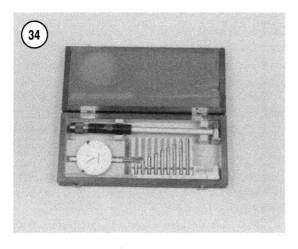

Compression Gauge

A compression gauge (**Figure 35**) measures combustion chamber (cylinder) pressure, usually in psi or kg/cm^2. The gauge adapter is either inserted or screwed into the spark plug hole to obtain the reading. Disable the engine so it does not start and hold the throttle in the wide-open position when performing a compression test. An engine that does not have adequate compression cannot be properly tuned. Refer to Chapter Three.

Multimeter

A multimeter (**Figure 36**) is an essential tool for electrical system diagnosis. The voltage function indicates the voltage applied or available to various electrical components. The ohmmeter function tests circuits for continuity and measures the resistance of a circuit.

Some manufacturers' specifications for electrical components are based on results using a specific test meter. Results may vary if a meter not recommended by the manufacturer is used. Such requirements are noted when applicable.

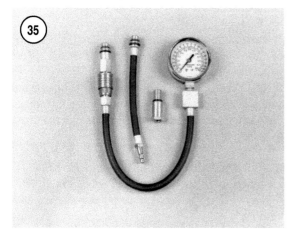

Ohmmeter (analog) calibration

Each time an analog ohmmeter is used or if the scale is changed, the ohmmeter must be calibrated.

Digital ohmmeters do not require calibration.
1. Make sure the meter battery is in good condition.
2. Make sure the meter probes are in good condition.
3. Touch the two probes together and observe the needle location on the ohms scale. The needle must align with the 0 mark to obtain accurate measurements.
4. If necessary, rotate the meter ohms adjust knob until the needle and 0 mark align.

ELECTRICAL SYSTEM FUNDAMENTALS

A thorough study of the many types of electrical systems used in today's motorcycles is beyond the scope of this manual. However, a basic understanding of electrical basics is necessary to perform simple diagnostic tests.

Refer to *Electrical Testing* in Chapter Two for typical test procedures and equipment. Refer to Chapter Nine for specific system test procedures.

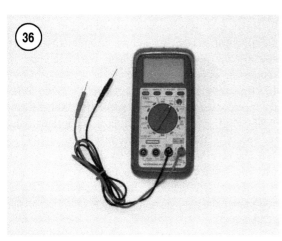

Cylinder Bore Gauge

A cylinder bore gauge is similar to a dial indicator. The gauge set shown in **Figure 34** consists of a dial indicator, handle, and different length adapters (anvils) to fit the gauge to various bore sizes. The bore gauge is used to measure bore size, taper and out-of-round. When using a bore gauge, follow the manufacturer's instructions.

Voltage

Voltage is the electrical potential or pressure in an electrical circuit and is expressed in volts. The more pressure (voltage) in a circuit, the more work can be performed.

Direct current (DC) voltage means the electricity flows in one direction. All circuits powered by a battery are DC circuits.

Alternating current (AC) means the electricity flows in one direction momentarily and then switches to the opposite direction. Alternator output is an example of AC voltage. This voltage must be changed, or rectified, to direct current to operate in a battery powered system.

Resistance

Resistance is the opposition to the flow of electricity within a circuit or component. It is measured in ohms. Resistance causes a reduction in available current and voltage.

Resistance is measured in an inactive circuit with an ohmmeter. The ohmmeter sends a small amount of current into the circuit and measures how difficult it is to push the current through the circuit.

An ohmmeter, although useful, is not always a good indicator of a circuit's actual ability under operating conditions. This is because of the low voltage (6-9 volts) the meter uses to test the circuit. The voltage in an ignition coil secondary winding can be several thousand volts. Such high voltage can cause the coil to malfunction, even though it tests acceptable during a resistance test.

Resistance generally increases with temperature. Perform all testing with the component or circuit at room temperature. Resistance tests performed at high temperatures may indicate high resistance readings and cause unnecessary replacement of a component.

Amperage

Amperage is the unit of measurement for the amount of current within a circuit. Current is the actual flow of electricity. The higher the current, the more work can be performed up to a given point. If the current flow exceeds the circuit or component capacity, it will damage the system.

SERVICE METHODS

Most of the procedures in this manual are straightforward and can be performed by anyone reasonably competent with tools. However, consider personal capabilities carefully before attempting any operation involving major disassembly.

1. In this manual, the term *Front* refers to the front of the motorcycle. The front of any component is the end closest to the front of the motorcycle. *Left* and *right* refer to the position of the parts as viewed by the rider sitting on the seat facing forward.

2. Whenever servicing an engine or suspension component, secure the motorcycle in a safe manner.

3. Label all similar parts for location and mark all mating parts for position. If possible, photograph or draw the number and thickness of any shim as it is removed. Identify parts by placing them in sealed and labeled plastic bags. It is possible for carefully laid out parts to become disturbed, making it difficult to reassemble the components correctly without a diagram.

4. Label disconnected wires and connectors with masking tape and a marking pen. Connectors must be reconnected to their mates. Do not rely on memory alone.

5. Protect finished surfaces from physical damage or corrosion. Keep gasoline and other chemicals off painted surfaces.

6. Use penetrating oil on frozen or tight bolts. Avoid using heat where possible. Heat can warp, melt or affect the temper of parts. Heat also damages the finish of paint and plastics.

7. When a part is a press fit or requires a special tool for removal, the information or type of tool is identified in the text. Otherwise, if a part is difficult to remove or install, determine the cause before proceeding.

8. To prevent objects or debris from falling into the engine, cover all openings.

9. Read each procedure thoroughly and compare the illustrations to the actual components before starting the procedure. Perform the procedure in sequence.

10. Recommendations are occasionally made to refer service to a dealership or specialist. In these cases, the work can be performed more economically by the specialist than by the home mechanic.

11. The term *replace* means to discard a defective part and replace it with a new part. Overhaul means to remove, disassemble, inspect, measure, repair and/or replace parts as required to recondition an assembly.

12. Some operations require using a hydraulic press. If a press is not available, have these operations performed by a shop equipped with the necessary equipment. Do not use makeshift equipment that may damage the motorcycle.

13. Repairs are much faster and easier if the motorcycle is clean before starting work. Degrease the motorcycle with a commercial degreaser; follow the directions on the container for the best results. Clean all parts with cleaning solvent when removing them. Refer to *Cleaning Parts* in *Safety* in this chapter.

CAUTION
Do not direct high-pressure water at steering bearings, fuel hoses, wheel bearings, suspension and electrical components. Water may force grease out of the bearings and possibly damage the seals.

14. If special tools are required, have them available before starting the procedure. When special tools are required, they are described at the beginning of the procedure.

15. Make diagrams of similar-appearing parts. For instance, crankcase bolts are often not the same lengths. Do not rely on memory alone. Carefully laid out parts can become disturbed, making it difficult to reassemble the components correctly.

16. Make sure all shims and washers are reinstalled in the same location and position.

17. Whenever rotating parts contact a stationary part, look for a shim or washer.

18. Use new gaskets if there is any doubt about the condition of old ones.

19. Replace self-locking fasteners, with new ones. Do not install standard fasteners in place of self-locking ones.

20. Use grease to hold small parts in place if they tend to fall out during assembly. Do not apply grease to electrical or brake components.

Heating Components

WARNING
Wear protective gloves to prevent burns and injury when heating parts.

CAUTION
Do not use a welding torch when heating parts. A welding torch applies excessive heat to a small area very quickly, which can damage parts.

A heat gun or propane torch is required to disassemble, assemble, remove and install some parts and components in this manual. Read the safety and operating information supplied by the manufacturer of the heat gun or propane torch while also noting the following:

1. The work area should be clean and dry. Remove all combustible components and materials from the work area. Wipe up all grease, oil and other fluids from parts. Check for leaking or damaged fuel system components. Repair or remove these parts before beginning work.

2. Never use a flame near the battery, fuel tank, fuel lines or other flammable materials.

3. When using a heat gun, remember that the temperature can be in excess of 540° C (1000° F).

4. Have a fire extinguisher near the job.

5. Always wear protective goggles and gloves when heating parts.

6. Before heating a part installed on the motorcycle, check areas around the part and those parts *hidden from view* that could be damaged or possibly ignite. Do not heat surfaces than can be damaged by heat. Shield materials near the part or area to be heated. For example, cables and wiring harnesses.

7. Before heating a part, read the entire procedure to make sure the required tools are available. This allows quick work while the part is at its optimum temperature.

8. The amount of heat recommended to remove or install a part is typically listed in the procedure. However, before heating parts without a specific recommendation, consider the possible effects. To avoid damaging a part, monitor the temperature with heat sticks or an infrared thermometer, if possible. Another way, though not as accurate, is to place tiny drops of water on the part. When the water starts to sizzle, the part is hot enough. Keep the heat in motion to prevent overheating.

Removing Frozen Fasteners

If a fastener cannot be removed, several methods may be used to loosen it. First, apply penetrating oil such as Liquid Wrench or WD-40. Apply it liberally and let it penetrate for 10-15 minutes. Rap the fastener several times with a small hammer. Do not hit it hard enough to cause damage. Reapply the penetrating oil if necessary.

For frozen screws, apply penetrating oil as described, and then insert a screwdriver into the slot and rap the top of the screwdriver with a hammer. This loosens the rust so the screw can be removed in the normal way. If the screw head is too damaged to use this method, grip the head with locking pliers and twist the screw out.

Avoid applying heat unless specifically instructed. Heat may melt, warp or remove the temper from parts.

Removing Broken Fasteners

If the head breaks off a screw or bolt, several methods are available for removing the remaining portion. If a large portion of the remainder projects out, try gripping it with locking pliers. If the projecting portion is too small, file it to fit a wrench or cut a slot in it to fit a screwdriver (**Figure 37**).

If the head breaks off flush, use a screw extractor. To do this, center punch the exact center of the remaining portion of the screw or bolt (A, **Figure 38**). Drill a small hole into the screw (B, **Figure 38**) and tap the extractor into the hole (C). Back the screw out with a wrench on the extractor (D, **Figure 38**).

Repairing Damaged Threads

Occasionally, threads are stripped through carelessness or impact damage. Often the threads can be repaired by running a tap (for internal threads on nuts) or die (for external threads on bolts) through the threads (**Figure 39**). To clean or repair spark plug threads, use a spark plug tap.

If an internal thread is damaged, it may be necessary to install a Helicoil or some other type of thread insert. Follow the manufacturer's instructions when installing their insert.

Stud Removal/Installation

A stud removal tool (**Figure 40**) is available from most tool suppliers. This tool makes the removal and installation of studs easier. If one is not available, thread two nuts onto the stud and tighten them against each other. Remove the stud by turning the lower nut (**Figure 41**).

1. Measure the height of the stud above the surface.
2. Thread the stud removal tool onto the stud and tighten it, or thread two nuts onto the stud.
3. Remove the stud by turning the stud remover or the lower nut.
4. Remove any threadlocking compound from the threaded hole. Clean the threads with an aerosol parts cleaner.
5. Install the stud removal tool onto the new stud or thread two nuts onto the stud.
6. Apply threadlocking compound to the threads of the stud.
7. Install the stud and tighten with the stud removal tool or the top nut.
8. Install the stud to the height noted in Step 1 or its torque specification.
9. Remove the stud removal tool or the two nuts.

Removing Hoses

When removing stubborn hoses, do not exert excessive force on the hose or fitting. Remove the hose clamp and carefully insert a small screwdriver or pick tool between the fitting and hose. Apply a spray lubricant under the hose and carefully twist the hose off the fitting. Clean any corrosion or rubber hose material from the fitting with a wire brush. Clean the

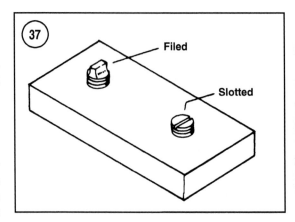

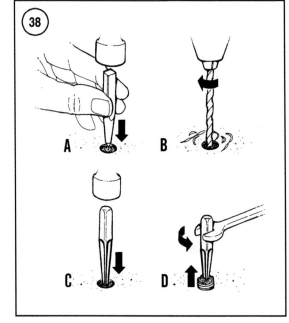

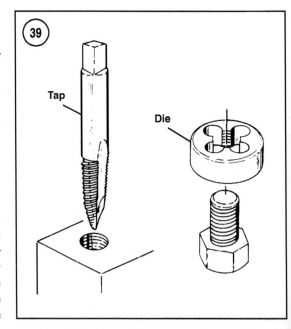

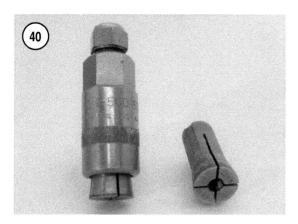

40

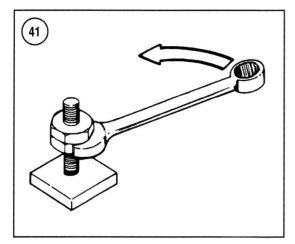

41

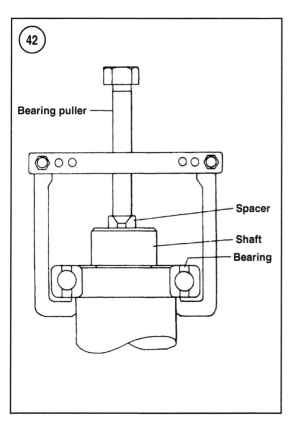

42

Bearing puller

Spacer

Shaft

Bearing

inside of the hose thoroughly. Do not use any lubricant when installing the hose (new or old). The lubricant may allow the hose to come off the fitting, even with the clamp secure.

Bearings

Bearings are precision parts, they must receive proper lubrication and maintenance. If a bearing is damaged, replace it immediately. When installing a new bearing, take precautions to avoid damaging it. Bearing replacement procedures are included in the individual chapters where applicable; however, use the following sections as a guideline.

Unless otherwise specified, install bearings with the manufacturer's mark or number facing outward.

Removal

While bearings are normally removed only when damaged, there may be times when it is necessary to remove a bearing that is in good condition. However, improper bearing removal will damage the bearing and possibly the shaft or case. Note the following when removing bearings:

1. Before removing the bearings, note the following:
   a. Refer to the bearing replacement procedure in the appropriate chapter for any special instructions.
   b. Remove any seals that interfere with bearing removal. Refer to *Seal Removal/Installation* in this section.
   c. When removing more than one bearing, identify the bearings before removing them. Refer to the bearing manufacturer's numbers on the bearing.
   d. Note and record the direction in which the bearing numbers face for proper installation.
   e. Remove any set plates or bearing retainers before removing the bearings.

2. When using a puller to remove a bearing from a shaft, take care that the shaft is not damaged. Always place a piece of metal between the end of the shaft and the puller screw. In addition, place the puller arms next to the inner bearing race. Refer to **Figure 42**.

3. When using a hammer to remove a bearing from a shaft, do not strike the hammer directly against the shaft. Instead, use a brass or aluminum spacer between the hammer and shaft (**Figure 43**). Make sure to support both bearing races with wooden blocks as shown.

4. The ideal method of bearing removal is with a hydraulic press. Note the following when using a press:

a. Always support the inner and outer bearing races with a suitable size wooden or aluminum spacer (**Figure 44**). If only the outer race is supported, pressure applied against the balls and/or the inner race will damage them.
b. Always make sure the press ram (**Figure 44**) aligns with the center of the shaft. If the ram is not centered, it may damage the bearing and/or shaft.
c. The moment the shaft is free of the bearing, it drops to the floor. Secure or hold the shaft to prevent it from falling.
d. When removing bearings from a housing, support the housing with 4 × 4 in. wooden blocks to prevent damage to gasket surfaces.

Installation

1. When installing a bearing into a housing, apply pressure to the *outer* bearing race (**Figure 45**). When installing a bearing onto a shaft, apply pressure to the inner bearing race (**Figure 46**).
2. When installing a bearing as described in Step 1, some type of driver is required. Never strike the bearing directly with a hammer or it will damage the bearing. When installing a bearing, use a piece of pipe or a driver with a diameter that matches the bearing inner race. **Figure 47** shows the correct way to use a driver and hammer to install a bearing.
3. Step 1 describes how to install a bearing into a case half or over a shaft. However, when installing a bearing over a shaft and into a housing at the same time, a tight fit is required for both outer and inner bearing races. In this situation, install a spacer underneath the driver tool so that pressure is applied evenly across both races. Refer to **Figure 48**. If the outer race is not supported as shown, the balls will push against the outer bearing race and damage it.

Interference fit

1. Follow this procedure when installing a bearing over a shaft. When a tight fit is required, the bearing inside diameter is smaller than the shaft. In this case, driving the bearing onto the shaft using normal methods may cause bearing damage. Instead, heat the bearing before installation. Note the following:
a. Secure the shaft so it is ready for bearing installation.
b. Clean all residues from the bearing surface of the shaft. Remove burrs with a file or sandpaper.
c. Fill a suitable pot or beaker with clean mineral oil. Place a thermometer rated above 120° C (248° F) in the oil. Support the thermometer

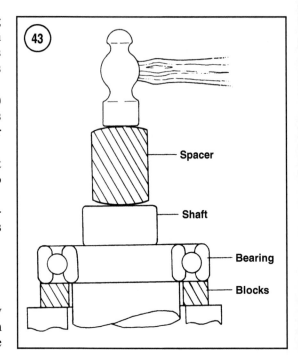
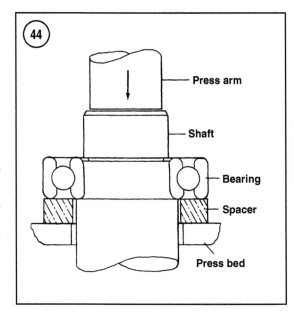
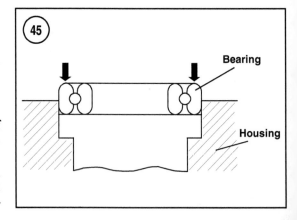

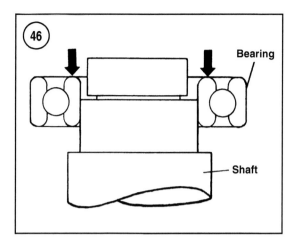

46

Bearing

Shaft

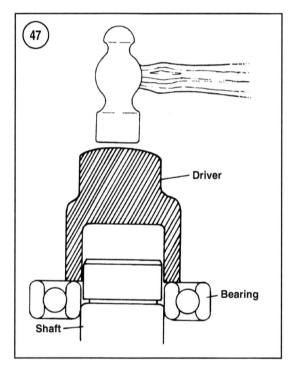

47

Driver

Bearing

Shaft

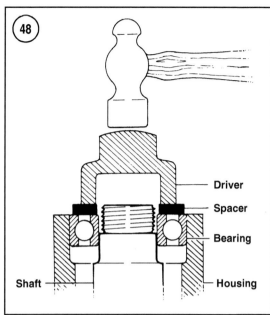

48

Driver

Spacer

Bearing

Shaft

Housing

ing with a slight interference fit. Driving the bearing into the housing using normal methods may damage the housing or cause bearing damage. Instead, heat the housing before the bearing is installed. Note the following:

CAUTION
Before heating the housing in this procedure, wash the housing thoroughly with detergent and water. Rinse and rewash the cases as required to remove all traces of oil and other chemical deposits.

a. Heat the housing to approximately 100° C (212° F) in an oven or on a hot plate. To check the temperature, fling tiny drops of water on the housing. If they sizzle and evaporate immediately, the temperature is correct. Heat only one housing at a time.

CAUTION
Do not heat the housing with a propane or acetylene torch. Never bring a flame into contact with the bearing or housing. The direct heat will destroy the case hardening of the bearing and will likely warp the housing.

so it does not rest on the bottom or side of the pot.

d. Remove the bearing from its wrapper and secure it with a piece of heavy wire bent to hold it in the pot. Hang the bearing in the pot so it does not touch the bottom or sides of the pot.

e. Turn the heat on and monitor the thermometer. When the oil temperature rises to approximately 120° C (248° F), remove the bearing from the pot and quickly install it. If necessary, place a socket on the inner bearing race and tap the bearing into place. As the bearing chills, it will tighten on the shaft, so installation must be done quickly. Make sure the bearing is installed completely.

2. Follow this step when installing a bearing into a housing. Bearings are generally installed in a hous-

b. Remove the housing from the oven or hot plate, and hold onto the housing with welding gloves.

NOTE
Remove and install the bearings with a suitable size socket and extension.

c. Hold the housing with the bearing side down and tap the bearing out. Repeat for all bearings in the housing.

d. Before heating the bearing housing, place the new bearing in a freezer if possible. Chilling a bearing slightly reduces its outside diameter while the heated bearing housing assembly is slightly larger due to heat expansion. This makes bearing installation easier.

NOTE
Always install bearings with the manufacturer's mark or number facing outward.

e. While the housing is still hot, install the new bearing(s) into the housing. Install the bearings by hand, if possible. If necessary, lightly tap the bearing(s) into the housing with a driver placed on the outer bearing race (**Figure 45**). Do not install new bearings by driving on the inner bearing race. Install the bearing until it seats completely.

Seal Removal/Installation

Seals (**Figure 49**) contain oil, water, grease or combustion gases in a housing or shaft. Improperly removing a seal can damage the housing or shaft. Improperly installing the seal can damage the seal. Note the following:

1. Prying is generally the easiest and most effective method of removing a seal from the housing. However, always place a rag underneath the pry tool (**Figure 50**) to prevent damage to the housing. Note the seal's installed depth or if it is installed flush.

2. Pack waterproof grease into the seal lips before the seal is installed.

3. In most cases, install seals with the manufacturer's numbers or marks facing out.

4. Install seals with a socket or driver placed on the outside of the seal as shown in **Figure 51**. Drive the seal squarely into the housing until it is to the correct depth or flush (**Figure 52**) as noted during removal. Never install a seal by hitting against the top of it with a hammer.

STORAGE

Several months of non-use can cause a general deterioration of the motorcycle. This is especially true in areas of extreme temperature variations. This deterioration can be minimized with careful preparation for storage. A properly stored motorcycle is much easier to return to service.

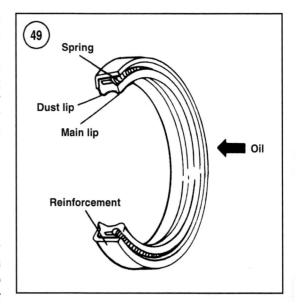

Storage Area Selection

When selecting a storage area, consider the following:

1. The storage area must be dry. A heated area is best but not necessary. It should be insulated to minimize extreme temperature variations.

2. If the building has large window areas, mask them to keep sunlight off the motorcycle.

3. Avoid buildings in industrial areas where corrosive emissions may be present. Avoid areas close to saltwater.

4. Consider the area's risk of fire, theft or vandalism. Check with an insurer regarding motorcycle coverage while in storage.

Preparing the Motorcycle for Storage

The amount of preparation a motorcycle should undergo before storage depends upon the expected length of non-use, storage area conditions and per-

sonal preference. Consider the following list the minimum requirement.

1. Wash the motorcycle thoroughly. Make sure all dirt, mud and road debris is removed.

2. Start the engine and allow it to reach operating temperature. Drain the engine oil regardless of the riding time since the last service. Fill the engine with the recommended type of oil.

3. Fill the fuel tank with fuel mixed with a fuel stabilizer. Mix the fuel and stabilizer in the ratio recommended by the stabilizer manufacturer. Run the engine for a few minutes so the stabilized fuel can enter the fuel injection system.

4. Remove the spark plugs and pour a tablespoon (45-60 ml) of engine oil into the cylinders. Place a rag over the openings and slowly turn the engine over to distribute the oil. Reinstall the spark plugs.

5. Remove the battery. Store the battery in a cool and dry location. Charge the battery once a month.

6. Use oily rags to cover the muffler output opening and intake openings in the air filter housing.

7. Apply a protective substance to the plastic and rubber components. Make sure to follow the manufacturer's instructions for each type of product being used.

8. Place the motorcycle on its centerstand. Rotate the front tire periodically to prevent a flat spot from developing and damaging the tire.

9. Cover the motorcycle with old bed sheets or something similar. Do not cover it with any plastic material that will trap moisture.

Returning the Motorcycle to Service

The amount of service required when returning a motorcycle to service after storage depends on the length of non-use and storage conditions. In addition to performing the reverse of the above procedure, make sure the brakes, clutch, throttle and engine stop switch work properly before operating the motorcycle. Refer to Chapter Three and evaluate the service intervals to determine which areas require service.

Table 1 VEHICLE DIMENSIONS AND WEIGHT

Overall length	2490 mm (98.0 in.)
Overall width	980 mm (38.6 in.)
Overall height	
XVS13A models	
2007-2009	1115 mm (43.9 in.)
2010	1145 mm (45.1 in.)
XVS13CT models	1520 mm (59.8 in.)
Seat height	
2007-2009 models	715 mm (28.1 in.)
2010 models	690 mm (27.2 in.)
Wheelbase	1690 mm (66.5 in.)
Ground clearance	145 mm (5.71 in.)
Weight (with oil and fuel)	
XVS13A models	303 kg (668 lbs.)
XVS13CT models	323 kg (712 lbs.)

Table 2 METRIC, DECIMAL AND FRACTION EQUIVALENTS

mm	in.	Nearest fraction	mm	in.	Nearest fraction
1	0.0394	1/32	26	1.0236	1 1/32
2	0.0787	3/32	27	1.0630	1 1/16
3	0.1181	1/8	28	1.1024	1 3/32
4	0.1575	5/32	29	1.1417	1 5/32
5	0.1969	3/16	30	1.1811	1 3/16
6	0.2362	1/4	31	1.2205	1 7/32
7	0.2756	9/32	32	1.2598	1 1/4
8	0.3150	5/16	33	1.2992	1 5/16
9	0.3543	11/32	34	1.3386	1 11/32
10	0.3937	13/32	35	1.3780	1 3/8
11	0.4331	7/16	36	1.4173	1 13/32
12	0.4724	15/32	37	1.4567	1 15/32
13	0.5118	1/2	38	1.4961	1 1/2
14	0.5512	9/16	39	1.5354	1 17/32
15	0.5906	19/32	40	1.5748	1 9/16
16	0.6299	5/8	41	1.6142	1 5/8
17	0.6693	21/32	42	1.6535	1 21/32
18	0.7087	23/32	43	1.6929	1 11/16
19	0.7480	3/4	44	1.7323	1 23/32
20	0.7874	25/32	45	1.7717	1 25/32
21	0.8268	13/16	46	1.8110	1 13/16
22	0.8661	7/8	47	1.8504	1 27/32
23	0.9055	29/32	48	1.8898	1 7/8
24	0.9449	15/16	49	1.9291	1 15/16
25	0.9843	31/32	50	1.9685	1 31/32

Table 3 CONVERSION FORMULAS

Multiply:	By:	To get the equivalent of:
Length		
Inches	25.4	Millimeter
Inches	2.54	Centimeter
Miles	1.609	Kilometer
Feet	0.3048	Meter
Millimeter	0.03937	Inches
Centimeter	0.3937	Inches
Kilometer	0.6214	Mile
Meter	3.281	Feet
Fluid volume		
U.S. quarts	0.9463	Liters
U.S. gallons	3.785	Liters
U.S. ounces	29.573529	Milliliters
Imperial gallons	4.54609	Liters
Imperial quarts	1.1365	Liters
Liters	0.2641721	U.S. gallons
Liters	1.0566882	U.S. quarts
Liters	33.814023	U.S. ounces
Liters	0.22	Imperial gallons
Liters	0.8799	Imperial quarts
Milliliters	0.033814	U.S. ounces
Milliliters	1.0	Cubic centimeters
Milliliters	0.001	Liters
Torque		
Foot-pounds	1.3558	Newton-meters
Foot-pounds	0.138255	Meters-kilograms
Inch-pounds	0.11299	Newton-meters
Newton-meters	0.7375622	Foot-pounds
Newton-meters	8.8507	Inch-pounds
Meters-kilograms	7.2330139	Foot-pounds

(continued)

Table 3 CONVERSION FORMULAS (continued)

Multiply:	By:	To get the equivalent of:
Volume		
Cubic inches	16.387064	Cubic centimeters
Cubic centimeters	0.0610237	Cubic inches
Temperature		
Fahrenheit	(°F − 32) × 0.556	Centigrade
Centigrade	(°C × 1.8) + 32	Fahrenheit
Weight		
Ounces	28.3495	Grams
Pounds	0.4535924	Kilograms
Grams	0.035274	Ounces
Kilograms	2.2046224	Pounds
Pressure		
Pounds per square inch	0.070307	Kilograms per square centimeter
Kilograms per square centimeter	14.223343	Pounds per square inch
Kilopascals	0.1450	Pounds per square inch
Pounds per square inch	6.895	Kilopascals
Speed		
Miles per hour	1.609344	Kilometers per hour
Kilometers per hour	0.6213712	Miles per hour

Table 4 TECHNICAL ABBREVIATIONS

A	Ampere
AC	Alternating current
A.h	Ampere hour
AT sensor	Air temperature sensor
C	Celsius
cc	Cubic centimeter
CDI	Capacitor discharge ignition
cid	Cubic inch displacement
CKP sensor	Crankshaft position sensor
cm	Centimeter
CT sensor	Coolant temperature sensor
cu. in.	Cubic inch and cubic inches
cyl.	Cylinder
DC	Direct current
ECM	Electronic control module
ECU	Electronic control unit
F	Fahrenheit
fl. oz.	Fluid ounces
ft.	Foot
ft.-lb.	Foot pounds
gal.	Gallon and gallons
H/A	High altitude
hp	Horsepower
Hz	Hertz
IAP sensor	Intake air pressure sensor
ID	Inside diameter
in.	Inch and inches
in.-lb.	Inch-pounds
in. Hg	Inches of mercury
k	One-thousand ohms (2k = 2000 ohms)
kg	Kilogram
kg/cm^2	Kilogram per square centimeter
kgm	Kilogram meter
km	Kilometer
km/h	Kilometer per hour
kPa	Kilopascals
kW	Kilowatt

(continued)

Table 4 TECHNICAL ABBREVIATIONS (continued)

L	Liter and liters
L/m	Liters per minute
lb.	Pound and pounds
m	Meter
mL	Milliliter
mm	Millimeter
N•m	Newton meter
O_2	Oxygen
OD	Outside diameter
oz.	Ounce and ounces
psi	Pounds per square inch
pt.	Pint and pints
qt.	Quart and quarts
rpm	Revolution per minute
SCCR	Starting circuit cutoff relay
SCCS	Starting circuit cutoff system
TDC	Top dead center
TP sensor	Throttle position sensor
V	Volt
W	Watt

Table 5 GENERAL TORQUE RECOMMENDATIONS*

Bolt diameter (mm)	N•m	in.-lb.	ft.-lb.
6	6	53	–
8	15	–	11
10	30	–	22
12	55	–	40
14	85	–	63
16	130	–	96

*Use for fasteners without a specified torque.

CHAPTER TWO

TROUBLESHOOTING

The troubleshooting procedures in this chapter described symptoms of typical problems and logical methods for isolating their causes. There may be several ways to resolve a problem, but only a systematic approach avoids wasted time and unnecessary parts replacement.

Begin troubleshooting by precisely describing the symptoms of the problem and the conditions under which they occur. Gather as much information as possible, never assume anything and do not overlook the obvious.

An engine needs three basic requirements to run properly: correct air/fuel mixture, compression and a spark at the proper time. If any element is missing, the engine will not run. If a quick check does not resolve the problem, turn to the troubleshooting procedure that most closely describes the symptoms of the failure, and perform the indicated tests.

In most cases, expensive and complex test equipment is not needed to determine if repairs can be performed at home. A few simple checks can prevent an unnecessary repair charge. On the other hand, be realistic and do not attempt repairs beyond one's capabilities.

ENGINE STARTING

System Operation

The positions of the sidestand, clutch and neutral switches affect engine starting. Refer to *Ignition and Starting Cutoff Systems* in Chapter Three.

Note the following before starting the engine:

1. The engine cannot start when the sidestand is down and the transmission is in gear.

2. The engine can start when the sidestand is down and the transmission is in neutral. The engine will stop, however, if the transmission is put in gear while the sidestand is down.

3. The engine can start when the sidestand is down and the transmission is in neutral if the clutch lever is pulled in.

4. The engine will also start if the sidestand is up, the transmission is in gear and the clutch lever is pulled

in. However, the engine will stop if the sidestand is moved down.

Normal Start

1. Shift the transmission into neutral.
2. Turn the ignition switch on.
   a. The neutral indicator light should turn on.
   b. The oil lever warning light, fuel level warning light, coolant temperature warning light, and engine trouble warning light should all turn on for a few seconds and then turn off.
3. Make sure the engine stop switch (A, **Figure 1**) is in the run position.
4. Press the starter switch (B, **Figure 1**) and start the engine. Do not open the throttle when pressing the starter switch.
5. Warm the engine until it responds cleanly to the throttle.
6. If the engine idles at a fast speed for more than five minutes or if the throttle is repeatedly snapped on and off at normal air temperatures, the exhaust pipes may discolor.

Engine Flooded

If the engine will not start and if a strong gasoline smell is present, the engine is probably flooded. To start a flooded engine:
1. Turn the engine stop switch to the off position.
2. Open the throttle fully.
3. Turn the ignition switch to the on position and operate the starter switch for 5 seconds.
4. Wait 10 seconds, and turn the engine stop switch to the run position.
5. Open the throttle slightly, and press the starter switch.
6. If the engine starts but idles roughly, vary the throttle position slightly until the engine idles and responds smoothly.

ENGINE WILL NOT START

Identifying the Problem

When the engine does not start, perform the following tests in the given order. They help determine if the problem is caused by a mechanical, fuel or electrical failure, and then identify the relevant troubleshooting procedure for further testing.

If the engine starts but idles or runs roughly, refer to *Engine Performance* in this chapter.
1. Refer to *Engine Starting* in this chapter to make sure all switches and starting procedures are correct.

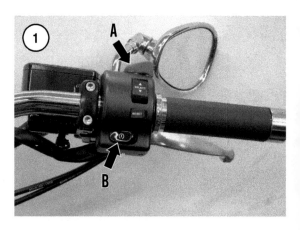

2. If the starter does not operate, troubleshoot the starting system as described in *Electrical Troubleshooting* in this chapter.
3. If the starter operates, and the engine seems flooded, refer to *Engine Flooded* in *Engine Starting* in this chapter.
4. Make sure the tank has sufficient fuel. Turn the ignition switch on and check the fuel level warning light. The fuel level is low if the warning light remains on.
5. Remove the fuel tank (Chapter Eight). Make sure the electrical connectors (**Figure 2**) are securely mated to each ignition coil terminal. Also confirm that each spark plug cap is securely connected to its spark plug.
6. Test the ignition system by performing the spark test described in this section. If the test produces a good spark, proceed to Step 7. If the spark is weak or if there is no spark, troubleshoot the ignition system as described in *Electrical Troubleshooting* in this chapter.
7. Check engine compression as described in Chapter Three. If the compression is low, check for one or more of the following:
   a. Leaking cylinder head gasket(s).
   b. Cracked or warped cylinder head(s).
   c. Worn piston rings, pistons and cylinders.
   d. Valve stuck open.
   e. Worn or damaged valve seat(s).
   f. Incorrect valve timing.

Spark Test

A spark test determines if the ignition system is producing adequate spark. The following procedure describes the uses of a spark tester. If this tester is not available, use a new spark plug.
1. Remove the fuel tank (Chapter Eight).
2. Remove the finished covers (Chapter Four).

WARNING
Disable the fuel system. Otherwise, fuel will enter into the cylinders when the

engine is turned over during the spark test, flooding the cylinders and creating explosive fuel vapors.

3. Disconnect the fuel injection fuse. Refer to *Fuses* in Chapter Nine.

4. Remove the spark plugs as described in Chapter Three.

5. Set the spark tester gap to 6.0 mm (0.24 in.), and insert the spark tester into the spark plug cap. Touch the tester base to a good engine ground. Position the tester so the electrode can be seen.

> *WARNING*
> *Mount the spark tester, away from the spark plug holes in the cylinder head so the tester cannot ignite the mixture in the cylinder. If the engine is flooded, do not perform this test. The firing of the spark tester can ignite fuel that is ejected through the spark plug holes.*

6. Shift the transmission into neutral, turn the ignition switch on and place the engine stop switch in the run position.

> *WARNING*
> *Do not hold the spark plugs, tester, wire or connector. Serious electrical shock may result.*

7. Press the starter button to turn the engine over. A fat blue spark must be evident across the tester terminals.

8. Repeat this test for the remaining cylinder.

9. If the spark is good, the ignition system is functioning properly. Check for one or more of the following possible malfunctions:
   a. Obstructed fuel line or fuel valve.
   b. Flooded engine.
   c. Damaged fuel pump system.
   d. Low compression or engine damage.

10. If the spark is weak or if there is no spark in one or both cylinders, troubleshoot the ignition system

as described in *Electrical Troubleshooting* in this chapter.

11. Reconnect the fuel injection fuse.

Engine is Difficult to Start

1. After attempting to start the engine, remove one of the spark plugs as described in Chapter Three, and check for the presence of fuel on the plug tip. Note the following:
   a. If no fuel is visible on the plug, remove the other spark plug. If there is no fuel on this plug, perform Step 2.
   b. If there is fuel on the plug tip, go to Step 5.
   c. If there is an excessive amount of fuel on the plug, check for a clogged or plugged air filter or for incorrect throttle valve operation (stuck open).

2. Make sure there is sufficient fuel in the fuel tank. Check the tank for a clogged fuel hose, breather hose or rollover valve.

3. Troubleshoot the fuel pump as described in *Fuel Pump Troubleshooting* in this chapter.

4. Check for a clogged or damaged fuel valve or fuel-valve hose.

5. Perform the spark test as described in this section. Note the following:
   a. If the spark is weak or if there is no spark, go to Step 6.
   b. If the spark is good, go to Step 8.

6. If the spark is weak or if there is no spark, check the following:
   a. Fouled spark plug(s).
   b. Damaged spark plug(s).
   c. Loose or damaged spark plug wire(s) or cap(s).
   d. Loose or damaged ignition coil.
   e. Damaged ECU.
   f. Damaged CKP sensor.
   g. Faulty ignition coil(s).
   h. Damaged engine stop switch.
   i. Damaged ignition switch.
   j. Dirty or loose-fitting terminals.

7. If the engine turns over but does not start, perform an engine compression test (Chapter Three). Check for the following possible malfunctions:
   a. Leaking cylinder head gasket.
   b. Incorrect valve clearance.
   c. Bent or stuck valve(s).
   d. Worn valve guide(s).
   e. Incorrect valve timing. Worn cylinders and/or pistons rings.
   f. Improper valve-to-seat contact.

8. If the spark is good, try starting the engine by following normal starting procedures. If the engine starts but then stops, check for the following conditions:
   a. Incorrect fast idle valve operation.

b. Leaking or damaged intake manifold.

c. Contaminated fuel.

d. Incorrect ignition timing due to failed ignition system component.

Engine Does Not Crank

If the engine will not turn over, check for one or more of the following:

1. Troubleshoot the starting system as described in *Electrical Troubleshooting* in this chapter.

2. Faulty starter clutch.

3. Seized pistons(s).

4. Seized crankshaft bearings.

5. Broken connecting rod.

6. Locked-up transmission or clutch assembly.

ENGINE PERFORMANCE

Refer to the relevant checklist when the engine runs but performs poorly.

Engine Idles Poorly

1. Engine:
   a. Clogged air filter element.
   b. Improperly adjusted valve clearance.
   c. Poorly seating valves.
   d. Defective valve guides.
   e. Worm camshafts.
2. Fuel system:
   a. Unsynchronized throttle valve.
   b. Damaged or cracked vacuum hose.
   c. Leaking throttle body joints.
   d. Improperly adjusted throttle cable free play.
   e. Flooded throttle body.
3. Electrical system:
   a. Fouled or improperly gapped spark plug(s).
   b. Faulty spark plug cap.
   c. Faulty ignition coil.
   d. Faulty CKP sensor.
   e. Faulty ECU.
   f. Broken or missing alternator Woodruff key.

Low or Poor Engine Power

1. Securely support the motorcycle with the rear wheel off the ground, and spin the rear wheel by hand. If the wheel spins freely, perform Step 2. If the wheel does not spin freely, check for the following conditions:
   a. Dragging rear brake.
   b. Excessive rear axle torque.
   c. Worn or damaged rear wheel bearings.

2. Check the tire pressure. If pressure is normal, perform Step 3. If pressure is low, adjust the pressure (Chapter Eleven).

3. Ride the motorcycle, and accelerate rapidly from first to second gear. If the engine speed reduces when the clutch is released, perform Step 4. If the engine speed does not change when the clutch is released, check for the following:
   a. Slipping clutch.
   b. Worn or warped plain plates or friction discs.
   c. Weak clutch spring.
   d. Incorrect clutch cable free play.
   e. Check the engine oil for additives.

4. Ride the motorcycle, and accelerate lightly. If the engine speed increases relative to throttle operation, perform Step 5. If engine speed does not increase, check for the following:
   a. Clogged air filter.
   b. Fuel flow restricted.
   c. Clogged muffler.
   d. Faulty fuel pump.
   e. Faulty relay unit (starting circuit cutoff relay side).

5. Check for one of the following:
   a. Incorrect ignition timing due to a malfunctioning ignition component.
   b. Improperly adjusted valves or worn valve seats.
   c. Low engine compression.
   d. Clogged fuel injectors.
   e. Fouled spark plugs.
   f. Incorrect spark plug heat range.
   g. Incorrect oil level.
   h. Contaminated oil.
   i. Worn or damaged valve train assembly.
   j. Engine overheating. Refer to *Engine Overheating* in this section.

6. If the engine knocks when accelerating or when running at high speed, check for the following:
   a. Incorrect type of fuel.
   b. Advanced ignition timing caused by malfunctioning ignition component.
   c. Excessive carbon buildup in the combustion chamber.
   d. Worn pistons and/or cylinder bores.

Poor Medium and High Speed Performance

1. Engine:
   a. Clogged air filter element.
   b. Improperly adjusted valve clearance.
   c. Poorly seating valves.
   d. Defective valve guides.
   e. Worm camshafts.
   f. Worn pistons or rings.
2. Fuel system:
   a. Unsynchronized throttle valve.

b. Damaged or cracked vacuum hose.
c. Leaking throttle body joints.
d. Improperly adjusted throttle cable free play
e. Flooded throttle body.
f. Check the fuel pump as described in *Fuel Pump Troubleshooting* in this chapter.
3. Electrical system:
   a. Test the ignition system as described in *Electrical Troubleshooting* in this chapter.
   b. Test the starting system as described in *Electrical Troubleshooting* in this chapter.

Engine Overheating

1. Engine:
   a. Clogged coolant passages.
   b. Heavy carbon deposits in combustion chamber.
   c. Worn or damaged cylinder head and piston.
2. Fuel system:
   a. Worn or damaged throttle body joint.
   b. Clogged air filter.
3. Electrical system:
   a. Incorrect spark plug gap.
   b. Improper spark plug heat range.
   c. Faulty fan relay.
   d. Faulty coolant temperature sensor.
   e. Faulty ECU.
4. Cooling system:
   a. Low coolant level.
   b. Leaking radiator.
   c. Bent or damaged radiator fins.
   d. Defective radiator cap.
   e. Damaged water pump.
   f. Thermostat stuck closed.
   g. Damaged or improperly connected hose or pipe.
5. Chassis:
   a. Dragging brakes.
   b. Slipping clutch.

Engine Runs Roughly

1. Incorrect valve timing.
2. Fuel system:
   a. Clogged air filter.
   b. Contaminated fuel.
   c. Clogged fuel line.
   d. Fouled spark plugs.
3. Electrical system:
   a. Loose battery cable connection(s).
   b. Short circuit from damaged wire insulation.
   c. Loose or defective ignition circuit wire.
   d. Defective ignition coil.
   e. Faulty ECU.

Engine Lacks Acceleration

1. Clogged fuel line.
2. Improper ignition timing caused by faulty ignition system component.
3. Dragging brake(s).
4. Slipping clutch.

Engine Backfires

1. Improper ignition timing caused by faulty ignition system component.
2. Incorrect throttle body adjustment.
3. Lean fuel mixture.

Engine Misfires During Acceleration

1. Improper ignition timing caused by faulty ignition system component.
2. Excessively worn or defective spark plug(s).
3. Incorrect throttle body adjustment.

ENGINE NOISES

Unusual noises often indicate a developing problem. Investigate any new noise as soon as possible. A minor problem, if corrected, could prevent more extensive damage.

Use a mechanic's stethoscope or a small section of hose held near your ear (not directly on your ear) with the other end close to the source of the noise to isolate the location. Determining the exact cause of a noise can be difficult. If this is the case, consult a professional mechanic to determine the cause. Do not disassemble major components until all other possibilities have been eliminated.

Consider the following when troubleshooting engine noises:

1. A knocking or pinging during acceleration may be caused by the use of a lower-than-recommended octane fuel. It may also be caused by poor fuel, a spark plug of the wrong heat range or carbon buildup in the combustion chamber.
2. Slapping or rattling noises at low speed or during acceleration may be caused by excessive piston-to-cylinder wall clearance (piston slap). Piston slap is easier to detect when the engine is cold and before the pistons have expanded. Once the engine has warmed up, piston expansion reduces piston-to-cylinder clearance.
3. Knocking or rapping while decelerating is usually caused by excessive rod bearing clearance.
4. Persistent knocking and vibration occurring every crankshaft rotation is usually caused by worn rod or

main bearing(s). It can also be caused by broken piston rings or damaged piston pins.

5. A rapid on-off squeal may be a compression leak around the cylinder head gasket or spark plug(s).

6. If there is valve train noise, check for the following:

   a. Excessive valve clearance.
   b. Excessively worn or damaged camshaft.
   c. Damaged cam chain tensioner.
   d. Worn or damaged valve lifters and/or shims.
   e. Damaged valve bore(s) in cylinder head.
   f. Valve sticking in guide.
   g. Broken valve spring.
   h. Low oil pressure.
   i. Clogged cylinder oil hole or oil passage.
   j. Excessively worn or damaged timing chain or sprockets.

7. For rattles, start checking at the source of the sound. This may require the removal of covers or other components.

ENGINE LUBRICATION

Insufficient engine lubrication quickly leads to engine seizure. Check the engine oil level before each ride, and top off the oil as described in Chapter Three. Oil/water pump assembly service appears in Chapter Five.

Oil Consumption High or Engine Smokes Excessively

1. Too much oil.
2. Worn or damaged piston rings.
3. Worn valve guides.
4. Worn or scored cylinders.
5. Worn valve stem.
6. Faulty valve seal.

Excessive Engine Oil Leaks

1. Clogged air filter breather hose.
2. Loose engine parts.
3. Damaged gasket-sealing surfaces.

Low Oil Pressure

1. Low oil level.
2. Damaged oil/water pump assembly.
3. Clogged oil strainer screen.
4. Clogged oil filter.
5. Internal oil leaks.
6. Incorrect type engine oil being used.
7. Oil pressure relief valve stuck open.

High Oil Pressure

1. Incorrect type engine oil being used.
2. Clogged oil filter, oil gallery or metering orifices.
3. Oil pressure relief valve stuck closed.

No Oil Pressure

1. Damaged oil/water pump.
2. Excessively low oil level.
3. Damaged oil/water pump drive shaft.
4. Damaged oil/water pump drive sprocket.
5. Incorrect oil/water pump installation.

Oil Level Too Low

1. Low oil level.
2. Worn piston rings.
3. Worn cylinder.
4. Worn valve guides.
5. Worn valve stem seals.
6. Incorrectly installed piston rings.
7. External oil leaks.
8. Oil leaking into the cooling system.

Oil Contamination

1. Blown head gasket allowing coolant to leak into the engine.
2. Water contamination.
3. Oil and filter not changed at specified intervals or when operating conditions demand more frequent changes.

CYLINDER LEAKDOWN TEST

A cylinder leakdown test locates compression leaks caused by leaking valves, blown head gaskets or broken, worn or stuck piston rings. The test applies compressed air through the cylinder and then measuring the leak rate as a percentage.

A cylinder leakdown tester and an air compressor are needed to perform this test.

1. Run the engine until it is warm. Turn it off.
2. Remove the air filter housing (Chapter Eight). Secure the throttle at its wide-open position.
3. Set the No. 1 cylinder (front) to top dead center on the compression stroke as described in *Valve Clearance* in Chapter Three.
4. Remove the spark plug from the No. 1 cylinder.
5. Thread the tester's adapter into the No. 1 cylinder spark plug hole following the manufacturer's instructions. Connect the leakdown tester onto the adapter. Connect an air compressor hose onto the tester's fitting.

6. If the engine is not too hot, remove the radiator cap. Refer to *Cooling System Precautions* in Chapter Ten.

> *WARNING*
> *The crankshaft may spin when compressed air is applied to the cylinder. Remove any tools attached to the end of the crankshaft. To prevent the engine from turning over as compressed air is applied to the cylinder, shift the transmission into fifth gear and have an assistant apply the rear brake.*

7. Apply compressed air to the leakdown tester following the tester manufacturer's instructions. Read the leak rate on the gauge. For a new or rebuilt engine, a loss of 0 to 5 percent per cylinder is desirable. A loss of 6 to 14 percent is acceptable and means the engine is in good condition.
8. With air pressure still applied, use a mechanic's stethoscope to listen for air leaks in the following areas:
   a. Air leaking through the exhaust pipe indicates a leaking exhaust valve.
   b. Air leaking through the throttle bodies indicates a leaking intake valve.
   c. Air leaking through the crankcase breather suggests worn piston rings or a worn cylinder bore.
9. Remove the leakdown tester, and repeat the test for the other cylinder. Note the difference between the cylinders. On a used engine, a pressure loss of 10 percent or less between cylinders is satisfactory. A pressure loss exceeding 10 percent between cylinders points to an engine in poor condition.

CLUTCH

Basic clutch troubles and their causes are listed in this section. Clutch service is found in Chapter Six.

Clutch Lever Hard to Pull In

1. Clutch cable requires lubrication.
2. Clutch cable improperly routed or bent.
3. Damaged pull rod bearing.

Clutch Slip

If the engine speed increases without an increase in motorcycle speed, the clutch is probably slipping. Some main causes of clutch slipping are:
1. Incorrect clutch cable adjustment.
2. Improperly assembled clutch.
3. Weak clutch springs.
4. Worn plain plate or friction disc.

5. Damaged pressure plate.
6. Improper oil level.
7. Improper oil viscosity.
8. Deteriorated or contaminated engine oil (engine oil additive being used).

Clutch Drag

A clutch is dragging when the clutch will not disengage or when the motorcycle creeps with the transmission in gear. Some causes of clutch drag are:
1. Incorrectly adjusted cluch cable.
2. Incorrect oil viscosity.
3. Engine oil level too high.
4. Deteriorated or contaminated engine oil (engine oil additive being used).
5. Incorrectly assembled clutch.
6. Uneven clutch spring tension.
7. Warped plain plate, friction disc or pressure plate.
8. Swollen friction disc.
9. Bent pull rod.
10. Damaged clutch hub.
11. Damaged primary driven gear bushing.
12. Clutch index marks not properly aligned.

TRANSMISSION AND SHIFT MECHANISM

Transmission symptoms are sometimes hard to distinguish from clutch symptoms. Common transmission and shift mechanism troubles and their checks are listed below. Refer to Chapter Seven for transmission and shift mechanism service. Prior to working on the transmission, make sure the clutch and shift mechanism assemblies are working properly. Refer to Chapter Six for clutch service procedures.

Transmission Jumps out of Gear

1. External shift mechanism:
   a. Incorrect shift pedal position.
   b. Damaged stopper bolt.
   c. Weak or damaged stopper lever spring.
   d. Weak or damaged gearshift linkage springs.
2. Internal shift mechanism:
   a. Bent or worn shift fork.
   b. Bent shift fork shaft.
   c. Loose or damaged shift cam.
   d. Damaged shift drum grooves.
3. Transmission:
   a. Worn gear dogs or slots.
   b. Gear groove worn.

Difficult Shifting

1. Refer to *Clutch Drag* in *Clutch* in this chapter.

2. Weak or damaged gearshift linkage springs.
3. Internal shift mechanism:
    a. Bent shift fork shaft.
    b. Bent or damaged shift fork.
    c. Damaged shift-fork guide pin.
    d. Damaged shift drum grooves.
4. Transmission:
    a. Worn gear dogs or slots.
    b. Gear groove worn.

Shift Pedal Does Not Move or Return

1. Shift mechanism:
    a. Shift shaft incorrectly installed.
    b. Bent shift shaft.
    c. Weak or damaged shift shaft return spring.
    d. Improper shift rod adjustment.
    e. Bend shift fork shaft.
    f. Damaged shift fork.
2. Transmission:
    a. Seized transmission gear.
    b. Improperly assembled transmission.

Incorrect Shift Lever Operation

1. Improperly adjusted shift pedal rod.
2. Bent shift lever.
3. Stripped shift lever splines.
4. Damaged shift lever linkage.

Excessive Gear Noise

1. Worn bearings.
2. Worn or damaged gears.
3. Excessive gear backlash.

FUEL SYSTEM

Engine Will Not Start

If the engine will not start and the electrical and mechanical systems are operating correctly, check the following:
1. Contaminated or old fuel.
2. Clogged fuel line.
3. Air leak at the intake manifold, air filter or throttle body assembly.
4. Clogged fuel injector.
5. Sticking or damaged fuel injector.
6. Damaged fuel pump.

Engine Starts but Idles and Runs Poorly or Stalls

An engine that idles roughly or stalls may have one or more of the following problems:

1. Contaminated or old fuel.
2. Clogged fuel line.
3. Improper throttle cable free play.
4. Incorrect throttle body synchronization.
5. Incorrect idle speed.
6. Intake air leak at the intake manifold, air filter or throttle body assembly.
7. Clogged fuel injector.
8. Sticking or damaged fuel injector.

Poor Fuel Mileage and Engine Performance

1. Infrequent tune-ups. Compare the service records with the maintenance schedule in Chapter Three.
2. Clogged air filter.
3. Clogged fuel system.
4. Damaged pressure regulator.
5. Faulty fuel pump.

Engine Backfires or Misfires During Acceleration

1. Lean fuel mixture.
2. Incorrect throttle body synchronization.
3. Ignition system malfunction.
4. Faulty vacuum hoses.
5. Vacuum leaks at the throttle body, throttle body joints or intake manifold.
6. Fouled spark plug(s).

FUEL PUMP TROUBLESHOOTING

When troubleshooting the fuel pump, refer to the wiring diagram at the end of this book. Perform these test procedures in the listed sequence. Each test presumes that the components tested in earlier steps are working properly. The tests can yield invalid results if they are performed out of sequence. If a test indicates that a component is working properly, reconnect the electrical connections and proceed to the next step.
1. Check the main, ignition and fuel injection system fuses. Replace any blown fuses as described in Chapter Nine.
2. Perform the battery open voltage test (Chapter Nine). Recharge or replace the battery as needed.
3. Check the continuity of the main switch and the engine stop switch (Chapter Nine). Replace a switch that fails its continuity test.
4. Perform the relay-unit fuel pump test (Chapter Nine). Replace the relay unit if it is faulty.
5. Inspect the fuel pump as described in *Fuel Pump* (Chapter Eight).
6. On 2007-2009 models, perform the diode 2 test (Chapter Nine). Replace diode 2 as needed.

7. Check all the wires and connectors in the fuel pump system. Repair or replace any wire or connector as needed.

8. The ECU is faulty. Take the motorcycle to a dealership for further ECU testing.

ELECTRICAL TESTING

This section describes the basics of electrical testing and the use of test equipment.

Preliminary Checks and Precautions

Perform the following before starting electrical troubleshooting:

1. Check the main fuse (Chapter Nine). If the fuse is blown, replace it.

2. Check the individual fuses mounted in the fuse box (Chapter Nine). Inspect the suspected fuse, and replace it if blown.

3. Inspect the battery (Chapter Nine). Make sure it is fully charged, and that the battery leads are clean and securely attached to the battery terminals.

4. Disconnect each electrical connector in the suspect circuit, and inspect the terminals in the connector. A bent pin will not connect to its mate in the female side of the connector causing an open circuit.

5. Make sure the female terminal on the end of each wire is pushed all the way into the plastic housing. If not, carefully push them in with a narrow blade screwdriver.

6. Check all electrical wires where they join with the individual metal terminals in both the male and female housings.

> *NOTE*
> *Dielectric grease is special grease that can be used on electrical components such as connectors and battery connections. Dielectric grease can be purchased at automotive part stores.*

7. Make sure all electrical terminals within the housing are clean and free of corrosion. Clean them and pack the connectors with dielectric grease.

8. Push the connector halves together. Make sure the terminals are fully engaged and locked together.

9. Never pull the electrical wires when disconnecting an electrical connector. Only pull the connector plastic housing.

10. Never use a self-powered test light on circuits that contain solid-state devices. The solid-state device may be damaged.

Electrical Component Replacement

Most motorcycle dealerships and parts suppliers will not accept the return of any electrical part. If the exact cause of an electrical system malfunction cannot be determined, have a dealership retest the specific system to verify the test results. If a new electrical component is installed and the system still does not work, the unit, in all likelihood, cannot be returned for a refund.

Consider any test results carefully before replacing a component that tests only slightly out of specification, especially resistance. A number of variables can affect test results dramatically. These include: the test meter's internal circuitry, ambient temperature, and the conditions under which the machine has been operated. All instructions and specifications have been checked for accuracy. However, successful test results depend - to a great degree - upon individual accuracy.

Back Probing

Some tests require back probing a connector. In these instances, insert a needle probe or a small wire into the connector at the indicated terminal, and connect the multimeter test probe to the needle probe or wire. The needle probe or wire must not exceed 0.5 mm (0.02 in.) in diameter.

Make sure the needle probe or wire contacts the metal part of the terminal. Exercise caution so the needle does not deform the terminals in the connector.

Test Light or Voltmeter

A test light can be constructed from a 12-volt light bulb with a pair of test leads carefully soldered to the bulb. To check for voltage in a circuit, attach one lead to ground and the other lead to various points along the circuit. The bulb lights when voltage is present.

A voltmeter is used in the same manner as the test light. The voltmeter, unlike the test light, also indicates how much voltage is present at each test point. When using a voltmeter, attach the positive test lead to the component or wire to be checked and the negative test lead to a good ground (**Figure 3**).

Ammeter

An ammeter measures the flow of current (amperes) in a circuit (**Figure 4**). When connected in series in a circuit, the ammeter determines if current is flowing through the circuit and if that current flow is within specification. Current flow is often referred to as current draw. Comparing actual current draw in the circuit or component to the manufacturer's specified current draw provides useful diagnostic information.

Self-powered Test Light

A self-powered test light can be constructed from a 12-volt light bulb, a pair of test leads and a 12-volt battery. When the test leads are touched together the light bulb should go on.

Use a self-powered test light as follows:

1. Touch the test leads together to make sure the light bulb turns on. If not, correct the problem before using the test light in a test procedure.
2. Disconnect the motorcycle's battery or remove the fuse(s) that protects the circuit to be tested.
3. Select two points within the circuit where there should be continuity.
4. Attach one lead of the self-powered test light to each point.
5. If there is continuity, the self-powered test light bulb will turn on.
6. If there is no continuity, the self-powered test light bulb will not come on indicating an open circuit.

Ohmmeter

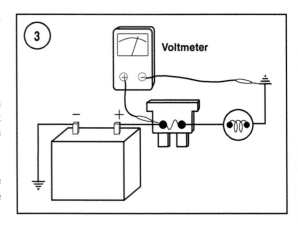

CAUTION
Never connect an ohmmeter to a circuit which has power applied to it. Always disconnect the battery negative lead before using an ohmmeter.

An ohmmeter measures the resistance (in ohms) to current flow in a circuit or component. Like the self-powered test light, an ohmmeter contains its own power source and should not be connected to a live circuit.

Ohmmeters may be analog type (needle scale) or digital type (LCD or LED readout). Both types of ohmmeters have a switch that allows you to select different ranges of resistance for accurate readings. The analog ohmmeter also has a set-adjust control which is used to zero or calibrate the meter (digital ohmmeters do not require calibration).

An ohmmeter is used by connecting its test leads to the terminals or leads of the circuit or component to be tested (**Figure 5**). If an analog meter is used, it must be calibrated by touching the test leads together and turning the set-adjust knob until the meter needle reads zero. When the leads are uncrossed, the needle should move to the other end of the scale indicating infinite resistance.

During a continuity test, a reading of infinity indicates that there is an open in the circuit or component. A reading of zero indicates continuity, that is, there

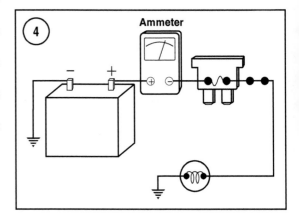

is no measurable resistance in the circuit or component being tested. If the meter needle falls between these two ends of the scale, this indicates the actual resistance present in the circuit. To determine the resistance, multiply the meter reading by the ohmmeter scale. For example, a meter reading of 5 multiplied by the R × 1,000 scale is 5,000 ohms of resistance.

Jumper Wire

A jumper wire is a simply way to bypass a potential problem when troubleshooting. If a faulty circuit works properly with a jumper wire installed, an open exists between the two jumper points in the circuit.

To troubleshoot with a jumper wire, first use the wire to determine if the problem is on the ground side or the load side of a device. In the example shown in **Figure 6**, test the ground by connecting a jumper between the lamp and a good ground. If the lamp comes on, the problem is the connection between the lamp and ground. If the lamp does not come on with the jumper installed, the lamp's connection to ground is good so the problem is between the lamp and the power source.

To isolate the problem, connect the jumper between the battery and the lamp. If it comes on, the problem is between these two points. Next, connect

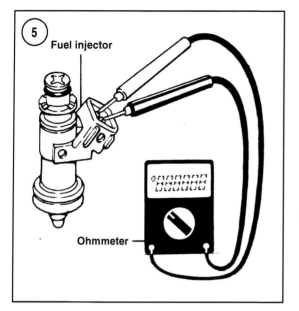

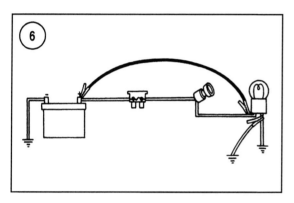

Voltage Test

Unless otherwise specified, all voltage tests are made with the electrical connectors still connected. Back probe the connector and make sure the test lead touches the electrical wire or metal terminal within the connector housing. Touching the wire insulation yields a false reading. Refer to *Back Probing* in this section.

Always check both sides of the connector. One side may be loose or corroded thus preventing electrical flow through the connector. This type of test can be performed with a test light or a voltmeter. A voltmeter gives the best results.

NOTE
If using a test light, it does not make any difference which test lead is attached to ground.

1. Attach the voltmeters negative test lead to a good ground (bare metal). If necessary, scrape away paint from the frame or engine (retouch later with paint). Make sure the part used for ground is not insulated with a rubber gasket or rubber grommet.
2. Attach the voltmeter positive test lead to the point (electrical connector, etc.) to be checked (**Figure 3**).
3. Turn the ignition switch on. If using a test light, the test light will come on if voltage is present. If using a voltmeter, note the voltage reading. The reading should be within 1 volt of battery voltage (12 volts). If the voltage is 11 volts or less, a problem exists in the circuit.

Voltage Drop Test

Since resistance causes voltage to drop, a voltmeter can be used to determine resistance in an active circuit. This is called a voltage drop test. A voltage drop test measures the difference between the voltage at the beginning of the circuit and the available voltage at the end of the circuit while the circuit is operating.

If the circuit has no resistance, there is no voltage drop so the voltmeter indicates 0 volts. The greater the resistance in a circuit, the greater the voltage drop reading. A voltage drop of 1 or more volts indicates that a circuit has excessive resistance.

It is important to note that a 0 reading on a voltage drop test is good. Battery voltage, on the other hand, indicates an open circuit. A voltage drop test is an excellent way to check the condition of solenoids, relays, battery cables and other high-current electrical components.

1. Connect the voltmeter positive test lead to the end of the wire or device closest to the battery.

the jumper between the battery and the fuse side of the switch. If the lamp comes on, the switch is good. By successively moving the jumper from one point to another, the problem can be isolated to a particular place in the circuit.

Pay attention to the following when using a jumper wire:

1. Make sure the jumper wire gauge (thickness) is the same as that used in the circuit being tested. Smaller gauge wires will rapidly overhead and could melt.
2. Install insulated boots over alligator clips. This prevents accidental grounding, sparks or possible shock when working in cramped quarters.
3. Jumper wires are temporary test measures only. Do not leave a jumper wire installed as a permanent solution. This creates a severe fire hazard that could easily lead to complete loss of the motorcycle.
4. When using a jumper wire always install an inline fuse/fuse holder (available at most auto supply stores or electronic supply stores) to the jumper wire.
5. Never use a jumper wire across any load (a component that is connected and turned on). This would result in a direct short and will blow the fuse(s).

2. Connect the voltmeter negative test lead to the ground side of the wire or device (**Figure 7**).

3. Turn the components on in the circuit.

4. The voltmeter should indicate 0 volts. If there is a drop of 1 volt or more, a problem exists within the circuit. A voltage drop reading of 12 volts indicates an open in the circuit.

Peak Voltage Test

A peak voltage test checks the voltage output of a component at normal cranking speed. This test accurately measures a component's output voltage under operating conditions.

A given peak voltage specification is a minimum value. If the measured voltage meets or exceeds this specification, the test results are satisfactory. The tested component is operating within specification. In some instances, the measured voltage may greatly exceed the minimum specification.

The Yamaha Model 88 Multimeter (part No. YU-A1927 or 90890-03174) with the peak voltage adapter, or an equivalent multimeter and peak voltage adapter, are needed to perform a peak voltage test. Refer to the manufacturer's instructions when using these tools.

Continuity Test

A continuity test is used to determine the integrity of a circuit, wire or component. A circuit has continuity if it forms a complete circuit; that is if there are no opens in either the electrical wires or components within the circuit. A circuit with an open, on the other hand, has no continuity.

A continuity test can be performed with a self-powered test light or an ohmmeter. An ohmmeter gives the best results. If using an analog ohmmeter, calibrate the meter by touching the leads together and turning the calibration knob until the meter reads zero.

1. Disconnect the negative cable from the battery (Chapter Nine).

2. Attach a test lead to one end of the part or circuit to be tested.

3. Attach the remaining test lead to the other end of the part or circuit to be tested.

4. The self-powered test light comes on if there is continuity. An ohmmeter reads 0 or very low resistance if there is continuity. A reading of infinite resistance indicates no continuity; the circuit has an open.

Short-to-Ground Test

1. Disconnect the negative cable from the battery (Chapter Nine).

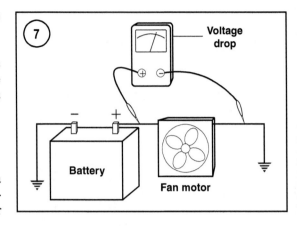

2. Disconnect the electrical connector from each end of the suspect circuit (A and C, **Figure 8**).

3. If the circuit branches off to include other components, disconnect the connectors of these components as well.

4. Connect an ohmmeter test probe to a terminal in one end of the circuit (A, **Figure 8**). Connect the other ohmmeter test probe to a good ground.

5. If continuity is indicated, a short-to-ground exists between A and C, **Figure 8**.

6. Disconnect the connector B, **Figure 8**, and check the continuity between A and ground. If continuity is present, the short is between points A and B, **Figure 8**. If no continuity is present, the short is between, B and C, **Figure 8**.

Testing For a Short with a Test Light or Voltmeter

1. Remove the blown fuse from the fuse panel (Chapter Nine).

2. Connect the test light or voltmeter across the fuse terminals in the fuse panel. Turn the ignition switch on and check for battery voltage (12 volts).

3. With the test light or voltmeter attached to the fuse terminals, wiggle the wiring harness of the suspect circuit at 6 in. (15.2 cm) intervals. Start next to the fuse panel and work away from the panel.

4. Watch the test light or voltmeter while moving along the harness. If the test light blinks or if the needle on the voltmeter moves when the harness is wiggled, a short-to-ground exists at that point in the harness.

ELECTRICAL TROUBLESHOOTING

Before troubleshooting an electrical problem, turn to the wiring diagrams at the end of the book and identify the components, connector and wiring in the suspect circuit. Determine how the circuit should work by tracing the current path from the power source through the circuit components to ground. Also

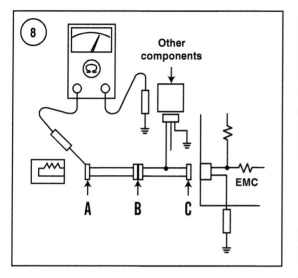

check any circuits that share the same fuse, ground or switch. If the other circuits work properly and the shared wiring is okay, the fault must be in the wiring used only by the suspect circuit. If all related circuits are faulty at the same time, the probable cause is a poor ground connection or a blown fuse(s).

As with all troubleshooting, analyze typical symptoms in a systematic manner. Never assume anything, and do not overlook the obvious, like a blown fuse or an electrical connector that has separated. Test the simplest and most obvious items first and try to make tests at easily accessible points on the motorcycle.

The troubleshooting procedures for various electrical systems are listed below. Start with the first inspection in the list, and perform the indicated check(s). If a test indicates that a component is working properly, reconnect the electrical connections and proceed to the next step. Systematically work through the troubleshooting checklist until the problem is identified. Repair or replace faulty parts as described in the appropriate section of the manual.

Perform these procedures in the listed sequence. Each test presumes that the components tested in the earlier steps are working properly. The tests can yield invalid results if they are performed out of sequence.

Ignition System

1. Check the ignition and main fuses (Chapter Nine). Replace any fuse as needed.
2. Perform the battery open voltage test (Chapter Nine). Charge or replace the battery as needed.
3. Check the spark plug gaps (Chapter Three). Regap or replace the plugs.
4. Perform the spark test as described in this chapter. The ignition system is working properly if a spark jumps the specified gap.

5. Perform the spark plug cap resistance test (Chapter Nine). Replace any cap that is out of specification.
6. Perform the ignition coil resistance test (Chapter Nine). Replace any coil that is out of specification.
7. Perform the crankshaft position sensor resistance test (Chapter Nine). Replace the sensor if it is out of specification.
8. Check the continuity of the following switches (Chapter Nine). Replace a switch that fails any portion of its test.
   a. Main switch.
   b. Engine stop switch.
   c. Neutral switch.
   d. Sidestand switch.
9. Perform the relay unit test (Chapter Nine). Replace the relay unit if it fails any portion of this test.
10. Perform the lean angle sensor output voltage test (Chapter Eight). Replace the sensor if it is out of specification.
11. Check all the wiring and connectors in the ignition system. Repair any faulty wire or connector.
12. Take the motorcycle to a dealership for ECU testing.

Starting System

1. Check the ignition and main fuses (Chapter Nine). Replace any fuse as needed.
2. Perform the battery open voltage test (Chapter Nine). Charge or replace the battery as needed.
3. Perform the starter operations test (Chapter Nine). If the starter operates, perform Step 5. If the starter does not operate, perform Step 4.
4. Disassemble and inspect the starter as described in Chapter Nine. Repair or replace the starter as needed.
5. Perform the starting circuit cutoff relay (SCCR) test and the relay unit diode test as described in *Relay Unit* in Chapter Nine. Replace the relay unit if it fails any portion of either test.
6. Perform the diode 1 test (Chapter Nine). Replace diode 1 as needed.
7. On 2007-2009 models, perform the diode 2 test (Chapter Nine). Replace diode 2 as needed.
8. Perform the starter relay test (Chapter Nine). Replace a faulty starter relay.
9. Check the continuity of the following switches (Chapter Nine). Replace a switch that fails any portion of its test.
   a. Main switch.
   b. Engine stop switch.
   c. Neutral switch.
   d. Sidestand switch.
   e. Clutch switch.
   f. Starter switch.
10. Check all the wiring and connectors in the starting system. Repair any faulty wire or connector.

Charging System

1. Check the ignition and main fuses (Chapter Nine). Replace any fuse as needed.
2. Perform the battery open voltage test (Chapter Nine). Charge or replace the battery as needed.
3. Perform the stator resistance test (Chapter Nine). Replace a faulty stator.
4. Perform the charging voltage test (Chapter Nine). Replace a voltage regulator/rectifier that is out of specification.
5. Check all the wiring and connectors in the charging system. Repair any faulty wire or connector.

Lighting System

The lighting system includes the headlight, high beam indicator light, taillight, license plate light, position light, meter light, and the optional accessory light (where equipped).
1. Check the bulb and each socket in the affected circuit.
2. Check the main, headlight, signal system, ignition and taillight fuses (Chapter Nine). Replace any blown fuse.
3. Perform the battery open circuit voltage test (Chapter Nine). Charge or replace the battery as needed.
4. Check the continuity of the following switches (Chapter Nine). Replace a switch that fails any portion of its test.
    a. Main switch
    b. Dimmer switch.
5. Perform the headlight relay test (Chapter Nine). Replace the relay if it fails any portion of this test.
6. Check all the wiring and connectors in the lighting system. Repair any faulty wire or connector.
7. Take the unit to a dealership for ECU or meter assembly testing.

Signal System

The signal system includes the turn signal lights, brake light, meter indicator lights, the horn and speedometer. Troubleshoot a signal system failure by performing the following.
1. Check the main, ignition, signal system and backup fuses (Chapter Nine). Replace any fuse as needed.
2. Perform the battery open voltage test (Chapter Nine). Charge or replace the battery as needed.
3. Check the continuity of the main switch (Chapter Nine). Replace a faulty switch.
4. Check all the wiring and connectors in the signal system. Repair any faulty wire or connector.
5. Locate the subsection that best describes the symptoms of the problem, and perform the indicated tests.

The horn does not sound

1. Check the continuity of the horn switch (Chapter Nine). Replace the left handlebar switch as necessary.
2. Perform the horn test (Chapter Nine). Replace the horn if resistance is out of specification.
3. Check all the wiring and connectors in the signal system. Repair any faulty wire or connector.

The brake light does not turn on

1. Check the brake light bulb and socket. Replace either as needed (Chapter Nine).
2. Check the continuity of the front and rear brake light switches (Chapter Nine). Replace any switch that fails the continuity test.
3. Check all the wiring and connectors in the signal system. Repair any faulty wire or connector.

A turn signal light or turn signal indicator light does not flash

1. Check the turn signal light bulb and socket. Replace either as needed (Chapter Nine).
2. Check the continuity of the turn signal switch (Chapter Nine). Replace the switch if it is faulty.
3. Perform the turn signal relay voltage test (Chapter Nine). Replace the relay if the input or output voltage is out of specification.
4. Check all the wiring and connectors in the signal system. Repair any faulty wire or connector.
5. If the wiring is good, take the meter assembly to the dealership for testing.

The neutral indicator light does not turn on

1. Check the continuity of the neutral switch (Chapter Nine). Replace the switch if it is out of specification.
2. Perform the relay unit diode test (Chapter Nine). Replace the relay unit if it fails any portion of this test.
3. Check all the wiring and connectors in the signal system. Repair any faulty wire or connector.
4. If the wiring is good, take the meter assembly to the dealership for testing.

The oil level warning light does not turn on

1. Perform the oil level switch resistance test (Chapter Nine). Replace the switch if it is out of specification.
2. Check all the wiring and connectors in the signal system. Repair any faulty wire or connector.

3. If the wiring is good, take the meter assembly to the dealership for testing.

The fuel level warning indicator light does not turn on

1. Perform the fuel level sender test (Chapter Eight). Replace the sender if it is out of specification.
2. Check all the wiring and connectors in the signal system. Repair any faulty wire or connector.
3. If the wiring is good, take the meter assembly to the dealership for testing.

The coolant temperature warning light does not turn on

1. Perform the coolant temperature (CT) sensor test (Chapter Ten). Replace the sensor if it is out of specification.
2. Check all the wiring and connectors in the signal system. Repair any faulty wire or connector.
3. If the wiring is good, take the motorcycle to a dealership for ECU and meter assembly testing.

The speedometer does not operate

1. Perform the speed sensor voltage test (Chapter Nine). Replace the sensor if it is out of specification.
2. Check all the wiring and connectors in the signal system. Repair any faulty wire or connector.
3. If the wiring is good, take the motorcycle to a dealership for ECU and meter assembly testing.

COOLING SYSTEM TROUBLESHOOTING

Radiator Fan Does Not Turn On

1. Check the main, ignition and fan fuses (Chapter Nine). Replace any blown fuse.
2. Perform the battery open circuit voltage test (Chapter Nine). Charge or replace the battery as needed.
3. Check the continuity of the main switch (Chapter Nine). Replace the switch if it is faulty.
4. Perform the radiator fan operation test (Chapter Ten). Replace the fan if it does not operate.
5. Perform the radiator fan relay test (Chapter Ten). Replace the relay if it is faulty.
6. Perform the coolant temperature (CT) sensor resistance test (Chapter Ten). Replace the sensor if it is out of specification.
7. Check all the wiring and connectors in the cooling system. Repair any faulty wire or connector.

8. If the wiring is good, take the motorcycle to a dealership for ECU testing.

FRONT SUSPENSION AND STEERING

Poor handling may be caused by improper tire pressure, a damaged/bent frame or front steering components, a worn front fork assembly, worn wheel bearings or dragging brakes.

Steering is Sluggish

1. Tire pressure too low.
2. Worn or damaged tire.
3. Damaged steering head bearings.
4. Incorrect steering stem adjustment (too tight).
5. Improperly installed upper or lower fork bridge.

Steering to One Side

1. Bent front or rear axle.
2. Bent frame or fork(s).
3. Worn or damaged wheel bearings.
4. Worn or damaged swing arm pivot bearings.
5. Damaged steering head bearings.
6. Bent swing arm.
7. Incorrectly installed wheels.
8. Front and rear wheels are not aligned.
9. Uneven front fork adjustment.
10. Front fork legs positioned unevenly in the fork bridges.

Leaking Fork Leg

1. Oil level too high.
2. Damaged or rusty fork tube.
3. Cracked or damaged fork slider.
4. Damaged or improperly installed oil seal.
5. Loose damper rod Allen bolt.
6. Damaged Allen bolt or copper washer.
7. Cracked or torn fork cap O-ring.

Front Suspension Noise

1. Low fork oil capacity.
2. Loose mounting fasteners.
3. Damaged fork(s) or rear shock absorber.

Wheel Wobble/Vibration

1. Unbalanced tire and wheel.
2. Damaged tire(s).
3. Damaged wheel rim(s).
4. Loose or damaged wheel bearing(s).

5. Loose front or rear axle.
6. Loose swing arm pivot bolt.

Hard Suspension (Front Fork)

1. Insufficient tire pressure.
2. Incorrect weight fork oil.
3. Worn or damaged fork tube bushing or slider bushing.
4. Plugged fork oil passage.
5. Binding slider.
6. Bent fork tubes.
7. Incorrect steering head bearing adjustment.
8. Damaged steering head bearings.
9. Damaged damper rod.

Hard Suspension (Rear Shock Absorber)

1. Excessive rear tire pressure.
2. Incorrect shock adjustment.
3. Poorly lubricated suspension components.
4. Bent or damaged shock absorber.
5. Damaged shock absorber bushing(s).
6. Damaged swing arm pivot bearings.

Soft Suspension (Front Fork)

1. Insufficient tire pressure.
2. Insufficient fork oil level.
3. Incorrect oil viscosity.
4. Weak or damaged fork springs.

Soft Suspension (Rear Shock Absorbers)

1. Insufficient rear tire pressure.
2. Incorrect shock absorber adjustment.
3. Weak or damaged shock absorber spring.
4. Damaged shock absorber.
5. Leaking damper unit.

BRAKE

The front and rear brake assemblies are critical to riding performance and safety. Inspect the front and rear brakes frequently, and repair any problem immediately. When adding or changing the brake fluid, use only DOT 4 brake fluid from a closed container. Refer to Chapter Fourteen for additional information on brake fluid selection and brake service.

When checking brake pad wear, verify that the brake pads in each caliper contact the disc squarely. If one of the brake pads is wearing unevenly, suspect a warped brake disc or a damaged caliper.

Brake Drag

1. Clogged brake hydraulic system.
2. Sticking caliper pistons.
3. Sticking master cylinder piston.
4. Incorrectly installed brake caliper.
5. Warped brake disc.
6. Incorrect wheel alignment.
7. Contaminated brake pad and disc.
8. Excessively worn brake disc or pad.
9. Caliper not sliding correctly.

Brakes Grab

1. Contaminated brake pads and disc.
2. Incorrect wheel alignment.
3. Warped brake disc.
4. Caliper not sliding correctly.

Brake Squeal or Chatter

1. Contaminated brake pads and disc.
2. Incorrectly installed brake caliper.
3. Warped brake disc.
4. Incorrect wheel alignment.

Soft or Spongy Brake Lever or Pedal

1. Low brake fluid level.
2. Air in brake hydraulic system.
3. Leaking brake hydraulic system.
4. Clogged brake hydraulic system.
5. Worn brake caliper seals.
6. Worn master cylinder seals.
7. Sticking caliper piston.
8. Sticking master cylinder piston.
9. Damaged front brake lever.
10. Damaged rear brake pedal.
11. Contaminated brake pads and disc.
12. Excessively worn brake disc or pad.
13. Warped brake disc.

Hard Brake Lever or Pedal Operation

1. Clogged brake hydraulic system.
2. Sticking caliper piston.
3. Sticking master cylinder piston.
4. Worn caliper piston seal.
5. Glazed or worn brake pads.
6. Damaged front brake lever.
7. Damaged rear brake pedal.
8. Caliper not sliding correctly.

CHAPTER THREE

LUBRICATION, MAINTENANCE
AND TUNE-UP

Tables 1-5 are at the end of this chapter.

MAINTENANCE SCHEDULE

Table 1 shows the specified maintenance schedule. If the motorcycle is operated in extreme conditions, including, high humidity, blowing dirt and dust and/or excessive heat, the services should be performed more frequently.

Most of the procedures in **Table 1** are described in this chapter. Those procedures that require more than minor disassembly are covered in the appropriate chapter of this manual. Refer to the *Table of Contents* or *Index* to locate a particular procedure.

CYLINDER NUMBERING AND
ENGINE ROTATION

The front cylinder is the No. 1 cylinder; the rear is No. 2.

The engine's positive rotation is counterclockwise when viewed from the left side. Use the flywheel nut to rotate the crankshaft manually, and always turn the crankshaft counterclockwise.

TUNE-UP

When performing a tune-up, service the following items as described in this chapter.

Perform engine tune-up procedures at the intervals specified in **Table 1**.

1. Air filter.
2. Spark plugs.
3. Engine compression test.
4. Engine oil and filter.
5. Ignition timing.
6. Valve clearance.
7. Throttle valve synchronization.
8. Brake system.
9. Suspension components.
10. Tires and wheels.
11. Fasteners.

AIR FILTER

The air filter removes debris from the incoming air before it enters the throttle bodies. Without an air filter, very fine dirt particles could enter the engine and rapidly wear the piston rings, cylinders and bearings. Never run the motorcycle without the air filter element properly installed.

Removal/Inspection/Installation

Remove and inspect the air filter at the interval in **Table 1**. Replace the air filter if it is soiled, severely clogged or broken in any area.

1. Securely support the motorcycle on a level surface.

2. Check that the ignition switch is off.

3. Remove the cover bolts (A, **Figure 1**) and pull the air filter cover (B) from the housing. Discard the cover O-ring.

4. Remove the air filter element (**Figure 2**).

5. Wipe the interior of the air filter housing (A, **Figure 3**) and housing cover with a shop rag dampened with cleaning solvent. Remove any debris that may have passed through a broken element.

6. Inspect the air filter element (A, **Figure 4**) for tears or other damage that would allow unfiltered air to pass into the engine. Also check the element gasket (B, **Figure 4**) for tears. Replace the element if necessary.

7. Gently tap the air filter element to loosen the dust.

8. Installation is the reverse of removal. Note the following:

    a. Install the air filter so the post (C, **Figure 4**) on the filter element slides into the hole (B, **Figure 3**) in the housing.

    b. Make sure the filter element seals against the housing.

    c. Install a new cover O-ring.

    d. Tighten the air filter cover bolts securely.

ENGINE COMPRESSION TEST

An engine compression test checks the condition of the rings, head gasket, piston and cylinder. Record the compression reading during each tune-up. Compare the current reading with those taken during earlier tune-ups. The comparison helps identify any developing problems.

Use a screw-in type compression gauge with a flexible adapter (**Figure 5**) when performing this test. Check the rubber gasket on the end of the adapter before each use. This gasket seals the cylinder to ensure accurate compression readings.

1. Before starting this test, confirm that:

    a. The cylinder head nuts and bolts are tightened to the specified torque. Refer to Chapter Four.

    b. The valves are properly adjusted as described in this chapter.

    c. The battery is fully charged (Chapter Nine) to ensure proper cranking speed.

2. Warm the engine to normal operating temperature, and turn the engine off.

3. Remove the spark plugs as described in this chapter.

4. Insert the spark plug into its spark plug cap, and ground the spark plugs against the cylinder head (**Figure 6**).

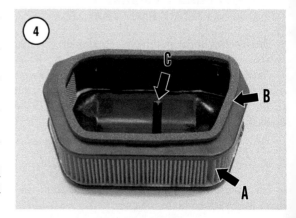

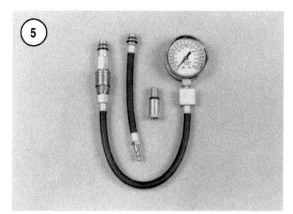

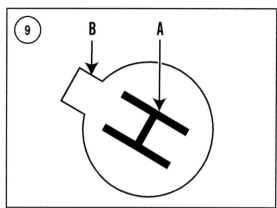

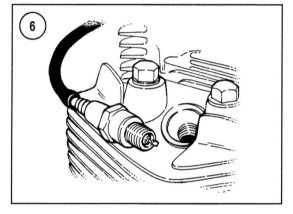

5. Install the compression gauge (**Figure 7**) into the spark plug following manufacturer's instructions. Be sure the gauge is properly seated in the cylinder head.
6. Completely open the throttle, and crank the engine until there is no further rise in pressure. Remove the gauge, and record the reading.
7. Repeat Steps 3-6 for the other cylinder.
8. Standard compression pressure is specified in **Table 4**. If a low reading (10 percent or more) is obtained on one of the cylinders, it indicates valve or ring trouble. To determine which, pour about a teaspoon of engine oil through the spark plug hole onto the top of the piston, then take another compression test and record the reading. If the compression returns to normal, the rings are worn or defective. If compression does not increase, the valves are leaking. The compression between cylinders should not vary by more than 10 percent.

IGNITION TIMING INSPECTION

The ignition timing is non-adjustable. The timing can be checked to make sure all ignition components are operating correctly.
1. Start the engine and let it reach normal operating temperature. Shut the engine off.
2. Remove the finished covers from the front cylinder (Chapter Four).
3. Remove the timing inspection plug (Chapter Five).
4. Connect a digital tachometer following the manufacturer's instructions.
5. Connect a timing light to the No. 1 spark plug wire (front cylinder) following the manufacturer's instructions.
6. Start the engine, and let it idle at the idle speed in **Table 4**.
7. Aim the timing light at the timing window (A, **Figure 8**). The timing is correct if the timing mark (A, **Figure 9**) on the flywheel aligns with the cutout in the timing window (B).

8. If the timing is incorrect, a problem exists in the ignition system. Follow the ignition system troubleshooting procedures in Chapter Two. The ignition timing cannot be adjusted.

9. Shut off the engine, and disconnect the timing light and tachometer. Install the removed parts.

10. Install the timing inspection plug (Chapter Five).

VALVE CLEARANCE

Adjustment

Perform the valve clearance measurement and adjustment with the engine at room temperature, below 95° F (35° C). Adjust the valves at the interval noted in **Table 1**.

The tappet adjusting tool (Yamaha part No.: YM-04154, YM-A5970 or 90890-04154), or its equivalent, is needed for valve adjustment.

1. Remove the rider's seat and left engine cover (Chapter Fifteen).

2. Remove the fuel tank, throttle body, and the intake manifold (Chapter Eight).

3. Remove the finished covers from both cylinders (Chapter Four).

4. Remove the spark plug from each cylinder as described in this chapter.

5. Remove the timing inspection plug and the flywheel bolt plug as described in *Inspection Plugs* in Chapter Five.

> *NOTE*
> *Valves can be adjusted while the engine is in the frame. The engine is shown removed for photographic clarity.*

6. Unscrew the tappet cover bolts (A, **Figure 10**), and remove the intake and exhaust tappet covers (B) from each cylinder.

7. Use the flywheel bolt (B, **Figure 8**) to turn the crankshaft counterclockwise until the front cylinder TDC mark (A, **Figure 11**) on the flywheel aligns with the cutout in the alternator cover.

> *NOTE*
> *A cylinder at TDC on the compression stroke has free play in both rocker arms, which indicates that both valves are closed.*

8. Check that the front cylinder is at TDC by pressing each rocker arm. The intake and exhaust rocker arms should have free play. If both rocker arms do not have free play, rotate the engine counterclockwise an additional 360° until they do.

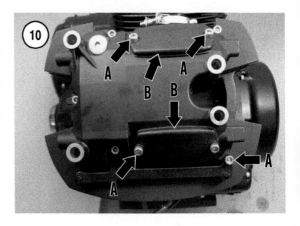

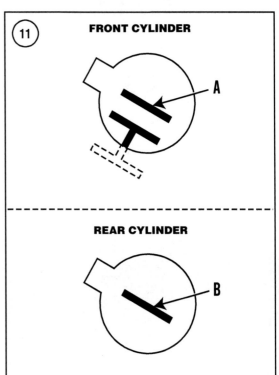

FRONT CYLINDER

REAR CYLINDER

9. Check the clearance of front-cylinder intake and exhaust valves by performing the following:

   a. Insert a feeler gauge (A, **Figure 12**) between the valve stem and the adjuster end.

   b. The clearance is correct if a slight drag is felt on the feeler gauge when it is inserted and withdrawn. The correct valve clearance for the intake and exhaust valves are listed in **Table 4**.

   c. Repeat substep a and substep b for each remaining valve in the front cylinder.

10. If necessary, adjust the valve clearance by performing the following:

   a. Loosen the locknut on the valve adjuster (B, **Figure 12**).

   b. With the feeler gauge between the valve stem and the adjuster end, turn the valve adjuster to obtain the specified clearance.

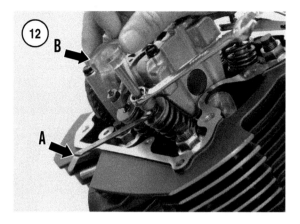

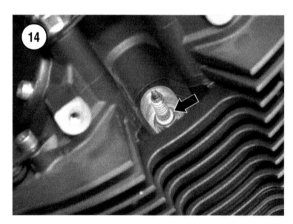

c. Hold the adjuster to prevent it from turning, and tighten the valve adjuster locknut to 14 N•m (10 ft.-lb.).

d. Recheck the valve clearance. If the clearance changed when the locknut was tightened, loosen the nut and repeat the adjustment procedure.

11. Use the flywheel bolt to turn the crankshaft counterclockwise until the rear cylinder is at top dead center on the compression stroke.

    a. If not already there, set the front cylinder to TDC by rotating the engine counterclockwise until the front-cylinder TDC mark (A, **Figure**

11) on the flywheel aligns with the alternator cover cutout.

    b. Rotate the crankshaft another 300° counterclockwise until the rear-cylinder TDC mark on the flywheel (B, **Figure 11**) aligns with the cutout in the alternator cover.

    c. Check that the rear cylinder is at TDC by pressing each rocker arm. The intake and exhaust rocker arms should have free play. If both rocker arms do not have free play, rotate the engine counterclockwise an additional 360° until they do.

12. Perform Step 9 and Step 10 to check and adjust each intake and exhaust valve in the rear cylinder.

13. Reinstall each tappet cover (B, **Figure 10**). Tighten the tappet cover bolts (A, **Figure 10**) to 10 N•m (89 in.-lb.).

14. When the clearance of each valve is within specification, reinstall the removed parts by reversing the removal procedure. Pay attention to the following:

    a. Use a new O-ring when installing the timing inspection plug and the flywheel bolt plug. Lubricate each O-ring with lithium-soap grease.

    b. Tighten the timing inspection plug to the 6 N•m (53 in.-lb.); the flywheel bolt plug to 10 N•m (89 in.-lb.).

    c. Tighten the spark plugs to the 13 N•m (115 in.-lb.).

SPARK PLUGS

Inspect and replace the spark plugs at the intervals specified in **Table 1**.

Removal

Reading a spark plug can help determine the operating condition of a cylinder. As each spark plug is removed, label it with its cylinder number.

1. Remove the finished covers as described in Chapter Four.

2. Pull the spark plug cap (**Figure 13**) from the plug. Label the caps so they will be reinstalled on the correct spark plug.

CAUTION
Whenever a spark plug is removed, dirt around it can fall into the plug hole. This can cause engine damage.

3. Use compressed air to blow debris from the spark plug tunnel.

4. Install a spark plug socket onto the spark plug (**Figure 14**). Make sure it is correctly seated on the

plug. Install socket handle, and turn the spark plug about halfway out its hole.

5. Blow out the spark plug tunnel with compressed air to remove any debris that was trapped below the spark plug hex fitting.

6. Remove the spark plug. Label the spark plug "front" or "rear" cylinder so the plug can be identified. The cylinder identification will be helpful if spark plug reading reveals a problem in a cylinder.

7. Repeat Steps 2-6 for the remaining spark plug.

8. Inspect each plug carefully. Look for a broken center porcelain insulator, excessively eroded electrodes and excessive carbon or oil fouling.

9. Inspect each spark plug cap for damage. If damaged, test the cap as described in Chapter Nine.

10. Measure the spark plug gap as described in this section. Adjust the gap as necessary.

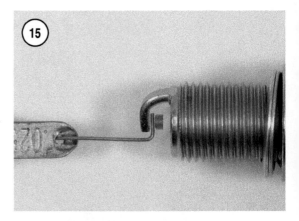

Installation

1. Apply a light coat of antiseize compound to the threads of the spark plug. Do not use engine oil on the plug threads.

2. Install the plug until it seats in the spark plug hole in the cylinder head. Tighten the plug to 13 N•m (115 in.-lb.). Do not overtighten a spark plug.

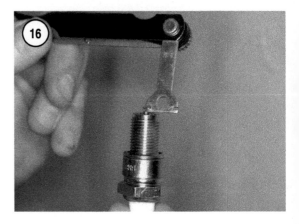

> *NOTE*
> *Push the spark plug cap all the way down to make full contact with the spark plug post. If the cap does not completely contact the plug, the engine may cut out at high engine speeds.*

3. Refer to the marks made during removal and press each spark plug cap (**Figure 13**) onto the correct spark plug. Rotate the assembly slightly in both directions and make sure it is attached to the spark plug.

4. Install the finished covers as described in Chapter Four.

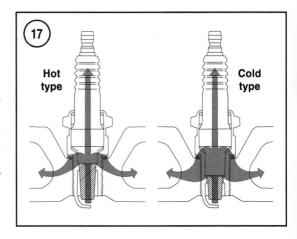

Gap

A spark plug should be carefully gapped to ensure a reliable, consistent spark. Always use a spark plug gapping tool and a wire feeler gauge to measure and adjust the gap.

1. Remove the new spark plugs from the boxes. If installed, unscrew the small adapter from the end of each plug. This adapter is *not* used.

2. Insert a wire feeler gauge between the center and side electrode of the plug (**Figure 15**). The specified gap is listed in Table 4. If the gap is correct, a slight drag will be felt as the wire is pulled through the gap. If there is no drag or if the gauge does not pass through the gap, bend the side electrode with a gaping tool (**Figure 16**) and set the gap to specification.

Heat Range Selection

Spark plugs are available in various heat ranges that are hotter or colder than the plugs originally installed by the manufacturer. Select a plug with a heat range designed for the load and conditions under which the motorcycle will be operated. A plug with an incorrect heat range can foul, overheat and cause piston damage.

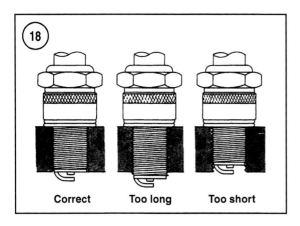

Correct   Too long   Too short

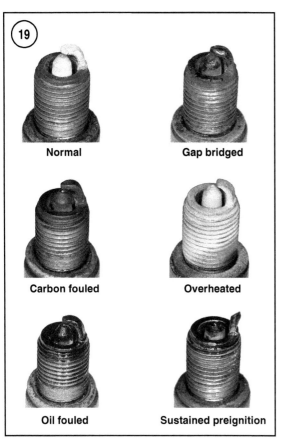

Normal   Gap bridged

Carbon fouled   Overheated

Oil fouled   Sustained preignition

Refer to **Table 4** for the specified spark plug.

Reading

Reading the spark plugs can provide information about spark plug operation, air/fuel mixture composition and engine conditions (such as oil consumption or pistons). Before checking the spark plugs, operate the motorcycle under a medium load for approximately 6 miles (10 km). Avoid prolonged idling before shutting off the engine. Remove the spark plugs as described in this chapter. Examine each plug and compare it to those shown in **Figure 19**.

Normal condition

Light tan- or gray-colored deposits on the firing tip and no abnormal gap wear or erosion indicate good engine, ignition and air/fuel mixture conditions. A plug with the proper heat range is being used. It may be serviced and returned to use.

Carbon fouled

Soft, dry, sooty deposits covering the entire firing end of the plug are evidence of incomplete combustion. Even though the firing end of the plug is dry, the deposits decrease the plug's insulation. The carbon forms an electrical path that bypasses the electrodes resulting in a misfire. One or more of the following conditions can cause carbon fouling:
1. Rich air/fuel mixture.
2. Spark plug heat range too cold.
3. Clogged air filter.
4. Improperly operating ignition component.
5. Ignition component failure.
6. Low engine compression.
7. Prolonged idling.

Oil fouled

An oil fouled plug has a black insulator tip, a damp oily film over the firing end and a carbon layer over the entire nose. The electrodes are not worn. Oil fouled plugs can be cleaned in an emergency, but it is better to replace them. Correct the cause of the fouling before returning the engine to service. Common causes for this condition are:
1. Incorrect air/fuel mixture.
2. Faulty fuel injection system.
3. Low idle speed or prolonged idling.
4. Ignition component failure.
5. Spark plug heat range too cold.
6. Engine still being broken in.
7. Valve guides worn.

In general, use a hot plug for low speeds and low temperatures. Use a cold plug for high speeds, high engine loads and high temperatures. Refer to **Figure 17**. Do not change the spark plug heat range to compensate for adverse engine or fuel conditions.

A plug should operate hot enough to burn off unwanted deposits, but not so hot that it is damaged or causes preignition. To determine if plug heat range is correct, remove each spark plug and examine the insulator.

When replacing plugs, make sure the reach (**Figure 18**) is correct. A longer than standard plug could interfere with the piston and cause engine damage.

8. Piston rings worn or broken.

Gap bridging

Plugs with this condition have deposits building up between the electrodes. The deposits reduce the gap and eventually close it entirely. If this condition is encountered, check for excessive carbon or oil in the combustion chamber. Be sure to locate and correct the cause of this condition.

Overheating

Badly worn electrodes and premature gap wear are signs of overheating, along with a gray or white blistered porcelain insulator surface. This condition is commonly caused by a spark plug with a heat range that is too hot. If the spark plug heat range is correct, consider the following causes:
1. Lean air/fuel mixture.
2. Faulty fuel injection operation.
3. Improperly operating ignition component.
4. Engine lubrication system malfunction.
5. Cooling system malfunction.
6. Engine air leak.
7. Improper spark plug installation (overtightening).
8. No spark plug gasket.

Worn out

Corrosive gases formed by combustion and high voltage sparks have eroded the electrodes. A spark plug in this condition requires more voltage to fire under hard acceleration. Install a new spark plug.

Preignition

If the electrodes are melted, preignition is almost certainly the cause. Check for throttle body mounting or intake manifold leaks and advanced ignition timing. The plug heat range may also be too hot. Find the cause of the preignition before returning the engine into service. Refer to *Engine Performance* in Chapter Two.

ENGINE OIL

Oil Level Check

Engine oil level is checked through the inspection window (A, **Figure 20**) in the alternator cover.
1. Start the engine, and let it reach normal operating temperature.
2. Stop the engine, and let the oil settle.

CAUTION
If the motorcycle is not parked correctly, an incorrect oil level reading will be observed.

3. Have an assistant hold the motorcycle so it stands *straight up and level*.
4. The oil level should be between the maximum and minimum window marks. If necessary, remove the oil filler cap (B, **Figure 20**) and add enough of the specified oil (**Table 3**) to raise the oil to the proper level. Do not overfill the crankcase.
5. Reinstall the oil filler cap, and tighten it securely.

Oil and Filter Change

The recommended oil and filter change interval is specified in **Table 1**. This assumes that the motorcycle is operated in moderate climates. If the motorcycle is operated under dusty conditions, the oil will get dirty more quickly and should be changed more frequently than recommended.

Use only the specified engine oil (**Table 3**). The classification is stamped on top of the can or printed on the label. Try to use the same brand of oil at each oil change, and avoid the use of oil additives. They may cause clutch damage.

NOTE
Some service stations and oil retailers accept used engine oil for recycling. Do not discard oil with the household trash or pour it onto the ground. Never add brake fluid, fork oil or any other type of petroleum-based fluid to engine oil intended for recycling. Most oil recycles will not accept the oil contaminated by other fluids.

1. Start the engine and run it until it reaches normal operating temperature, then turn the engine off.
2. Securely support the motorcycle on a level surface.
3. Place a drain pan under the oil drain bolt and filter. Remove the oil drain bolt (A, **Figure 21**) from the left side of the crankcase.
4. Let the oil drain for at least 15-20 minutes.
5. Inspect the sealing washer on the oil drain bolt. Replace the washer if its condition is in doubt.
6. Install the oil drain bolt and washer. Tighten the bolt to 43 N•m (32 ft.-lb.).
7. To replace the oil filter, perform the following:
   a. Install a socket-type oil filter wrench onto the oil filter (B, **Figure 21**), and turn the filter *counterclockwise* until oil begins to run out.

b. Wait until the oil stops, and then completely unscrew and remove the filter. Hold it with the open end facing up.
c. Hold the filter over the drain pan, and pour out any remaining oil. Place the old filter in a heavy-duty, reclosable plastic bag and seal the bag. Discard the filter properly.
d. Thoroughly clean the filter's seat on the crankcase. This surface must be clean to achieve a good oil seal.
e. Apply a light coat of clean engine oil to the rubber seal on the new filter.
f. Turn the oil filter onto the threaded stud.
g. Tighten the filter by hand until the rubber gasket contacts the crankcase surface, and then tighten to 17 N•m (12.5 ft.-lb.).
8. Remove the oil filler cap (B, **Figure 20**), and insert a funnel into the oil filler hole. Fill the crankcase with the correct weight and quantity of oil (**Table 3**). Turn in the oil filler cap securely.
9. Check the oil pressure by performing the following:
   a. Slightly loosen the oil check bolt on each cylinder head (front cylinder: **Figure 22**; rear cylinder **Figure 23**).
   b. Start the engine, and let it idle. Oil should seep from each loosened oil check bolt. If it does not do so within one minute, turn the engine off and inspect the oil lines, oil filter and oil pump for damage.
   c. Turn the engine off, and Tighten the oil check bolts to 15 N•m (11 ft.-lb.).
10. Check for oil leaks. Once the oil has settled, check the oil level as described in this section. Adjust the oil level if necessary.

CLUTCH CABLE FREE PLAY

Adjustment

Adjust the clutch cable free play at the interval indicated in **Table 1**. The clutch will not engage or disengage properly if the free play is not maintained within specification.

NOTE
This clutch release mechanism loosens as the engine warms up. Therefore, set the free play to the minimum setting.

Measure clutch cable free play at the end of the hand lever (**Figure 24**). If the clutch lever free play is outside the specified range (**Table 4**), adjust free play by performing the following:
1. At the clutch hand lever, pull the rubber boot (A, **Figure 25**) back from the adjuster.

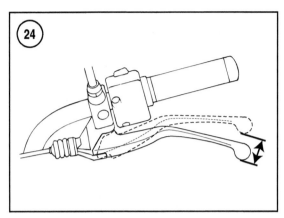

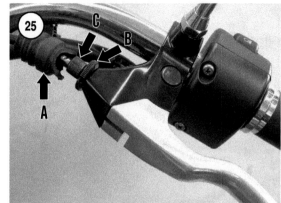

2. Loosen the clutch cable locknut (B, **Figure 25**).

3. Turn the adjuster (C, **Figure 25**) in or out to set the free play.

4. Tighten the locknut, and reinstall the rubber boot.

NOTE
2010 models do not have a mid-cable adjuster.

5. On 2007-2009 models, if the proper free play cannot be achieved at the hand lever adjuster, adjust the clutch release mechanism by performing the following:

    a. Remove the frame neck covers (Chapter Eight).

    b. Slide the rubber cover (A, **Figure 26**) off the mid-cable adjuster.

    c. Loosen the locknut (B, **Figure 26**) and turn the clutch cable adjuster (C) in either direction until the free play is within specification.

    d. Tighten the clutch adjuster locknut securely and reinstall the rubber cover.

6. Recheck the amount of free play at the hand lever and perform any minor adjustments at the lever.

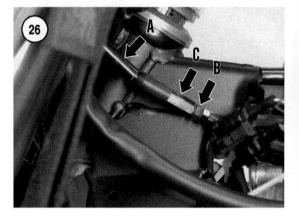

SHIFT PEDAL HEIGHT

Adjustment

Check the shift pedal height at the intervals specified in **Table 1**.

The shift pedal height is determined by the shift rod installed length (**Figure 27**). This equals the distance from the center of the shift pedal pivot to the center of the shift lever pivot (A, **Figure 28**). If the measured length is not within the range specified in **Table 4**, adjust the installed length by performing the following:

1. Loosen the locknut (B, **Figure 28**) at each end of the shift rod. The forward locknut uses left-hand threads.

2. Turn the shift rod (C, **Figure 28**) to attain the desired length.

3. Tighten each shift rod locknut to 8 N•m (71 in.-lb.).

FUEL AND EXHAUST SYSTEMS

Fuel Line Check

Inspect the condition of all the fuel and vacuum lines for cracks or deterioration at the intervals specified in **Table 1**. Replace hoses and lines as necessary. Make sure the hose clamps are in place and holding securely.

Exhaust System Check

Check the exhaust system at the intervals specified in **Table 1**. Inspect the exhaust system for dents and other damage. Check for leaks at all fittings. Replace any gaskets as necessary. Refer to **Table 5** and tighten all exhaust system fasteners to specification.

Evaporative Emissions Control System (California Models)

At the service intervals in **Table 1**, check all of the EVAP hoses for cracks or deterioration. Check the EVAP canister for loose connections or signs of damage. Refer to Chapter Eight.

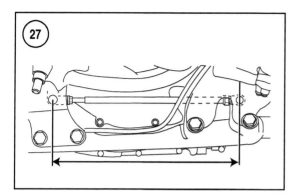

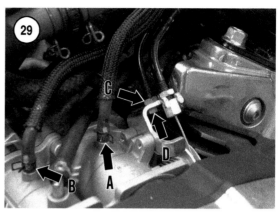

THROTTLE VALVE SYNCHRONIZATION

Synchronize the throttle valves at the interval specified in **Table 1**.

Synchronizing the throttle valves makes sure that one cylinder does not try to run faster than the other.

The carburetor synchronizer (Yamaha part No.: YU-44456), vacuum gauge (Yamaha part No.: 90890-03094), or an equivalent tool is needed for this procedure.

NOTE
Before synchronizing the throttle valves, check the ignition timing and valve clearances. Adjust the valves as necessary.

1. Securely support the motorcycle on a level surface.
2. Start the engine, and warm it up to operating temperature.
3. Remove the rider's seat (Chapter Fifteen).
4. Remove the fuel tank (Chapter Eight).
5. Disconnect the front-cylinder intake air pressure (IAP) hose (A, **Figure 29**) from its fitting on the front throttle body. Label the hose and fitting. Repeat this for the rear cylinder IAP hose (B, **Figure 29**).
6. Connect the hoses of a vacuum gauge to the throttle body fittings.
7. Connect a digital tachometer following the manufacturer's instructions.

8. Reinstall the fuel tank (Chapter Eight).
9. Start the engine and check engine idle speed. If the idle speed is out of specification (**Table 4**), use the air screws to adjust idle speed. Note the following:
   a. Insert a screwdriver through the hole in the front of the air filter housing (A, **Figure 30**) to adjust the air screw on the front-cylinder throttle body (B). Use the hole on the rear of the housing (C, **Figure 30**) to adjust the rear-cylinder air screw (D).
   b. Adjust the front- and rear-cylinder air screws by equal amounts. When adjusting idle, make small adjustments in one throttle body's air screw and then make the same adjustment at the other body's air screw.
10. Once idle speed is within specification, check the intake vacuum pressure at idle. The intake vacuum pressure of each cylinder should be within the range specified in **Table 4**.

NOTE
To gain the utmost in engine performance and efficiency, adjust the air screws so that the gauge readings are as close to each other as possible.

11. If the difference between the vacuum readings in the two cylinders is greater than 1.33 kPa, (10 mm Hg [0.4 in. Hg]), adjust the air screws (B and D, **Figure 30**) to synchronize the throttle valves. Note the following:
   a. Use the throttle body with the lowest reading as the standard.
   b. Adjust the air screw on the throttle body with the higher vacuum until the intake vacuum reading in the two throttle bodies are equal or as close as possible.
   c. If vacuum pressure of the lower reading is out of specification, turn the air screw of this throttle body until the reading is within specification. Now adjust the air screw on the second throttle body until its vacuum reading equals that of the first.

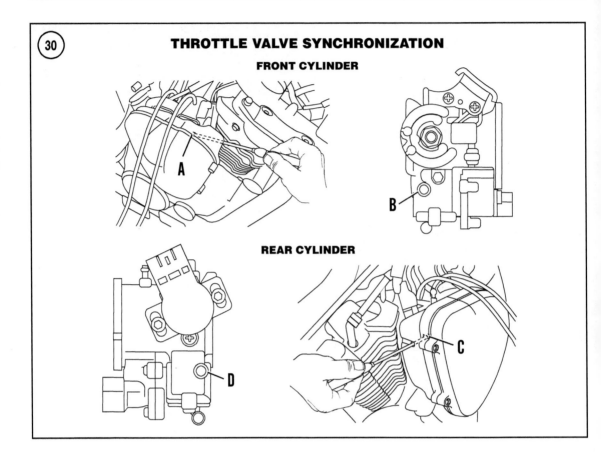

THROTTLE VALVE SYNCHRONIZATION

FRONT CYLINDER

REAR CYLINDER

12. Once the throttle valves are synchronized, check the idle speed. If necessary, use the air screws to fine tune the idle as described in Step 9.

13. Repeat Steps 9-11 until the throttle valves are synchronized and the idle speed is within specification.

14. Stop the engine and detach the equipment.

15. Reinstall the hose (A and B, **Figure 29**) of each IAP sensor to the fitting on the correct throttle body.

16. Check and adjust the throttle cable free play as described in this chapter.

THROTTLE CABLE FREE PLAY

Inspection

Check for smooth throttle operation from fully closed to fully open. Turn the handlebars, and check throttle operation at various steering positions. The throttle grip must return to the fully closed position without any hesitation.

Inspect the throttle cables for damage, wear or deterioration. Make sure the throttle cables are not kinked at any place.

If the throttle grip returns to the fully closed position smoothly and if the cables do not appear to be damaged, the throttle cables as described in this chapter. Replace the throttle cables as described in Chapter Eight.

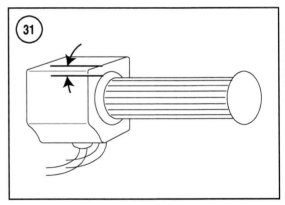

Check free play at the throttle grip flange (**Figure 31**). Too much free play causes delayed throttle response; too little free play causes unstable idling. Adjust the free play if it is outside the range specified in **Table 4**.

Adjustment

Verify throttle cable adjustment at the intervals specified in **Table 1**.

1. Remove the fuel tank (Chapter Eight).

2. Synchronize the throttle valves as described in this chapter.

3. At the handlebar, make sure the throttle cable locknut (A, **Figure 32**) is tight against adjuster.

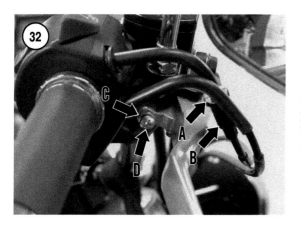

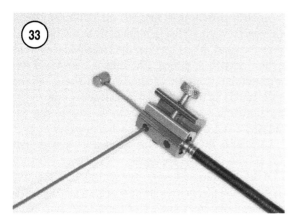

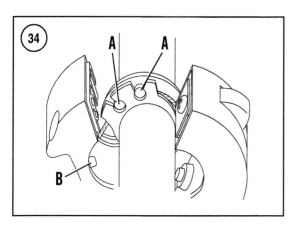

4. Perform the following at the throttle body:
   a. Loosen the locknut (C, **Figure 29**) on the pull cable.
   b. Turn the pull cable adjuster (D, **Figure 29**) in either direction until free play at the throttle grip is within specification (**Table 4**).
   c. Tighten the pull cable locknut securely.
5. If the correct amount of free play cannot be achieved at the throttle body, perform the following at the handlebar:
   a. Slide the cable holder away from the adjusters.
   b. Loosen the pull cable locknut (A, **Figure 32**).

   c. Turn the pull cable adjuster (B, **Figure 32**) in either direction until free play is within specification.
   d. Tighten the locknut securely, and slide the cable holder back to its original position.
6. Operate the throttle a few times. The cable free play should be within specification. If not, the throttle cables may have stretched. Replace the cables as described in Chapter Eight.

WARNING
If idle speed increases when the handlebar is turned to right or left, check the throttle cable routing. Do not ride the motorcycle in this unsafe condition.

7. Start the engine and let it idle in neutral. Turn the handlebar from steering lock to steering lock and listen to the engine. If idle speed changes as the handlebar is turned, the throttle cable is routed incorrectly or there is insufficient cable free play. Make the necessary corrections.
8. Test ride the motorcycle at slow speeds to confirm that the throttle operates correctly. Readjust the cables as necessary.

CONTROL CABLE LUBRICATION

CAUTION
Do not lubricate nylon-lined cables. These are generally used dry. Oil and most cable lubricants will cause liner expansion, pinching the liner against the cable. When installing nylon-lined and other aftermarket cables, follow the cable manufacturer's instructions.

Lubricate non-nylon lined control cables at the intervals specified in **Table 1** or if they become stiff or sluggish. When lubricating a cable, also inspect it for fraying and check the cable sheath for chafing.

The main cause of cable breaks or cable stiffness is improper lubrication. Periodic lubrication lengthens service life. Lubricate cables with a cable lubricant and a cable lubricator as shown in **Figure 33**. Only use the specified lubricant on control cables (**Table 3**).

Throttle Cable

1. Remove the mounting screws and separate the halves of the right handlebar switch as described in Chapter Nine.
2. Disengage the ends (A, **Figure 34**) of both the pull and push cables from the throttle drum.
3. Attach a cable lubricator to the cable following the manufacturer's instructions.

4. Insert the nozzle of the lubricant can into the lubricator, press the button on the can and hold it down until the lubricant begins to flow out of the other end of the cable **Figure 33**.

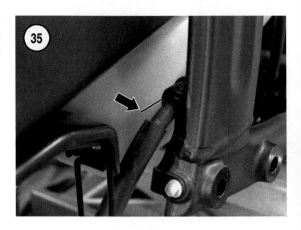

> *NOTE*
> *Place a shop cloth at the throttle body end of the cable to catch all excess lubricant that flows out.*

> *NOTE*
> *If lubricant does not flow out the end of the cable, check the entire cable for fraying, bending or other damage.*

5. Remove the lubricator, reconnect the cables, and adjust the throttle cable as described in this chapter. When installing the right handlebar assembly, be sure the pin (B, **Figure 34**) on the switch assembly aligns with the hole in the handlebar.
6. Adjust the throttle cable free play as described in this chapter.

Clutch Cable

1. At the handlebar, slide the clutch lever boot (A, **Figure 25**) away from the adjuster.
2. Loosen the clutch cable locknut (B, **Figure 25**) and rotate the adjuster (C) to provide maximum slack in the cable.
3. Disconnect the cable end from the clutch hand lever.
4. Attach a cable lubricator to the cable following the manufacturer's instructions.
5. Insert the nozzle of the lubricant can into the lubricator (**Figure 33**), press the button on the can and hold it down until the lubricant begins to flow out of the other end of the cable.

> *NOTE*
> *Place a shop cloth at the clutch lever end of the cable to catch all excess lubricant that flows out.*

> *NOTE*
> *If lubricant does not flow out the end of the cable, check the entire cable for fraying, bending or other damage.*

6. Remove the lubricator, reconnect the cable end to the clutch lever, and adjust the clutch cable free play as described in this chapter.

IGNITION AND STARTING CUTOFF SYSTEMS

The ignition circuit cutoff system uses the position of the sidestand switch and the neutral switch to control current flow through the ignition system. Current flows from the ignition coils to the ECU and fires the spark plugs if either the sidestand switch or neutral switch is closed. The engine can run if the transmission is in gear (neutral switch open) and the sidestand is up (sidestand switch closed) or the transmission is in neutral (neutral switch closed) and the sidestand is down (sidestand switch open).

Current is interrupted and the spark plugs do not fire if both switches are open.

A second related system, the starting circuit cutoff system (SCCS), controls the flow of current to the starter based upon the positions of the neutral and clutch switches. The starting circuit cutoff relay (SCCR) in the relay unit closes and the starter can operate if the transmission is in neutral (neutral switch closed), or the clutch lever is pulled in (clutch switch closed) and the sidestand is up (the sidestand switch is closed).

Regularly check the status of these systems at the intervals specified in **Table 1** by performing the following test.

Cutoff System Test

1. Securely support the motorcycle on a level surface with both wheels on the ground.
2. Start the engine and let it warm up. Turn the engine off.
3. Check the neutral switch by performing the following:
   a. Make sure the engine stop switch is turned to run.
   b. Move the sidestand to the down position.
   c. Turn the ignition switch on.
   d. Shift the transmission into neutral.
   e. Press the starter button. The engine should start. If it does not start, the neutral switch is probably faulty. Inspect the switch as described in Chapter Nine.
4. Check the sidestand switch by performing the following:

a. Raise the sidestand to the up position.
b. Shift the transmission in neutral.
c. Start the engine, and let it idle.
d. Pull in and hold the clutch lever. Shift the transmission into gear.
e. While holding the clutch lever in, move the sidestand down. The engine should stop.
f. If the engine does not stop when the sidestand is lowered, the sidestand switch is probably faulty. Inspect the switch as described in Chapter Nine.

5. Check the clutch switch by performing the following:
a. Raise the sidestand to the up position.
b. Pull in and hold the clutch lever.
c. Press the starter button while holding the clutch lever in. The engine should start. If it does not start, the clutch switch is probably faulty. Inspect the switch as described in Chapter Nine.

COOLING SYSTEM

Check, inspect and service the cooling system at the intervals specified in **Table 1**. Refer to *Safety* in Chapter One and *Cooling System Precautions* in Chapter Ten.

WARNING
Never remove the radiator cap or disconnect any coolant hose while the engine and radiator are hot. Scalding fluid and steam may be blown out under pressure and cause serious injury.

WARNING
Coolant is toxic and must never be discharged into storm sewers, septic systems, waterways or onto the ground. Pour used coolant into the original container and dispose of it according to local regulations. Do not store coolant where it is accessible to children or pets.

CAUTION
Coolant can damage painted surfaces. Immediately wash coolant spills with soapy water and rinse the area thoroughly.

Coolant Selection

CAUTION
Many coolant solutions contain silicate inhibitors to protect aluminum parts from corrosion damage. However, silicate inhibitors cause premature wear of water pump seals. Do not use coolant solutions that contain silicate inhibitors.

Use a 50:50 mixture of distilled water and antifreeze with corrosion inhibitors. Use only soft or distilled water. Never use tap or saltwater; these damage engine parts. Distilled (or purified) water can be purchased at supermarkets or drug stores in gallon containers. Never use alcohol-based antifreeze. Never allow the mixture to become less than 50 percent antifreeze or greater than 60 percent antifreeze.
Cooling system capacities are in **Table 3**.

Coolant Level

The coolant reservoir sits inside the rear frame member on the right side. Keep the coolant level in the reservoir at the full mark.
The coolant level should be checked when the engine is cold.
1. Securely support the motorcycle on a level surface.
2. Check the coolant level in the coolant reservoir. It should be between the FULL (**Figure 35**) and LOW level lines on the reservoir.
3. If coolant level is below the low level line, perform the following:
a. Remove coolant reservoir cap cover (Chapter Ten).
b. Remove the reservoir cap (**Figure 36**), and add coolant to the reservoir until the fluid level rises to the FULL mark.
c. Reinstall the reservoir cap, and the coolant reservoir cap cover (Chapter Ten).
d. Tighten the reservoir cap cover bolts to 4 N•m (35 in.-lb.).

Coolant Change

Drain and refill the cooling system at the interval listed in **Table 1**.

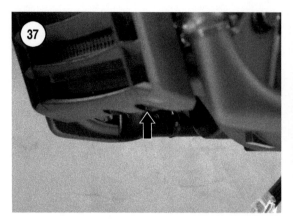

At times, the cooling system must be drained when another part of the engine is being serviced. If the coolant is still in good condition, it can be reused if it is not contaminated. In these instances, drain the coolant into a clean pan, and store it a clean container.

Perform the following procedure when the engine is cold.

1. Securely support the motorcycle on a level surface.

2. Remove the fuel tank (Chapter Eight).

3. Remove the coolant reservoir cover (Chapter Ten).

4. Place a drain pan under the drain bolt (**Figure 37**) on the left side of the radiator.

5. Remove the drain bolt and its copper washer from the radiator. Discard the copper washer.

6. Disconnect the radiator output hose (**Figure 38**) from its engine fitting.

7. Remove the radiator cap and let the coolant completely drain from the radiator and engine.

8. Remove the coolant reservoir (Chapter Ten), and pour out the coolant in the reservoir. Reinstall the reservoir. Tighten the coolant reservoir bolt, brake hose holder bolt, and brake hose guide bolts to 7 N•m (62 in.-lb.).

9. Reinstall the drain bolt (**Figure 37**) with a new copper washer. Tighten the coolant drain bolt to 2 N•m (18 in.-lb.).

10. Reconnect the radiator output hose (**Figure 38**) to its engine fitting. Tighten the hose clamp securely.

11. Place a funnel into the radiator filler neck (**Figure 39**) and slowly refill the radiator and engine with a 50:50 mixture of coolant and distilled water. Add the mixture slowly so it will expel as much air as possible from the cooling system. **Table 3** lists engine coolant capacity.

12. Sit on the motorcycle and slowly rock it from side to side to help expel air from the engine, radiator and coolant hoses.

13. Top off the radiator as necessary.

> *WARNING*
> *Do not start and run the motorcycle in an enclosed area. The exhaust gases contain carbon monoxide, a colorless, odorless, poisonous gas. Carbon monoxide levels build quickly in a small, enclosed area and can cause unconsciousness and death in a short time.*

14. After filling the radiator, leave the radiator cap off and bleed the cooling system by performing the following:

  a. Connect a remote fuel tank, and start the engine. Let it idle for 2-3 minutes.

  b. Snap the throttle a few times to bleed air from the cooling system. Add coolant to raise the level to the bottom of the filler neck.

  c. Turn off the engine once the coolant level becomes stabile.

15. Install the radiator cap. Turn the radiator cap clockwise to the first stop. Then push the cap down and turn it clockwise until it stops.

16. Add coolant to the reservoir until the fluid level reaches the FULL level line (**Figure 35**).

17. Start the engine and let it run at idle speed until the engine reaches normal operating temperature.

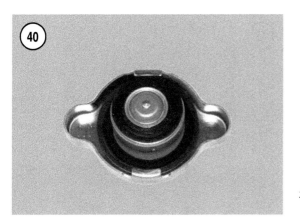

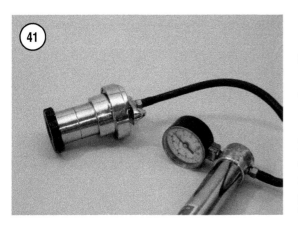

Snap the throttle several times, and turn off the engine.

18. Wait several minutes so the coolant can settle, and check the coolant level in the reservoir. If necessary, add coolant to the reservoir, not to the radiator.

19. Test ride the motorcycle and readjust the coolant level in the reservoir as required.

Cooling System Check

1. Remove the fuel tank (Chapter Eight).

2. Check all cooling system hoses for damage or deterioration. Replace any hose that is questionable. Make sure all hose clamps are tight. Refer to Chapter Eight.

3. Clean any dirt and debris from the radiator core. Use a whiskbroom, compressed air or low-pressure water. If an object has hit the radiator, carefully straighten the fins with a screwdriver.

4. Pressure test the radiator cap by performing the following:

   a. Remove the radiator cap (**Figure 40**) from the radiator.

   b. Use a cooling system tester to pressure test the radiator cap (**Figure 41**) following the tester manufacturer's instructions. Slowly pressurize the cap and stop when the pressure is within the

radiator cap opening pressure range specified in **Table 4**. The cap must hold this pressure for at least 10 seconds. Replace the radiator cap if it does not hold pressure or if opening pressure is outside the specified range.

> *CAUTION*
> *Do not exceed the indicated test pressure. If test pressure exceeds the specifications, the radiator may be damaged.*

5. Reinstall the radiator cap.

TIRES AND WHEELS

Check the tires and wheels at the intervals specified in **Table 1**.

Tire Pressure

Check and adjust tire pressure to accommodate load, which is to total weight of the rider, passenger, cargo and accessories. Check tire pressure when the temperature of the tire equals ambient air temperature. The specified tire pressures are shown in **Table 2**.

> *NOTE*
> *After checking and adjusting the tire pressure, reinstall the air valve cap. The cap prevents small pebbles and/or dirt from collecting in the valve stem. A dirty valve stem could leak or cause inaccurate tire pressure readings.*

Tire Inspection

The likelihood of tire failure increases with tread wear. Check tire tread for excessive wear, deep cuts, embedded objects such as stones, nails, etc. Also check for high spots that indicate internal tire damage. Replace tires that show high spots or swelling. If a nail or other object punctures the tire, mark its location with a light crayon before pulling it out. This will help locate the hole for repair. Refer to Chapter Eleven for tire changing procedures.

Measure tread wear (**Figure 42**) at the center of the tire tread with a tread depth gauge or small ruler. Because tires sometimes wear unevenly, measure wear at several points. Replace the tires if any tread depth measurement is less than specified in **Table 2** or it the tread is worn to the tire's wear indicators.

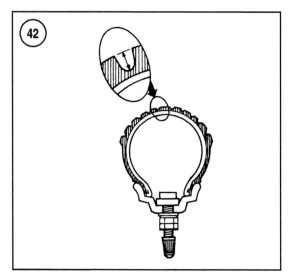

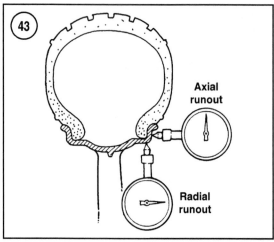

Wheel Inspection

Frequently inspect the wheels for cracks, warping, or dents. A damaged wheel may cause an air leak.

Wheel runout is the amount of wobble a wheel shows as it rotates. To quickly check runout, simply support the motorcycle with the wheel off the ground. Slowly turn the wheel while holding a pointer solidly against a fork leg or the swing arm with the other end against the rim. If you suspect that either axial runout (side-to-side movement) or radial runout (up-and-down movement) exceeds the specification in **Table 2**, measure axial and radial runout (**Figure 43**) as described in Chapter Ten.

FRONT FORK

Fork Oil Change

The manufacturer does not provide an oil change interval for the front fork. Nonetheless, it is a good practice to change the fork oil once a year. If the fork oil becomes contaminated with dirt or water, change it immediately.

Changing the fork oil requires disassembling and assembling the fork leg. Refer to *Front Fork* in Chapter Twelve.

Check

Check front fork operation and for leaks at the intervals specified in **Table 1**.
1. Securely support the motorcycle on a level surface.
2. Inspect each fork leg for scratches or other damage.
3. Apply the front brake and pump the fork up and down as vigorously as possible. Check for smooth fork operation, and check for any oil leaks.

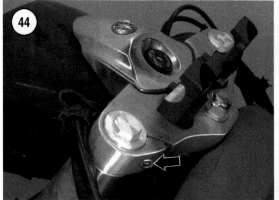

WARNING
If any of the mentioned hardware is loose, refer to Chapter Twelve for correct tightening procedures and torque specifications.

4. Make sure the upper (**Figure 44**) and lower (**Figure 45**) fork bridge clamp bolts are tightened to specification (Chapter Twelve).
5. Make sure the handlebar clamp bolts (**Figure 46**) are tight, and that handlebar is securely held in place.
6. Make sure the front axle clamp bolt (A, **Figure 47**) and axle (B) are tight.

STEERING HEAD

Inspections

1. Check the steering head for looseness at the intervals specified in **Table 1** or when one of the following conditions exist:
    a. The handlebar vibrates more than normal.
    b. The front fork makes a clicking or clunking noise when the front brake is applied.
    c. The steering feels tight or slow.

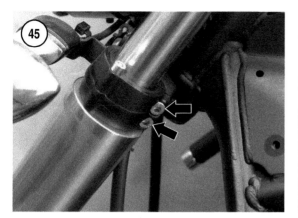

d. The motorcycle does not want to steer straight on level road surfaces.

2. Securely support the motorcycle on a level surface with the front tire off the ground.

3. Check the bearing preload by performing the following:

a. Center the front wheel. Push lightly against the left handlebar grip to start the wheel turning to the right, then let go. The wheel should continue turning under its own momentum until the fork leg hit its stop.

b. Center the wheel, and push lightly against the right handlebar grip.

c. If the front wheel does not turn all the way to the stop when you lightly push a handlebar grip, the steering is too tight. Adjust the steering head bearings as described in *Installation/Assembly* in *Steering Stem* in Chapter Twelve.

4. Check the bearing free play by performing the following:

a. Center the front wheel. Grasp the bottom of the two fork sliders, and try to rock the forks back and forth. There should be little or no rocking in the steering head. If any play is felt, the steering head is too loose.

b. Adjust the steering head bearings as described in *Installation/Assembly* in *Steering Stem* in Chapter Twelve.

REAR SUSPENSION

Inspection

Inspect the rear suspension at the interval specified in **Table 1**.

1. Securely support the motorcycle with both wheels on the ground. Check the shock absorber by bouncing on the seat several times.

2. Securely support the motorcycle with the rear wheel off the ground. Refer to *Motorcycle Stand* in Chapter Eleven.

3. While an assistant steadies the motorcycle, push hard on the rear wheel (sideways) to check for side play in the rear swing arm bearings.

4. Check the shock absorber for oil leaks or other damage.

> *WARNING*
> *If any of the mentioned fasteners are, refer to Chapter Thirteen for correct tightening procedures and torque specifications.*

5. Check the shock absorber, suspension linkage, rear axle and swing arm hardware. Make sure all fasteners are tight.

Shock Absorber Spring Preload Adjustment

> *CAUTION*
> *Never turn the cam ring beyond the maximum or minimum position.*

The spring preload can be adjusted to nine different positions to suit riding, load and speed conditions. The fourth position is the factory default

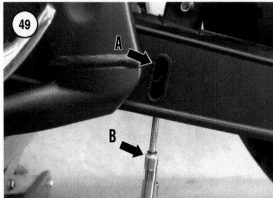

setting. Lower numbered settings soften the preload; higher settings stiffen preload.

1. Remove the muffler and rear cylinder exhaust pipe (Chapter Eight).

2. Remove the coolant reservoir cover (Chapter Ten), and disconnect the fuel hose from the subtank.

3. Retrieve the spanner wrench and extension from the tool kit.

4. Stand on the right side of the motorcycle, and adjust the preload by rotating the cam ring (**Figure 48**) on the shock absorber to achieve the desired preload.

DRIVE BELT

Free Play Adjustment

The belt tension gauge (Yamaha part No. YM-03170 or 90890-03170, or its equivalent) is needed to check the deflection.

Check drive belt free play when the engine is cold and the belt dry. Check and adjust the drive belt at the intervals specified in **Table 1**.

1. Securely support the motorcycle on a suitable stand with the rear wheel off the ground. Refer to *Motorcycle Stand* in Chapter Eleven.

2. Rotate the rear wheel and check the belt tension. Locate the belt's tightest point, and rotate the wheel so the tight point is at the center of the lower belt run.

3. Observe the belt position through the window (A, **Figure 49**) in the lower drive belt guard. Use chalk or similar removable marker to mark the position of the belt.

4. Use the belt tension gauge (B, **Figure 49**) to apply 4.5 kg (10 lb.) of force to the middle of the lower belt run. Make another mark near the window to indicate the position of the drive belt.

5. Each gradation on the window equals 5 mm (0.20 in.). Calculate the deflection by subtracting the measurement in Step 3 from the measurement in Step 4.

6. The calculated free play should be within the specified range (**Table 4**). If necessary, adjust the free play by performing the following:

    a. Loosen the rear axle nut (A, **Figure 50**).

    b. Loosen the drive belt adjuster locknut (B, **Figure 50**) on each side of the swing arm.

    c. Turn the drive belt adjuster (C, **Figure 50**) on each side an equal number to turns to obtain the correct belt free play. Use the alignment marks on the belt pullers (D, **Figure 50**) to assure both pullers are in the same position.

    d. Tighten the drive belt adjuster locknuts to 16 N•m (12 ft.-lb.).

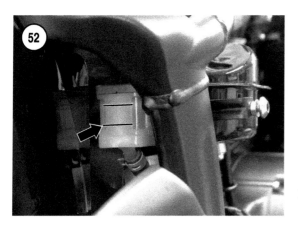

e. Recheck the belt free play.

f. Once free play is within specification, tighten the rear axle nut to 150 N•m (110 ft.-lb.).

BRAKES

WARNING
Only use the specified brake fluid (Table 4) from a sealed container. Others may vaporize and cause brake failure. Do not mix different brands or types of brake fluid as they may not be compatible.

CAUTION
Be careful when handling brake fluid. Do not spill it on painted or plated surfaces or plastic parts as it will destroy the surface. Wash the area immediately with soapy water and thoroughly rinse it off.

Perform all the brake checks and replacement procedures at the intervals specified in **Table 1**.

Brake Hoses and Seals

Check the brake hoses between the master cylinder and each brake caliper. If there are any leaks, tighten the connections and bleed the brakes as described in Chapter Fourteen. If this does not stop the leak or if a line is damaged, cracked, or chafed, replace the hose(s) and/or seals, and then bleed the brake system.

Brake Fluid Level Check

The fluid level should be kept above the low mark on the reservoir. If the brake fluid level reaches the low level mark (front: **Figure 51** rear: **Figure 52**), correct the fluid level by adding fresh brake fluid.
1. Securely support the motorcycle on level ground.
2A. When adding fluid to the front master cylinder, position the handlebars so the master cylinder reservoir is level.
2B. On the rear master cylinder:
    a. Remove the reservoir bolt (**Figure 53**) and move the reservoir (**Figure 54**) rearward.
    b. Have an assistant hold the reservoir level while the top cover is removed.
3. Clean any dirt from the area around the top cover prior to removing the cover.
4. Remove the top cover, diaphragm plate and the diaphragm.
5. Add brake fluid from a sealed brake fluid container.
6. Reinstall the diaphragm, diaphragm plate and the top cover.

Brake Pad Inspection

Inspect the brake pads for excessive or uneven wear, scoring and oil or grease on the friction surface.
1. Securely support the motorcycle on level ground.
2A. On front calipers:
    a. Look into the caliper assembly, and inspect the wear grooves (**Figure 55**, typical).

b. Replace both pads in both front calipers if any pad is worn to the bottom of the wear grooves.

c. If uncertain about the state of the friction material, remove the brake pads (Chapter Fourteen) and measure pad thickness with a vernier caliper. Replace all the front brake pads if any pad is worn to the wear limit (**Table 4**).

2B. On rear caliper:

a. Remove the brake pads (Chapter Fourteen).

b. Measure the pad thickness with a vernier caliper.

c. Replace both pads if the pad thickness equals or is less than the wear limit (**Table 4**).

Front Brake Lever Free Play
(2007-2009 Models)

> *NOTE*
> *Front brake lever free play is not adjustable on 2010 models.*

The front brake lever free play is the distance the brake lever moves before the master piston starts moving. Brake lever free play is measured at the end of the hand lever (**Figure 56**).

1. Push the brake lever forward, away from the handle grip.

2. Pull the lever, and measure free play.

3. If free play is outside the range specified in **Table 4**, perform the following:

a. Loosen the brake adjuster locknut. (C, **Figure 32**).

b. Turn the adjuster (D, **Figure 32**) in or out until free play is within the specification.

4. After adjusting free play, spin the wheel and check for any brake drag. Readjust free play as necessary.

Rear Brake Pedal Height Adjustment

1. Securely support the motorcycle so that it sits straight up.

2. Check the end of the brake pushrod. It must be visible through the hole in the push-rod clevis (A, **Figure 57**). If it is not, adjust the brake pedal by performing the following:

a. Loosen the adjuster locknut (B, **Figure 57**) on the rear master cylinder clevis. Turn the adjuster (C, **Figure 57**) until the pushrod end is visible through the clevis hole (A).

b. Tighten the locknut to 16 N•m (12 ft.-lb.).

3. After adjusting the brake pedal, make sure the rear brake does not drag. Readjust the brake pedal height as necessary.

4. Adjust the rear brake light as described in this section.

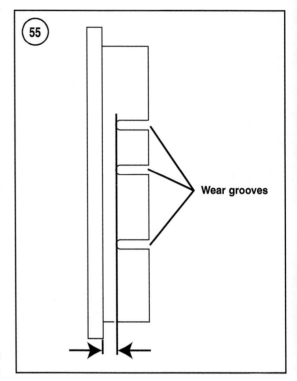

Wear grooves

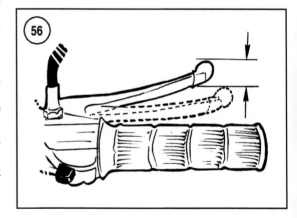

Rear Brake Light Switch Adjustment

> *WARNING*
> *Do not ride the motorcycle if the rear brake light does not operate properly.*

1. Turn the ignition switch on.

2. Depress the brake pedal. The brake light should come when the brake pedal is depressed but just before the rear brake is applied. If necessary, adjust the switch by performing the following:

a. Hold the rear brake light switch body (A, **Figure 58**), and turn the adjuster nut (B) until the brake light operates properly.

b. Turn the nut clockwise and the brake light comes on sooner; counterclockwise and the light comes on later.

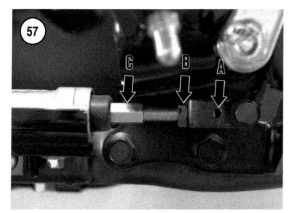

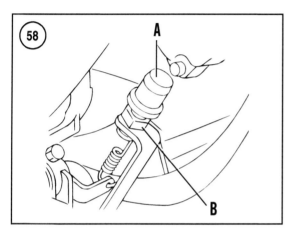

SIDESTAND

Inspection

Check the operation of the sidestand and the sidestand switch at the service interval listed in **Table 1**. Perform the following:

1. Securely support the motorcycle on a level surface.

2. Operate the sidestand, and check its movement and spring tension. Replace the spring if it is weak or damaged.

3. Lubricate the sidestand pivot surfaces with lithium soap grease.

4. Check the sidestand switch as described in *Ignition and Starting Cutoff Systems* in this chapter.

5. If loosened, tighten the sidestand nut to 56 N•m (41 ft.-lb.).

GENERAL LUBRICATION

Swing Arm Bearing Lubrication

Clean the swing arm bearings in solvent and pack them with lithium-soap grease at the intervals specified in **Table 1**. The swing arm must be removed to service the bearings. Refer to Chapter Thirteen.

Steering Stem Bearing Lubrication

Remove, clean and lubricate the steering stem bearings with lithium-soap grease at the interval specified in **Table 1**. Refer to Chapter Twelve.

Wheel Bearing Inspection/Lubrication

Worn wheel bearings cause excessive wheel play that results in vibration and other steering troubles. Inspect and lubricate the wheel bearings at the intervals specified in **Table 1**. Refer to Chapter Eleven.

Miscellaneous Lubrication Points

Unless otherwise indicated, lubricate the following items at the intervals specified in **Table 1** with lithium-soap grease: O-rings, oil seal lips, shift pedal shaft, brake pedal shaft, footrest pivots, clutch lever, front brake lever, control cable ends and the sidestand bolt and sliding surfaces.

FASTENERS

Check the tightness of all fasteners, including:
1. Engine mounting hardware.
2. Engine crankcase covers.
3. Handlebar and front fork.
4. Gearshift lever.
5. Drive belt components.
6. Brake pedal and lever.
7. Exhaust system.
8. Lighting equipment.

Table 1 MAINTENANCE SCHEDULE*

Odometer reading	Procedure
Initial 600 miles (1000 km) or 1 month	Check the valve clearance; adjust as necessary. Change engine oil and filter.
	(continued)

Table 1 MAINTENANCE SCHEDULE* (continued)

Odometer reading	Procedure
Initial 600 miles (1000 km) or 1 month (continued)	
	Check clutch and shifting operation; adjust the cable free play or replace the cable as necessary. Check the shift pedal height.
	Check the throttle operation. Lubricate the throttle grip as necessary. Check cable free play; adjust as necessary.
	Check the operation and fluid level of the front and rear brakes. Replace the pads if necessary.
	Check the drive belt free play. Adjust as necessary.
	Check the steering head bearings for smoothness or excessive play. Adjust as necessary.
	Check the operation of the front and rear brake light switches. Adjust as necessary.
	Check the operation of the ignition circuit cutoff and starting system; repair as necessary.
	Check the operation of all lights and switches. Adjust the headlight as needed.
	Lubricate all control cables.
	Check all fasteners. Tighten them as necessary.
2500 miles (4000 km)	Check the drive belt free play. Adjust as necessary.
4000 miles (7000 km) or 7 months	Check the valve clearance; adjust as necessary.
	Check the condition of the spark plugs; clean and adjust the gap as necessary.
	Check the crankcase breather hose for cracks or damage: replace as necessary.
	Check the fuel and vacuum lines for cracks or damage; replace as necessary.
	Check throttle valve synchronization; adjust as necessary.
	Check the exhaust system for leaks. Retighten hardware and/or replace gaskets as necessary.
	Change engine oil and filter.
	Check the air filter; replace if damaged.
	Check the operation of the front and rear brakes; replace the pads if necessary.
	Check brake fluid level in each master cylinder; adjust as necessary.
	Check the operation of the front and rear brake light switches. Adjust as necessary.
	Check clutch and shifting operation; adjust the cable free play or replace the cable as necessary. Check the shift pedal height.
	Check the brake hoses for cracks or damage. Replace as necessary.
	Lubricate the pivots in the brake and clutch levers with lithium-soap grease.
	Lubricate the brake pedal and shift pedal pivot shafts with lithium-soap grease.
	Check the operation of the sidestand. Lightly lubricate the pivot and contact surfaces with lithium-soap grease.
	Check the operation of the ignition and starting circuit cutoff system; repair as necessary.
	Check the operation of the front fork, and check for oil leaks.
	Check the condition of the coolant hoses. Replace as necessary.
	Check the steering head bearings for smoothness or excessive play. Adjust as necessary.
	Check the operation of the shock absorber, and check for leaks.

(continued)

Table 1 MAINTENANCE SCHEDULE* (continued)

Odometer reading	Procedure
4000 miles (7000 km) or 7 months (continued)	Check the wheel bearings for wear or damage. Replace if necessary. Check the wheels for runout and balance. Replace as necessary. Check tire tread for wear or damage. Replace as necessary. Check and adjust tire pressure. Check all fasteners. Tighten them as necessary. Check the operation of all lights and switches. Adjust the headlight as needed. Check the operation of the throttle. Lubricate the throttle grip as necessary. Check cable free play; adjust as necessary. Lubricate all control cables.
8000 miles (13,000 km) or 12 months	Perform the 4000 mile (7000 km) checks. Replace the spark plugs. Check the swing arm bearings. Lubricate with lithium-soap grease as needed.
12,000 miles (19,000 km) or 19 months	Perform the 4000 mile (7000 km) checks. On California models, check the EVAP system for damage. Replace hoses or parts as needed.
16,000 miles (25,000 km) or 24 months	Perform the 4000 mile (7000 km) checks. Replace the spark plugs. Repack the swing arm pivot bearings with lithium-soap grease. Repack the steering head bearings with lithium-soap grease. Lubricate the suspension linkage with lithium-soap grease. Change the coolant. Replace the brake fluid in the front and rear brakes. Replace the seals in each brake caliper.
20,00 miles (31,000 km) or 31 months	Perform the 4000 mile (7000 km) checks.
Every 4 years	Replace the brake hoses.

*Consider this maintenance schedule a guide to general maintenance and lubrication intervals. Address items more frequently if the motorcycle is exposed to mud, water, sand, high humidity or if run harder than normal.

Table 2 TIRE SPECIFICATIONS

Item	Specification
Front Tire	
Type	Tubeless
Size	130/90-16M/C 67H
Model	
Dunlop	D404F X
Bridgestone	EXEDRA G721
Wear limit	1.0 mm (0.04 in.)
Rear Tire	
Type	Tubeless
Size	170/70B 16M/C 75H
Model	
Dunlop	K555
Bridgestone	EXEDRA G722 G
Wear limit	1.0 mm (0.04 in.)

(continued)

Table 2 TIRE SPECIFICATIONS (continued)

Item	Specification
Tire inflation pressure (cold)[1]	
Front	250 kPa (36 psi)
Rear	280 kPa (41 psi)
Maximum load[2]	
XVS13A models	210 kg (463 lb.)
XVS13CT models	190 kg (419 lb.)
Wheel runout limit	
Radial	1.0 mm (0.04 in.)
Lateral	0.5 mm (0.02 in.)

1. Tire inflation pressures apply to original equipment tires only. Aftermarket tires may require different pressures. Refer to the tire manufacturer's specifications.
2. Load equals the total weight of rider, passenger, accessories and all cargo.

Table 3 RECOMMENDED LUBRICANTS AND FLUIDS

Brake fluid	DOT 4
Cable lubricant	Cable lubricant or engine oil
Coolant quantity	
Total system capacity	2.10 L (2.22 qt.)
Radiator capacity	0.55 L (0.58 qt.)
Reservoir capacity (to FULL level line)	0.45 L (0.48 qt.)
Coolant temperature	90-100° C (194-212° F)
Engine oil	
Classification	API SG or SH, JASO MA
Viscosity	SAE 20W40
Quantity	
Oil change only	3.20 L (3.38 qt.)
Oil and filter change	3.40 L (3.59 qt.)
When totally dry	3.70 L (3.91 qt.)
Oil temperature	70-80° C (158-176° F)
Fuel	Regular unleaded
Pump octane	86 (R+M) / 2 method
Research octane	91 or higher
Fuel tank capacity	
Total	18.5 L (4.89 gal.)
Reserve	3.7 L (0.98 gal.)

Table 4 MAINTENANCE SPECIFICATIONS

Item	Specification
Brake lever free play (at lever end)	2-5 mm (0.08-0.20 in.)
Brake pad wear limit	0.8 mm (0.03 in.)
Clutch cable free play (at lever end)	5-10 mm (0.20-0.39 in.)
Compression pressure	
Standard pressure @ sea level	1450 kPa (210 psi) @ 400 rpm
Minimum-Maximum pressure	1200-1500 kPa (170-218 psi)
Drive belt free play	
Motorcycle on the sidestand	5.0-7.0 mm (0.20-0.28 in.)
Motorcycle on a suitable stand	4.0-6.0 mm (0.16-0.24 in.)
Engine idle speed	950-1050 rpm
Intake vacuum pressure	32.0-37.3 kPa (240-280 mm Hg)
Ignition minimum spark gap	6 mm (0.24 in.)
Ignition timing	5° B.T.D.C. @ 1000 rpm. Not adjustable.
Radiator cap opening pressure	93.3-122.7 kPa (13.5-17.8 psi)
Rim runout wear limit	
Radial	1.0 mm (0.04 in.)
Axial	0.5 mm (0.02 in.)
Shift rod installed length	255-259 mm (10.04-10.20 in.)

(continued)

Table 4 MAINTENANCE SPECIFICATIONS (continued)

Item	Specification
Shock absorber spring preload settings	
Minimum (softest)	1
Standard	4
Maximum (hardest)	9
Spark plug	
Recommended plug	NGK LMAR7A-9
Spark plug gap	0.8-0.9 mm (0.031-0.035 in.)
Throttle cable free play (at the flange)	4-6 mm (0.16-0.24 in.)
Valve clearance	
Intake	0.09-0.13 mm (0.0035-0.0051 in.)
Exhaust	0.14-0.18 mm (0.0055-0.0071 in.)

Table 5 MAINTENANCE TORQUE SPECIFICATIONS

Item	N•m	in.-lb.	ft.-lb.
Alternator damper cover bolt	7	62	–
Coolant reservoir cap cover bolt	4	35	–
Cooling system			
Coolant drain bolt	2	18	–
Coolant reservoir bolt*	7	62	–
Drive belt adjuster locknut	16	–	12
Exhaust system			
Exhaust header nuts	20	–	15
Exhaust header studs	15	–	11
Exhaust pipe clamp bolts	12	106	–
Exhaust pipe guard bolts	7	62	–
Exhaust-pipe-guard clamp screws	6	53	–
Muffler bracket bolts	53	–	39
Muffler bolts	35	–	26
Muffler clamp bolts	12	106	–
Flywheel bolt plug	10	89	–
Oil check bolt	15	–	11
Oil drain bolt	43	–	32
Oil filter	17	–	12.5
Rear axle nut	150	–	110
Rear brake hose guide bolt	7	62	–
Rear brake hose holder bolt	7	62	–
Rear brake pushrod adjuster			
locknut	16	–	12
Shift rod locknuts	8	71	–
Sidestand nut	56	–	41
Spark plugs	13	115	–
Tappet cover bolts	10	89	–
Timing inspection plug*	6	53	–
Valve adjuster locknut	14	–	10

*Refer to text.

CHAPTER FOUR

ENGINE TOP END

The engine is a liquid-cooled, 4-stroke, single overhead camshaft (SOHC), V-twin. Two main bearings support the crankshaft in a vertically split crankcase.

This chapter covers the camshafts, valves, cylinder heads, cylinder block, piston, and rings. Refer to Chapter Three for valve adjustment.

Tables 1-3 are at the end of this chapter.

FINISHED COVERS

A finished cover sits atop each side of the front and rear cylinder heads. Each of the fours covers is unique and mounts to one side of a particular head. The following procedure applies to each finished cover.

Removal/Installation

1. Securely support the motorcycle on a level surface.
2. Remove the fuel tank and air filter housing (Chapter Eight).
3. Remove each finished cover bolt (**Figure 1**) and its washers.
4. Pull the cover from the motorcycle. Account for the spacer and damper behind each bolt.

5. Installation is the reverse of removal. Tighten the finished cover bolts to 8 N•m (71 in.-lb.).

CYLINDER HEAD COVER

Removal/Installation

1. Remove the engine (Chapter Five).
2. Remove the tappet cover bolts (A, **Figure 2**, typical) and pull the tappet cover (B) and cover O-ring from each side of the cylinder head.
3. Evenly loosen the cylinder head cover bolts in a crisscross pattern, and remove the bolts. The front cylinder head cover uses seven cover bolts (A, **Figure 3**); the rear cover uses eleven (A, **Figure 4**).
4. Mark the finished cover bracket on the exhaust side of the front cylinder head cover (B, **Figure 3**) and on the exhaust side of the rear cylinder head cover (B, **Figure 4**). They are not interchangeable.
5. Remove the cylinder head cover and the cover gasket from the cylinder head. Account for the locating dowels.
6. Installation is the reverse of removal.
   a. Install a new cylinder head gasket.
   b. Install each finished cover bracket onto the correct cylinder head cover.

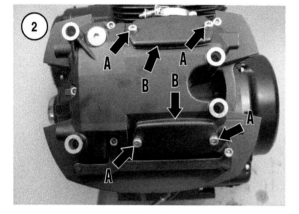

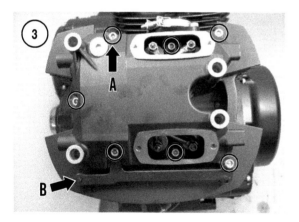

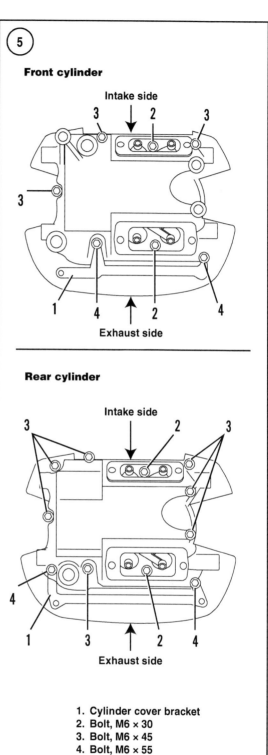

Front cylinder

Rear cylinder

1. Cylinder cover bracket
2. Bolt, M6 × 30
3. Bolt, M6 × 45
4. Bolt, M6 × 55

c. Three different length bolts secure the cover in place. Refer to **Figure 5**. Install each bolt in the correct location.

d. Following a crisscross pattern, evenly tighten the cylinder head cover bolts in two-to-three stages. Tighten the bolts to 10 N•m (89 in.-lb.).

e. Install a new O-ring with each tappet cover. Lubricate the O-ring with lithium- soap grease, and tighten the tappet cover bolts to 10 N•m (89 in.-lb.).

CAM CHAIN TENSIONER

Removal

CAUTION
Never remove a cam chain tensioner while the engine is in the frame. The cylinder head cover must be removed to reset the tensioner.

1. Remove the engine (Chapter Five).
2. Remove the cylinder head cover from the cylinder being serviced.
3. Remove the timing inspection plug (A, **Figure 6**) and the flywheel bolt plug (B) as described in *Inspection Plugs* in Chapter Five.

CAUTION
A particular cylinder must be set to TDC on the compression stroke when its cam chain tensioner is removed or installed.

4A. Set the front cylinder to TDC on the compression stroke by performing the following:
   a. Use the flywheel bolt to rotate the engine counterclockwise (when viewed from the left side) until the front cylinder TDC mark (A, **Figure 7**) aligns with the cutout in the alternator cover.
   b. The timing mark on the front cylinder cam chain sprocket (A, **Figure 8**) should also align with the timing mark on its camshaft carrier (B).
4B. Set the rear cylinder to TDC on the compression stroke by performing the following:
   a. Use the flywheel bolt to rotate the engine counterclockwise (when viewed from the left side)

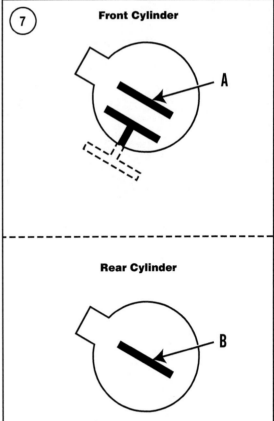

until the front cylinder TDC mark (A, **Figure 7**) aligns with the cutout in the alternator cover.
   b. Rotate the engine an additional 300° counterclockwise until the rear cylinder TDC mark (B, **Figure 7**) aligns with the cutout in the alternator cover.
   c. The timing mark on the rear cylinder cam-chain sprocket (A, **Figure 8**) should also align with the pointer on its camshaft carrier (B).

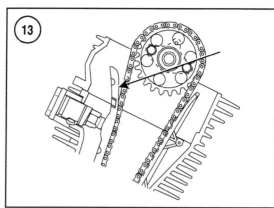

5. Make sure the appropriate cylinder is at TDC on the compression stroke by pressing each rocker arm. Both the intake and exhaust rocker arms should have free play. If they do not, rotate the engine an additional 360° until they do.

6. Remove the cam chain tensioner housing bolts (A, **Figure 9**), and pull the tensioner (B) from its base on the rear side of the cylinder. Discard the housing gasket.

7. Remove the base bolt (A, **Figure 10**), and pull the cam chain tensioner base (B) from the rear of the cylinder. Watch for the locating pin. Note that the tensioner base is marked F (front cylinder) or R (rear cylinder).

8. Remove the base gasket (A, **Figure 11**) and locating pin (B). Discard the gasket.

Installation

1. Lock the plunger by performing Step 7 of *Assembly* in this section.

2. Make sure the cylinder is still at top dead center on the compression stroke. If necessary perform Step 4A or Step 4B of *Removal* in this section.

3. Install the locating pin (B, **Figure 11**) and a new base gasket (A) onto the port in the cylinder.

4. Set the correct tensioner base (B, **Figure 10**) into place on the cylinder port, and install the base bolt (A). Finger-tighten the bolt.

5. Install a new housing gasket (**Figure 12**) onto the cam chain tensioner housing, and seat the housing (B, **Figure 9**) in the base. Make sure the arrow on the tensioner housing points up.

6. Install the cam chain housing tensioner bolts (A, **Figure 9**).

7. Tighten the cam chain tensioner bolts (A, **Figure 9**) and the base bolt (C) to 10 N•m (89 in.-lb.).

8. Release the tensioner plunger by pressing the rear cam chain guide rearward and then releasing the guide (**Figure 13**).

9. Install the cylinder head cover as described in this chapter.

10. Install both inspection plugs (A and B, **Figure 6**), alternator damper and its cover as described in *Inspection Plugs* in Chapter Five.

Disassembly

> *CAUTION*
> *Pressing the plunger into the housing releases tensioner clip No. 1. At this point, the plunger is free and can fly from the housing.*

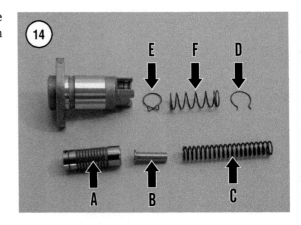

1. Set the tension body upright on the bench.
2. Press the plunger into the housing and hold the plunger in place.
3. Squeeze the arms of tensioner clip No. 2, and remove the plunger (A, **Figure 14**), spring seat (B), and inner spring (C) from the tensioner housing.
4. Remove tensioner clip No. 1 (D, **Figure 14**), tensioner clip No. 2 (E), and the outer spring (F) from the housing.

Assembly

1. Drain the oil from the tensioner housing, and set it upright on the bench.
2. Install the outer spring into the tensioner housing (**Figure 15**).

3. Install tensioner clip No. 2 (E, **Figure 14**) with its arms facing up, and seat the arms in the lower slot (A, **Figure 16**) in the tensioner housing.
4. Install tensioner clip No. 1 (D, **Figure 14**) so its arm sit in the upper slot (B, **Figure 16**) of the housing. Make sure the arms of clip No. 1 engage the grooves in the sides of the upper slot.
5. Install the tensioner inner spring (A, **Figure 17**) and spring seat (B) into the housing.
6. Set the plunger (**Figure 18**) over the spring seat.

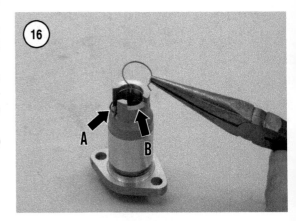

> *WARNING*
> *Do not push the plunger once it has been locked into place in the following step. Doing so releases the plunger. It will be ejected from the housing.*

7. Lock the plunger into place by performing the following:
   a. While squeezing the arms of clip No. 2 (**Figure 19**), press the plunge into the housing until the plunger's upper groove aligns with clip No 1.
   b. Continue holding the plunger in place, and press the arms of clip No. 1 (**Figure 20**) together until the clip seats in the plunger groove.
   c. While keeping clip No. 1 engaged in the groove, slowly release the plunger until it locks.

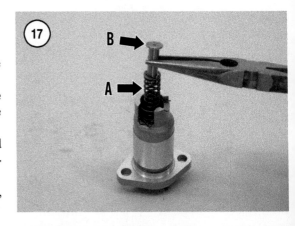

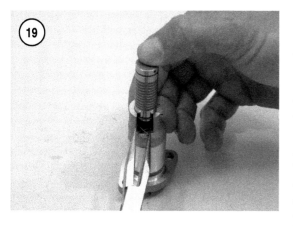

CAMSHAFT CARRIER

The camshaft and rocker arms mount inside a carrier in each cylinder head. The carrier must be removed and disassembled to access the camshaft and rocker arms.

Refer to **Figure 21**.

Removal

The magneto & rotor holder (Yamaha part No. YU-01235), or equivalent holder, is needed for this procedure.

If both camshaft carriers require service, remove and service the front-cylinder carrier and then the rear-cylinder carrier.

1. Remove the engine (Chapter Five).
2. Set the front cylinder to TDC on the compression stroke and remove the cam chain tensioner from the front cylinder as described in this chapter.

> NOTE
> *The front- and rear-cylinder carriers are identical. However, the camshafts are not. The front-cylinder camshaft is identified by a dot on the shaft (**Figure 22**).*

3. Hold the camshaft sprocket with the special tool, and remove sprocket bolts (**Figure 23**).
4. Remove the front-cylinder camshaft sprocket from between the cam chain runs.
5. Tie a safety wire around the cam chain and secure the wire to the engine so the chain will not fall into the crankcase.
6. Reverse the tightening sequence shown in **Figure 24**, and evenly loosen the camshaft carrier bolts in two-to-three stages. Remove the bolts (**Figure 25**), and lift the carrier from the front cylinder head. Account for the dowels (**Figure 26**). They may come out with the carrier.
7. Perform Steps 2-6 and remove the camshaft carrier from the rear cylinder.

Installation

1. Use the flywheel nut to rotate the engine counterclockwise (when viewed from the left side) until the front cylinder TDC mark (A, **Figure 7**) aligns with the cutout in the alternator cover.
2. Make sure the dowels (**Figure 26**) are in place in the cylinder head or the carrier.
3. Set the front cylinder camshaft carrier into the front cylinder head. Make sure the camshaft has the front cylinder ID mark (**Figure 22**).
4. Apply engine oil to the threads of the camshaft carrier bolt, and install the bolts (**Figure 25**).
5. Following the sequence shown in **Figure 24**, evenly tighten the camshaft carrier bolts in two-to-three stages to 10 N•m (89 in.-lb.).
6. Pull the cam chain tight against the timing sprocket, and untie the safety wire.
7. Fit the camshaft sprocket between the runs of the cam chain, and seat the sprocket on the camshaft. The timing mark on the sprocket (A, **Figure 8**) must align with the pointer on the camshaft carrier (B).
8. Install the camshaft sprocket bolts. Hold the sprocket with the special tool, and tighten the cam-

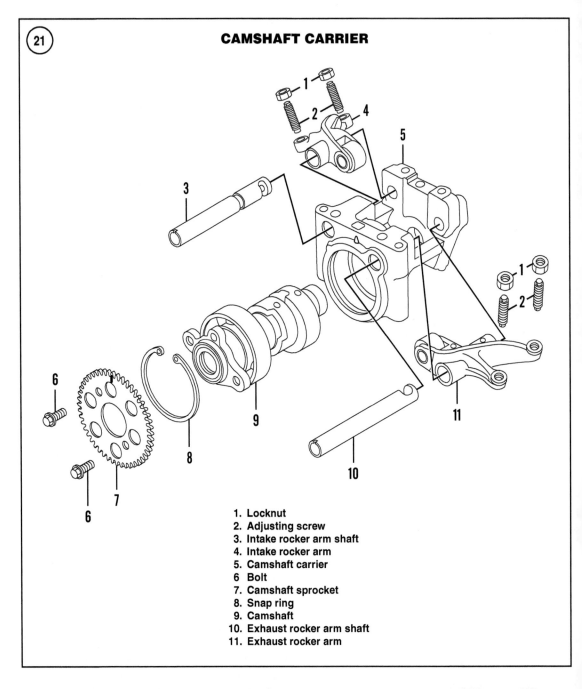

CAMSHAFT CARRIER

1. Locknut
2. Adjusting screw
3. Intake rocker arm shaft
4. Intake rocker arm
5. Camshaft carrier
6 Bolt
7. Camshaft sprocket
8. Snap ring
9. Camshaft
10. Exhaust rocker arm shaft
11. Exhaust rocker arm

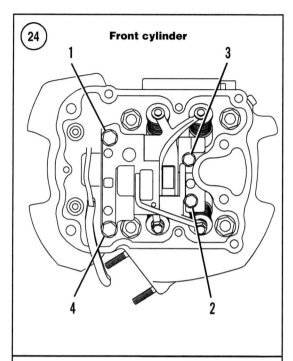

Front cylinder

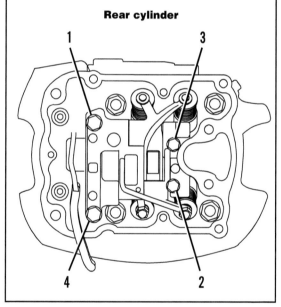

Rear cylinder

shaft sprocket bolts (**Figure 23**) to 20 N•m (15 ft.-lb.).

9. Install the cam chain tensioner into the front cylinder as described in this chapter.

10. Rotate the crankshaft 300° counterclockwise until the rear cylinder TDC mark (B, **Figure 7**) aligns with the slot on the alternator cover.

11. Perform Steps 2-9 and install the camshaft carrier, camshaft sprocket and cam chain tensioner into the rear cylinder.

12. Install the inspection plugs and alternator cover (Chapter Five).

Disassembly/Assembly

A slide hammer bolt (6 mm): (Yamaha part No. YU-01083-1 or 90890-01083) and weight (Yamaha part No.YU-01083-3 or 90890-0184), or equivalent tools, are needed for this procedure.

Refer to **Figure 21**.

NOTE
*The center ear on the camshaft sprocket boss (A, **Figure 27**) must face up and align with the arrow (B) on the carrier when the camshaft is removed or in-*

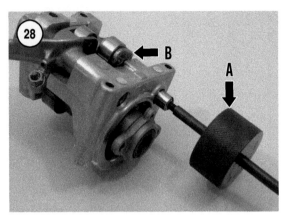

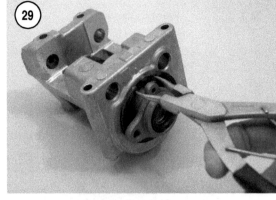

stalled. This positions the cam lobes so they will not be marred.

1. Use a slide hammer (A, **Figure 28**) to remove a rocker arm shaft, and lift the rocker arm (B) from the carrier.

2. Repeat Step 1 and remove the remaining shaft and rocker arm.

3. Remove the snap ring from the carrier (**Figure 29**).

4. Rotate the camshaft so the center ear (A, **Figure 27**) aligns with the pointer (B) on the carrier, and remove the camshaft from the carrier.

5. Installation is the reverse of removal.

    a. Lubricate the camshaft lobes and journals with molybdenum disulfide oil.

    b. Lubricate the rocker arm shaft with engine oil.

    c. The intake rocker arm shaft is identified by a groove (A, **Figure 30**). Use each shaft with the correct rocker arm.

    d. Position each rocker arm (C, **Figure 27**) so its slot runs vertically. This positions each rocker arm shaft so its cutout (B, **Figure 30**) faces the center of the carrier. A carrier bolt passes through each cutout and locks the shafts in place.

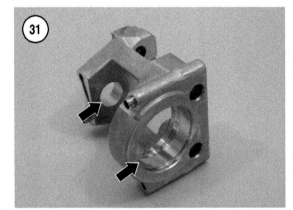

Camshaft Inspection

1. Clean all parts in solvent, and blow them dry with compressed air.

2. Inspect the carrier's camshaft bosses (**Figure 31**) for wear and scoring. Replace the carrier if necessary.

3. Check the camshaft lobes for wear. The lobes should not be scored, and the edges should be square. Slight damage can be removed with silicon carbide oil stone. Use No. 100-120 grit initially, and then polish the lobe with No. 280-320 grit.

4. Measure the cam lobe height (**Figure 32**) and width (**Figure 33**). Replace the camshaft if a lobe is worn beyond the service limit specified in **Table 2**.

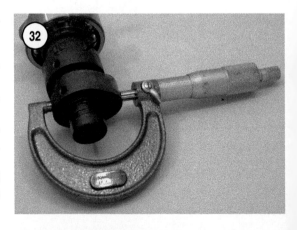

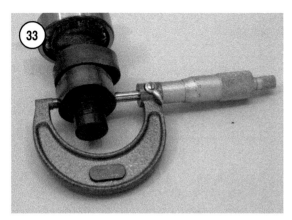

5. Measure the outside diameter of the camshaft journal (A, **Figure 34**). Replace if not within specification (**Table 2**).

6. Rotate the camshaft bearing (B, **Figure 34**) and check for binding or excessive noise. Replace the camshaft as necessary.

7. Inspect the teeth of the camshaft sprocket (**Figure 35**). If a tooth is broken, cracked or if more than 1/4 of a tooth has worn away, replace the camshaft sprocket and cam chain as a set.

Rocker Arm Inspection

Replace if any measurement is not within specification (**Table 2**).

1. Clean all parts in solvent and dry them thoroughly with compressed air.

2. Inspect the rocker arm roller (A, **Figure 36**). It should turn smoothly, and it should not be unevenly worn or discolored.

3. Inspect each valve adjuster (B, **Figure 36**) where it rides on the valve stem. Replace if scratched, pitted, or if shows signs of overheating (blue discoloration).

4. Measure the inside diameter of the rocker arm bore (C, **Figure 36**).

5. Inspect the rocker arm shaft for overheating (blue discoloration), excessive wear or scratches.

6. Measure the outside diameter of the rocker arm shaft (**Figure 37**).

7. Calculate the rocker-arm-to-rocker-shaft clearance by subtracting the shaft outside diameter (Step 6) from the rocker-arm-bore inside diameter (Step 4). If the clearance is less than the service limit, replace the part that is out of specification.

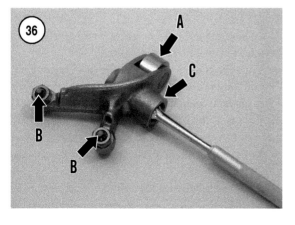

CYLINDER HEAD

Refer to **Figure 38**.

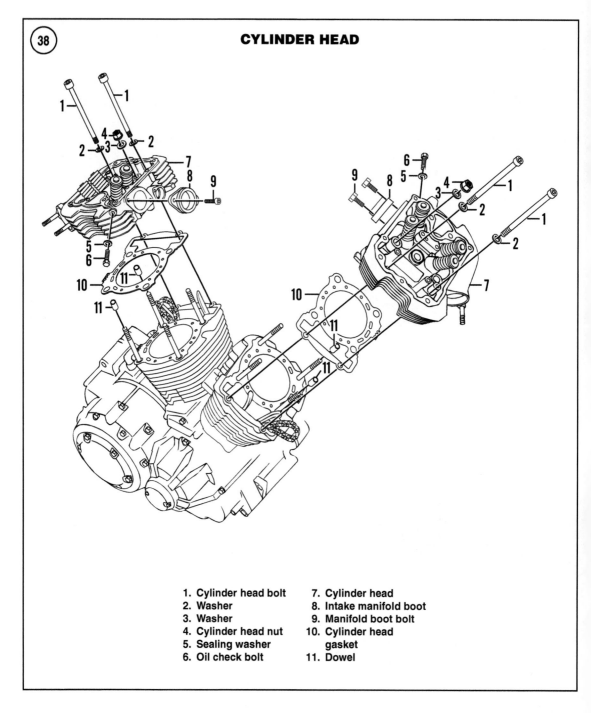

CYLINDER HEAD

1. Cylinder head bolt
2. Washer
3. Washer
4. Cylinder head nut
5. Sealing washer
6. Oil check bolt
7. Cylinder head
8. Intake manifold boot
9. Manifold boot bolt
10. Cylinder head gasket
11. Dowel

Removal

1. Remove the engine (Chapter Five).

2. Remove the cam chain tensioner and the camshaft carrier (this chapter) from the cylinder being serviced.

3. Reverse of the tightening sequence shown in **Figure 39**, and evenly loosen the cylinder head nuts and bolts in 1/2-turn increments.

4. Remove the nuts (A, **Figure 40**) and bolts (B) from the cylinder head. Account for the washer installed with each fastener.

5. Loosen the cylinder head by tapping around its perimeter with a plastic mallet.

6. Untie the cam-chain safety wire from the engine.

7. Pull the cylinder head straight up and off the cylinder studs. Account for the dowels (A, **Figure 41**) on the two exhaust-side studs. Pass the cam chain and safety wire through the cam chain tunnel while removing the head, and retie the safety wire to the engine.

8. Remove and discard the cylinder head gasket (B, **Figure 41**).

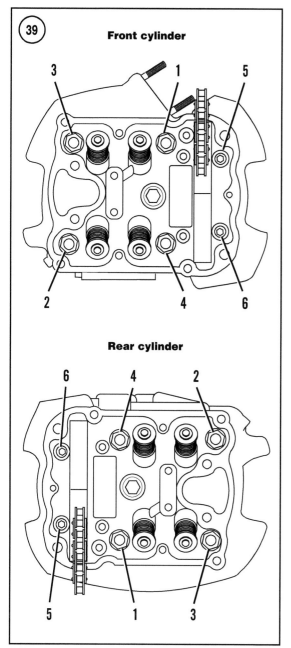

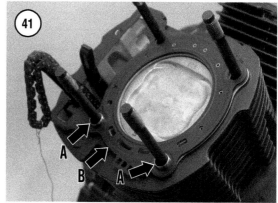

CAUTION
The cylinder head fasteners must be evenly tightened in sequence as described below. The head could be damaged if it is not tightened properly.

5. Following the sequence shown in **Figure 39**, tighten the cylinder head fasteners in two to three stages to: cylinder head nuts to 65 N•m (48 ft.-lb.); cylinder head bolts to 13 N•m (115 in.-lb.).

Cylinder Head Leak Test

Perform this test before removing the valves or cleaning the cylinder head.

1. Position the cylinder head so the exhaust port faces up. Pour solvent or kerosene into the exhaust port (**Figure 42**).

2. Turn the head over slightly, and check the exhaust valve areas in the combustion chamber. If the valves and seats are in good condition, no leaks past the valve seats will be found. If any area is wet, the valve seat is not sealing correctly. Remove the valve, and inspect the valve and seat for wear or damage as described in this section.

3. Pour solvent into the intake port, and check the intake valves.

Installation

1. Fit the dowels (A, **Figure 41**) over the studs noted during removal, and install a new cylinder head gasket (B).

2. Lower the cylinder head part way down the cylinder studs, feed the cam chain and safety wire up through the cam chain tunnel in the head, and seat the head on the cylinder block.

3. Pull the cam chain taut and make sure it still properly engages the timing sprocket on the crankshaft. Secure the cam chain safety wire to the engine.

4. Lubricate the washers and the threads of the cylinder-head nuts and bolts with engine oil.

Inspection

1. Perform the cylinder head leak test as described in this section.

2. Remove all gasket material from the mating surfaces on the cylinder head and cylinder block.

CAUTION
Cleaning the combustion chamber with the valves removed can damage the valve seat surfaces. A damaged valve seat will cause poor valve seating.

3. Without removing the valves, remove all carbon deposits from the combustion chambers (A, **Figure 43**). Use a fine wire brush dipped in solvent or make a scraper from hardwood. Take care not to damage the head, valves or spark plug threads.

4. Examine the spark plug threads (B, **Figure 43**) in the cylinder head for damage. If damage is minor or if the threads are dirty or clogged with carbon, use a spark-plug thread tap to clean the threads. If the damage is severe, restore the threads by installing a steel thread insert. Thread insert kits can be purchased at automotive supply stores or they can be installed at a dealership.

5. After all carbon is removed from the combustion chambers and valve ports, clean the entire head in solvent.

6. Clean away all carbon on the piston crowns. Do not remove the carbon ridge at the top of the cylinder bore.

7. Inspect the intake manifold boots for cracks or other damage that would allow unfiltered air into the engine. If necessary, remove the boots. Lubricate the cylinder head mating surface of each boot with engine oil. Install each boot in its original location, and tighten the intake manifold boot bolts to 10 N•m (89 in.-lb.).

8. Check for cracks in the combustion chambers and exhaust ports. A cracked head must be replaced.

9. Inspect the threads on the exhaust pipe mounting studs. Clean the threads with an appropriate size metric die. Replace a stud if damage is severe.

10. After the head has been thoroughly cleaned, place a straightedge across the gasket surface at several points. Measure the warp by inserting a feeler gauge (**Figure 44**) between the straightedge and the cylinder head at each location. If warp exceeds the service limit listed in **Table 2**, the cylinder head must be replaced or resurfaced. Consult a dealership.

VALVES AND VALVE COMPONENTS

Complete valve service requires a number of special tools. The following procedure describes how to

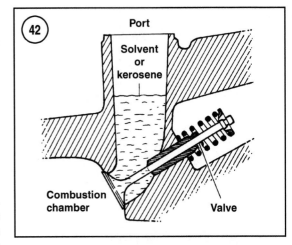

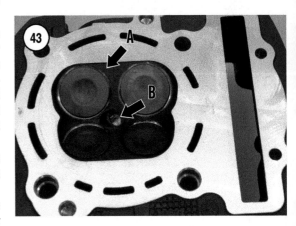

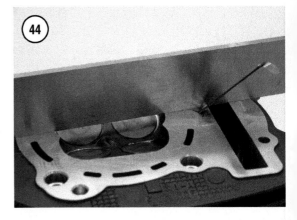

check valve components and determine the needed service.

A valve spring compressor (Yamaha part No. YM-04019 or 90890-04019) and valve spring compressor 26-mm adapter (Yamaha part No. YM-01253-1 or 90890-01243), or equivalent tools, are needed to remove and install the valves.

Valve Removal

Refer to **Figure 45**.

45 **VALVE ASSEMBLY**

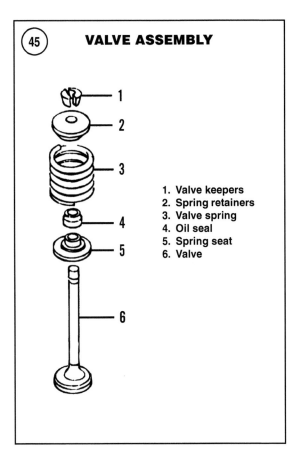

1. Valve keepers
2. Spring retainers
3. Valve spring
4. Oil seal
5. Spring seat
6. Valve

46 **VALVE LIFTER BORE PROTECTOR**

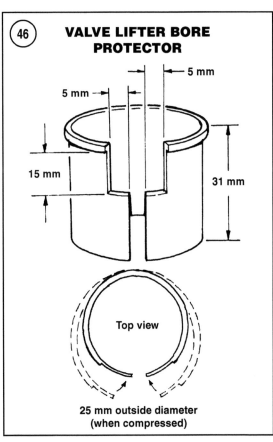

Top view

25 mm outside diameter
(when compressed)

47

CAUTION
Keep the components of each particular valve assembly together. Do not mix components from different valve assemblies. Excessive wear may result.

1. Remove the cylinder head, and perform the *Cylinder Head Leak Test* as described in *Cylinder Head* in this chapter.

NOTE:
*Fashion a bore protector from a plastic 35-mm film canister by cutting out the bottom of the canister and part of its side (**Figure 46**). Cutaway enough material so the canister can slide between the valve assembly and the side of the bore. The plastic canister protects the bore from potential marring by the valve spring compressor.*

2. Fit a bore protector between the valve assembly and the bore.
3. Install a valve spring compressor squarely over the valve retainer. Be sure the opposite end of the compressor rests against the valve head.

CAUTION
To avoid loss of spring tension, do not compress the valve spring any more than necessary to remove the valve keepers.

4. Tighten the compressor until the valve keepers separate from the valve stem. Remove both valve keepers with a magnet or needlenose pliers (**Figure 47**).

CAUTION
Remove any burrs from the valve stem grooves before removing the valve. Burrs on the valve stem will damage the valve guide when the stem passes through it.

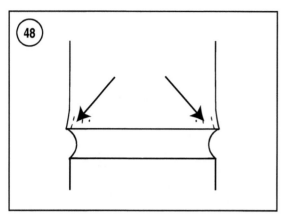

5. Inspect the valve stem grooves for burrs (**Figure 48**). Remove any burrs and then remove the valve spring compressor.

6. Remove the spring retainer (**Figure 49**) and valve spring (**Figure 50**).

7. Remove the oil seal (**Figure 51**) from the valve guide. Discard the oil seal.

8. Remove the spring seat (**Figure 52**).

9. Rotate the valve (**Figure 53**) slightly, and remove it from the cylinder head.

> *CAUTION*
> *All the components of each valve assembly must be kept together (**Figure 54**). Place each set in a divided carton or into separate small boxes. Label the set so you will know what cylinder it came from and whether it is an intake or an exhaust valve. This keeps parts from getting mixed up and makes installation simpler. Do not mix components from different valve assemblies; excessive wear may result.*

10. Repeat Steps 1-9 for the remaining valve assemblies. Keep the parts from each valve assembly separate.

Valve Installation

1. Clean the end of the valve guide.

2. Install the spring seat (**Figure 52**), and seat it in the cylinder head.

3. Apply molybdenum disulfide oil to a new oil seal. Push the seal straight down onto the valve guide until the seal bottoms (**Figure 55**).

4. Apply molybdenum disulfide oil to the valve stem. Install the valve partway into the guide (**Figure 53**). Slowly turn the valve as it enters the oil seal, and continue turning the valve until it is completely installed.

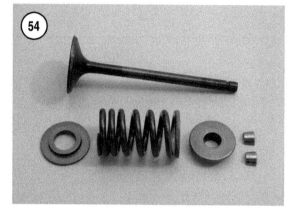

5. Install the valve spring (**Figure 50**) so the end with the closer wound coils faces the combustion chamber.

6. Seat the spring retainer (**Figure 49**) on top of the spring.

7. Fit a bore protector between the valve assembly and the bore.

8. Install a valve spring compressor squarely over the valve retainer. Be sure the opposite end of the compressor sits against the valve head.

CAUTION
To avoid loss of spring tension, do not compress the springs any more than necessary to install the valve keepers.

9. Compress the valve springs with a valve spring compressor, and install the valve keepers (**Figure 47**).

10. When both valve keepers are seated around the valve stem, slowly release the compressor. Remove the compressor, and inspect the keepers (**Figure 56**). Tap the end of the valve stem with a soft-faced mallet to assure that the keepers are properly seated (**Figure 57**).

11. Repeat steps 1-10 for the remaining valves.

12. Install the cylinder head and camshaft carrier as described in this chapter.

13. Adjust the valve clearance as described in Chapter Three.

Valve Inspection

CAUTION
*Replace any valve that is out of specification or worn to the service limit (**Table 2**). Always replace the valve guide when replacing a valve. Do not install a new valve into an old guide. Excessive wear will result.*

Replace components that are not within specification (**Table 2**).

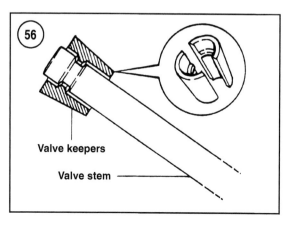

Valve keepers

Valve stem

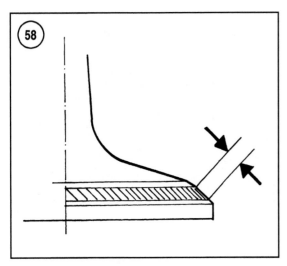

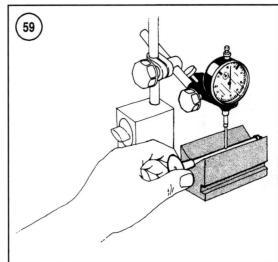

1. Clean the valve in solvent. Do not gouge or damage the valve-seating surface.

2. Inspect the contact surface of each valve (**Figure 58**) for burning. Minor roughness or pitting can be removed by lapping the valve as described in this section. Excessive unevenness indicates that the valve is not serviceable.

3. Inspect the valve stem for wear and roughness. Measure the runout as shown in **Figure 59**.

4. Measure the outside diameter of the valve stem (**Figure 60**).

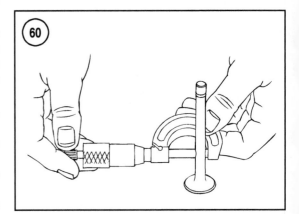

5. Remove all carbon and varnish from the valve guides with a stiff spiral wire brush.

6. Measure the inside diameter of the valve guide with a small hole gauge (**Figure 61**), and then measure the gauge with a micrometer. Take a measurement at the top, middle, and bottom of the guide. Replace the valve guide if any measurement is outside the specified range.

7. Subtract the valve stem outside diameter (Step 4) from the valve guide inside diameter (Step 5). The difference is the valve stem-to-guide clearance. Replace the valve guide if the valve stem-to-guide clearance exceeds the service limit.

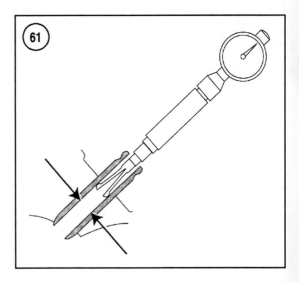

NOTE
If a small hole gauge is unavailable, perform Step 8 to check valve stem-to guide clearance, perform step 8. Measure the valve stem diameter before performing this test. This test is only accurate if the valve stem is within specification.

8. Insert the valve into its guide, and attach a dial indicator as show in **Figure 62**. Hold the valve slightly off its seat and rock it sideways in two directions while watching the dial indicator. Compare the valve movement to the valve stem-to-guide clearance specification in **Table 2**. If the valve movement is

outside the specified valve-stem-to-guide clearance range, replace the valve guide. As a final check, have the valve guides measured at a dealership.

9. Check the valve spring as follows:
   a. Inspect the valve spring for bends or other signs of distortion.

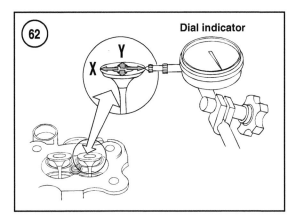

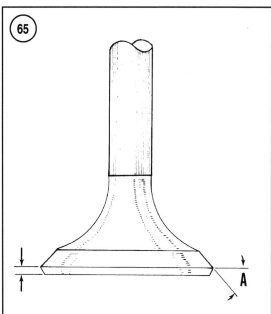

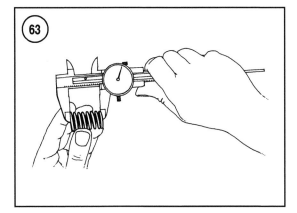

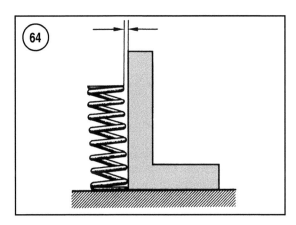

12. Inspect each valve seat (**Figure 66**) in the cylinder head. If a seat is burned or worn, it must be reconditioned. This should be performed by a service or machine shop. Seats and valves in near-perfect condition can be reconditioned by lapping as described in this section.

b. Measure each valve spring free length (**Figure 63**). Replace the spring if its free length is less than the service limit.

c. Use a square to measure the tilt of each spring (**Figure 64**).

d. Replace any defective or worn spring.

10. Measure the valve margin thickness (A, **Figure 65**) with a vernier caliper. Replace the valve and valve guide if the margin thickness is worn to the service limit.

11. Check the spring seat, spring retainer and valve keepers for cracks or other damage.

Valve Guide
Removal/Installation

Replace the valve guide when valve stem-to-guide clearance is excessive. If a valve guide is replaced, also replace its respective valve.

1. The following special tools are needed to for this service.

a. 6 mm valve guide remover (Yamaha YM-04064-A or 90890-04064).

b. 6 mm valve guide installer (Yamaha YM-0465-A or 90890-04065).

c. 6 mm valve guide reamer (Yamaha YM-04066 or 90890-04066).

NOTE:
The valve guides contract when they are cooled, which reduces the overall diameter of the guide. On the other hand, heating the cylinder head slightly increase the diameter of the guide bore due to expansion. Since the valve guides have a slight interference fit, cooling the guides and heating the head makes installation easier.

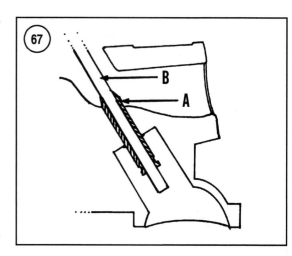

2. Remove the intake manifold boot from the cylinder head.

CAUTION
Do not heat the cylinder head with a torch. Never bring a flame into contact with the cylinder head. Direct flame can warp the cylinder head.

CAUTION
Residual oil or solvent odor may remain in the oven after heating the cylinder head.

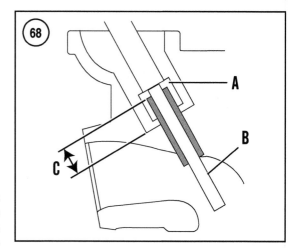

3. Place the cylinder head in a shop oven and warm it to 212° F (100° C). Check the temperature of the cylinder head by flicking tiny drops of water onto the head. The cylinder head is heated to the proper temperature if the drops sizzle and evaporates immediately.

WARNING
Wear protective gloves when performing this procedure. The cylinder head will be very hot.

4. Remove the cylinder head from the oven and place it onto wooden blocks with the combustion chamber facing up.
5. From the combustion side of the head, drive the old valve guide (A, **Figure 67**) out of the cylinder head with the 6-mm valve guide remover (B) and a hammer.
6. Remove and discard the valve guide.
7. After the cylinder head cools, check the guide bore for carbon or other contamination. Clean the bore thoroughly.
8. Reheat the cylinder head as described in step 2.
9. Remove the cylinder head from the oven and place it onto wooden blocks with the combustion chamber facing down.
10. Remove one valve guide from the freezer.

CAUTION
Failure to lubricate the new valve guide and guide bore will result in damage to the cylinder head and/or valve guide.

11. Apply clean engine oil to the new valve guide and to the valve guide bore in the cylinder head.
12. From the top side of the cylinder head (camshaft side), drive the new valve guide into the cylinder head with the a hammer, the 6 mm (0.31 in.) valve guide installer (A, **Figure 68**) and the valve guide remover. (B). Drive the valve guide into the bore until the guide's installed height (C, **Figure 68**) is within specification (**Table 2**).
13. After the cylinder head has cooled down, ream the new valve guides as follows:
   a. Apply cutting oil to both the new valve guide and to the valve guide reamer.

CAUTION
Always rotate the valve guide reamer clockwise. The valve guide will be damaged if the reamer is rotated counterclockwise.

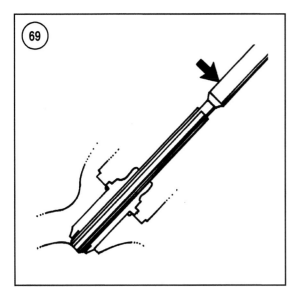

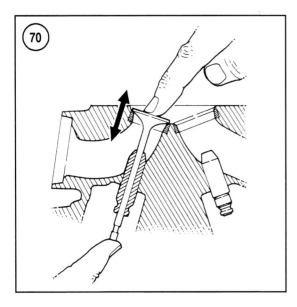

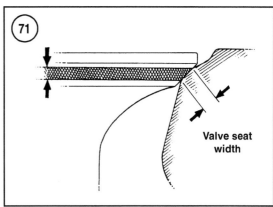

Valve seat
width

15. Clean the cylinder head and valve guides with solvent to wash out all metal particles. Dry the head with compressed air.

16. Lightly oil the valve guides to prevent rust.

17. Inspect the valve seats as described in this section.

18. Install the intake manifold boot. Lubricate the manifolds with engine oil, and tighten the intake manifold boot bolts to 10 N•m (89 in.-lb.).

Valve Seat Inspection

1. Remove the valves as described in this section.

2. Check the valve seal with marking compound by performing the following:

    a. Clean all carbon deposits from the valve face with solvent or detergent. Completely dry the valve face.

    b. Spread a thin layer of marking compound evenly on the valve face.

    c. Insert the valve into its guide.

    d. Support the valve by hand (**Figure 70**), and tap the valve up and down in the cylinder head. Do not rotate the valve; a false impression will result.

    e. Remove the valve and examine the impression left by the marking compound. If the impression left in the dye on the valve or in the cylinder head is not even and continuous and if the valve seat width (**Figure 71**) is not within specification (**Table 2**), replace the cylinder head. The manufacturer does not provide tools or cutter angles for valve seat reconditioning.

3. Examine the valve seat in the cylinder head (**Figure 66**). It should be smooth and even, with a polished seating surface.

4. Measure the valve seat width (**Figure 71**).

5. If the valve seat is within specification (**Table 2**), install the valves as described in this chapter.

6. If the valve seat is not correct, replace the cylinder head.

    b. Insert the 6 mm (0.31 in.) valve guide reamer from the top side (**Figure 69**), and rotate the reamer clockwise. Continue to rotate the reamer and work it down through the entire length of the new valve guide. Continue to apply additional cutting oil during this procedure.

    c. Rotate the reamer clockwise until it has traveled all the way through the new valve guide.

    d. Rotate the reamer clockwise, and completely withdraw the reamer from the valve guide.

    e. Measure the inside diameter of the valve guide with a small hole gauge (**Figure 61**). Measure the gauge with a micrometer, and compare the measurement to the specification in **Table 2**. Replace the valve guide if it is not within specification.

14. If necessary, repeat steps 1-12 for any other valve guide.

Valve Seat Lapping

Valve lapping can restore the valve seat without machining if the amount of wear or distortion is not too great. Lapping is also recommended after the valve seat has been refaced or when a new valve and valve guide have been installed.

1. Apply a light coating of fine grade valve lapping compound on the seating surface of the valve.

2. Apply molybdenum disulfide oil to the valve stem, and insert the valve into the cylinder head.

3. Wet the suction cup of the valve lapping tool (**Figure 72**) and stick it onto the valve head.

4. Lap the valve to the valve seat (**Figure 73**) by performing the following:

    a. Lap the valve by rotating the lapping stick between your hands in both directions.

    b. Every 5 to 10 seconds, stop and rotate the valve 180° in the valve seat.

    c. Continue lapping until the contact surfaces of the valve and the valve seat in the cylinder head are a uniform gray. Stop as soon as they turn this color to avoid removing too much material.

5. Thoroughly clean the cylinder head and all valve components in solvent, followed by a wash with detergent and hot water.

6. After the lapping has been completed and the valve assemblies have been reinstalled into the cylinder head, the valve seat should be tested. Check the seat by performing the *Cylinder Head Leak Test* in *Cylinder Head* in this chapter. If fluid leaks past any of the seats, disassemble that valve assembly and repeat the lapping procedure until there are no leaks.

7. After the cylinder head and valve components are cleaned in detergent and hot water, apply a light coat of engine oil to all bare metal surfaces to prevent rust.

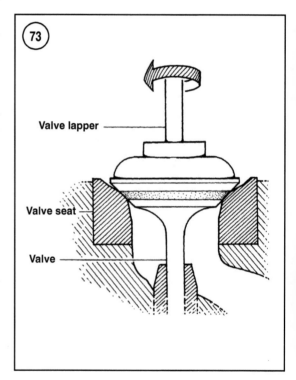

Valve lapper

Valve seat

Valve

CYLINDER BLOCK

Refer to **Figure 74**.

Removal

1. Remove the cylinder head and head gasket as described in this chapter.

2. If still installed, remove the front cam-chain guide from the cylinder block. Note that the guide's upper boss rests in a cutout in the block (**Figure 75**).

3. Loosen the cylinder block by tapping around its perimeter with a plastic mallet.

4. Pull the cylinder block straight up, and lift it off the piston and cylinder studs. Feed the cam chain and safety wire through the cam chain tunnel, and retie the wire to the engine.

5. Remove the dowels (A, **Figure 76**), and discard the base gasket (B).

6. Slip a length of hose over the each crankcase studs so the piston or rings will not be marred if the piston accidentally strikes a stud.

7. Inspect the cylinder as described in this section.

Installation

1. Clean any gasket residue from the top and bottom gasket surfaces of the cylinder block.

2. Install the dowels (A, **Figure 76**) and new base gasket (B).

3. Liberally lubricate the cylinder with engine oil.

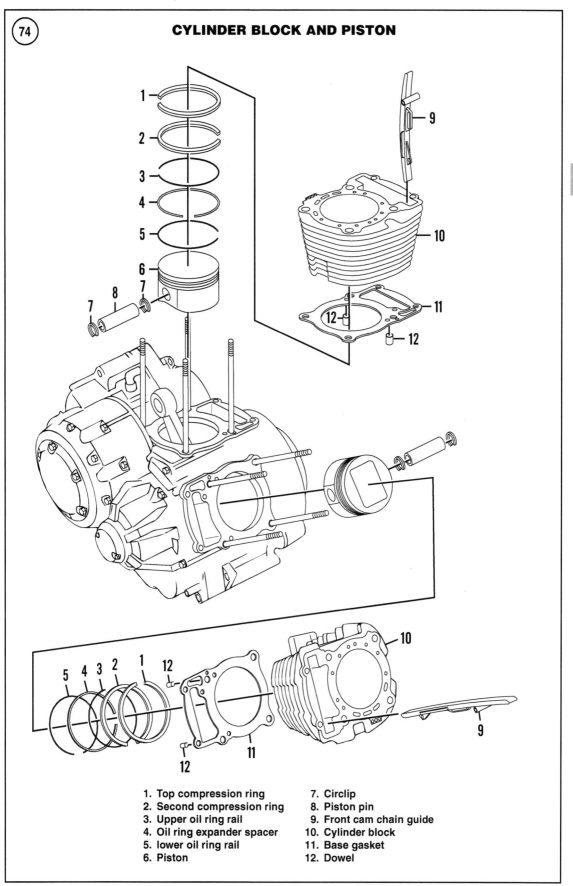

CYLINDER BLOCK AND PISTON

1. Top compression ring
2. Second compression ring
3. Upper oil ring rail
4. Oil ring expander spacer
5. lower oil ring rail
6. Piston
7. Circlip
8. Piston pin
9. Front cam chain guide
10. Cylinder block
11. Base gasket
12. Dowel

4. Rotate the crankshaft so the piston sits at top dead center.

CAUTION
*A cutout on the camshaft-tunnel side of the cylinder sleeve does not have a chamfer (**Figure 77**). This cutout can catch a piston ring end during cylinder installation. Reposition a ring as necessary to prevent this.*

5. Check the position of each piston ring end gap. If necessary, adjust a piston ring so its end gap sits outside of the cutout (**Figure 77**).
6. Start the cylinder block down the crankcase studs. Position the cam chain and rear cam chain guide so they will pass through the cam chain tunnel in the block.

7. Lower the cylinder until the piston rings are within the cylinder sleeve (**Figure 78**). Use a pistons ring compressor or fingers to compress each ring as it enters the cylinder.
8. Run the cam chain and safety wire up through the cam chain tunnel in the cylinder block, and secure the safety wire to the outside of the engine.
9. Lower the cylinder block all the way down onto the crankcase.
10. Install the front cam chain guide so its boss rests in the cylinder cutout (**Figure 75**).
11. Install the cylinder head as described in this chapter.
12. Follow the break-in procedure in Chapter Five.

Inspection

If the cylinder bore is damaged or out of specification (**Table 2**), replace the cylinder block, piston and rings as a set. The cylinder cannot be bored. Oversized pistons and rings are not available from the manufacturer.
1. Remove all gasket residue from the top and bottom gasket surfaces (A, **Figure 79**) on the cylinder block. Apply a gasket remover or use solvent and soak any old gasket material. If necessary, use a dull, broad-tipped chisel and gently scrape off all gasket residue. Do not gouge the sealing surface. An oil leaks will result.

2. Wash the cylinder block in solvent to remove any oil or carbon particles. The cylinder bore must be cleaned thoroughly before attempting any measurement otherwise incorrect readings may be obtained.
3. Inspect the cylinder wall (B, **Figure 79**) for scratches.
4. Measure the inside diameter of the cylinder bore with a cylinder bore gauge (**Figure 80**). Measure the bore at the top, center and bottom of the cylinder. At

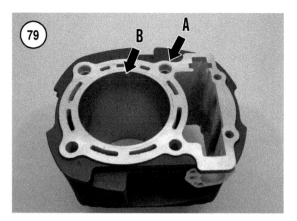

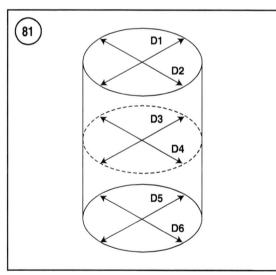

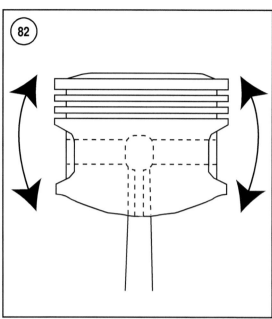

c. Out of round equals the largest of the measurements taken parallel to the crankshaft (D1, D3 or D5) minus the smallest of the measurements taken 90° to the crankshaft (D2, D4 or D6).

6. If the either the cylinder bore, taper or out-of-round is out of specification, replace the cylinder block.

7. Calculate the piston-to-cylinder clearance as described in *Piston Clearance* in *Pistons and Rings* in this chapter.

PISTONS AND RINGS

Refer to **Figure 74**.

Piston Removal

1. Remove the cylinder head and cylinder block as described in this chapter.

2. Lightly mark the top of the piston with an F or R (front or rear) and an arrow indicating its orientation within the cylinder so it can be reinstalled in the correct cylinder.

WARNING
The edges of all piston rings are very sharp. Be careful when handling them.

3. Before removing the piston, hold the connecting rod tightly and rock the piston (**Figure 82**). Any rocking motion (do not confuse with the normal sliding motion) indicates wear on the piston pin, piston pin bore or connecting rod small-end bore (more likely a combination of these). If necessary, replace the piston and piston pin as a set.

each height, measure the bore in two axes: parallel to the crankshaft and 90° to the crankshaft. Refer to **Figure 81**. Record all six measurements: D1-D6.

5. Calculate cylinder bore, taper or out-of-round.

    a. Cylinder bore equals the largest of the six inside diameter measurements (D1-D6).

    b. Taper equals the largest of the top measurements (D1 or D2) minus the largest of the bottom measurements (D5 or D6).

4. Stuff clean shop rags into the crankcase opening to prevent objects from falling into the crankcase (**Figure 83**).

5. Remove a circlip (**Figure 84**) from one side of the piston pin bore with a small screwdriver or scribe. Hold a thumb over one edge of the clip so it will not spring out of the piston. Deburr the piston pin and the circlip groove as necessary.

6. From the other side, push the piston pin out of the piston by hand. If the pin is tight, remove it with the homemade tool shown in **Figure 85**. Do not drive out the piston pin. This could damage the piston pin, connecting rod, or piston.

7. Lift the piston from the connecting rod, and remove the remaining circlip from the piston. Discard both piston pin circlips.

8. Mark the piston pin and piston so they can be reassembled as a set.

9. If the piston is going to be left off for some time, protect the connecting rod by slipping a piece of foam insulation tube over the rod small end.

Piston Installation

1. Rotate the engine so the connecting rod sits at top dead center.

2. Install a new piston pin circlip into one side of the piston. Position the circlip so its end gap is at least 3 mm (0.12 in.) away from the piston notch (**Figure 86**).

3. Apply clean engine oil to the inside surface of the connecting rod small end.

4. Apply fresh engine oil to the piston pin, and install the pin into the piston until it is flush with the inside of the piston-pin boss (**Figure 87**).

5. Place the piston onto the connecting rod so the arrow on the piston crown (A, **Figure 88**).

> *CAUTION*
> *When installing the piston pin, do not push the pin too far into the piston. The piston pin circlip installed in Step 2 will be forced into the piston metal, destroying the clip groove and loosening the clip.*

6. Line up the piston pin with the hole in the connecting rod, and push the piston pin through the connecting rod (**Figure 89**). Jiggle the piston as necessary until the piston pin enters the connecting rod. Do not use force during installation or damage may occur.

7. Push the piston pin until it bottoms against the pin clip on the other side of the piston. If the piston pin does not slide easily, install it with the homemade tool (**Figure 85**) used during removal but eliminate the piece of pipe. Pull the piston pin in until it stops.

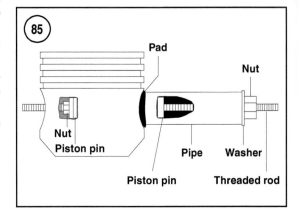

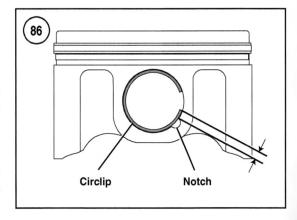

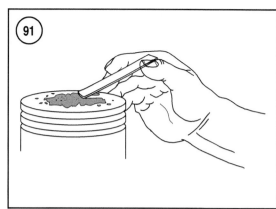

4

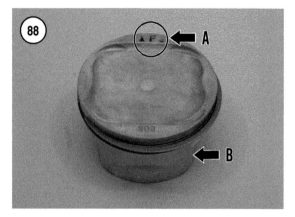

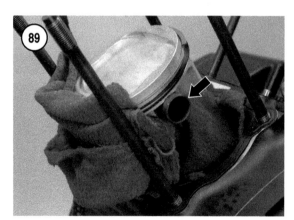

8. After the piston is installed, recheck and make sure that the arrow on the piston crown (**Figure 90**) points to the front side of the cylinder.

9. Install the second piston pin circlip (**Figure 84**) into the groove in the piston. Be sure the circlip's end gap is at least 3 mm (0.12 in.) away from the notch in the piston (**Figure 86**). Make sure both piston pin circlips are seated in their respective grooves.

10. Check the installation by rocking the piston back and forth around the pin axis and from side to side along the axis. It should rotate freely back and forth but not from side to side.

11. If necessary, install the piston rings as described in this section.

12. Install the cylinder and cylinder head as described in this chapter.

Piston Inspection

1. Carefully clean the carbon from the piston crown (**Figure 91**) with a chemical remover or with a soft scraper. Remark the piston as soon as it is cleaned. Do not remove or damage the carbon ring around the circumference of the piston above the top ring. If the piston, rings and cylinder are within specification and can be reused, removal of the carbon ring from the top of the piston or removal of the carbon ridge from the top of the cylinder wall will promote excessive oil consumption.

> *CAUTION*
> *Do not wire brush the piston skirts.*

2. After cleaning the piston, examine the crown. It should show no signs of wear or damage.

3. Examine each ring groove for burrs, dented edges and wide wear. Pay particular attention to the top compression ring groove. It usually wears more than the others. Since the oil rings are constantly bathed in oil, these rings and grooves wear little compared to compression rings and their grooves. If the oil ring groove shows signs of wear or if the oil ring assem-

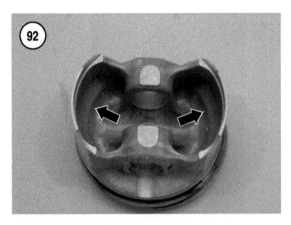

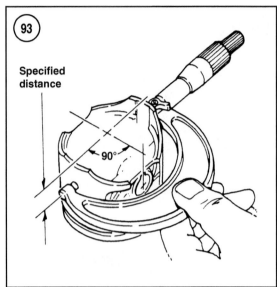

Specified
distance

90°

bly is tight and difficult to remove, the piston skirt
may have collapsed. If so, replace the piston.

4. Check the oil control holes (**Figure 92**) in the
piston for carbon or oil sludge buildup. If necessary,
clean the holes and blow them out with compressed
air.

NOTE
If the piston skirt is worn or scuffed un-
evenly from side-to-side, the connect-
ing rod may be bent or twisted.

5. Check the piston skirt (B, **Figure 88**) for galling
and abrasion, which may have been caused by piston
seizure. If a piston shows signs of partial seizure (bits
of aluminum build-up on the piston skirt), the piston
should be replaced. When replacing a piston, lightly
hone the cylinder with a bottlebrush hone.

6. Check the circlip groove on each side of the piston for wear or other damage. Install a new circlip
into each piston circlip groove and try to move the
clip from side to side. If the circlip has any side play,
the groove is worn and the piston must be replaced.

7. Measure the outside diameter of the piston across
the skirt at right angles to the piston pin bore. Measure
the piston at a point 8 mm (0.31 in.) up from the bottom of the piston skirt (**Figure 93**). Record the reading for the piston-to-cylinder clearance calculation.

8. Calculate the piston-to-cylinder clearance as described in this section.

Piston-to-Cylinder Clearance

1. Make sure the pistons and cylinder walls are clean
and dry.

2. Measure the inside diameter of the cylinder and
determine the cylinder bore as described in Step 4
and Step 5A of *Cylinder Inspection*. Record the reading.

3. Measure the outside diameter of the piston as described in Step 7 of *Piston Inspection*. Record the
measurement.

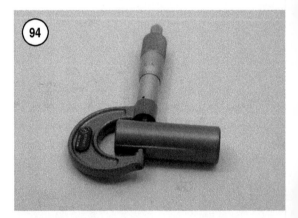

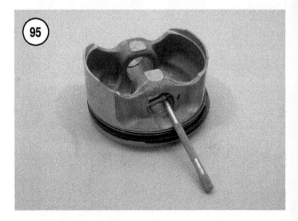

4. Piston-to-cylinder clearance is the difference between the piston outside diameter and the cylinder
bore inside diameter. Subtract the outside diameter
of the piston (Step 3) from the cylinder bore inside
diameter (Step 2). If the piston-to-cylinder clearance
is out of specification (**Table 2**), replace cylinder,
piston and rings as a set. Oversized pistons are not
available.

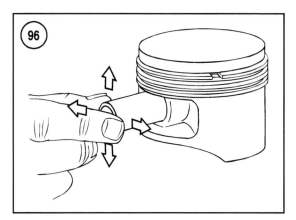

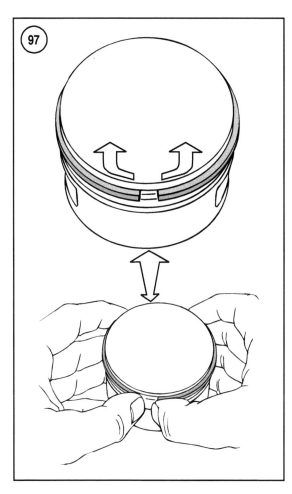

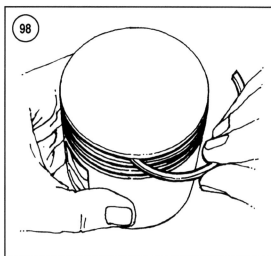

5. Calculate piston pin-to-piston-bore clearance by subtracting the piston pin outside diameter from the piston pin bore inside diameter If the clearance is not within specification (**Table 2**), replace the piston and piston pin as a set.

6. Oil the piston pin, and install it in the connecting rod as described in this section. Slowly rotate the piston pin and check for radial and lateral play (**Figure 96**). If any play exists, the connecting rod should be replaced (providing the piston pin outside diameter is within the specification in **Table 2**).

7. Inspect the connecting rod as described in Chapter Five.

Piston Ring
Removal/Inspection

A 3-ring assembly is used with each piston. The top and second rings are compression rings. The lower ring is an oil control ring assembly consisting of two ring rails and an expander spacer.

> *WARNING*
> *The edges of all piston rings are very*
> *sharp. Be careful when handling them.*

1. Remove the compression rings with a ring expander tool or by spreading the ends with your thumbs just enough to slide the ring up over the piston (**Figure 97**). Repeat for the remaining rings.

2. Remove all carbon buildup from the ring grooves with a broken piston ring (**Figure 98**). Do not remove aluminum material from the ring grooves. This increases ring side clearance.

3. Inspect the grooves for burrs, nicks or broken and cracked lands. Recondition or replace the piston if necessary.

Piston Pin Inspection

1. Clean the piston pin in solvent, and dry it thoroughly.

2. Inspect the piston pin for chrome flaking or cracks. Replace the pin if necessary.

3. Measure the outside diameter of the piston pin (**Figure 94**). Replace the piston and piston pin if the pin diameter is out of specification (**Table 2**).

4. Measure the inside diameter of the piston pin bore in the piston with a small bore gauge (**Figure 95**).

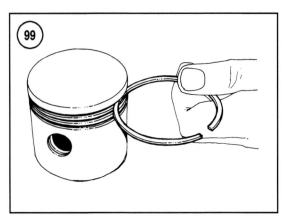

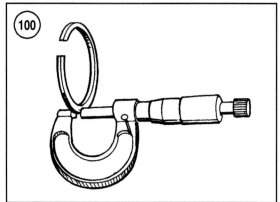

4. Roll each ring around its piston groove as shown in **Figure 99** to check for binding. Minor binding may be cleaned up with a fine-cut file.

5. Measure the thickness of each ring (**Figure 100**). If the thickness is less than specified (**Table 2**), the ring(s) must be replaced.

> *NOTE*
> *When checking the oil control ring assembly, measure the end gap of each oil ring rail. The end gap of the expander spacer cannot be measured. If either ring rail has excessive end gap, replace the entire oil ring assembly.*

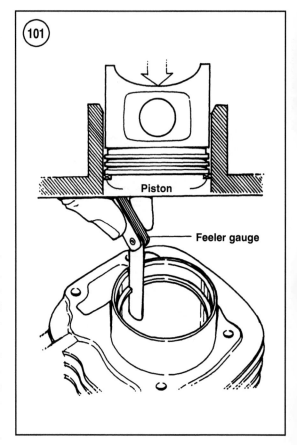

Piston

Feeler gauge

6. Place each ring, one at a time, into the cylinder, and push the ring to a point 10 mm (0.39 in.) below the top of the cylinder. Push the ring with the crown of the piston to ensure that the ring is square in the cylinder bore. Measure the ring end gap with a flat feeler gauge (**Figure 101**). If the gap is out of specification (**Table 2**), replace the rings.

7. Install the piston rings as described in this section and measure the side clearance of each ring in its groove with a flat feeler gauge (**Figure 102**). If the clearance is greater than specified (**Table 2**), replace the piston and rings as a set.

8. When installing new rings, measure their end gaps as described in Step 6, and compare the measurements to the dimensions given in **Table 2**. If the end gap is greater than specified, return the rings for another set(s). If the end gap is smaller than specified (**Table 2**), secure a small file in a vise, grip the ring with your fingers, and enlarge the gap (**Figure 103**).

Piston Ring Installation

> *CAUTION*
> *When installing any ring, liberally lubricate the ring and piston groove with clean engine oil.*

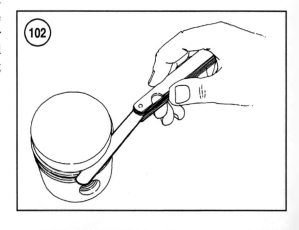

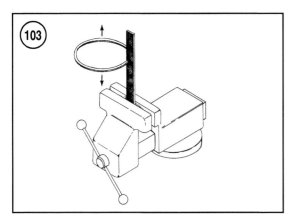

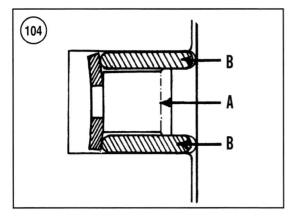

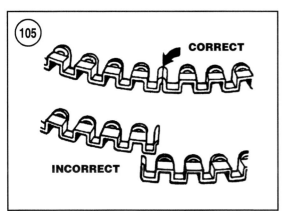

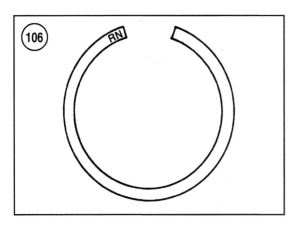

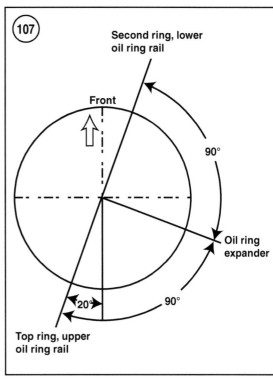

1. Install the oil control ring assembly into the bottom ring groove. Install the oil ring expander spacer first (A, **Figure 104**), and then install each ring rail (B). Make sure the ends of the expander spacer butt together (**Figure 105**). They should not overlap. If reassembling used parts, install the ring rails as they were removed.

2. Install the second compression ring, and then install the top ring. Carefully spread the ends of each ring with your thumbs and slip the ring over the top of the piston (**Figure 97**). Install each compression ring with its manufacturing marks (**Figure 106**) facing up.

3. Make sure the rings are seated completely in their grooves all the way around the piston and that the ends are distributed around the piston.

4. Check the side clearance of each ring as shown in **Figure 102**. If side clearance is not within the specification shown in **Table 2**, re-examine the condition of the piston and rings.

> *CAUTION*
> *A cutout on the camshaft-tunnel side of the cylinder sleeve does not have a chamfer (**Figure 77**). This cutout can catch a piston ring end during cylinder installation. Reposition a ring as necessary to prevent this.*

5. Distribute the ring gaps around the piston as shown in **Figure 107**.

6. Follow the break-in procedure in Chapter Five.

Table 1 GENERAL ENGINE SPECIFICATIONS

Engine type	4-stroke, liquid-cooled, SOHC, V-twin
Number of cylinders	2
Bore × stroke	100.0 mm × 83.0 mm (3.94 in. × 3.27 in.)
Displacement	1304 cc (80 cu. in.)
Compression ratio	9.50:1
Compression pressure	
Standard pressure @ sea level	1450 kPa (210 psi) @ 400 rpm
Minimum-Maximum pressure	1200-1500 kPa (170-215 psi)
Ignition timing	5° B.T.D.C. @ 1000 rpm. Not adjustable.

Table 2 ENGINE TOP END SPECIFICATIONS

Item	New mm (in.)	Service limit mm (in.)
Cylinder head warp	–	0.03 mm (0.0012 in.)
Camshaft		
Cam lobe height		
Intake	42.988-43.088 (1.6924-1.6964)	42.888 (1.6885)
Exhaust	43.156-43.256 (1.6991-1.7030)	43.056 (1.6951)
Cam lobe width		
Intake	37.045-37.145 (1.4585-1.4624)	36.945 (1.4545)
Exhaust	37.118-37.218 (1.4613-1.4653)	37.018 (1.4574)
Camshaft journal		
outside diameter	20.959-20.980 (0.8252-0.8260)	–
Rocker arm		
Rocker arm bore		
inside diameter	12.000-12.018 (0.4724-0.4731)	–
Rocker arm shaft		
outside diameter	11.976-11.991 (0.4715-0.4721)	–
Rocker-arm-to-rocker-shaft		
clearance	0.009-0.042 (0.0004-0.0017)	0.095 (0.0037)
Valves		
Valve clearance (cold)		
Intake	0.09-0.13 (0.0035-0.0051)	–
Exhaust	0.14-0.18 (0.0055-0.0071)	–
Valve stem runout	–	0.010 (0.0004)
Valve stem outside diameter		
Intake	5.975-5.990 (0.2352-0.2358)	5.945 (0.2341)
Exhaust	5.960-5.975 (0.2346-0.2352)	5.930 (0.2335)
Valve guide inside diameter		
(intake and exhaust)	6.000-6.012 (0.2362-0.2367)	6.050 (0.2382)
Valve guide installed height	14.5-14.9 (0.571-0.587)	–
Valve stem-to-guide clearance		
Intake	0.010-0.037 (0.0004-0.0015)	0.080 (0.0031)
Exhaust	0.025-0.052 (0.0010 -0.0020)	0.10 (0.0039)
Valve seat width	1.00-1.20 (0.0394-0.0472)	–
Valve margin thickness	1.15-1.45 (0.0453-0.0571)	–
Valve springs		
Free length	42.43 (1.67)	40.31 (1.59)
Installed length	35.00 (1.38)	–
Valve spring tilt		2.5°/1.9 mm (0.075 in.)
Cylinder		
Bore inside diameter	100.000-100.010 (3.9370-3.9374)	–
Taper	–	0.050 (0.0020)
Out of round	–	0.050 (0.0020)
Pistons		
Outside diameter[1]	99.955-99.970 (3.9352-3.9358)	–
Piston-to-cylinder clearance	0.030-0.055 (0.0012-0.0022)	0.15 (0.0059)
Piston offset	0.50 (0.0197)	–
Piston pin bore inside diameter	23.004-23.015 (0.9057-0.9061)	23.045 (0.9073)
Piston pin outside diameter	22.991-23.000 (0.9052-0.9055)	22.971 (0.9044)
Piston pin-to-piston-bore		
clearance	0.004-0.024 (0.00016-0.00094)	0.074 (0.00291)
	(continued)	

Table 2 ENGINE TOP END SPECIFICATIONS (continued)

Item	New mm (in.)	Service limit mm (in.)
Piston rings		
Side clearance		
Top	0.030-0.080 (0.0012-0.0032)	0.130 (0.0051)
Second	0.030-0.070 (0.0012-0.0028)	0.130 (0.0051)
Ring thickness		
Top	1.20 (0.05)	–
Second	1.20 (0.05)	–
Oil ring rail	2.50 (0.10)	–
Ring end gap[2]		
Top	0.20-0.35 (0.0079-0.0138)	0.60 (0.0236)
Second	0.45-0.060 (0.0177-0.0236)	0.95 (0.0374)
Oil ring rail	0.20-0.70 (0.0079-0.0276)	–

1. Measured 8.0 mm (0.31 in.) from bottom of piston skirt.
2. Measure 10.0 mm (0.39 in.) below the top of the cylinder.

Table 3 ENGINE TOP END TORQUE SPECIFICATIONS

Item	N•m	in.-lb.	ft.-lb.
Cam chain guide bolt	10	89	–
Cam chain tensioner housing bolt	10	89	–
Cam chain tensioner bolts	10	89	–
Cam-chain-tensioner base bolt	10	89	–
Camshaft carrier bolts*	10	89	–
Camshaft sprocket bolts	20	–	15
Cylinder head blind plug	6	53	–
Cylinder head cover bolts	10	89	–
Cylinder head bolts*	13	115	–
Cylinder head nuts*	65	–	48
Damper cover bolt	7	62	–
Finished cover bolts	8	71	–
Flywheel bolt plug	10	89	–
Intake manifold boot bolt	10	89	–
Oxygen sensor	44	–	32.5
Oil check bolt	15	–	11
Spark plug	13	115	–
Tappet cover bolts*	10	89	–
Timing inspection plug	6	53	–
Valve adjuster locknut	14	–	10

*Refer to text.

CHAPTER FIVE

ENGINE LOWER END

This chapter describes the service procedures for the following lower end components:
1. Flywheel and starter gears.
2. Starter clutch.
3. Balancer assembly.
4. Cam chain and guides.
5. Oil/water pump.
6. Crankcase.
7. Crankshaft.
8. Connecting rods.

The text makes frequent references to the left and right sides of the engine. This refers to the engine as it sits in the frame not as it sits on the workbench.

The external gearshift, clutch, throttle body/injectors, starter/clutch and alternator can be serviced with the engine in the frame.

Tables 1-3 are at the end of this chapter.

ENGINE

Removal

Refer to **Figure 1**.

1. Securely support the motorcycle on a level surface.
2. Drain the engine oil and remove the oil filter. Drain the coolant. Refer to Chapter Three.
3. Remove the rider's seat, left engine cover, both side covers and the sidestand (Chapter Fifteen).
4. Remove the battery cover, battery, battery box, horn and starter (Chapter Nine).

CAUTION
Stuff clean shops rags into the intake manifold boots to keep debris out of the engine.

5. Remove the frame neck covers, fuel tank, exhaust system, air filter housing, throttle body and the intake manifold (Chapter Eight).
6. Remove the finished covers from each cylinder head (Chapter Four).
7. Remove the engine pulley, the pulley housing, and the shift pedal/floorboard assembly (Chapter Seven).
8. Remove the radiator and coolant reservoir cover (Chapter Ten).
9. Drain the fluid from the rear brake (Chapter Fourteen).

CAUTION
Once a brake or reservoir hose is disconnected from the rear brake master cylinder, immediately seal the hose in a plastic bag so brake fluid will not leak onto the motorcycle.

10. Remove the banjo bolt (A, **Figure 2**), and disconnect the brake hose from the rear brake master cylinder. Account for the two sealing washers.
11. Disconnect the reservoir hose (B, **Figure 2**) from its fitting on the rear brake master cylinder.
12. Remove the coolant-reservoir-cover bracket bolts (A, **Figure 3**), and suspend the bracket (B) and brake hoses out of the way.

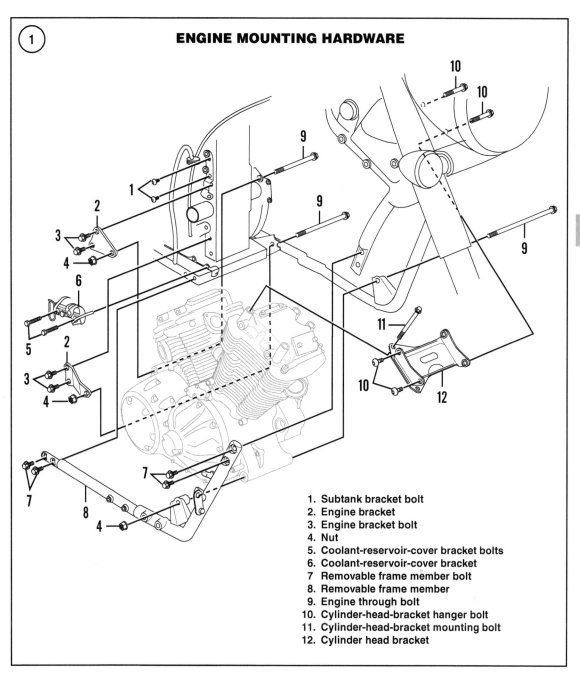

ENGINE MOUNTING HARDWARE

1. Subtank bracket bolt
2. Engine bracket
3. Engine bracket bolt
4. Nut
5. Coolant-reservoir-cover bracket bolts
6. Coolant-reservoir-cover bracket
7. Removable frame member bolt
8. Removable frame member
9. Engine through bolt
10. Cylinder-head-bracket hanger bolt
11. Cylinder-head-bracket mounting bolt
12. Cylinder head bracket

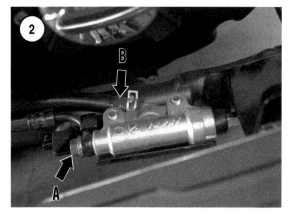

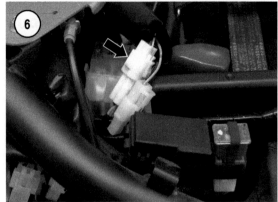

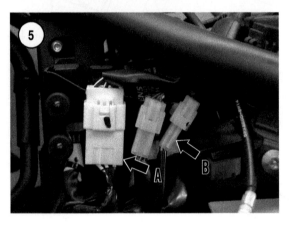

13. Pull the spark plug cap from each spark plug.

14. Separate the halves of the following electrical connectors:

   a. Oil level switch connector (**Figure 4**).

   b. Stator connector (A, **Figure 5**).

   c. Crankshaft position sensor connector (B, **Figure 5**).

   d. Speed sensor connector (**Figure 6**).

   e. Rear brake light switch connector (**Figure 7**).

   f. Neutral switch connector (**Figure 8**).

   g. Release any clamps that secure the wires to the frame. Note the routing of the wires.

15. Disconnect the crankcase breather hose (A, **Figure 9**) from its crankcase fitting, and remove the heat shield (B).

16. Release the clutch cable from the cable holder (A, **Figure 10**), and disconnect the cable end from the clutch release lever (B). On 2007-2009 models, if necessary, loosen the mid-cable adjuster (**Figure 11**) to create additional slack. 2010 models do not have a mid-cable adjuster.

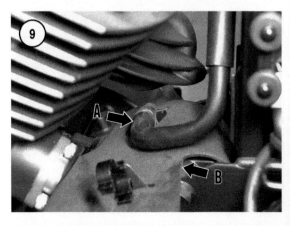

17. Loosen the subtank bracket bolts (A, **Figure 12**), but leave the bracket (B) in place. When necessary slide the bracket up to access the engine bracket bolts.

18. Place a hydraulic jack under the crankcase to support the engine once the mounting bolts are removed.

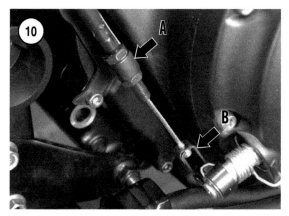

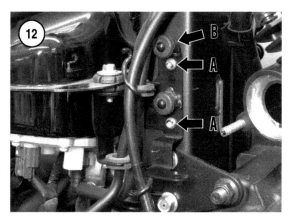

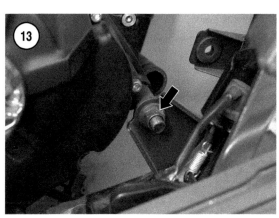

19. Check that all cables, wires, and hoses are disconnected from the engine and safely secured out of the way.

20. Remove the nut from the front engine through bolt (**Figure 13**). Leave bolt in place.

21. Remove the front (**Figure 14**) and rear (**Figure 15**) removable frame member bolts.

22. Remove the removable frame member along with the floorboard and brake master cylinder.

23. Loosen all the remaining engine mounting fasteners.

24. Remove the nut (A, **Figure 16**) from each rear engine through bolt.

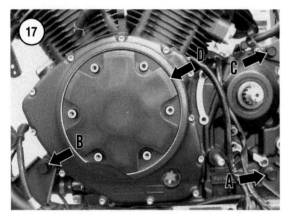

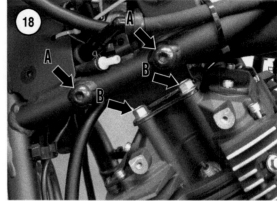

25. Remove the engine bracket bolts (B, **Figure 16**), and remove the lower engine bracket (C) from the right side.

26. Remove the engine upper bracket bolts (D, **Figure 16**), and remove the upper engine bracket (E). Slide the subtank bracket (B, **Figure 12**) up to access the engine bracket bolts.

27. Pull the lower, rear engine through bolt (A, **Figure 17**) from the left side.

28. Remove the cylinder-head-bracket hanger bolts from the left side (A, **Figure 18**) and from the right side (A, **Figure 19**).

29. Pull the front engine through bolt (B, **Figure 17**), and the upper, rear engine through bolt (C). The engine is now free.

30. Slightly lower the engine so the cylinder head bracket can be removed.

31. Remove the cylinder-head-bracket mounting bolts from the left (B, **Figure 18**) and right sides (B, **Figure 19**), and remove the cylinder head bracket.

32. With the help of an assistant, lower the jack, and roll it from the right side. Lift the engine off the jack and remove it to the bench.

33. While the engine is removed for service, check all the frame's engine mounts for cracks or other damage. If any cracks are found, take the frame assembly to a dealership for further examination.

Installation

1. Set the front cylinder head bracket onto the front cylinder head. Install the cylinder-head-bracket mounting bolts (B, **Figure 18** and B, **Figure 19**), and tighten them to 30 N•m (22 ft.-lb.).

2. With the aid of an assistant, set the engine on a hydraulic jack and roll the engine into place beneath the frame.

3. While your assistant holds the engine, raise the hydraulic jack until the cylinder head bracket aligns with its frame mounts.

4. Apply threadlocking compound to the threads of the cylinder-head-bracket hanger bolts (A, **Figure 18** and A, **Figure 19**), and install the bolts onto each side of the bracket. Finger-tighten the bolts at this time.

5. Fit the lower engine bracket (C, **Figure 16**) into place on the frame. Apply threadlocking compound to the threads of the engine bracket bolts (B, **Figure 16**), and finger-tighten the bolts.

6. Fit the upper engine bracket (E, **Figure 16**) into place. Apply threadlocking compound to the threads of the bolts (D, **Figure 16**) and finger tighten the bolts.

7. Install each rear engine through bolt (A and C, **Figure 17**) from the right side. Finger-tighten a nut onto each bolt (A, **Figure 16**).

8. Set the removable frame member into place on the right side, and install the front (**Figure 14**) and rear (**Figure 15**) removable frame member bolts. Apply threadlocking compound to and finger-tighten each bolt.

9. Install the front engine through bolt (B, **Figure 17**) from the right side, and install a nut (**Figure 13**) onto the bolt.

10. Tighten the fasteners to specification in the given order.

   a. The engine bracket bolts to 48 N•m (35 ft.-lb.).

   b. The removable frame member bolts to 48 N•m (35 ft.-lb.).

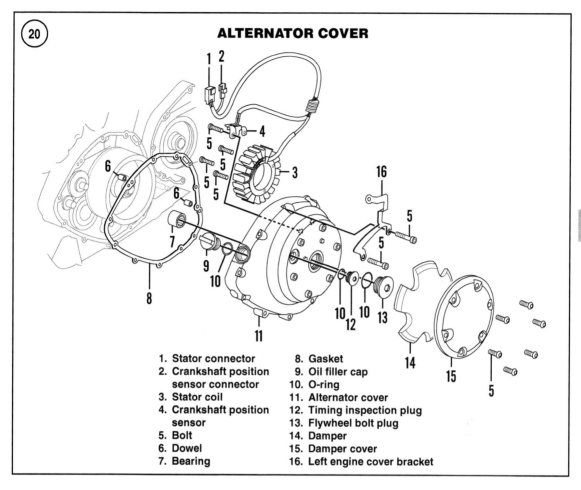

ALTERNATOR COVER

20

1. Stator connector
2. Crankshaft position sensor connector
3. Stator coil
4. Crankshaft position sensor
5. Bolt
6. Dowel
7. Bearing
8. Gasket
9. Oil filler cap
10. O-ring
11. Alternator cover
12. Timing inspection plug
13. Flywheel bolt plug
14. Damper
15. Damper cover
16. Left engine cover bracket

c. The cylinder-head-bracket hanger bolts to 48 N•m (35 ft.- lb.).

d. The nut on each engine through bolt to 88 N•m (65 ft.-lb.).

11. Install the subtank bracket (B, **Figure 12**) and the coolant-reservoir-cover bracket (B, **Figure 3**) to the right side of the frame. Tighten each bracket bolt to 7 N•m (62 in.-lb.).

12. Connect the neutral switch connector (**Figure 8**) to the neutral switch. Route the cable along the path noted during removal.

13. Reconnect the halves of the following connectors:

a. Oil level switch connector (**Figure 4**).

b. Stator connector (A, **Figure 5**).

c. Crankshaft position sensor connector (B, **Figure 5**).

d. Speed sensor connector (**Figure 6**).

e. Rear brake light switch connector (**Figure 7**).

14. Connect the spark plug cap to each spark plug.

15. Connect the reservoir hose (B, **Figure 2**) to its fitting on the rear brake master cylinder.

16. Connect the brake hose to the rear brake master cylinder. Use a new sealing washer on each side of the hose fitting, and tighten the banjo bolt (A, **Figure 2**) to 30 N•m (22 ft.-lb.).

17. Install the radiator and coolant reservoir cover (Chapter Ten).

18. Install the engine pulley, the pulley housing, and the shift pedal/floorboard assembly (Chapter Seven).

19. Install the finished covers onto each cylinder head (Chapter Four).

20. Install the intake manifold, throttle body, air filter housing, exhaust system, fuel tank and frame neck covers (Chapter Eight).

21. Install the starter, horn, battery box, battery and battery cover (Chapter Nine).

22. Install the sidestand, both side covers, the left engine cover and the rider's seat (Chapter Fifteen).

23. Add brake fluid and bleed the rear brake (Chapter Fourteen.

24. Add engine oil and coolant (Chapter Three).

25. Start the engine and check for oil, coolant or exhaust leaks.

INSPECTION PLUGS

Removal/Installation

Refer to **Figure 20**.

1. Remove the damper cover bolts (A, **Figure 21**). Remove the damper cover (B, **Figure 21**) and the damper from the alternator cover.

2. Remove the timing inspection plug (A, **Figure 22**) from the alternator cover. If necessary, also remove the flywheel bolt plug (B, **Figure 22**). Discard the O-ring installed with each plug.

3. Installation is the reverse of removal.
   a. Install a new O-ring onto each plug. Lubricate the O-ring with lithium-soap grease.
   b. Tighten the timing inspection plug to 6 N•m (53 in.-lb.).
   c. Tighten the flywheel bolt plug to 10 N•m (89 in.-lb.).
   d. Install the alternator cover damper and damper cover. Tighten the damper cover bolts (A, **Figure 21**) to 7 N•m (62 in.-lb.).

ALTERNATOR COVER

Removal/Installation

Refer to **Figure 20**.

The stator assembly, which includes the stator coil and the crankshaft position (CKP) sensor, sits inside the alternator cover. Refer to Chapter Nine for stator assembly service procedures.

1. Securely support the motorcycle in an upright position.

2. Disconnect the negative cable from the battery (Chapter Nine).

3. Drain the engine oil (Chapter Three).

4. Remove the left engine cover (Chapter Fifteen).

5. Remove the engine pulley cover and the shift pedal/footrest assembly (Chapter Seven).

6. Disconnect the halves of the stator connector (A, **Figure 5**) and the crankshaft position sensor connector (B). Note how the stator cable is routed through the engine. It must be rerouted along the same path.

7. Remove the alternator cover bolts (C, **Figure 21**). Note the location of the left engine cover bracket (D, **Figure 21**). It must be reinstalled under the same cover bolts.

8. Remove the alternator cover from the crankcase. Account for the dowels (A, **Figure 23**) behind the cover.

9. Remove and discard the gasket.

10. Installation is the reverse of removal.
   a. Apply Yamaha Bond No. 1215 to the stator wire damper (**Figure 24**).
   b. Install a new alternator cover gasket.
   c. Tighten the alternator cover bolts to 10 N•m (89 in.-lb.).
   d. Route the stator wire along the path noted during removal. Connect the halves of the stator

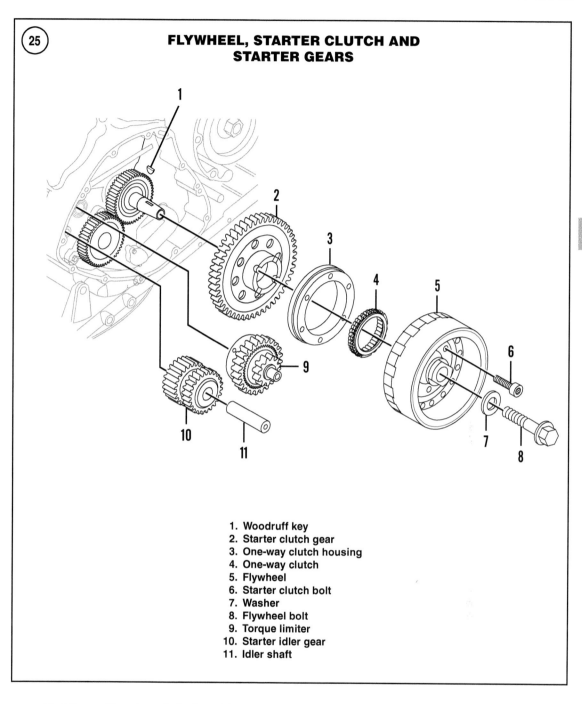

25

FLYWHEEL, STARTER CLUTCH AND STARTER GEARS

1. Woodruff key
2. Starter clutch gear
3. One-way clutch housing
4. One-way clutch
5. Flywheel
6. Starter clutch bolt
7. Washer
8. Flywheel bolt
9. Torque limiter
10. Starter idler gear
11. Idler shaft

(A, **Figure 5**) and crankshaft position sensor connector (B).

FLYWHEEL AND STARTER GEARS

The sheave holder (Yamaha part No. YS-01880-A or 90890-01701) and flywheel puller (Yamaha part No. YU-33270-B or 90890-01362), or equivalent tools, are needed.

Refer to **Figure 25**.

Removal

1. Remove the alternator cover as described in this chapter.

2. Remove every other starter clutch bolt (B, **Figure 23**). If the starter clutch will be serviced, loosen the three remaining bolt but leave them in place.

NOTE
Install the sheave holder so it sits completely flat against the flywheel. Do not let the sheave holder sit across any raised portion of the flywheel.

3. Hold the flywheel with the sheave holder. Remove the flywheel bolt (C, **Figure 23**) and its washer. If a flywheel holder is unavailable, hold the bolt boss with a 32-mm wrench.

4. Install the puller bolts into the three open starter clutch bolt holes, and install the flywheel puller. (**Figure 26**). Protect the crankshaft end by inserting an appropriate size socket between the puller center screw and the crankshaft. Make sure the puller parallels the flywheel.

5. Turn the puller's center screw, and drive the flywheel off the crankshaft. If necessary, adjust the puller bolts to keep the puller parallel to the flywheel.

6. Remove the Woodruff key (A, **Figure 27**) and the starter clutch gear (B) from the crankshaft.

7. Remove the washer (A, **Figure 28**) from the crankshaft.

8. Remove the torque limiter (B, **Figure 28**) and its washer (C).

9. Remove the starter idler gear (A, **Figure 29**) and the idler shaft (B) from the crankcase.

10. Inspect the flywheel as described in this section.

Installation

1. Install the washer (A, **Figure 28**) onto the crankshaft, and seat it against the balancer drive gear.

2. Apply engine oil to the idler shaft and to the torque limiter shaft.

3. Position the starter idler gear (A, **Figure 29**) in the crankcase. Install the idler shaft (B, **Figure 29**) so it sits in the shaft boss in the crankcase.

4. Install the torque limiter (B, **Figure 28**) so its shaft sits in the crankcase boss, and install the washer (C). Make sure the torque limiter teeth engage those of the starter idler gear.

5. Install the starter clutch gear (B, **Figure 27**), and press Woodruff key (A) into the crankshaft keyway.

6. Install the flywheel by performing the following:

   a. Align the flywheel slot with the Woodruff key, and slide the flywheel onto the crankshaft so the rollers in the one way clutch (A, **Figure 30**) rest against the edge of the starter-clutch-gear bearing surface (C, **Figure 27**).

   b. Simultaneously rotate the starter clutch gear clockwise while facing the engine and gently press the flywheel in until the one-way clutch rollers slide onto the bearing surface and bottoms against the starter clutch gear. Refer to A, **Figure 31**.

7. Apply engine oil to the threads of the flywheel bolt and to the washer.

8. Install the flywheel bolt into the crankshaft taper.

9. Hold the flywheel with the sheave holder, and tighten the flywheel bolt (C, **Figure 23**) to 90 N•m

(66 ft.-lb.). Make sure the sheave holder does not cross any raised portion of the flywheel.

10. Install the three starter clutch bolts (B, **Figure 23**). Apply threadlocking compound to the threads of each bolt, and tighten each starter clutch bolt to 24 N•m (18 ft.-lb.).

11. Install the alternator cover as described in this chapter.

Inspection

Replace any part that is worn or damaged.

1. Clean the parts in solvent and dry them with compressed air.

> *WARNING*
> *Replace a cracked or chipped flywheel. A damaged flywheel can fly apart at high speed, throwing metal fragments into the engine. Do not attempt to repair a damaged flywheel.*

2. Inspect the flywheel (B, **Figure 31**) for cracks or breaks. Be sure the magnet is free of all metal parts.

3. Check the flywheel tapered bore (B, **Figure 30**) and the crankshaft taper for damage.

4. Inspect the threads of the flywheel bolt. Replace the bolt if the threads are stretched or damaged.

5. Slide the idler shaft (A, **Figure 32**) within the starter idler gear (B). It should slide smoothly.

6. Inspect the teeth of the starter idler gear (B, **Figure 32**) and torque limiter (**Figure 33**).

7. Inspect the idler gear shaft (A, **Figure 32**) and the bearing surface of the starter idler gear for nicks or other signs of damage.

8. Perform the *Starter Clutch Operation Test* as described in *Starter Clutch* in this chapter.

STARTER CLUTCH

Removal/Installation

Refer to **Figure 25**.

1. Remove the flywheel as described in this chapter.

2. Remove the remaining starter clutch bolts from the flywheel.

3. Remove the starter clutch from the back of the flywheel.

4. Remove the one-way clutch from the one-way housing (C, **Figure 30**). Note that the side of the one-way clutch with the arrow faces the flywheel.

5. Installation is the reverse of removal. Note the following:

   a. Seat the one-way clutch into the housing so the side with the arrow will face the flywheel when installed.

b. Apply threadlocking compound to the threads of each starter clutch bolt, and install the bolts.

c. Hold the flywheel with the sheave holder, and tighten all starter clutch bolts to 24 N•m (18 ft.-lb.).

Inspection

1. Inspect the teeth (A, **Figure 34**) of the starter clutch gear. Replace the gear if any teeth are worn, broken or missing.

2. Inspect the bearing surface (B, **Figure 34**) of the starter clutch gear for nicks or scratches. Replace the starter clutch gear if it shows signs of wear.

> *NOTE*
> *The one-way clutch and one-way clutch housing are not available separately. If either part is worn or damaged, replace both as an assembly.*

3. Inspect the rollers in the one-way clutch (A, **Figure 30**) for wear or damage. All the rollers should rotate freely. Replace the one-way clutch and housing if damage or wear is noted.

Operation Test

1. Install the starter clutch gear into the one-way clutch by performing the following:

a. Set the flywheel assembly face down on the bench.

b. Set the starter clutch gear onto the one-way clutch so the gear's bearing surface (B, **Figure 34**) rests atop rollers (A, **Figure 30**) in the one-way clutch.

c. Rotate the starter clutch gear counterclockwise and gently press the gear down until it bottoms within the one-way clutch. Refer to **Figure 35**.

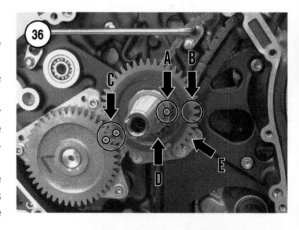

2. Hold the flywheel, and turn the starter clutch gear counterclockwise. The gear should turn freely within the starter clutch.

3. Hold the flywheel, and turn the starter clutch gear clockwise. It should not turn in this direction.

> *NOTE*
> *The one-way clutch and one-way clutch housing are not available separately. If either part is worn or damaged, replace the starter clutch assembly.*

4. The one-way clutch is faulty if it fails either test.

BALANCER ASSEMBLY

Removal/Installation

Left side

1. Remove the flywheel and starter gears as described this chapter.

2. Rotate the engine until the indexing dot on the crankshaft (A, **Figure 36**) sits at 3 o'clock. When the crankshaft is in this position, the projection on the balancer drive gear (B, **Figure 36**) sits opposite the crankshaft's indexing dot (A), and the indexing dot on the balancer drive gear aligns with the dot on the balancer driven gear (C). Both sets of marks must be properly aligned during assembly.

3. Remove the snap ring (D, **Figure 36**) and slide the balancer drive gear (E) from the crankshaft taper.

4. Remove the balancer assembly bolts (A, **Figure 37**), and remove the balancer assembly (B) from the crankcase. Note that the balancer journal engages the bearing in the crankcase (A, **Figure 38**), and the assembly dowels engages the crankcase bosses (B).

5. Installation is the reverse of removal.

  a. If necessary, rotate the engine so the indexing dot on the crankshaft (A, **Figure 36**) sits at 3-o'clock.

  b. Lubricate the balancer journal with engine oil.

  c. Apply threadlocking compound to the balancer assembly bolts. Tighten them to 12 N•m (106 in.-lb.).

  d. Lubricate the inner circumference of the balancer drive gear (A, **Figure 39**) with engine oil.

  e. Install the balancer drive gear so its projection (B, **Figure 36**) sits opposite the crankshaft indexing dot (A), and the marks on the drive and driven gears align (C).

  f. Install a new snap ring (D, **Figure 36**).

Right side

1. Remove the clutch and primary drive gear (Chapter Six).

2. Slide the straight key (A, **Figure 40**) from the crankshaft keyway, and remove the balancer drive gear (B) from the crankshaft.

3. Remove the balancer assembly bolts (A, **Figure 41**), and remove the balancer assembly (B) from the crankcase.

4. Installation is the reverse of removal.

  a. Apply engine oil to the balancer journal.

  b. Install the balancer assembly so the journal engages the balancer bearing (A, **Figure 42**) and the dowels engage the crankcase bosses (B).

c. Apply threadlocking compound to the threads of the balancer assembly bolts (A, **Figure 41**), and tighten the bolts to 12 N•m (106 in.-lb.).

d. Install the balancer drive gear (B, **Figure 40**) onto the crankshaft so the drive gear's keyway aligns with the crankshaft keyway and the indexing mark on the drive gear aligns with the mark on the driven gear (C). Rotate the crankshaft or driven gear as needed so the marks and keyways align, and install the straight key (A, **Figure 40**).

Inspection

1. Inspect the teeth of the balancer drive (A, **Figure 39**) and driven gears (B).

2. Inspect the balancer journal for scoring or other signs of wear.

3. Check the balancer bearing (A, **Figure 38** or A, **Figure 42**) by rotating its inner race. It should turn smoothly without excessive noise.

4. Inspect the straight key for nicks, rounded edges or other signs of wear. If worn replace the key and inspect the keyway in the right balancer drive gear, the primary drive gear, primary-drive-gear spacer and the crankshaft.

5. Replace worn or damaged parts as necessary.

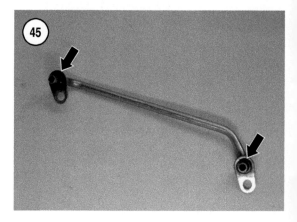

CAM CHAIN AND CHAIN GUIDES

Removal/Installation

1. Remove the engine as described in this chapter.

2. Remove the cylinder head (Chapter Four) from the cylinder being serviced.

3. Remove the front cam chain guide from the cylinder block, and remove the block (Chapter Four). Note that the stop on the front guide sits in the cutout in the cylinder block (**Figure 43**).

4. Refer to *Balancer Assembly* in this chapter, and remove the balancer drive gear from the appropriate side of the crankshaft.

5. Remove the cam chain guide bolts (C, **Figure 42**), and lift the rear cam chain guide (D) from the tunnel.

6A. To remove the front-cylinder cam chain, disengage the chain from the timing sprocket on the right side of the crankshaft, and remove the cam chain.

6B. Remove the rear-cylinder cam chain by performing the following:

   a. Remove the oil delivery pipe bolts (A, **Figure 44**), and pull the oil delivery pipe No. 1 (B)

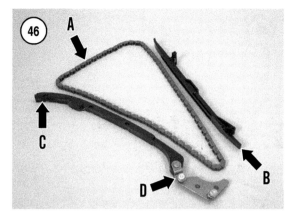

Tie one end of a safety wire to the cam chain, and secure the to the engine.

c. After installing the rear-cylinder cam chain, install the oil delivery pipe No. 1 (B, **Figure 44**) so its rear fitting passes through the cam chain run. Lubricate new O-rings with lithium-soap grease, and seat the O-rings onto the oil delivery pipe fittings (**Figure 45**). Apply threadlocking compound to the threads of the oil delivery pipe bolts (A, **Figure 44**), and tighten the bolts to 10 N•m (89 in.-lb.).

d. Install the cylinder block, front cam chain guide and cylinder head as described in Chapter Four. Keep the cam chain taut against its timing sprocket when the chain is fed through the cam chain tunnel of the block and cylinder head. Secure the safety wire to the engine so the chain remains engaged with the sprocket.

Inspection

1. Inspect the cam chain (A, **Figure 46**) for wear, stretching or link damage.
2. Inspect the sliding surface of the front (B, **Figure 46**) and rear (C) cam chain guide.
3. Inspect the pivot point (D, **Figure 46**) on the rear chain guide (C). Be sure the pivot moves freely.
4. Inspect the camshaft sprocket (**Figure 47**) and the respective crankshaft timing sprocket for worn or broken teeth. Refer to *Crankshaft* in this chapter.
5. If the cam chain, cam sprocket or timing sprocket must be replaced, replace all three items as a set.

OIL/WATER PUMP DRIVE ASSEMBLY

The pump drive assembly consists of the oil/water pump drive chain, chain guide, drive sprocket and driven sprocket.

Removal

1. Remove the clutch (Chapter Six).
2. Remove the bolts (A, **Figure 48**), and pull the oil/water pump chain guide (B) from the left side of the crankcase.
3. Refer to *Flywheel* and *Starter Gears* in this chapter and hold the flywheel with a flywheel holder. Remove the oil/water pump driven sprocket bolt (**Figure 49**).
4. Remove the driven sprocket (A, **Figure 50**) from the end of the pump shaft, and remove the drive chain (B).
5. Slide the oil/water pump drive sprocket (A, **Figure 51**) from the mainshaft bushing.
6. Remove the bushing (A, **Figure 52**) and thrust plate (B) from the mainshaft.

from the crankcase. Note how the chain is situated around the oil delivery pipe.

b. Discard the O-ring (**Figure 45**) from the fitting at each end of the oil delivery pipe.

c. Remove the cam chain from the timing sprocket on the left side of the crankcase.

7. Installation is the reverse of removal.

a. Set the rear cam chain guide in place. Apply threadlocking compound to the threads of the cam chain guide bolts (C, **Figure 42**), and tighten the bolts to 10 N•m (89 in.-lb.).

b. Fit the cam chain onto the timing sprocket. Feed the chain through the cam chain tunnel.

Installation

1. Slide the thrust plate (B, **Figure 52**) onto the mainshaft. Seat the plate against the mainshaft bearing, and then install the bushing (A, **Figure 52**).

2. Slip the oil/water pump drive sprocket (A, **Figure 51**) onto the bushing so the tabs on the sprocket (B) face out.

3. Seat the drive chain (B, **Figure 50**) onto the drive sprocket so the chain engages the sprocket teeth.

4. Set the driven sprocket (A, **Figure 50**) between the runs of the drive chain, and seat the sprocket against the end of the pump shaft. Make sure the driven sprocket engages the drive chain.

5. Apply threadlocking compound to the threads of the driven sprocket bolt, and install the bolt (**Figure 49**). Hold the flywheel, and tighten the oil/water pump driven sprocket bolt to 15 N•m (11 ft.-lb.).

6. Install the chain guide (B, **Figure 48**). Apply threadlocking compound to the threads of the oil/water pump chain guide bolts (A, **Figure 48**), and tighten the bolts to 10 N•m (89 in.-lb.).

Inspection

1. Inspect the teeth on the oil/water pump drive sprocket (A, **Figure 53**) and driven sprocket (B) for worn or damage teeth.

2. Inspect the drive chain (C, **Figure 53**) and the drive sprocket bearing surface (D) for excessive wear or damage.

3. If any part is worn or damaged, replace the drive sprocket, driven sprocket and drive chain as a set.

OIL/WATER PUMP

The combination oil/water pump sits inside the crankcase.

Refer to **Figure 54**.

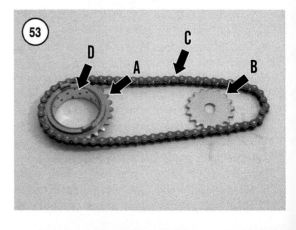

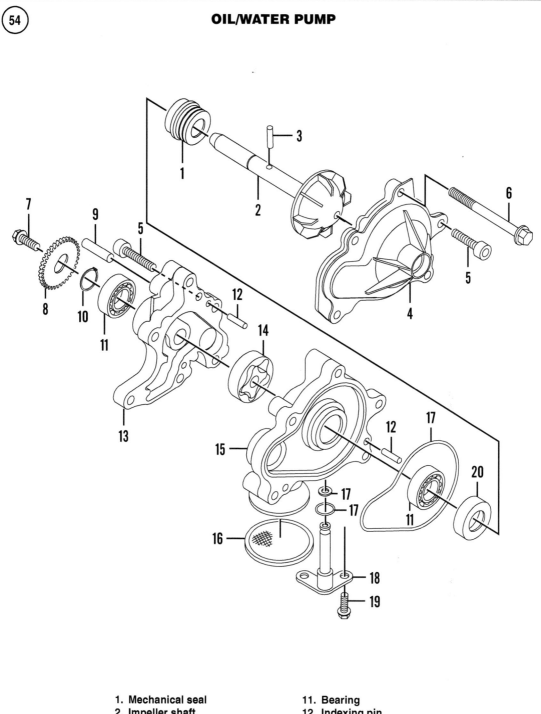

OIL/WATER PUMP

1. Mechanical seal
2. Impeller shaft
3. Pin
4. Water pump cover
5. Cover bolt
6. Oil/water pump mounting bolt
7. Sprocket bolt
8. Oil/water pump driven sprocket
9. Dowel pin
10. Snap ring
11. Bearing
12. Indexing pin
13. Oil pump cover
14. Oil pump rotors
15. Oil/Water pump housing
16. Oil strainer
17. O-ring
18. Drain cock
19. Drain cock bolt
20. Oil seal

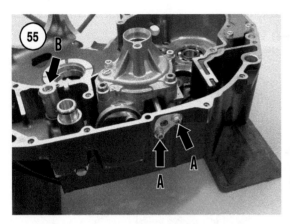

Removal

1. Remove the engine and separate the crankcase as described in this chapter.

2. Remove the drain cock bolts (A, **Figure 55**) and pull the drain cock from the crankcase half. Remove and discard the drain-cock O-rings (**Figure 56**).

3. Remove the oil/water pump mounting bolts (A, **Figure 57**), and lift the oil/water pump (B) from the right crankcase. Account for the dowels (A, **Figure 58**) behind the oil/pump.

4. Remove the coolant pipe No. 3 (A, **Figure 59**) from its fitting behind the pump. Remove and discard the O-ring (B, **Figure 59**) from each end of each coolant pipe.

5. If necessary, remove the oil pressure relief valve from the crankcase (B, **Figure 55**).

Installation

1. Inspect coolant pipe No. 3 (A, **Figure 59**) for nicks or other damage that could cause leaks. Replace the pipe if damaged.

2. Lubricate new coolant pipe O-rings with lithium-soap grease, and fit an O-ring (B, **Figure 59**) onto each end of the pipe.

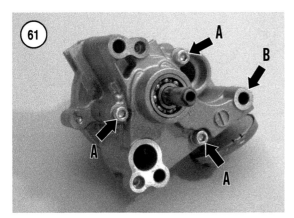

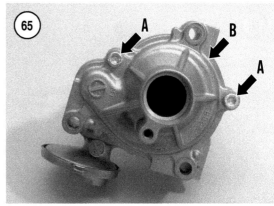

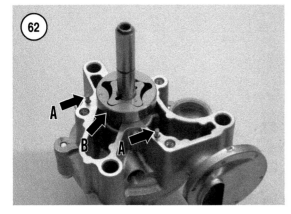

3. Press coolant pipe No 3 into its crankcase port (B, **Figure 58**) until it bottoms.

4. Apply a micro thin layer of sealant to the oil port (C, **Figure 58**) in the crankcase half.

5. Install the dowels (A, **Figure 58**) into the crankcase.

6. Seat the oil/water pump (B, **Figure 57**) in place so the port on the pump mates with the coolant pipe No. 3 (B, **Figure 58**) and the pump bosses engage the dowels (A, **Figure 58**).

7. Install the oil/water pump mounting bolts (A, **Figure 57**). Tighten the bolts to 24 N•m (17.5 ft.-lb.).

8. Lubricate a new O-ring with lithium-soap grease, and fit it onto the oil pressure relief valve. Press the valve (B, **Figure 55**) into its port in the right crankcase half.

9. Install new O-rings (**Figure 56**) onto the drain cock. Lubricate the O-rings with lithium-soap grease.

10. Insert the drain cock through the cutout in the crankcase, and seat the cock in the water pump port.

11. Tighten the drain cock bolts (A, **Figure 55**) to 10 N•m (89 in.-lb.).

12. Join the case halves as described in this chapter.

Disassembly

Since the oil/water pump is very inaccessible, consider replacing the unit rather than rebuilding it. Even a small loss of efficiency could require considerable work to correct.

1. Remove the snap ring (**Figure 60**) from the end of the pump shaft.

2. Remove the oil pump cover bolts (A, **Figure 61**), and lift the oil pump cover (B) from the pump housing. Account for the indexing pins (A, **Figure 62**) behind the cover.

3. Remove the outer rotor (B, **Figure 62**), inner rotor (**Figure 63**) and the pin (**Figure 64**) from the pump shaft.

4. Remove the water pump cover bolts (A, **Figure 65**), and remove the cover (B) from the pump housing.

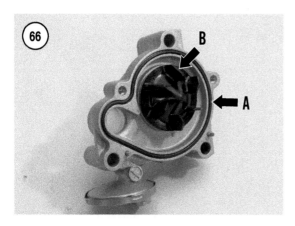

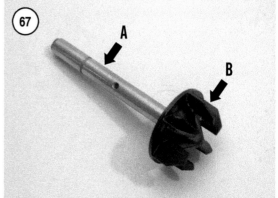

5. Remove and discard the O-ring (A, **Figure 66**).

6. Pull the impeller (B, **Figure 66**), and remove the pump shaft from the pump housing.

7. Inspect the oil and water pump components as described in this section.

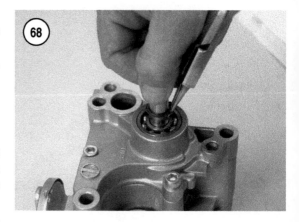

Assembly

1. Lubricate the pump shaft (A, **Figure 67**) with lithium-soap grease, and install the pump shaft from the water-pump side of the pump housing (B, **Figure 66**).

2. Lubricate a new O-ring with lithium-soap grease, and install the O-ring (A, **Figure 66**).

3. Fit the water pump cover (B, **Figure 65**) onto the pump housing.

4. Apply threadlocking compound to the threads of the water pump cover bolts (A, **Figure 65**), and tighten the bolts to 10 N•m (89 in.-lb.).

5. Turn the assembly over, and install the pin into the hole in the impeller shaft (**Figure 64**).

6. Lubricate the inner rotor with engine oil. Slide the rotor (**Figure 63**) over the shaft and onto the pin so the rotor cutouts engage the pin.

7. Lubricate the outer rotor with engine oil. Slide the rotor (B, **Figure 62**) onto the shaft until the outer rotor mates with the inner rotor.

8. Install the indexing pins (A, **Figure 62**) into the pump housing.

9. Seat the oil pump cover (B, **Figure 61**) onto the pump housing. Apply threadlocking compound to the threads of the oil pump cover bolts (A), and tighten bolts to 10 N•m (89 in.-lb.).

10. Pull the impeller shaft up, and install the snap ring (**Figure 68**) so it is completely seated in the shaft groove.

11. Check the pump operation by rotating the pump shaft. It should turn smoothly and without excessive noise.

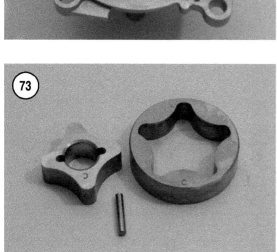

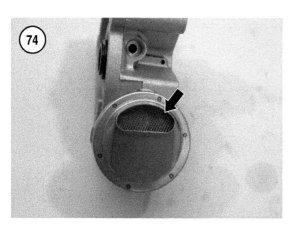

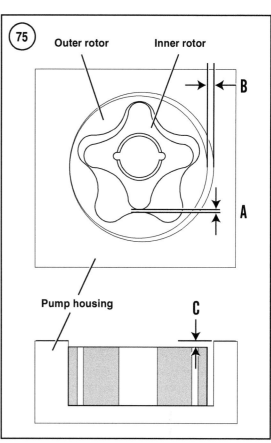

Inspection

Replace any part that is worn, damaged or out of specification.

1. Clean all parts in solvent, and dry them thoroughly with compressed air.

2. Inspect the oil pump side (**Figure 69**) and the water pump side (**Figure 70**) of the oil/water pump housing for cracks, corrosion or other damage.

3. Inspect the oil pump cover (**Figure 71**) and the water pump cover (**Figure 72**) for cracks, corrosion or other damage.

4. Inspect the oil pump rotors (**Figure 73**) for wear or abrasion.

5. Inspect the oil strainer (**Figure 74**) for tears or other damage that will admit contaminants into the pump.

6. Install the outer and inner rotors into the rotor housing.

7. Use a flat gauge to measure the clearance between the tip of the inner rotor and the outer rotor (A, **Figure 75**) and to measure the clearance between the outer rotor and the housing (B, **Figure 75**).

8. Measure the pump rotor depth, which is distance from the top of the oil pump cover to the top of the rotors (C, **Figure 75**).

9. Replace the rotors if any measurement exceeds the service limit in **Table 1**. If these measurements

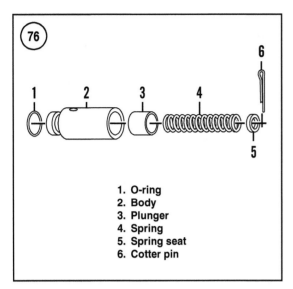

1. O-ring
2. Body
3. Plunger
4. Spring
5. Spring seat
6. Cotter pin

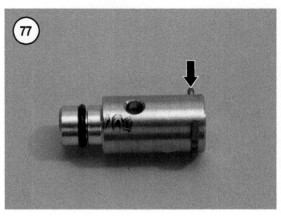

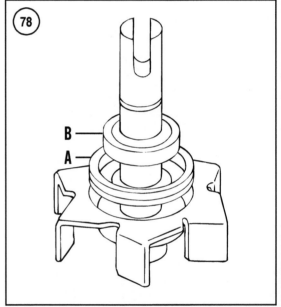

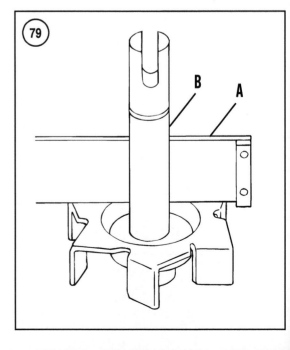

are still out of specification with the new rotors, replace the oil/water pump.

10. Use a wooden dowel to check the oil pressure
relieve valve. Press the dowel into the valve end, and
check the movement of the plunger. It should move
smoothly. If it does not, disassemble the valve by
performing the following. Refer to **Figure 76**.

CAUTION
*The oil pressure relief valve compo-
nents are under spring pressure. Be
careful when disassembling this valve.*

  a. Remove the cotter pin (**Figure 77**) from the oil
    pressure relief valve.
  b. Remove the spring seat, spring and plunger.
  c. Clean the components in solvent, and blow
    them dry with compressed air.
  d. If any component is scratched, nicked or dam-
    aged; replace the oil pressure relief valve.
    Replacement parts are unavailable.
  e. If the parts are in good condition, lubricate
    them with engine oil and reassemble the valve.
    Use a new cotter pin.

11. Inspect the mechanical seal (**Figure 70**) in the
oil/water pump housing for damage. If damaged, replace the seal as described in this section.

NOTE
*The mechanical seal must be removed
to inspect the oil seal.*

12. If necessary, remove the mechanical seal and
inspect the oil seal for damage as described in this
section.

13. Inspect the impeller (B, **Figure 67**) and shaft (A)
for wear or corrosion.

14. Check the impeller blades for corrosion or damage. If corrosion is minor, clean the blades. Replace

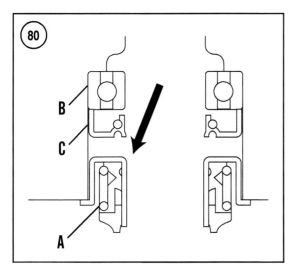

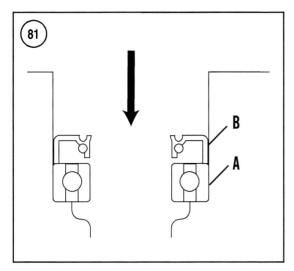

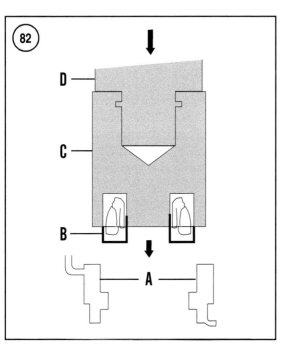

the impeller if corrosion is severe or if the blades are cracked or broken.

15. Inspect the rubber damper (A, **Figure 78**) and the damper holder (B) in the impeller. Replace the impeller if they are damaged or deteriorated.

16. Use a straightedge (A, **Figure 79**) to check the impeller shaft (B) tilt. Replace the impeller if tilt exceeds the maximum specification (**Table 1**).

Mechanical Seal, Oil Seal and Bearing Removal/Installation

1. The following special tools, or equivalent tool, are needed to install the mechanical seal:
   a. Mechanical seal installer (Yamaha part No. YM-33221-A or 90890-04078).
   b. Middle driven shaft bearing driver (Yamaha part No. YM-04058 or 90890-04058).

2. Insert a drift through the oil pump side of the oil/water pump housing, and carefully tap the mechanical seal (A, **Figure 80**) from the housing. If necessary, also drive the bearing (B, **Figure 80**) and oil seal (C) from the housing.

3. Clean and dry the inner bore of the body.

4. Install a new bearing as follows:
   a. Apply a light coat of engine oil to the outer surface of the new bearing.
   b. Place the bearing squarely against the bore opening.
   c. Select a bearing driver or socket that matches the bearing's outside diameter. Drive the bearing (A, **Figure 81**) into the bore until it bottoms.

5. Install the oil seal as follows:
   a. Apply tap water or coolant to the outer surface of the oil seal.
   b. Place the oil seal squarely against the bore opening so its closed side faces away from the bearing.
   c. Select a driver or socket that matches the seal's outside diameter, and drive the seal (B, **Figure 81**) into the bore until the seal bottoms against the bearing.

6. Install the mechanical seal as follows:

CAUTION
Do not lubricate the outer surface of the mechanical seal with oil or grease.

   a. Apply a light coat of Yamaha bond No. 1215 to the bore (A, **Figure 82**) in the pump housing.
   b. Seat the mechanical seal (B, **Figure 82**) squarely onto the bore opening.
   c. Use the Yamaha seal installer (C, **Figure 82**) and driver (D) to drive the mechanical seal into the bore.

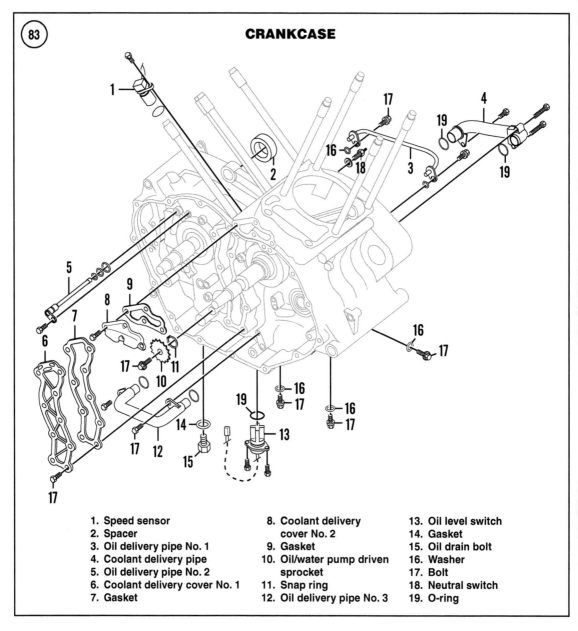

CRANKCASE

1. Speed sensor
2. Spacer
3. Oil delivery pipe No. 1
4. Coolant delivery pipe
5. Oil delivery pipe No. 2
6. Coolant delivery cover No. 1
7. Gasket
8. Coolant delivery cover No. 2
9. Gasket
10. Oil/water pump driven sprocket
11. Snap ring
12. Oil delivery pipe No. 3
13. Oil level switch
14. Gasket
15. Oil drain bolt
16. Washer
17. Bolt
18. Neutral switch
19. O-ring

d. If the special tools are unavailable, drive the seal with a socket that sits against the seal's outer rim.

CRANKCASE

Crankcase Separation

Refer to **Figure 83** and **Figure 84**.
1. Remove the engine as described in this chapter.
2. Remove the following exterior assemblies from the crankcase:
   a. Oil and oil filter (Chapter Three).
   b. Clutch and primary drive gear (Chapter Six).
   c. The oil/water pump drive assembly as described in this chapter.

d. Cylinder head, cylinder block and pistons from each cylinder (Chapter Four).
e. Flywheel and starter gears as described in this chapter.
f. Balancer assembly, cam chain and chain guides for each cylinder as described in this chapter.
g. External shift mechanism (Chapter Seven).
h. Oil level switch, neutral switch, and speed sensor (Chapter Nine).

3. Perform the following on the right side of the crankcase:
   a. Remove the oil delivery pipe bolt (A, **Figure 85**), and slide oil delivery pipe No. 2 from the crankcase. Remove and discard the O-rings (**Figure 86**) from delivery pipe No. 2.

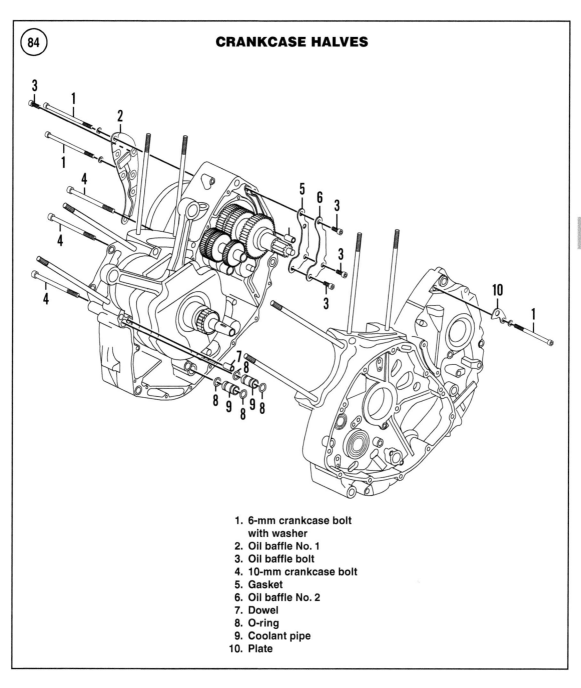

CRANKCASE HALVES

1. 6-mm crankcase bolt with washer
2. Oil baffle No. 1
3. Oil baffle bolt
4. 10-mm crankcase bolt
5. Gasket
6. Oil baffle No. 2
7. Dowel
8. O-ring
9. Coolant pipe
10. Plate

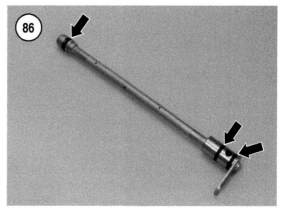

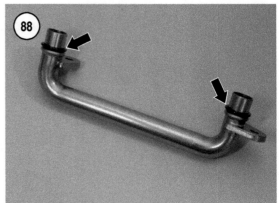

b. Remove the oil delivery pipe bolts (A, **Figure 87**), and pull oil delivery pipe No. 3 (B) from the right side of the crankcase. Remove and discard the O-ring (**Figure 88**) from each fitting on the deliver pipe.

4. Perform the following on the left side of the crankcase.

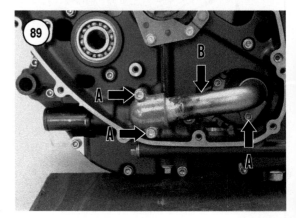

a. If still installed, remove oil delivery pipe No. 1 (B, **Figure 44**) from the left side. Refer to *Cam Chain and Guides* in this chapter.

b. Remove the coolant delivery pipe bolts (A, **Figure 89**), and pull the coolant delivery pipe (B) from the crankcase. Remove and discard the O-ring from each end of the pipe (**Figure 90**).

c. Remove the spacer (A, **Figure 91**).

5. Before removing the crankcase bolts, draw an outline of each case half on a piece of cardboard. Punch holes in the drawing corresponding to the bolt location in each crankcase half shown in **Figure 92**. As each bolt is removed, insert it, along with any washer, cable holder or plate, into its respective hole in the cardboard template so bolts can be quickly identified during assembly.

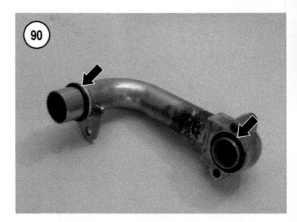

NOTE
*Two crankcase bolts pass through oil baffle No. 1 (A, **Figure 93**). This oil baffle, coolant delivery cover No. 1 (B, **Figure 93**) and coolant delivery cover No. 2 (C) do not need to be removed when splitting the case.*

6. Set the crankcase on the bench so the right side faces up. Following a crisscross pattern, evenly loosen the crankcase bolts in 1/4-turn increments. Once all the bolts are loose, remove the 10 × 110 mm crankcase bolts (A, **Figure 92**) and the 6 × 120 mm crankcase bolts (B).

7. Turn the crankcase over so the left side faces up. Following a crisscross pattern, evenly loosen the crankcase bolts in 1/4-turn increments. Once the

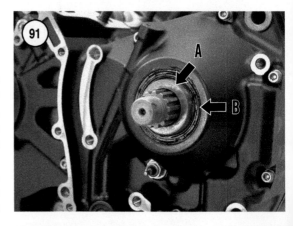

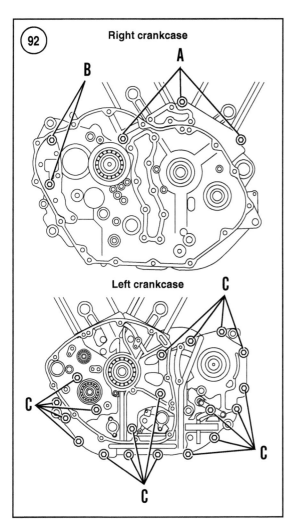

Right crankcase

A

B

Left crankcase

C

C

C

C

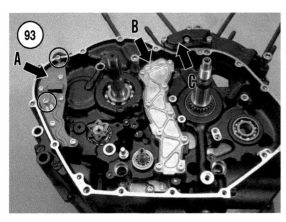

8. Separate the crankcase halves by carefully tapping around the crankcase perimeter with a plastic mallet. Do not use a metal hammer. Separate the crankcase halves by lifting the left case half off the right half.

9. Remove the dowels (A, **Figure 94**) from the crankcase.

10. Remove coolant pipe No. 1 (B, **Figure 94**) and coolant pipe No. 2 (C). Remove and discard the O-ring from each end of each pipe.

11. Oil baffle No. 2 (D, **Figure 94**) does not have to be removed. If necessary, remove the oil baffle bolts, and lift oil baffle No. 2 from the right crankcase half. Discard the oil baffle gasket.

Crankcase Joining

1. Clean and dry all crankcase bolts.

2. Clean the sealing surface of each crankcase half. Spray them with electric contact cleaner, and let them dry thoroughly.

3. If removed, install the oil baffles or coolant delivery covers by performing the following:

   a. Install oil baffle No. 2 (D, **Figure 94**) with a new gasket. Apply threadlocking compound to the threads of the oil baffle bolts, and tighten the bolts to 10 N•m (89 in.-lb).

   b. Fit oil baffle No. 1 (A, **Figure 93**) into place. Apply threadlocking compound to the threads of the oil baffle bolts, and tighten the bolts to 10 N•m (89 in.-lb). Two crankcase bolts will pass through this baffle.

   c. Install coolant delivery cover No. 1 (B, **Figure 93**) or coolant delivery cover No. 2 with a new gasket. Apply threadlocking compound to the threads of the coolant delivery cover bolts, and tighten the bolts to 10 N•m (89 in.-lb.).

4. Use engine oil to lubricate the bearings, including the inner races, in each crankcase half. Do not add so much oil that it will drip from the bearing when the case half is turned over.

bolts are all loose, remove the 6 × 80 mm crankcase bolts (C, **Figure 92**).

CAUTION
If the case halves must be pried apart, do so very carefully. The mating surfaces must not be damaged. If they are, the crankcase will leak and must be replaced.

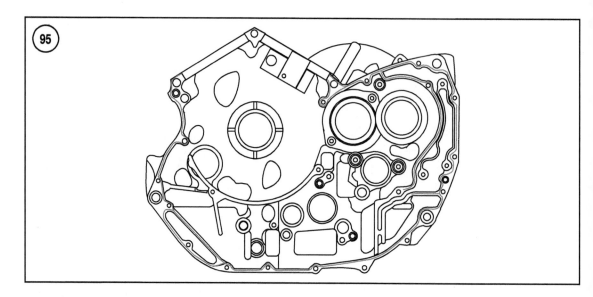

5. Apply engine oil to the crankshaft, transmission shafts and their journals in the right case half.

6. Install coolant pipe No. 1 (B, **Figure 94**) and coolant pipe No. 2 (C) into their bosses in the right crankcase half. Install a new O-ring onto each end of each coolant pipe. Lubricate these O-rings with lithium-soap grease.

7. Apply a thin coat of Yamaha Bond No. 1215 to the sealing surface of the right crankcase half where shown in **Figure 95**.

8. Install the dowels (A, **Figure 94**) into the right crankcase half.

> *CAUTION*
> *The crankcase halves should fit together without force. If the case halves do not completely mate with one another, do not attempt to pull them together with the crankcase bolts. Separate the case halves, and determine the cause of the interference. Do not risk damage by forcing the case halves together.*

9. Lower the left crankcase half onto the right half, and join both halves together. If necessary, gently tap them together with a plastic mallet.

10. Install the 6 × 80 mm crankcase bolts and washers (C, **Figure 92**) into their original locations. Install the cable holder (**Figure 96**) under the bolt above the countershaft.

11. Following a crisscross pattern, evenly tighten the left crankcase bolts in 1/4-turn increments. Tighten the bolts to 10 N•m (89 in.-lb.).

12. Turn the crankcase over so the right side faces up.

13. Install the 10 × 110 mm crankcase bolts (A, **Figure 92**) and the 6 × 120 mm crankcase bolts (B) into their original locations. Apply threadlocking compound to the threads of each 6 × 120 mm bolt.

14. Following a crisscross pattern, evenly tighten the right crankcase bolts in 1/4-turn increments. Tighten the 10-mm crankcase bolts (A, **Figure 92**) to 36 N•m (26.5 ft.-lb.). Tighten the 6-mm crankcase bolts (B, **Figure 92**) to 10 N•m (89 in.-lb.).

15. Perform the following to install oil deliver pipes No. 2 and No 3.

  a. Lubricate new O-rings with lithium-soap grease, and install them onto oil delivery pipe

No 2. (**Figure 86**) and oil delivery pipe No. 3 (**Figure 88**).

  b. Set oil delivery pipe No 2 (B, **Figure 85**) and oil delivery pipe No 3 (B, **Figure 87**) into place in the right crankcase.

  c. Apply threadlocking compound to the threads of the oil delivery pipe bolts (A, **Figure 85** and A, **Figure 87**). Tighten the bolts to 10 N•m.

16. Install the spacer (A, **Figure 91**) and seat it in the seal (B). Lubricate the spacer and seal with engine oil so the seal will not be damaged.

17. Install the coolant delivery pipe by performing the following.

  a. Lubricate new O-rings with lithium-soap grease, and install them onto each end of the pipe (**Figure 90**).

  b. Seat the coolant delivery pipe (B, **Figure 89**) in the left side of the crankcase. Apply threadlocking compound to the threads of the coolant delivery pipe bolts (A), and tighten the bolts to 10 N•m (89. in.-lb.).

18. Reverse Step 2 of the removal procedure, and install any remaining external assemblies.

19. Install the engine (Chapter Five).

20. Add oil and coolant (Chapter Three) and check for leaks.

Crankcase Disassembly

This procedure describes the removal of the crankshaft, transmission shaft assemblies and the internal shift mechanism after the crankcase has been split. Disassembly and inspection procedures for the transmission shafts and internal shift mechanism appear in Chapter Seven.

1. Separate the crankcase halves as described in this section.

CAUTION
Although the countershaft shift forks are identical, they have developed a wear pattern and should be reinstalled into the original locations. Label the shift forks during removal so each can be easily identified for assembly.

2. Remove the mainshaft shift-fork shaft (A, **Figure 97**) and the countershaft shift-fork shaft (B).

3. Rotate the shift forks so the engagement pins clear the shift drum (**Figure 98**), and lift the drum from the crankcase.

4. Remove the outermost countershaft shift fork (**Figure 99**) and label it *Left*. Remove the remaining countershaft shift fork (**Figure 100**) and label it *Right*. Remove the mainshaft shift fork (**Figure 101**) and label it *Center*.

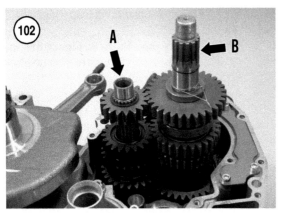

5. Simultaneously lift both the mainshaft assembly (A, **Figure 102**) and the countershaft (B) from the right crankcase half. Store each individual shaft assembly in a sealed and labeled plastic bag.

6. Lift the crankshaft (**Figure 103**) from the right crankcase half.

7. Remove the oil jet (**Figure 104**) from the land in each crankcase half. Make sure each jet is clear.

Crankcase Assembly

This procedure describes the installation of the crankshaft, transmission shaft assemblies, and internal shift mechanism.

NOTE
Coat all parts with engine oil before assembly.

1. Support the right crankcase half (**Figure 105**) on wooden blocks with its inboard side facing up.

2. Lubricate a new O-ring (**Figure 106**) with lithium-soap grease, and install the O-ring onto each oil jet.

3. Press each oil jet (**Figure 104**) into place so its indexing pin engages the hole in the crankcase half.

4. Install the crankshaft (**Figure 103**) so its clutch-side journal seats in the main bearing in the right crankcase. Position the right connecting rod so it sits in the rear-cylinder cutout of the right crankcase; the left rod in the front-cylinder cutout.

5. Make sure the washer is in place on the countershaft assembly.

6. Loop a safety wire around the right end of the countershaft and secure the washer and gears onto the countershaft so they will not fall out during installation (**Figure 107**).

7. Mesh the mainshaft and countershaft assemblies together, and simultaneously lower both assemblies into place in the right crankcase half (**Figure 108**). Make sure each shaft slides into its respective bearing.

8. Clip the safety wire and pull it out from under the countershaft. Completely seat each shaft into its bearing.

NOTE
Install each shift fork so the side with the embossed 3D8 facing the left side of the engine. Refer to the marks made during removal to identify the center, right and left shift forks.

9. Position the center shift fork (**Figure 101**) so its 3D8 mark faces up, and install the shift fork into the mainshaft 3rd-4th combination gear.

17. Once transmission operation has been confirmed, shift the transmission into neutral.

18. Join the crankcase halves as described in this chapter.

Crankcase Inspection

1. Using a scraper, remove all sealant residue from all crankcase mating surfaces.

> *WARNING*
> *When drying the bearings with compressed air, hold both races so the bearing will not rotate. The air jet will spin the bearings at excessive speeds. Since the bearings lack lubrication this rapid spinning will damage the bearings.*

10. Position the right shift fork (**Figure 100**) so its 3D8 mark faces up, and install the shift fork into the countershaft dog clutch.

11. Position the left shift fork (**Figure 99**) so its 3D8 mark faces up, and install the shift fork into countershaft fifth gear.

12. Rotate the shift forks outward as necessary so the shift drum can be lowered into place. Install the shift drum (**Figure 98**).

> *NOTE*
> *The shift drum is in neutral when its neutral dot is positioned as shown in C, **Figure 97**.*

13. Turn the shift drum to the neutral position. Rotate each shift fork so its guide pin engages the respective groove in the shift drum.

14. Install the mainshaft shift fork shaft (A, **Figure 97**) through the mainshaft shift fork, and seat it in the shaft boss.

15. Install the countershaft shift fork shaft (B, **Figure 97**) through both countershaft shift forks, and seat the shaft in its crankcase boss.

16. Spin the transmission shafts and use the shift drum to shift through the gears. Make sure the transmission shifts into all gears.

2. Clean both crankcase halves and all crankcase bearings with cleaning solvent. Thoroughly dry them with compressed air.

3. Clean all crankcase oil passages with compressed air.

4. Lightly oil the crankcase bearings with engine oil before checking the bearings in Step 5.

> *NOTE*
> *When replacing a bearing, also replace its mate in the opposite case half. Crankcase bearings should be replaced as a set.*

5. Rotate the bearings slowly by hand, and check them for roughness, pitting, galling and play. Replace any bearing that turns roughly or shows excessive play as described in this section.

6. Inspect the countershaft oil seal for wear or damage.

7. Inspect the crankcase studs. They must be straight, screwed tightly into the crankcase and their threads must be in good condition.

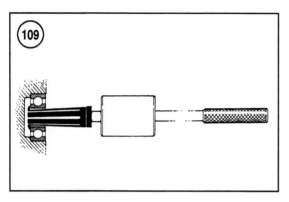

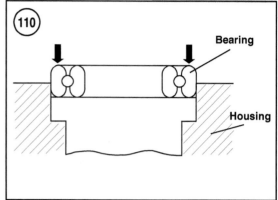

8. Inspect the mating surfaces of both crankcase halves. They must be free of gouges, burrs or any damage that could cause an oil leak.

9. Inspect the crankcase for cracks and fractures, especially in the lower areas where it is are vulnerable to rock damage.

10. Check the areas around the stiffening ribs and around bearing bosses for damage. Repair or replace the crankcase if necessary.

11. Check the threaded holes in both crankcase halves for thread damage, dirt or oil buildup. If necessary, clean or repair the threads with a suitable size metric tap. Coat the tap threads with kerosene or an aluminum tap fluid before use.

Crankcase Bearing
Removal/Installation

1. Before replacing the crankcase bearings, note the following:

   a. Because of the number of bearings used in the left and right crankcase halves, make sure to identify a bearing and note its location before removing it. Use the size code markings to identify a bearing.

   b. Refer to *Bearings* in *Service Methods* in Chapter One for general information on bearing removal and installation.

   c. Before heating the crankcase, remove each oil jet and its O-ring. Install new O-rings when reinstalling the oil jets.

   d. Heat the crankcase to approximately 205-257° F (95-125° C) in an shop oven or on a hot plate. Do not heat the crankcase with a torch. This type of localized heating may warp the crankcase.

   e. Drive the bearing out with a suitable size bearing driver, socket or a drift.

   f. After removing bearings, clean the crankcase half in solvent and dry it thoroughly.

   g. A blind bearing remover (**Figure 109**) is required to remove some of the blind bearings in the following procedures.

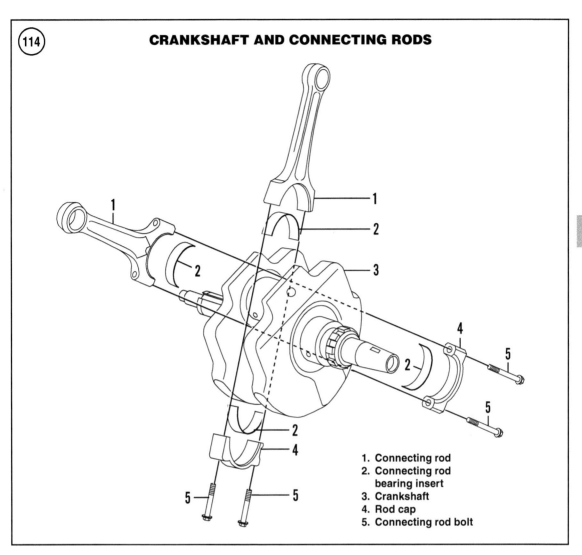

CRANKSHAFT AND CONNECTING RODS

(114)

1. Connecting rod
2. Connecting rod
   bearing insert
3. Crankshaft
4. Rod cap
5. Connecting rod bolt

2. When installing a new bearing into the crankcase, press the outer bearing race only (**Figure 110**). Use a bearing driver or socket that matches the outside diameter of the bearing.

Right crankcase half

1. Remove the bearing retainer, and press the mainshaft bearing (A, **Figure 111**) from the case half.
   a. Install the bearing retainer once the new mainshaft bearing is installed. Make sure the OUT stamp can be read once the retainer is installed.
   b. Apply threadlocking compound to the threads of the bearing retainer bolts, and tighten the bolts to 12 N•m (106 in.-lb.).
2. Use a blind bearing puller to remove the countershaft bearing (B, **Figure 111**).
3. Press the right balancer bearing (C, **Figure 111**) from the crankcase.

Left crankcase half

1. Remove the bearing retainer, and press the countershaft bearing (A, **Figure 112**) from the crankcase. Remove the countershaft spacer (A, **Figure 113**) and oil seal (B) before removing the countershaft bearing.
   a. Install the bearing retainer once the new countershaft bearing is installed. Make sure the OUT stamp can be read once the retainer is installed.
   b. Apply threadlocking compound to the threads of the bearing retainer bolts, and tighten the bolts to 12 N•m (106 in.-lb.).
2. Use a blind bearing puller to remove the mainshaft bearing (B, **Figure 112**) and the torque limiter bearing (C, **Figure 113**).
3. Press the left balancer bearing (C, **Figure 112**) from the crankcase.

CRANKSHAFT

Refer to **Figure 114**.

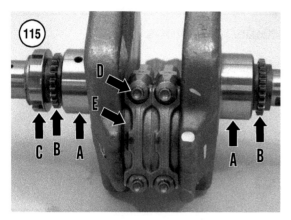

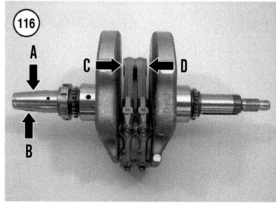

Removal/Installation

Remove and install the crankshaft as described in *Crankcase Disassembly* and *Crankcase Assembly* in this chapter.

Inspection

1. Clean the crankshaft thoroughly with solvent, and dry it with compressed air. Lightly oil the journal surfaces immediately to prevent rust.
2. Blow the oil passages clear with compressed air.
3. Visually inspect each crankshaft journal (A, **Figure 115**) for scratches, heat discoloration or other damage.
4. Check each timing sprocket (B, **Figure 115**) for excessive wear or tooth damage.
5. Inspect the flywheel taper (A, **Figure 116**), keyway (B) and all threads for wear or damage.
6. Inspect the dogs (C, **Figure 115**) for the left balancer drive gear.
7. Inspect the connecting rod big end for signs of seizure, bearing or thrust washer damage or for connecting rod damage.
8. Check the connecting rod small end for signs of excessive heat (blue coloration) or other damage.
9. Check the connecting-rod big-end side clearance. Slide the connecting rods to one side. Measure the big end side clearance (**Figure 117**) with a flat feeler gauge. If the clearance is outside the range specified in **Table 1**, replace the connecting rods and recheck the clearance. If the side clearance is still outside the specified range, replace the crankshaft.
10. Use V-blocks and a dial gauge to check the crankshaft runout (**Figure 118**). If the runout exceeds the service limit in **Table 1**, replace the crankshaft.
11. Measure the outside diameter of each crankshaft journal (**Figure 119**). Record the readings. Replace the crankshaft if either journal is out of specification (**Table 1**).

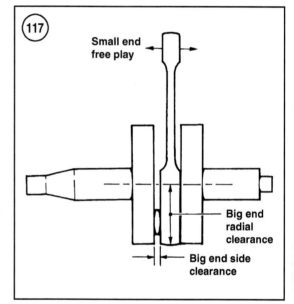

12. Measure the inside diameter of the crankshaft main bearing (D, **Figure 111**) in each crankcase half. Record the readings. Replace the case halves as a set if either bearing inside diameter is out of specification (**Table 1**).
13. Calculate the crankshaft oil clearance by subtracting the crankshaft journal outside diameter (Step 11) from the main bearing inside diameter (Step 12). Perform this calculation for the left and right sides.
14. If either oil clearance is out of specification (**Table 1**), replace the crankshaft and crankcase as a set.

CONNECTING RODS

Refer to **Figure 114**.

Removal

1. Separate the case halves and remove the crankshaft as described in this chapter.

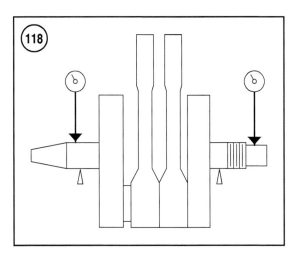

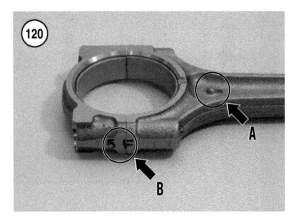

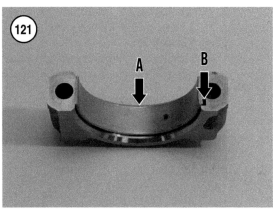

3. Remove the rod cap (E, **Figure 115**), and lift the connecting rod from the crankpin. Note that the raised dot on the connecting rod (A, **Figure 120**) faces the flywheel tapered end of the crankshaft.

CAUTION
*Keep each bearing insert (A, **Figure 121**) in its original place in the connecting rod or rod cap. If reusing bearing inserts, they must be installed in their original locations; otherwise rapid wear will occur.*

4. Mark the rod cap and bearing insert so they can be reinstalled in their original location.
5. A connecting rod and its cap are mated. Keep them together. Make sure the weight mark on the end of the rod cap matches the mark on the rod (B, **Figure 120**).
6. Repeat for the remaining connecting rod.

Installation

1. Install a bearing insert (A, **Figure 121**) into each connecting rod and cap. Make sure the tab (B, **Figure 121**) on the bearing insert locks into the cutout in the rod cap or connecting rod. If reusing the bearing inserts, install each in its original location as noted during removal.
2. Apply engine oil to the bearing surface of each insert.

CAUTION
*Installed each connecting rod so the side with the raised dot (A, **Figure 120**) faces the flywheel tapered end of the crankshaft.*

3. Refer to the marks made during removal, and position the connecting rod over the correct side of the crankpin. Set the connecting rod onto the crankpin so the side with the raised dot (A, **Figure 120**) faces the flywheel tapered end of the crankshaft (A, **Figure 116**).

CAUTION
*The two connecting rods must be reinstalled in their original positions, either on the flywheel taper side of the crankpin (C, **Figure 116**) or on the primary drive side (D). Before removal, mark each connecting rod and its cap so they can be installed onto the correct side of the crankpin.*

2. Remove the connecting rod cap bolts (D, **Figure 115**). Discard the bolts.

4. Fit the bearing cap onto the connecting rod. Make sure the I.D. numbers on the rod and cap align with each other (B, **Figure 120**).

5. Apply molybdenum disulfide grease to the threads of new connecting rod bolts, and evenly snug down the bolts.

6. Repeat Steps 1-5 for the remaining connecting rod.

7. Tighten the connecting rod bolts (D, **Figure 115**) to specification by performing the following:

    a. Tighten the connecting rod bolts to 15 N•m (11 ft.-lb.).

    b. Use a torque angle gauge (**Figure 122**) to tighten the connection rod bolts an additional 125-135°.

Inspection

Replace any connecting rod that is damaged or out of specification (**Table 1**).

1. Insert each connecting rod for damage.

2. Inspect the small end bore for wear or scoring. Measure the small end inside diameter (**Figure 123**).

3. If necessary, take the connecting rod to a machine shop and check for straightness.

4. Inspect the bearing inserts (A, **Figure 121**) for excessive wear, scoring or burning. The inserts can be reused if they are in good condition. If the bearing will be discarded, note its color code.

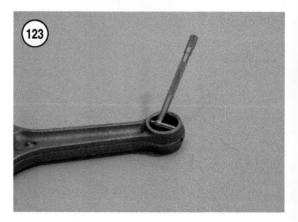

5. Oil the piston pin, and install it in the connecting rod small end. Slowly rotate the piston pin, and check for radial and lateral play (**Figure 124**). If any play exists, the connecting rod should be replaced (providing the piston pin outside diameter is within specification).

6. Check the connecting rod oil clearance as described in this section.

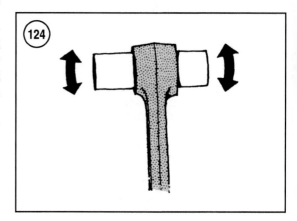

Oil Clearance

1. Wipe the bearing inserts and crankpins clean. Install the inserts (A, **Figure 121**) into their original connecting rod or rod cap.

2. Place a piece of Plastigage onto the crankpin so the Plastigage parallels to the crankshaft (**Figure 125**).

3. Install the connecting rods by perform Step 3-7 of *Installation* in this section.

CAUTION
Do not rotate the crankshaft while Plastigage is in place.

4. Remove the connecting rods as described in this section.

5. Determine the oil clearance by measuring the width of flattened Plastigage according to the man-

ufacturer's instructions (**Figure 125**). Replace the bearings if the connecting rod oil clearance is outside the range specified in **Table 1**.

6. Clean all Plastigage from the crankpin and bearing inserts. Install the connecting rods as described in this section.

Bearing Selection

Bearing inserts are identified by color. To determine the proper bearing inserts, calculate the bearing insert number as described below. Refer to **Table 2**,

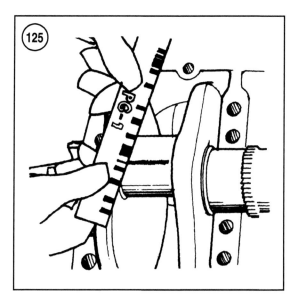

the number on the related connecting rod (B, **Figure 120**). For example, if the connecting rod is marked with a 5 and the related crankweb number is a *2*, 5 - 2 = 3. The new bearing insert number is *3*.

4. Refer to **Table 2** and use the bearing insert number to determine the color code for the bearing inserts. In the above example, brown bearing inserts would be installed in the connecting rod and cap.

NOTE
Determine the bearing insert number for both connecting rods. Then take insert numbers and colors to a dealership for bearing purchase.

5. Repeat Steps 1-4 for the other connecting rod.
6. After new bearings have been selected, recheck the oil clearance as described in this section. If clearance is still out of specification, take the crankshaft and connecting rods to a dealership for further service. The manufacturer does not provide connecting rod or crankpin service specifications.

BREAK-IN

Following cylinder servicing (boring, honing, new rings, etc.) and major lower end work, the engine should be broken in just as though it were new. The performance and service life of the engine greatly depends upon a careful and sensible break-in.

During the break-in period (the initial 1000 miles [1600 km]), periodically vary the speed of the motorcycle. Prolonged steady running at one speed, no matter how moderate, must be avoided. Also avoid prolonged full-throttle operation, hard acceleration or any situation that could result in excessive heat.

1. During the first 600 miles (1000 km) of operation, avoid running above 1/3 throttle.
2. Between 600 to 1000 miles (1000 – 1600 km) of operation, avoid running above 1/2 throttle.
3. At the end of the break-in period (1,000 miles [1600 km]), change the engine oil and oil filter.

and use the bearing number to identify the bearing color.
1. The connecting rods are marked with a number (B, **Figure 120**).
2. The crankweb is marked with a number (**Figure 126**) that relates to the connecting rod crankpin.
3. To select the proper bearing insert number, subtract the number on the crankweb (**Figure 126**) from

Table 1 ENGINE LOWER END SPECIFICATIONS

Item	New mm (in.)	Service limit mm (in.)
Connecting rods		
Oil clearance	0.030-0.054 (0.0012-0.0021)	–
Small end inside diameter	23.015-23.028 (0.9061-0.9066)	–
Big end side clearance	0.320-0.474 (0.0126-0.0187)	–
	(continued)	

Table 1 ENGINE LOWER END SPECIFICATIONS (continued)

Item	New mm (in.)	Service limit mm (in.)
Crankshaft		
Runout	–	0.020 (0.0008)
Journal outside diameter	49.968-49.980 (1.9672-1.9677)	–
Main bearing inside diameter	50.010-50.030 (1.9689-1.9697)	–
Oil clearance	0.030-0.060 (0.0012-0.0024)	–
Oil pump		
Type	Trochoid	
Inner-rotor-outer-to-outer-rotor		
tip clearance	Less than 0.12 (0.0047)	0.20 (0.0079)
Outer rotor to housing clearance	0.09-0.19 (0.0035-0.0075)	0.26(0.0102)
Pump rotor depth	0.06-0.13 (0.0024-0.0051)	0.20 (0.0079)
Waterpump impeller tilt	–	0.15 (0.006)

Table 2 CONNECTING ROD BEARING INSERT SELECTION

Connecting rod bearing number	Bearing insert color
1	Blue
2	Black
3	Brown
4	Green
5	Yellow
Connecting rod bearing number = The number on the connecting rod – the number on the crankweb	

Table 3 ENGINE LOWER END TORQUE SPECIFICATIONS

Item	N•m	in.-lb.	ft.-lb.
Alternator cover bolt	10	89	–
Balancer assembly bolts*	12	106	–
Bearing retainer bolts*	12	106	–
Brake hose banjo bolt*	30	–	22
Cam chain guide bolts*	10	89	–
Coolant delivery pipe bolts*	10	89	–
Coolant-reservoir-cover bracket bolts	7	62	–
Connecting rod bolt*			
Initial	15	–	11
Final	additional 125-135°		
Crankcase stud	15	–	11
Crankcase bolts*			
6 mm	10	89	–
10 mm	36	–	26.5
Damper cover bolts*	7	62	–
Drain cock bolts*	10	89	–
Engine mounting hardware			
Cylinder-head-bracket hanger bolts*	48	–	35
Cylinder-head-bracket mounting bolts	30	–	22
Engine bracket bolts*	48	–	35
Engine through bolt/nuts*	88	–	65
Removable frame member bolt	48	–	35
Flywheel bolt*	90	–	66
Flywheel bolt plug*	10	89	–
Neutral switch	20	–	15
Oil delivery pipe bolts*	10	89	–
Oil baffle bolts*	10	89	–
Oil drain bolt	43	–	32
Oil filter	17	–	12.5
Oil gallery bolts*	20	–	15
Oil level switch bolt	10	89	–
(continued)			

Table 3 ENGINE LOWER END TORQUE SPECIFICATIONS (continued)

Item	N•m	in.-lb.	ft.-lb.
Oil pump cover bolts (6 mm)*	10	89	–
Oil/water pump mounting bolts (8 mm)*	24	–	18
Oil/water pump chain guide bolts*	10	89	–
Oil/water pump driven sprocket bolts*	15	–	11
Starter clutch bolts*	24	–	18
Subtank bracket bolts	7	62	–
Timing inspection plug*	6	53	–
Water pump cover bolts (6 mm)*	10	89	–

*Refer to text.

CHAPTER SIX

CLUTCH AND PRIMARY DRIVE GEAR

Table 1 and **Table 2** are at the end of this chapter.

CLUTCH COVER

Removal/Installation

Refer to **Figure 1**.
1. Securely support the motorcycle on level ground.
2. Remove the muffler and exhaust pipe (Chapter Eight).
3. Drain the engine oil and remove the oil filter (Chapter Three).

NOTE
2010 models do not have a mid-cable adjuster.

4. Release the clutch cable from the cable holder (A, **Figure 2**), and disconnect the cable end from the clutch release lever (B). On 2007-2009 models, if necessary, loosen the mid-cable adjuster (**Figure 3**) to create additional slack.
5. Remove the clutch cover bolts (A, **Figure 4**), and pull the clutch cover (B) from the primary drive gear cover. Account for the dowels (A, **Figure 5**) behind the cover.
6. Remove and discard the clutch cover gasket (B, **Figure 5**).
7. Installation is the reverse of removal.
   a. Install the dowels (A, **Figure 5**) and a new gasket (B) into the crankcase.

   b. Install the clutch cover so the splines of the clutch release shaft (A, **Figure 6**) align with the splines of the clutch pull rod (C, **Figure 5**). Rotate the pull rod as necessary.
   c. Tighten the clutch cover bolts (A, **Figure 4**) to 10 N•m (89 in.-lb.).
   d. Adjust the clutch cable free play (Chapter Three).

Inspection

1. Inspect the clutch cover for cracks or other signs of damage.
2. Closely inspect the release shaft oil seal (A, **Figure 7**) in the clutch cover.
3. Inspect the clutch release mechanism for signs or wear or damage. Disassemble the mechanism as necessary as described in this chapter.

CLUTCH RELEASE MECHANISM

The clutch release mechanism mounts in the clutch cover on the right side of the crankcase. It is cable operated by the clutch lever on the left side of the handlebar.

Disassembly/Inspection/Assembly

Refer to **Figure 8**.

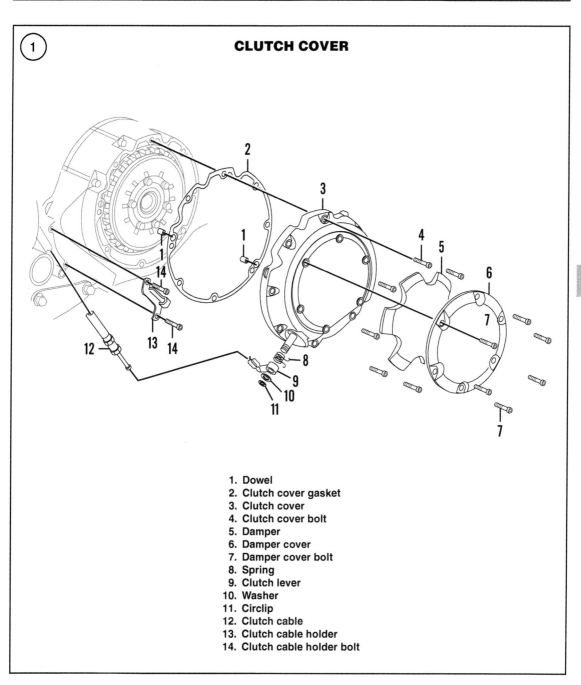

CLUTCH COVER

1. Dowel
2. Clutch cover gasket
3. Clutch cover
4. Clutch cover bolt
5. Damper
6. Damper cover
7. Damper cover bolt
8. Spring
9. Clutch lever
10. Washer
11. Circlip
12. Clutch cable
13. Clutch cable holder
14. Clutch cable holder bolt

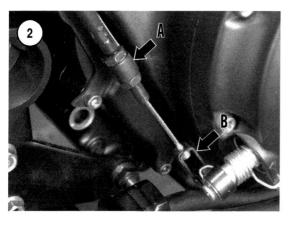

1. Remove the clutch cover as described in this chapter.

2. Remove the circlip and washer (B, **Figure 7**) from the clutch release shaft. Discard the circlip.

3. Slide the clutch lever (C, **Figure 7**) and the return spring (D) from the shaft. Note how the spring arms engage the clutch lever and the cover (E, **Figure 7**).

4. Remove the E-clip (B, **Figure 6**) and washer from the release shaft. Discard the E-clip.

5. Pull the release shaft (C, **Figure 6**) from the clutch cover.

6. Pry the oil seal from the clutch cover. Discard the oil seal.

7. Inspect the bearings for signs of wear or damage. Replace the bearings as needed.

8. Inspect the splines on the release shaft (A, **Figure 6**) for signs of wear of damage.

9. Inspect the pivot in the clutch case for elongation.

10. Inspect the clutch release shaft oil seal (A, **Figure 7**) for damage or brittleness.

11. Replace any part that is worn or damaged.

12. Assembly is the reverse of disassembly.

   a. Lubricate the release bearing with engine oil.

   b. Install a new oil seal. Pack the lips with lithium-soap grease.

   c. Install a new release shaft E-clip.

   d. Install the clutch lever (C, **Figure 7**) so its location mark (A, **Figure 9**) faces the clutch cover and so the indexing dot aligns (B) with the pointer on the cover (C). Make sure the spring arms engage the lever and cover (E, **Figure 7**) as noted during removal.

   e. Install a new clutch lever circlip.

CLUTCH CABLE

In time, the clutch cable will stretch to the point where it can no longer function and must be replaced.

Removal/Installation

1. Remove the fuel tank and the left frame neck cover (Chapter Eight).

2. Disconnect the clutch cable from the hand lever by performing the following:

   a. At the handlebar, slide the clutch cable boot (A, **Figure 10**) away from the adjuster.

   b. Loosen the clutch cable locknut (B, **Figure 10**) and rotate the adjuster (C) to provide maximum slack in the cable.

   c. Align the slots in the adjuster, locknut, and lever housing.

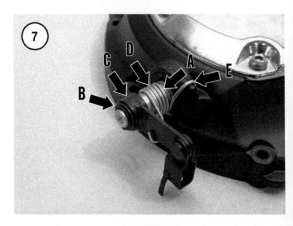

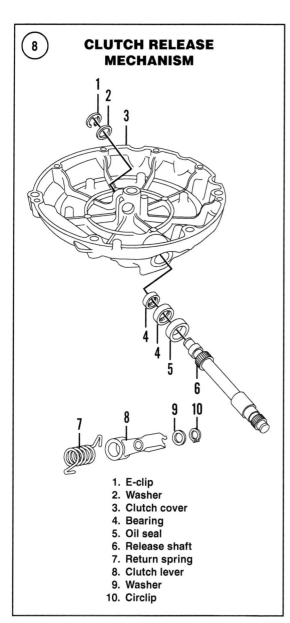

8 **CLUTCH RELEASE MECHANISM**

1. E-clip
2. Washer
3. Clutch cover
4. Bearing
5. Oil seal
6. Release shaft
7. Return spring
8. Clutch lever
9. Washer
10. Circlip

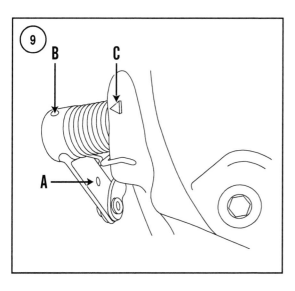

9

10

d. Disconnect the clutch cable end from the hand lever. Pass the cable through the aligned slots.

3. At the clutch cover, release the clutch cable from the cable holder (A, **Figure 2**), and disconnect the cable end from the clutch release lever (B).

NOTE
Make a drawing of the cable routing through the frame and note the location of any cable ties or holders. The new cable must be rerouted along the same path as the old cable.

4. Follow the cable from the release lever, along the frame main frame bone, and on to the clutch hand lever. Remove any cable ties that secure the clutch cable to the motorcycle.

5. Pull the clutch cable out from behind the steering head area, through the cable holder on the left fork leg.

6. Remove the cable and replace it with a new cable. Route the new cable along the path followed by the old cable. Secure the cable to the motorcycle at the same points noted during removal.

7. Connect the clutch cable to the clutch release lever and to the clutch hand lever. Lubricate the clutch cable ends with lithium-soap grease.

8. Adjust the clutch cable free play as described in Chapter Three.

CLUTCH

The wet, multi-plate clutch operates immersed in engine oil. It is mounted on the right side of the transmission mainshaft.

The clutch holding tool (Yamaha part No. YM-91042 or 90890-04086), a Grabbit, or an equivalent tool is needed for clutch service.

Removal

See **Figure 11**.

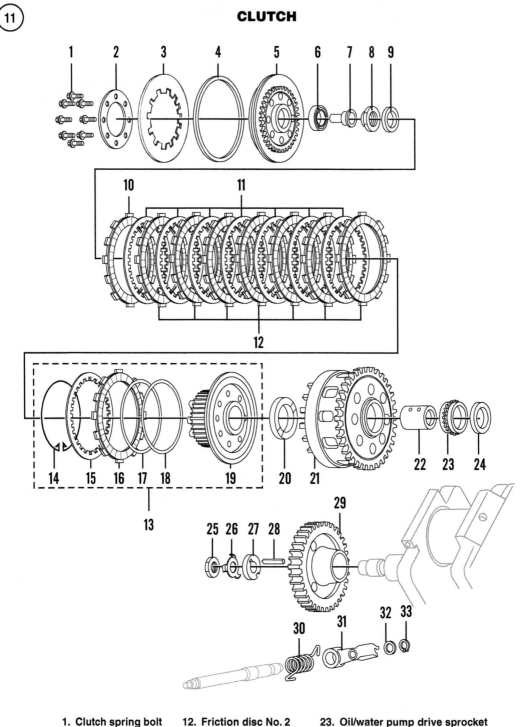

CLUTCH

1. Clutch spring bolt
2. Spring retainer
3. Clutch spring
4. Spring seat
5. Pressure plate
6. Bearing
7. Pull rod
8. Clutch nut
9. Spring washer
10. Friction disc No. 1
11. Plain plate

12. Friction disc No. 2
13. Hub assembly
14. Wire retainer
15. Plain plate
16. Friction disc No. 3
17. Damper spring
18. Damper spring seat
19. Clutch hub
20. Thrust washer
21. Clutch housing
22. Bushing

23. Oil/water pump drive sprocket
24. Thrust washer
25. Primary drive gear nut
26. Lockwasher
27. Spacer
28. Key
29. Primary drive gear
30. Return spring
31. Clutch lever
32. Washer
33. Circlip

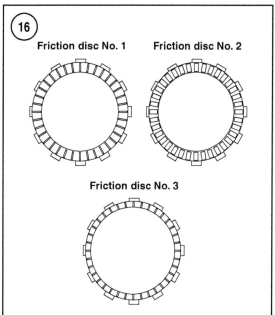

Friction disc No. 1   Friction disc No. 2

Friction disc No. 3

1. Remove the clutch cover as described in this chapter.
2. Evenly loosen clutch spring bolts (A, **Figure 12**) in a crisscross pattern. Remove the bolts and the spring retainer (B, **Figure 12**).
3. Remove the clutch spring (A, **Figure 13**) and spring seat (B).
4. Remove the pressure plate (**Figure 14**).
5. Remove the pull rod (**Figure 15**) from the back of the pressure plate.

NOTE
*Friction discs can be identified by their inside diameters and the shape of the friction material on the discs. Refer to **Figure 16**.*

6. Remove friction disc No. 1 (**Figure 17**) from the clutch housing. Note the tabs with a cutout fit in the clutch housing slots marked with an indexing dot (A, **Figure 18**).

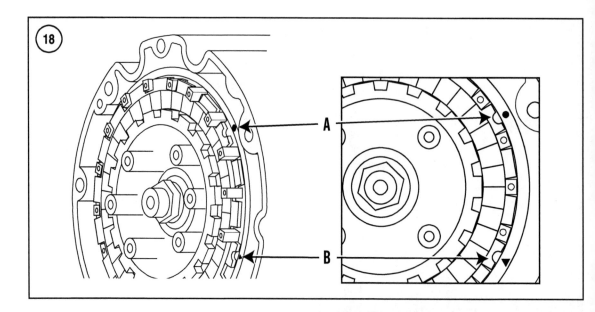

7. Remove the plain plate (**Figure 19**). Stack the plain plate on friction disc No. 1.

8. Remove friction disc No. 2 (**Figure 20**), and stack it on the plain plate. Note that tabs with the cutout fits in the clutch housing slots with the indexing triangle (B, **Figure 18**).

9. Continue to remove a plain plate and friction disc No. 2 until all the plates and discs are removed. Stack each disc and plate in the order of removal.

10. Unstake the clutch nut (**Figure 21**).

CAUTION
Do not clamp the clutch holding tool too tightly. The tool could damage the grooves in the clutch hub.

11A. Hold the clutch hub with a clutch holding tool, and loosen the clutch nut (**Figure 21**).

CAUTION
Do not *use a steel washer in the next step. Steel will damage the gear teeth.*

11B. If a clutch holder is not available, stuff a shop cloth, copper penny, or brass washer between the primary drive gear and the primary driven gear on the clutch housing. Loosen the nut. The washer holds the clutch during nut removal.

12. Remove the clutch nut (**Figure 21**), and spring washer. Note that the OUT on the spring washer faces out.

NOTE
The clutch hub assembly includes a damper assembly. The damper assembly does not need to be disassembled unless the clutch chatters severely.

13. Remove the clutch hub assembly (**Figure 22**). If necessary, disassemble the hub assembly by performing the following:

   a. Pull the ends of the wire retainer from the hole in the hub (A, **Figure 23**), and remove the wire retainer. Discard the retainer.

   b. Remove the plain plate (B, **Figure 23**) and friction disc No. 3 (C).

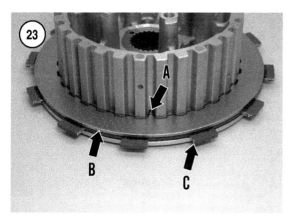

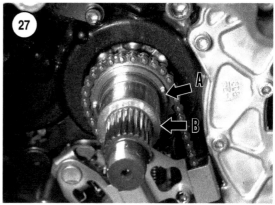

c. Remove the damper spring and the spring seat (**Figure 24**).

14. Remove the thrust washer (A, **Figure 25**) and the clutch housing (B). Note that the cutouts on the back of the clutch housing (A, **Figure 26**) engage the tabs of the oil/water pump drive sprocket (A, **Figure 27**).

Installation

1. If disassembled, assemble the clutch hub damper assembly by performing the following:

a. Install the spring seat and the damper spring onto the clutch hub (**Figure 24**). Install the damper spring so the manufacturer's marks face up away from the spring seat.

b. Install friction disc No. 3 (C, **Figure 23**) and a plain plate (B).

c. Seat one end of a new wire retainer through the hole in the clutch boss (A, **Figure 23**).

d. Press the wire retainer into the grooves around the circumference of the clutch hub, and then insert the remaining end of the wire retainer into the hole.

e. Make sure both ends of the wire retainer are securely locked in the clutch hub hole (**Figure 28**).

CAUTION
The clutch housing powers the oil/water pump drive gear. If the housing is not properly installed, the pump will not operate and the engine will not have oil pressure.

2. Install the clutch housing onto the transmission mainshaft by performing the following:

a. Apply engine oil to the bushing (B, **Figure 27**) on the mainshaft.

b. Align the slots in the clutch housing (A, **Figure 26**) with the tabs on the oil/water pump drive sprocket (A, **Figure 27**).

c. Slide the clutch housing (B, **Figure 25**) onto the mainshaft so the teeth of the primary driven gear (B, **Figure 26**) on the housing engage the teeth of the primary drive gear (**Figure 29**).

d. Gently push the clutch housing onto the mainshaft until the slots in the housing engage the tabs on the oil/water pump drive sprocket. The housing is properly installed when the end of the bushing (A, **Figure 30**) sits flush with the bottom of the clutch housing (B).

e. If necessary, use a pic tool against the oil pump chain (**Figure 31**) to rotate the drive sprocket while simultaneously pressing the clutch housing home.

3. Install the thrust washer (A, **Figure 25**) onto the mainshaft, and install the clutch hub (**Figure 22**).

4. Install the spring washer (**Figure 32**) so side of the washer marked OUT faces out.

5. Lubricate the threads of a new clutch nut with engine oil, and install the nut (**Figure 21**).

6. Use the same tool set-up used during removal to hold the clutch hub (**Figure 33**), and tighten the clutch nut to 125 N•m (92 ft.-lb.).

7. Stake the nut to lock it in place.

NOTE
Apply fresh engine oil to each friction disc to avoid clutch lock up. Install

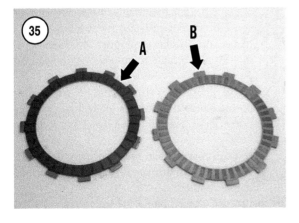

each friction disc No. 2 so the tabs with the cutouts sits in the clutch housing slots marked with the indexing triangle (B, Figure 18).

8. Install the first friction disc No. 2 (**Figure 20**) so the tabs with the cutout fit into the slots marked with the indexing triangle.

9. Install the first plain plate (**Figure 19**) and then install the next friction disc No. 2. Continue alternately installing a plain plate, then a friction disc No. 2 and then a plain plate.

10. After the last plain plate is installed, install friction disc No. 1 (**Figure 17**). Install disc No. 1 so the tabs with the cutout sit in the slots marked with the indexing dot (A, **Figure 18**).

11. Check that the marked tabs on all the friction disc No. 2s sits in the housing slot marked with a triangle (B, **Figure 18**). The marked tabs on the single friction disc No. 1 must sit in the slots marked with the indexing dot (A, **Figure 18**). If necessary, remove the friction discs and plain plates. Reinstall them correctly.

12. Lubricate the pull rod (**Figure 15**) with lithium-soap grease, and install it into the back of the pressure plate.

13. Install the pressure plate (**Figure 14**) onto the clutch hub.

14. Install the spring seat (**Figure 34**) onto the pressure plate, and seat the clutch spring (A, **Figure 13**) into the spring seat. Make sure the convex side of the spring faces out.

15. Apply threadlocking compound to the threads of the clutch spring bolts (A, **Figure 12**). Fit the spring plate (B, **Figure 12**) into place, and loosely install the clutch spring bolts (A).

16. Evenly snug down the bolts in a crisscross pattern. Tighten the clutch spring bolts (A, **Figure 12**) 8 N•m (71 in.-lb.).

17. Adjust the clutch cable free play as described in Chapter Three.

Inspection

1. Clean all clutch parts in a petroleum-based solvent such as a commercial solvent or kerosene. Thoroughly dry the parts with compressed air.

2. Inspect the friction plates. If any disc must be replaced, replace all the friction discs as a set.
    a. Check the friction material (A, **Figure 35**) for excessive wear, cracks, and other damage.
    b. Inspect the frictions disc tabs (B, **Figure 35**) for surface damage. Pay particular attention to the sides of the tabs where they slide along the clutch housing slots. If these tabs are not smooth, the clutch will not disengage and engage correctly.

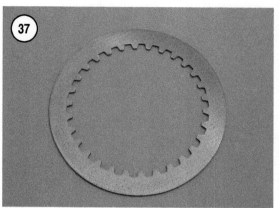

c. Measure the thickness of each friction plate (**Figure 36**) at four places around the disc. If any disc is worn to the service limit (**Table 1**), replace all the friction plates as a set.

d. Measure the inside diameter of each friction disc. If any disc is worn greater than the new dimension, replace all the friction discs.

3. Inspect the clutch plates as described below.

a. Check the inner splines of the plain plates (**Figure 37**). Minor roughness can be cleaned with an oilstone or fine file. If any one plate has excessive roughness or wear, replace all the plates as a set.

NOTE
The clutch plate thickness does not apply to clutch plate No. 1. Clutch plate No. 1 is considerable thicker than the seven standard clutch plates.

b. Measure the thickness of each plain plate at several places around the plate. If any plate is out of specification (**Table 1**), replace all the clutch plates as a set.

c. Check the plain plates for warp on a surface plate or a piece of plate glass (**Figure 38**). Replace all the plain plates as a set if the warp in any plate equals or exceeds the service limit in **Table 1**.

4. If clutch hub was disassembled, inspect friction disc No. 3 as described in Step 2. Inspect the plain plate as described in Step 3.

5. Inspect the clutch housing by performing the following:

a. Check the slots (A, **Figure 39**) for cracks, nicks or galling where they come in contact with the friction disc tabs. They must be smooth for chatter-free operation. If any excessive damage

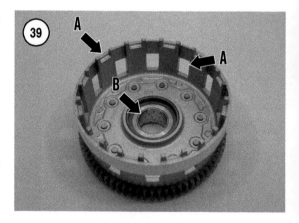

is evident, replace the clutch housing and inspect the friction disc tabs for excessive wear.

b. Inspect the bushing (B, **Figure 39**) in the housing for discoloration or other signs of heat damage.

c. Check the primary driven gear (B, **Figure 26**) on the clutch housing for tooth wear, damage or cracks. Replace the clutch housing if necessary.

d. If the primary driven gear is worn or damaged, also inspect the primary drive gear as described in this chapter.

6. Inspect the clutch hub for the following:

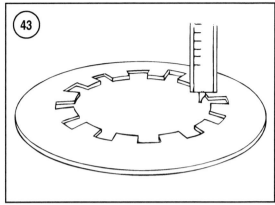

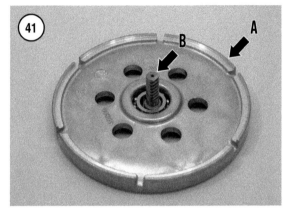

7. Check the pressure plate (A, **Figure 41**) for cracks, wear or galling.

8. Inspect the splines on the pull rod (B, **Figure 41**) for roughness or excessive wear.

9. Visually inspect the clutch spring (A, **Figure 42**) and spring seat (B) for cracks, wear and other signs of fatigue.

10. Measure the free height of the clutch spring with a vernier caliper (**Figure 43**). Replace the spring if its height is less than the service limit (**Table 1**).

11. Inspect the splines of the pull rod. Replace as necessary.

PRIMARY DRIVE GEAR COVER

Removal/Installation

Refer to **Figure 44**.

1. Remove the air filter housing, exhaust system and frame neck covers (Chapter Eight).

2. Drain the fluid from the rear brake (Chapter Fourteen).

> *CAUTION*
> *Once a brake or reservoir hose is disconnected from the rear brake master cylinder, immediately seal the hose in a plastic bag so brake fluid will not dribble onto the motorcycle.*

3. Remove the banjo bolt (A, **Figure 45**), and disconnect the brake hose from the rear-brake master cylinder. Account for the two sealing washers.

4. Disconnect the reservoir hose (B, **Figure 45**) from its fitting on the rear brake master cylinder.

5. Disconnect the rear brake light switch connector (**Figure 46**). Note the location of all clamps and then release any clamps that secure the wire to the removable frame member.

6. Check that all cables, wires, and hoses are disconnected from the removable frame member and safely moved out of the way.

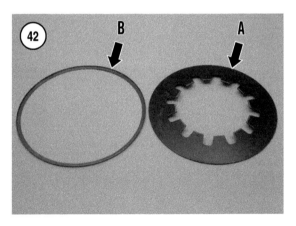

a. Check the grooves for cracks, nicks or galling (A, **Figure 40**) where they come in contact with the clutch plate splines. They must be smooth for chatter-free operation. If excessive damage is evident, the components must be replaced.

b. Inspect the posts (B, **Figure 40**) for wear or galling. If excessive damage is evident, replace the clutch boss.

c. Inspect the inner splines (C, **Figure 40**) in the hub for damage. Remove any small nicks with an oilstone. If damage is excessive, the clutch hub must be replaced.

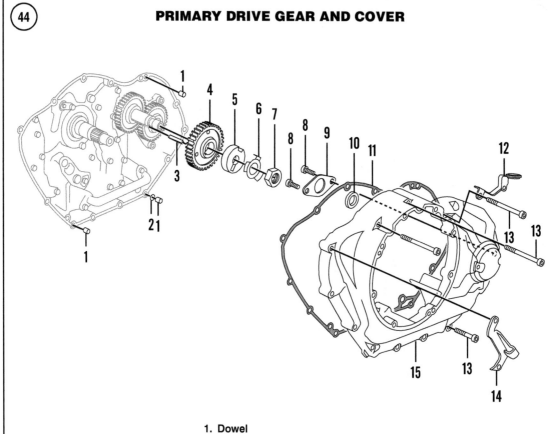

PRIMARY DRIVE GEAR AND COVER

1. Dowel
2. O-ring
3. Straight key
4. Primary drive gear
5. Spacer
6. Lockwasher
7. Primary drive gear nut
8. Retainer bolt
9. Seal retainer
10. Oil seal
11. Gasket
12. Air filter housing bracket
13. Primary drive gear cover bolts
14. Clutch holder bracket
15. Primary drive gear cover

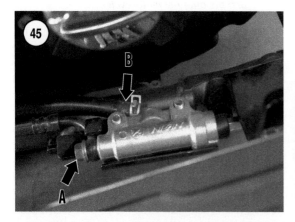

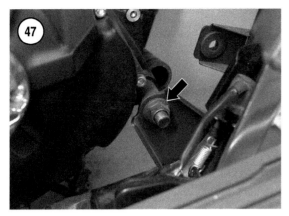

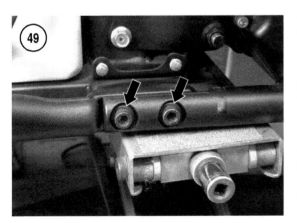

7. Remove the nut from the front engine through bolt (**Figure 47**). Leave the bolt in place.

8. Remove the front (**Figure 48**) and rear (**Figure 49**) removable frame member bolts.

9. Remove the removable frame member along with the floorboard and brake master cylinder.

10. Remove the cover bolts (A, **Figure 50**). Note the location of the clutch cable holder (B, **Figure 50**) and the air filter housing bracket (C). Each must be reinstalled in its original location.

11. Remove the primary drive gear cover (D, **Figure 50**) from the right side.

12. Remove the dowels (A and B, **Figure 51**) behind the cover. Remove and discard the O-ring installed on the lower front dowel (B, **Figure 51**).

13. Remove and discard the cover gasket.

14. Installation is the reverse of removal.

   a. Install a new O-ring with the front lower dowel (B, **Figure 51**). Lubricate the O-ring with lithium-soap grease.

   b. Pack the lips of the cover's oil seal (**Figure 52**) with lithium-soap grease.

   c. Install a new cover gasket.

   d. Tighten the primary drive gear cover bolts (A, **Figure 50**) to 10 N•m (89 in.-lb.).

   e. Apply threadlocking compound to the threads of the removable frame member

bolts (**Figure 48** and **Figure 49**), and tighten
the bolts to 48 N•m (35 ft.-lb.).

f. Tighten the front engine through bolt/nut
(**Figure 47**) to 88 N•m (65 ft.-lb.).

g. Install new sealing washers on the brake hose
banjo bolt (A, **Figure 45**), and tighten the banjo bolt to 30 N•m (22 ft.-lb.).

PRIMARY DRIVE GEAR

Refer to **Figure 44**.

Tools

A means to hold the flywheel or clutch is needed
to perform this service. Have the appropriate tools on
hand before starting.

1. A sheave holder (Yamaha part No. YU-01880-A
or 90890-01701) or its equivalent.

2. A clutch holding tool (Yamaha part No. YM-
91042 or 90890-04086), a Grabbit or an equivalent
clutch holder.

Removal

1. Remove the primary drive gear cover as described
in this chapter.

2. Bend the lockwasher tab (A, **Figure 53**) away
from the flat of the primary drive gear nut.

3A. Hold the clutch with a Grabbit, and remove the
primary drive gear nut (B, **Figure 53**).

3B. If the clutch has been removed, perform the following:

a. Remove the alternator cover (Chapter Five).

b. Hold the flywheel with the special tool. Make
sure the holder does not pass over any raised
portion of the flywheel.

c. Remove the primary drive gear nut (B, **Figure
53**).

4. Remove the lockwasher (**Figure 54**) and spacer
(**Figure 55**).

5. Remove the primary drive gear (A, **Figure 56**) from the crankshaft and make sure the straight key (B) does not fall out.

Installation

1. Install the primary drive gear (A, **Figure 56**) onto the crankshaft so the gear engages the straight key (B).

2. Install the spacer (**Figure 55**) onto the crankshaft so the spacer's slot engages the straight key.

3. Install a new lockwasher (**Figure 54**) so its tab engages the cutout in the spacer.

4. Apply engine oil to the threads of the primary drive gear nut, and turn the nut (B, **Figure 53**) onto the crankshaft.

5. Hold the engine with the tool used during removal, and tighten the primary drive gear nut to 100 N•m (74 ft.-lb.).

6. Bend a tab of the lockwasher (A, **Figure 53**) against a nut flat.

Inspection

Replace any part that is worn or damaged.

1. Inspect the primary drive gear (**Figure 57**) for broken or missing teeth. If found, replace the primary drive gear and inspect the primary driven gear on the clutch housing.

2. Inspect the straight key for nicks, rounded edges or other signs of wear. If worn replace the key and inspect the keyway in the primary drive gear, spacer and the crankshaft.

3. Inspect the threads of the primary gear nut.

Table 1 CLUTCH SPECIFICATIONS

Item	New mm (in.)	Service Limit mm (in.)
Friction disc		
Quantity		
Friction disc No. 1	1	
Friction disc No. 2	7	
Friction disc No. 3	1	
Thickness		–
Friction disc No. 1	2.90-3.10 (0.114-0.122)	2.80 (0.1102)
Friction disc No. 2	2.92-3.08 (0.115-0.121)	2.82 (0.1110)
Friction disc No. 3	2.90-3.10 (0.114-0.122)	2.80 (0.1102)
Inside diameter		
Friction disc No. 1	124 (4.88)	–
Friction disc No. 2	124 (4.88)	–
Friction disc No. 3	135 (5.31)	–
Plain plate		
Thickness	1.90-2.10 (0.075-0.083)	
Quantity	8	
Warp	–	0.20 (0.0079)
Clutch spring		
Free height	6.70 (0.26)	–
Minimum height	6.37 (0.25)	–
Quantity	1	–
Clutch lever free play		
At lever end	5-10 (0.20-0.39)	–

Table 2 CLUTCH AND PRIMARY DRIVE GEAR TORQUE SPECIFICATIONS

Item	N•m	in.-lb.	ft.-lb.
Brake hose banjo bolt*	30	–	22
Clutch cable holder bolt	10	89	–
Clutch cover bolts	10	89	–
Clutch nut*	125	–	92
Clutch spring bolts*	8	71	–
Removable frame member bolts*	48	–	35
Engine through bolt/nut	88	–	65
Primary drive gear cover bolts	10	89	–
Primary drive gear nut*	100	–	74
Shift-lever clamp bolt	10	89	–
*Refer to text.			

CHAPTER SEVEN

TRANSMISSION AND SHIFT MECHANISM

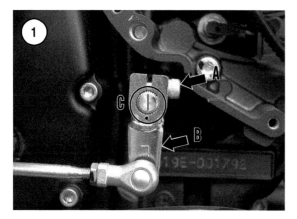

This chapter describes the service procedures for the transmission, engine pulley, and the internal and external shift mechanisms.

Table 1 and **Table 2** are at the end of this chapter.

SHIFT PEDAL/FLOORBOARD ASSEMBLY

1. Remove the sidestand (Chapter Fifteen).
2. Loosen the clamp bolt (A, **Figure 1**) on the shift lever (B), and slide the lever from the shift shaft. Note that the indexing dot on the shift lever aligns with the indexing line on the shift shaft (C, **Figure 1**).
3. On California models, disconnect the EVAP purge hose (A, **Figure 2**) and breather hose (B) from their respective fittings on the canister. Label each hose

and its fitting. They must be reconnected to the correct fitting.

4. Remove the floorboard bracket bolts (**Figure 3**). Lower the shift pedal/floorboard assembly from the frame.
5. Installation is the reverse of removal.
   a. Apply threadlocking compound to the threads of the floorboard bracket bolts (**Figure 3**), and tighten the bolts to 64 N•m (47 ft.-lb.).
   b. Install the shift lever onto the shift shaft. The indexing dot of the shift lever (B, **Figure 1**) must align with the line on the shift shaft (C).
   c. Tighten the shift shaft clamp bolt (A, **Figure 1**) to 10 N•m (89 in.-lb.).
   d. If necessary, adjust the shift pedal (Chapter Three).

ENGINE PULLEY COVER

Removal/Installation

Refer to **Figure 4**.
1. Securely support the motorcycle on level ground
2. Remove engine pulley cover bolts (**Figure 5**), and pull the cover assembly from the pulley housing.
   a. The outer pulley cover does not need to be removed.
   b. Account for the dowels (**Figure 6**) behind the inner cover.
3. Installation is the reverse of removal.
   a. Install the dowels (**Figure 6**).

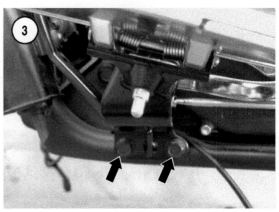

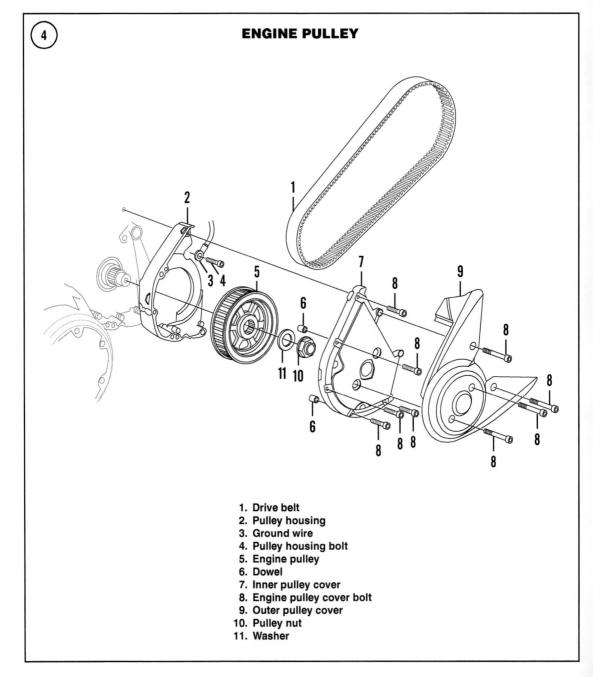

ENGINE PULLEY

1. Drive belt
2. Pulley housing
3. Ground wire
4. Pulley housing bolt
5. Engine pulley
6. Dowel
7. Inner pulley cover
8. Engine pulley cover bolt
9. Outer pulley cover
10. Pulley nut
11. Washer

b. Evenly snug down the engine pulley cover bolts (**Figure 5**). Tighten the bolts to 10 N•m (89 in.-lb.).

c. If removed, install the outer pulley cover onto the inner pulley cover. Evenly snug down the engine pulley cover bolts in the sequence shown in **Figure 7**. Tighten the bolts, in sequence, to 10 N•m (89 in.-lb.).

ENGINE PULLEY AND HOUSING

CAUTION
If the existing drive belt will be reused, it must be installed so it travels in the same direction. Mark the belt before removal.

Removal

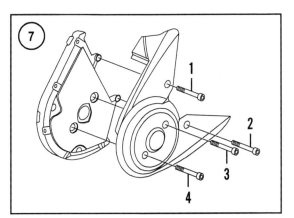

Refer to **Figure 4**.

1. Remove the engine pulley cover as described in this chapter.

2. If necessary, draw an arrow on the top of the drive belt to indicate the direction of forward rotation.

3. Unstake the engine pulley nut (A, **Figure 8**).

4. Have an assistant apply the rear brake, and remove the engine pulley nut. Discard the nut.

5. Remove the washer (B, **Figure 8**) from the countershaft. On 2008-2010 models, note that the outboard side of the washer is marked OUT.

6. Loosen the belt adjusters on the swing arm, and slide the wheel forward to create sufficient slack in the drive belt.

7. Slide the engine pulley (**Figure 9**) and belt from the transmission countershaft.

8. Remove the engine pulley from between the drive belt runs.

9. Remove the engine pulley housing by performing the following:

a. Remove the engine pulley housing bolts (**Figure 10**). Note that the upper rear housing bolt also secures the ground wire in place.

b. Pull the housing from the engine. Account for the damper (**Figure 11**) and dowel (**Figure 12**) behind the housing.

10. Inspect the teeth (A, **Figure 13**) and splines (B) of the engine pulley. If wear is excessive, replace the engine pulley, wheel pulley and drive belt as a set.

Installation

1. If removed, install the engine pulley housing by performing the following:

a. Fit the damper (**Figure 11**) onto the housing.

b. Make sure the dowel (**Figure 12**) is in place on the crankcase.

c. Fit the housing into place, and install the engine pulley housing bolts (**Figure 10**). Secure the ground wire behind the upper rear bolt noted during removal.

d. Tighten the engine pulley housing bolts to 24 N•m (18 ft.-lb.).

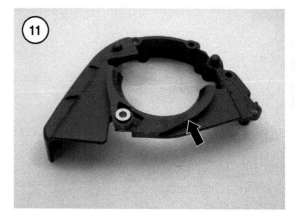

> *CAUTION*
> *Install the drive belt so it turns in the original direction. Do not twist the belt during installation.*

2. Fit the engine pulley (**Figure 9**) between the drive belt runs, and slide the pulley and belt onto the countershaft.

3. Install the washer (B, **Figure 8**) and a new nut (A) onto the countershaft. Note the following:

a. On 2007 models, apply threadlocking compound to the nut threads.

b. On 2008-on models, lubricate the washer and nut threads with engine oil. Install the washer so the side marked OUT faces out.

c. On all models, the shouldered side of the nut must face the washer.

4. Have an assistant apply the rear brake. Tighten the engine pulley nut to 140 N•m (103 ft.-lb.).

5. Stake the nut to both cutouts in the countershaft.

6. Install the engine pulley cover.

7. Adjust the drive belt free play (Chapter Three).

EXTERNAL SHIFT MECHANISM

Removal

Refer to **Figure 14**.

1. Securely support the motorcycle on level ground, and shift the transmission into neutral.

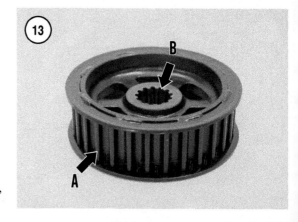

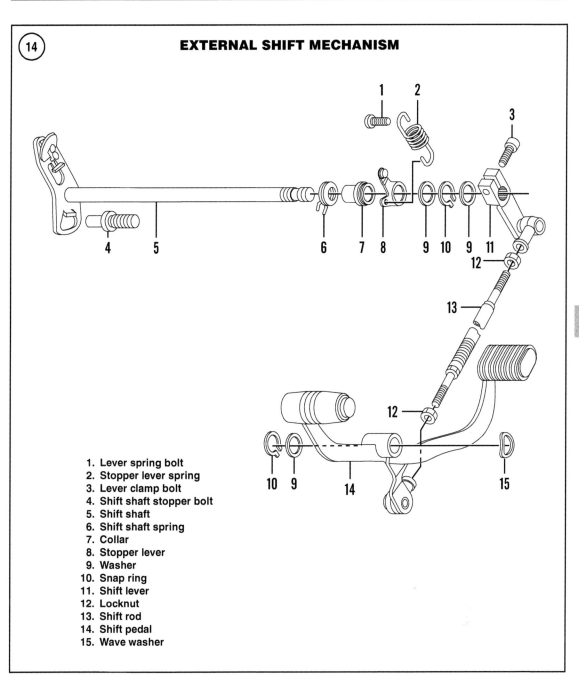

EXTERNAL SHIFT MECHANISM

1. Lever spring bolt
2. Stopper lever spring
3. Lever clamp bolt
4. Shift shaft stopper bolt
5. Shift shaft
6. Shift shaft spring
7. Collar
8. Stopper lever
9. Washer
10. Snap ring
11. Shift lever
12. Locknut
13. Shift rod
14. Shift pedal
15. Wave washer

2. Remove the engine pulley cover (this chapter), the primary drive gear cover (Chapter Six) and the sidestand (Chapter Fifteen).

3. Loosen the clamp bolt (A, **Figure 1**) on the shift lever (B), and slide the lever from the shift shaft. Note that the indexing dot on the shift lever aligns with the indexing line on the shift shaft.

4. Notice that the arms of the shift shaft spring (A, **Figure 15**) straddle the shift-shaft stopper bolt in the crankcase, and that the roller of the stopper lever (B) engages the detent in the shift cam.

5. Stuff a rag into the crankcase opening so parts cannot fall into the crankcase.

6. Disconnect the stopper lever spring from the post (**Figure 16**) in the crankcase.
7. Press the stopper lever (A, **Figure 17**) away from the shift cam, and pull the shift shaft assembly (B) from the crankcase. Remove the washer (A, **Figure 18**) that sits on the inboard side of the stopper lever.
8. If necessary, remove the shift-shaft stopper bolt (A, **Figure 19**) from the crankcase.

Installation

1. Pack the lips of the shift shaft oil seal with lithium-soap grease.
2. If removed, install the shift-shaft stopper bolt (A, **Figure 19**). Apply threadlocking compound to the bolt threads, and torque the shift shaft stopper bolt to 22 N•m (16).
3. Slide the washer (A, **Figure 18**) onto the shift shaft, and seat the washer against the stopper lever.
4. Insert the end of the shift shaft into the crankcase boss (B, **Figure 19**) and slide the assembly into the crankcase until the assembly bottoms. Note the following:
   a. The arms of the shift shaft spring (A, **Figure 15**) must straddle the stopper bolt.
   b. The shift pawls (B, **Figure 18**) must engage the pins on the shift cam.
   c. The roller (B, **Figure 15**) on the stopper lever must the engage the detent on the shift cam.
5. Hook the stopper lever spring (**Figure 16**) over the crankcase post.
6. Install the shift lever (B, **Figure 1**) onto the shift shaft so the indexing dot on the lever aligns with the line on the shift shaft (C). Tighten the shift shaft clamp bolt (A, **Figure 1**) to 10 N•m (89 in.-lb.).
7. Install the engine pulley cover (this chapter), the primary drive gear cover (Chapter Six) and the sidestand (Chapter Fifteen).

Disassembly/Assembly

1. Remove the washer (A, **Figure 18**) from the end of the shift shaft.
2. Remove the snap ring, stopper lever and spring, and the collar from the shift shaft.
3. Remove the shift shaft spring. Note that the arms of the spring straddle the tang (C, **Figure 18**) on the shift shaft.
4. Assembly is the reverse of disassembly.

Inspection

Replace any part that is worn or damaged.
1. Inspect the shift shaft for bends or damage.

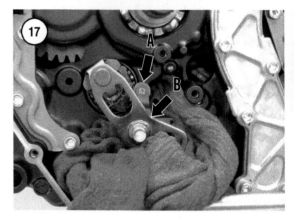

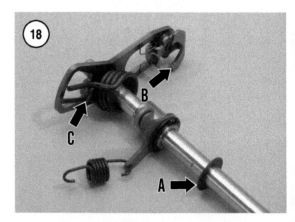

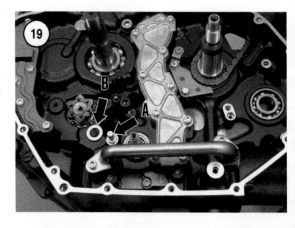

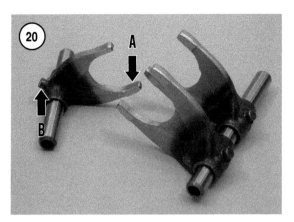

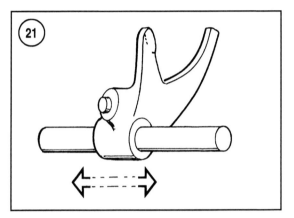

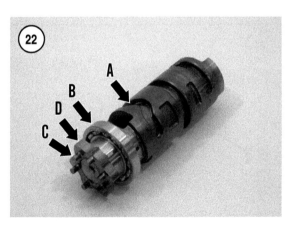

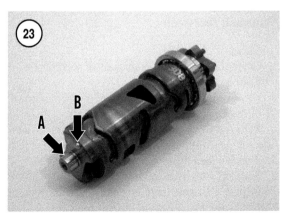

2. Inspect the shift pawls (B, **Figure 18**) for cracks or damage.

3. Check the stopper lever spring and the shift shaft spring for cracks or signs of fatigue.

4. Check the operation of the roller on the stopper lever. It should move smoothly.

5. Inspect the stopper lever for bends or other signs of damage.

INTERNAL SHIFT MECHANISM

Removal/Installation

Remove and install the internal shift mechanism as described in *Crankcase Disassembly* and *Crankcase Assembly* in *Crankcase* in Chapter Five.

Inspection

Replace any part that is worn or damaged.

1. Inspect each shift fork for signs of wear or cracking. Examine the fingers (A, **Figure 20**) and guide pin (B) on each fork. These surfaces should be smooth with no signs of wear or damage.

2. Make sure each fork slides smoothly on its shaft (**Figure 21**). If any binding is noted, replace the fork shaft and related shift fork(s).

3. Roll the shift fork shaft along a surface plate or piece of glass to check runout. Any clicking sounds indicate the shaft is bent and must be replaced.

4. Inspect the guide grooves in the shift drum (A, **Figure 22**) for excessive wear.

5. Spin the drum bearing (B, **Figure 22**), and check for excessive play or roughness.

6. Check the pins (C, **Figure 22**) and shift cam ramps (D) for wear.

7. Inspect the shift drum journal (A, **Figure 23**) for wear or discoloration.

8. Inspect the neutral post (B, **Figure 23**) for wear or damage.

TRANSMISSION

Removal/Installation

Remove and install the mainshaft and countershaft assemblies as described in *Crankcase Disassembly* and *Crankcase Assembly* in *Crankcase* in Chapter Five.

Troubleshooting

Refer to Chapter Two.

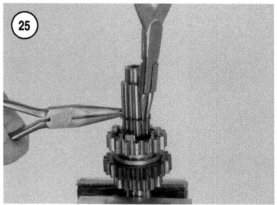

Service Notes

1. A large egg flat can be used to help maintain correct alignment and positioning of the parts. As each part is removed, set it into one of the depressions in the egg flat with the same orientation it had when on the transmission shaft. Refer to **Figure 24**. This is an easy way to retain the correct relationship of all parts.

2. The snap rings and circlips fit tightly on the transmission shafts. They usually become distorted during removal. Replace all snap rings and circlips during assembly.

3. Snap rings and circlips will turn and fold over, making removal and installation difficult. To ease replacement, open a snap ring with a pair of snap ring pliers while at the same time holding the back of the ring with conventional pliers (**Figure 25**).

4. Install a snap ring or circlip so its flat side faces away from the direction of thrust. Refer to **Figure 26**.

5. Position each snap ring or circlip so its end gap sits within a groove in the transmission shaft as shown in **Figure 27**.

6. Apply molybdenum disulfide oil to the each gear and bushing during assembly.

7. When installing a splined gear or a splined bushing onto a shaft, align the oil hole in the gear or bushing with an oil hole in the shaft.

8. The gears on a particular shaft can be identified by their diameter. On the mainshaft, first gear has the smallest diameter; sixth gear the largest. On the countershaft, sixth gear has the smallest diameter; first gear the largest.

9. If disassembling a used, high-mileage transmission for the first time, pay particular attention to any additional shims not shown in the illustrations or photographs. Additional shims may have been installed during a previous repair to compensate for wear. If the transmission is being reassembled with the old parts, install these shims in their original locations since the shims have developed a wear pattern. If new parts are being used, discard the additional shims.

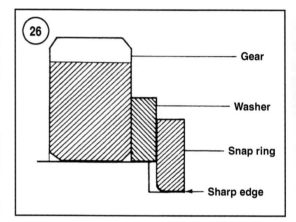

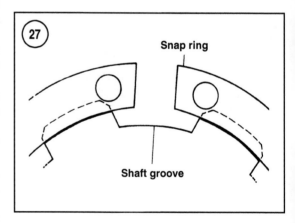

Mainshaft Disassembly

Refer to **Figure 28**.

1. Clean the assembled mainshaft in solvent. Dry it with compressed air.

2. Remove the circlip from the end of the mainshaft.

3. Slide second gear from the mainshaft.

4. Remove the circlip and slide the third/fourth combination gear from the mainshaft.

5. Remove the circlip and splined washer.

6. Slide off fifth gear and fifth-gear bushing.

7. Inspect the mainshaft assembly as described in *Transmission Inspection* in this section.

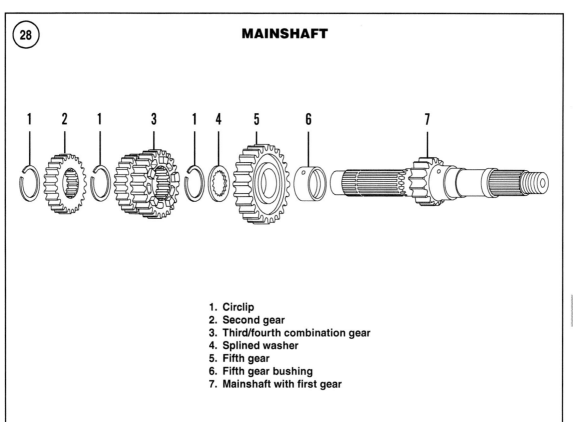

MAINSHAFT

1. Circlip
2. Second gear
3. Third/fourth combination gear
4. Splined washer
5. Fifth gear
6. Fifth gear bushing
7. Mainshaft with first gear

7

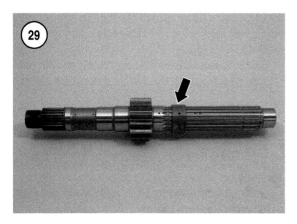

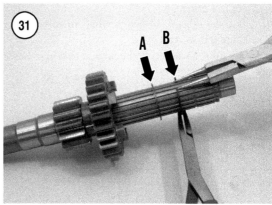

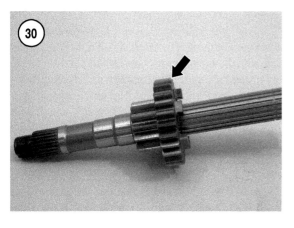

Mainshaft Assembly

Refer to **Figure 28**.

1. Apply a light coat of molybdenum disulfide oil to all sliding surfaces prior to installation.

2. Slide the fifth gear bushing (**Figure 29**) onto the mainshaft and up against first gear. Align the oil holes.

3. Install the fifth gear (**Figure 30**) onto the bushing so its engagement dogs face out away from first gear.

4. Install the splined washer (A, **Figure 31**) and a new circlip (B). Seat the circlip in the groove next to fifth gear.

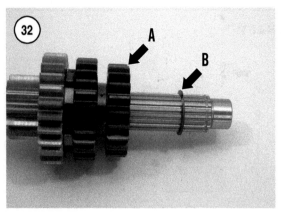

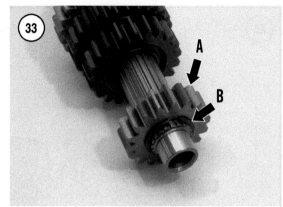

5. Install the third/fourth combination gear so the smaller (third) gear (A, **Figure 32**) faces out.
6. Install a new circlip (B, **Figure 32**), and completely seat it in the inner groove at the shaft's end.
7. Install second gear (A, **Figure 33**), and seat it against the circlip.
8. Install a new circlip (B, **Figure 33**), and seat it in the outer groove of the shaft.
9. Refer to **Figure 34** for the correct placement of the mainshaft gears. Make sure each gear properly engages an adjoining gear where applicable.

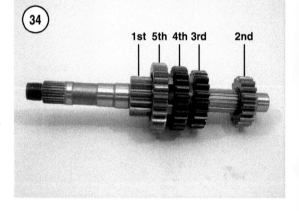

Countershaft Disassembly

Refer to **Figure 35**.
1. Clean the assembled countershaft in solvent, dry it with compressed air.
2. Slide off the washer, first gear and first gear bushing.
3. Slide off the fifth gear.
4. Remove the circlip.
5. Slide off the splined washer, the fourth gear and the fourth gear splined bushing.
6. Pull the lockwasher retainer until its arms release from the slots of the lockwasher, and remove the retainer.
7. Rotate the lockwasher in its groove until the splines of the retainer mesh with those of the countershaft, and remove the lockwasher.
8. Slide off the third gear and the third gear bushing.
9. Remove the splined washer and the circlip.
10. Remove the dog clutch, the circlip and the splined washer.
11. Slide second gear and the second gear bushing from the countershaft.
12. Remove the O-ring from the shaft.

Countershaft Assembly

1. Apply a light coat of clean molybdenum disulfide oil to all sliding surfaces before installing any parts.

2. Lubricate a new O-ring with lithium-soap grease, and install the O-ring (A, **Figure 36**) onto the countershaft.
3. Slide the second gear bushing (B, **Figure 36**) onto the countershaft, and seat it against the shaft's shoulder.
4. Install second gear with its flat side facing in, and seat second gear onto its bushing (**Figure 37**).
5. Install the splined washer (A, **Figure 38**) and a new circlip (B). Seat the circlip in the groove next to second gear.
6. Install the dog clutch (**Figure 39**) so the side with the shift fork groove faces out.
7. Install a new circlip (**Figure 40**) and seat it in the groove next to the dog clutch.
8. Install the splined washer (A, **Figure 41**) and third gear bushing (B). Align the oil hole in the bushing with the holes in the countershaft.
9. Install third gear (**Figure 42**) with its engagement slots facing in and seat third gear onto the bushing.
10. Install the lockwasher (**Figure 43**), and slide it onto the shaft so its sits in the groove next to third gear. Slightly rotate the lockwasher so it locks in the mainshaft groove and is held in place by the shaft splines.
11. Install the lockwasher retainer. Align the wide arm of the retainer with the wide slot in the lock-

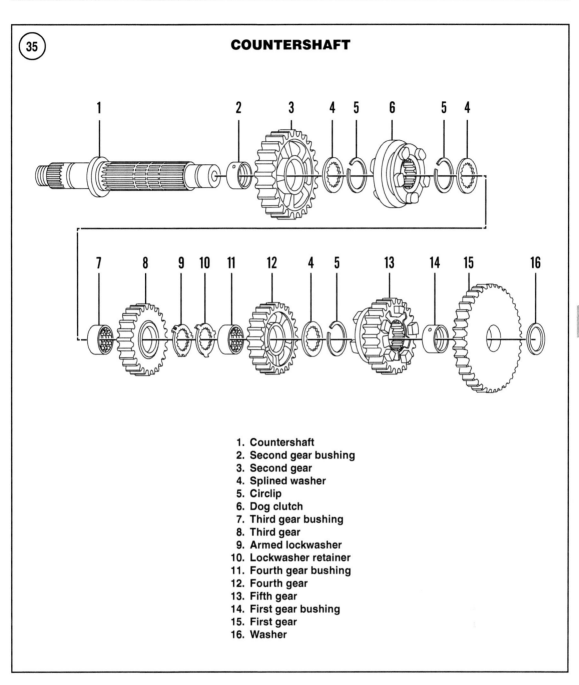

COUNTERSHAFT

1. Countershaft
2. Second gear bushing
3. Second gear
4. Splined washer
5. Circlip
6. Dog clutch
7. Third gear bushing
8. Third gear
9. Armed lockwasher
10. Lockwasher retainer
11. Fourth gear bushing
12. Fourth gear
13. Fifth gear
14. First gear bushing
15. First gear
16. Washer

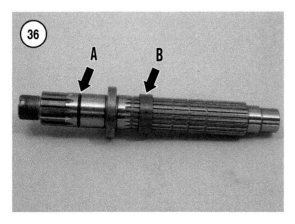

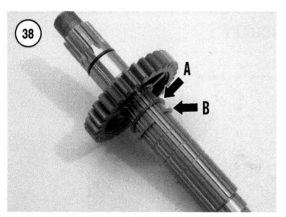

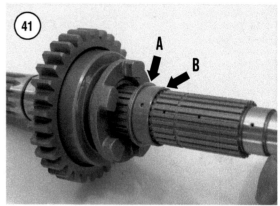

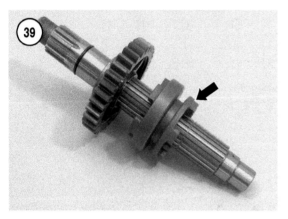

washer. Press the retainer (**Figure 44**) into place so
its locking arms engage the slots in the lockwasher.

12. Install fourth gear bushing (**Figure 45**), and seat
it against the lockwasher retainer.

13. Install the fourth gear so its engagement slots
face out (**Figure 46**), and seat fourth gear onto the
bushing.

14. Install the splined washer (A, **Figure 47**) and
new circlip (B). Seat the circlip in the groove next
to fourth gear.

15. Install the fifth gear (**Figure 48**) so the side with
the shift fork groove faces in. Align the oil hold in
the gear with the hole in the countershaft.

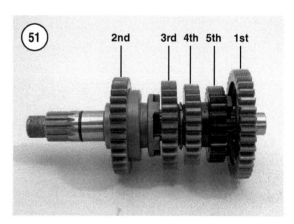

16. Install the first gear bushing (**Figure 49**).

17. Install first gear with the flat side facing out (A, **Figure 50**), and install the washer (B).

18. Refer to **Figure 51** for the correct placement of the countershaft gears. Make sure each gear engages properly an adjoining gear where applicable.

19. After both transmission shafts have been assembled, mesh the two assemblies together in the correct position (**Figure 52**). Check that the gear properly engages its mate on the other shaft. This is the last check before the shaft assemblies are installed in the crankcase. Make sure they are correctly assembled.

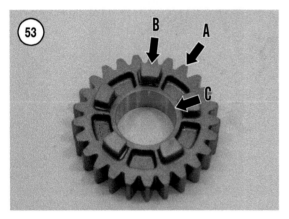

Transmission Inspection

1. Clean all parts in solvent and thoroughly dry them.

> *NOTE*
> *Any defective gear should be replaced. It is also a good idea to replace the gear's mate from the opposite shaft, even though the mate may not show as much wear or damage. Worn parts usually cause accelerated wear on new parts. Replace gears in sets to ensure proper mating and wear.*

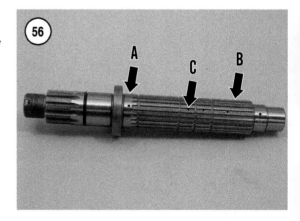

2. Inspect the gears for cracks or chips as well as for broken or burnt teeth (A, **Figure 53**).

3. Check the engagement dogs (B, **Figure 53**) and engagement slots (**Figure 54**). Replace any gear(s) with rounded or damaged edges on the dogs or within the slots.

4. Inspect the bearing surfaces (C, **Figure 53**) of all free-wheeling gears and bushings (**Figure 55**) for wear, discoloration and galling. Also inspect the respective shaft's bearing surfaces (A, **Figure 56**). If there is any metal flaking or visual damage, replace both parts.

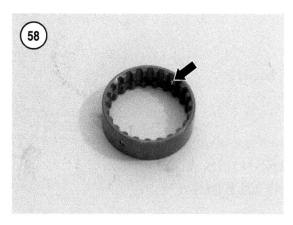

5. Inspect the splines (B, **Figure 56**) on each shaft for wear or discoloration. Also check the internal splines on the sliding gears (**Figure 57**) and splined bushings (**Figure 58**). If no visual damage is apparent, install each gear onto its respective shaft and work the gear back and forth to make sure it moves smoothly.
6. Make sure any oil hole in a gear, bushing or shaft (C, **Figure 56**) is clear.

7. Inspect each shift fork groove (**Figure 59**) for wear or damage. Replace the gear(s) if necessary.
8. Replace any washers that show wear.
9. Discard all circlips, and replace them during assembly.
10. If any transmission parts are worn or damaged, inspect the shift drum and shift forks as described in this chapter.

Table 1 TRANSMISSION AND SHIFT MECHANISM SPECIFICATIONS

Item	New	Service limit
Transmission gear ratios		
First gear	36/13 (2.769)	–
Second gear	32/18 (1.778)	–
Third gear	29/21 (1.381)	–
Fourth gear	29/26 (1.115)	–
Fifth gear	24/25 (0.960)	–
Primary reduction ratio	70/45 (1.556)	–
Secondary reduction ratio	70/30 (2.333)	–
Shift shaft	–	0.025 (0.0010)

Table 2 TRANSMISSION AND SHIFT MECHANISM TORQUE SPECIFICATIONS

Item	N•m	in.-lb.	ft.-lb.
Engine pulley cover bolts*	10	89	–
Engine pulley nut*	140	–	103
Engine pulley housing bolts	24	–	18
Floorboard bracket bolts*	64	–	47
Shift shaft clamp bolt	10	89	–
Shift shaft stopper bolt*	22	–	16
*Refer to text.			

CHAPTER EIGHT

AIR/FUEL, EMISSIONS AND EXHAUST SYSTEMS

This chapter describes the procedures for servicing the air and fuel delivery systems, emissions systems, and the exhaust system. This chapter also addresses troubleshooting for the fuel injection system.

Tables 1-3 are at the end of this chapter.

> *WARNING*
> *Some fuel may spill during fuel system service. Work in a well-ventilated area at least 50 feet from any sparks or flames, including gas-appliance pilot lights. Do not allow any smoking in the area. Keep a B:C rated fire extinguisher on hand.*

Refer to *Handling Gasoline Safely* in *Safety* in Chapter One.

FRAME NECK COVERS

Removal/Installation

Refer to **Figure 1**.

1. Remove the quarter turn fastener (A, **Figure 2**) and the bolt (B) from one frame neck cover. Account for the washer behind the bolt.
2. Repeat Step 1 on the other frame neck cover.
3. Pull the lower edge of each frame cover out. Disengage the tab on the left cover from the cutout in the right cover, and remove the covers. Account for the damper on the front mount of each cover.
4. Installation is the reverse of removal. Make sure the tops of the covers mate and the dampers are in place as noted during removal.

FUEL TANK

Removal/Installation

> *NOTE*
> *During removal, label each hose and its fitting. Also note how a hose is routed through the motorcycle. Each hose must be correctly routed and connected to the proper fitting during assembly.*

Refer to **Figure 1**.

1. Securely support the motorcycle in an upright position on a level surface.
2. Remove the rider's seat (Chapter Fifteen).
3. Disconnect the negative cable from the battery (Chapter Nine).
4. Open the fuel tank cap. Use a pump or siphon to remove the fuel from the tank. Store the fuel in a proper container.
5. Remove the frame neck covers as described in this chapter.
6. Remove the fuel tank bolts (**Figure 3**).

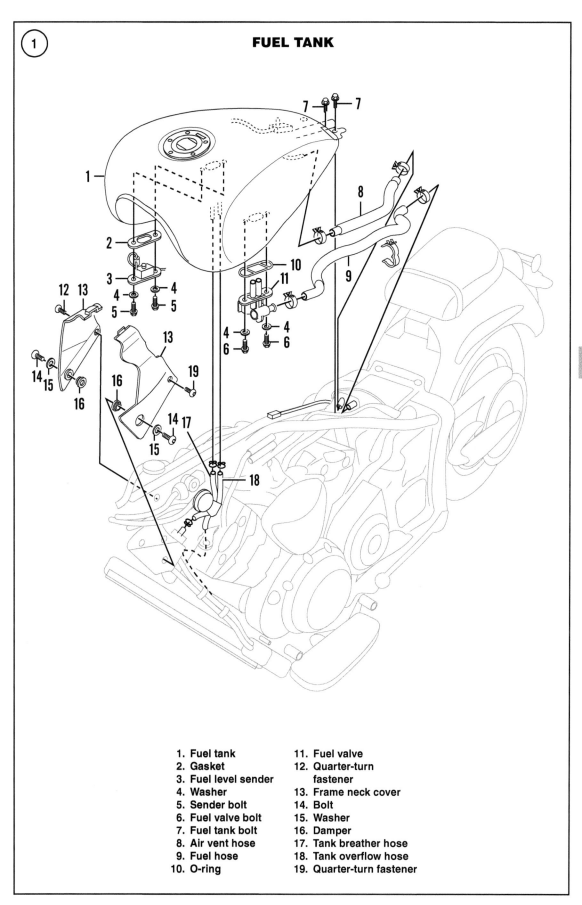

FUEL TANK

1. Fuel tank
2. Gasket
3. Fuel level sender
4. Washer
5. Sender bolt
6. Fuel valve bolt
7. Fuel tank bolt
8. Air vent hose
9. Fuel hose
10. O-ring
11. Fuel valve
12. Quarter-turn fastener
13. Frame neck cover
14. Bolt
15. Washer
16. Damper
17. Tank breather hose
18. Tank overflow hose
19. Quarter-turn fastener

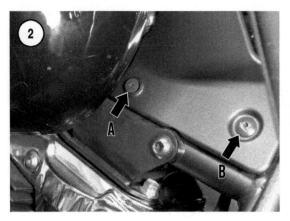

NOTE
The fuel valve lever is located on the inboard side of the fuel valve.

7. Stand on the left side of the motorcycle, and lift the rear of the fuel tank. Reach behind the fuel valve, and turn the valve (A, **Figure 4**) off.

8. Disconnect the fuel hose (B, **Figure 4**) from the fuel valve fitting. Be prepared to catch fuel that leaks from the hose.

9. Release the fuel level sender connector (A, **Figure 5**) from its mount on the tank bracket, and separate the halves of the connector.

10. Remove the mounting bolts (B, **Figure 5**), and lift the seat bracket (C) from the frame.

11. Release the clamp from the air vent hose (A, **Figure 6**), and disconnect the hose from the port on the subtank.

12. On California models, perform the following:
   a. Release the breather hose (A, **Figure 7**) from its clamp (B) on the left side of the steering head.
   b. Disconnect the tank-side of the breather hose (A, **Figure 8**) from the in-line fitting (B). Refer to A, **Figure 9**.

13. Follow the tank overflow hose (C, **Figure 8**), and release it from the clamps that secure the hoses to the left frame downtube. Pull the hose clear of the frame neck.

14. Lift the rear of the tank, pull the tank to the rear until it disengages from the damper (B, **Figure 9**) on each side of the motorcycle, and remove the fuel tank along with the air-vent and overflow hoses.

15. Installation is the reverse of removal.
   a. Route each hose along the path noted during removal.
   b. Reconnect each hose to the fitting noted during removal.
   c. Set the tank into place, and slide it forward until the tank engages the damper on each side.
   d. Tighten the fuel tank bolts (**Figure 3**) to 23 N•m (17 ft.-lb.).

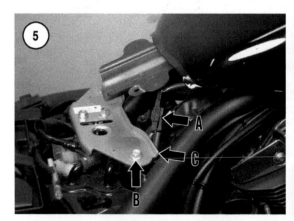

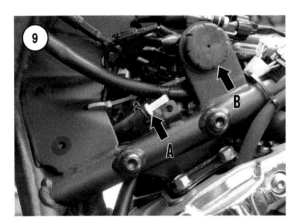

FUEL VALVE

Refer to **Figure 1**.

Removal/Installation

1. Remove the fuel tank as described in this chapter.
2. Set the fuel tank on a protective pad or blanket.
3. Drain the fuel into a clean, sealable container.
4. Position the tank so residual fuel will not spill from the tank when the fuel valve is removed.
5. Remove each fuel valve screw (**Figure 10**) and washer, and remove the valve and O-ring (10, **Figure 1**). Discard the O-ring.
6. The packing and fuel valve seal are the only replaceable parts in the fuel valve. To replace either, refer to **Figure 11** and perform the following:
    a. Remove the two pan head screws and disassemble the valve.
    b. Replace the packing or fuel valve seal.
    c. Assemble the fuel valve by reversing these disassembly steps. Tigthen the screws securely.
7. Install the fuel valve by reversing these removal steps. Note the following:
    a. Install a new O-ring (10, **Figure 1**) during installation.
    b. Tighten the fuel valve screws (**Figure 10**) to 7 N•m (62 ft.-lb.).
    c. After installing the fuel valve, pour a small amount of fuel into the tank and check for leaks. If a leak is present, solve the problem before installing the fuel tank.
    d. Check the new valve by performing fuel valve operation test as described in this section.

Operation Test

1. Disconnect the fuel hose (B, **Figure 4**) from the fitting on the fuel valve.
2. Connect a test hose to the fuel valve fitting and feed the other end of the hose into a suitable container.
3. Turn the fuel valve to *ON*, and check the container.
4. The valve is operating properly if fuel flows from the test hose. Replace a valve that fails this test.

FUEL LEVEL SENDER

Refer to **Figure 1**.

Removal/Installation

1. Remove the fuel tank as described in this chapter.
2. Set the fuel tank on a protective pad or blanket.

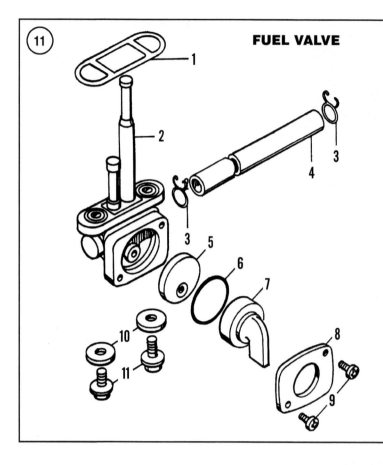

FUEL VALVE

1. O-ring
2. Fuel valve body
3. Clamp
4. Fuel hose
5. Valve packing
6. Valve seal
7. Lever
8. Plate
9. Pan head screw
10. Washer
11. Screw

3. Drain the fuel into a clean, sealable container.

4. Position the tank so residual fuel will not spill from the tank when the fuel level sender is removed.

5. Remove each fuel level sender bolt (**Figure 12**) and washer, and remove the sender and gasket. Discard the gasket (2, **Figure 1**).

6. Installation is the reverse of removal.

   a. Install a new gasket.

   b. Tighten the fuel level sender bolts to 8 N•m (71 in.-lb.).

Resistance Test

1. Remove the fuel level sender as described in this section.

2. Connect an ohmmeter's positive test probe to the green terminal in the sender side of the fuel level sender connector; connect the negative test probe to the connector's black terminal.

3. The sender is faulty if its resistance is outside the range specified in **Table 2**.

Fuel Level Warning Light Test

The self-diagnostic system uses the fuel level warning light to indicate the status of the fuel level sender circuit.

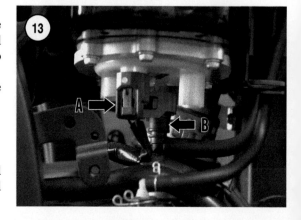

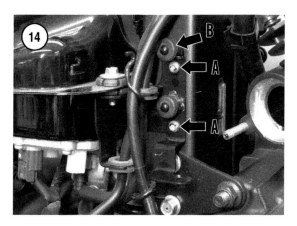

1. Turn the main switch on and watch the fuel level warning light.
2. The light should turn on for a few seconds and then turn off.
3. Replace the meter assembly (Chapter Nine) if the light does not turn on as described in Step 2.
4. If the fuel level warning light flashes eight times, goes out for three seconds and then repeats this cycle, the self-diagnostic system has detected an error in the fuel level sender. Replace the fuel level sender as described in this section.

SUBTANK

Removal

1. Remove the rider's seat and right side cover (Chapter Fifteen).
2. Remove the battery box (Chapter Nine).
3. Remove the fuel tank as described in this chapter.
4. Disconnect the fuel pump connector (A, **Figure 13**) from fuel pump.
5. Disconnect the fuel hose (B, **Figure 13**) from the output port on the fuel pump. Be prepared to catch fuel dribbling from the hose and pump.
6. Remove each subtank bolt (B, **Figure 6**). Account for the collar and damper installed with each bolt.
7. Remove the subtank bracket bolts (A, **Figure 14**).
8. Slide the subtank bracket (B, **Figure 14**) forward, and remove the subtank from the motorcycle.

Installation

1. Set the subtank into the frame.
2. Install the subtank bracket (B, **Figure 14**). Tighten the subtank bracket bolts (A) to 7 N•m (62 in.-lb.).
3. Install and tighten the subtank bolts (B, **Figure 6**) to 10 N•m (89 in.-lb.). Make sure a collar and damper are in place in each mount.
4. Securely connect the fuel hose (B, **Figure 13**) to the pump output port. Make sure the hose connector locks onto the pump fitting.
5. Connect the fuel pump connector (A, **Figure 13**) to the fuel pump.
6. Install the fuel tank as described in this chapter.
7. Install the battery box (Chapter Nine).
8. Install the right side cover and the rider's seat (Chapter Fifteen).

FUEL PUMP

Refer to **Figure 15**.

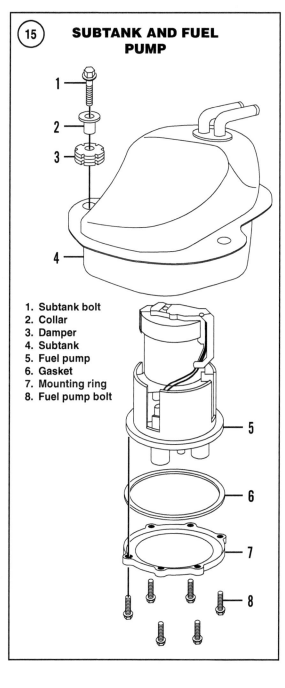

SUBTANK AND FUEL PUMP

1. Subtank bolt
2. Collar
3. Damper
4. Subtank
5. Fuel pump
6. Gasket
7. Mounting ring
8. Fuel pump bolt

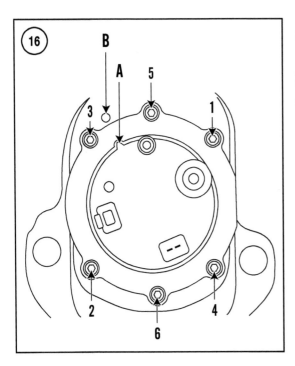

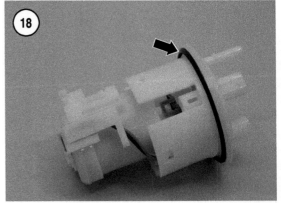

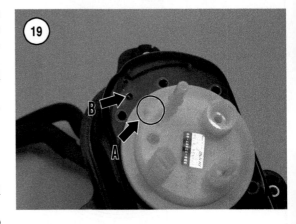

Removal

1. Remove the subtank as described in this chapter.
2. Invert the subtank, and set it on wood blocks. Support the subtank so its hose fittings and mounting surface will not be damaged.
3. Fit a gasket onto the mounting ring. Position the mounting ring (A, **Figure 16** or A, **Figure 19**) on to the pump so the cutout in the ring engages the indexing tab on the pump (B, **Figure 16** or B, **Figure 19**).
4. Remove the mounting ring (A, **Figure 17**) and gasket. Discard the gasket.
5. Lift the fuel pump, and remove it from the subtank. Discard the pump's O-ring (**Figure 18**).

Installation

1. Install a new O-ring (**Figure 18**) onto the fuel pump.
2. Set the pump into the subtank so the indexing tab on the pump (A, **Figure 19**) aligns with the indexing dot on the subtank (B).
3. Fit a new gasket into the mounting ring, and set the ring (A, **Figure 17**) onto the pump so the cutout in the ring engages the indexing tab on the pump (B).
4. Turn in the fuel pump bolts. Evenly snug down the bolts in the sequence shown in **Figure 16**. Tighten the bolts, in sequence, to 6 N•m (53 in.-lb.).

Inspection

1. Inspect the fuel pump for cracks, discoloration or other signs of damage. Replace a damaged pump.

2. Check each port for obstructions. Clear a port as needed. Replace the pump if a port cannot be cleared.
3. Check the input and output fuel hoses and the air breather hose for obstructions. Clear or replace a hose as needed.

Fuel Pressure Test

The fuel pressure adapter (Yamaha part No. YM-03176 or 90890-03176) and pressure gauge (Yamaha part No. YU-03153 or 90890-03153) are needed to perform this test.

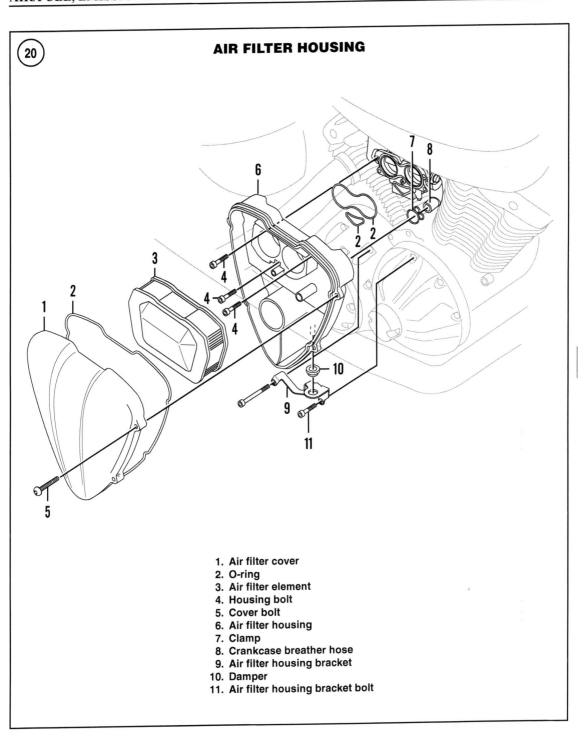

AIR FILTER HOUSING

20

1. Air filter cover
2. O-ring
3. Air filter element
4. Housing bolt
5. Cover bolt
6. Air filter housing
7. Clamp
8. Crankcase breather hose
9. Air filter housing bracket
10. Damper
11. Air filter housing bracket bolt

1. Remove the side cover from the right side.

2. Disconnect the fuel hose (B, **Figure 13**) from the output port on the pump. Be prepared to catch fuel dribbling from the hose and pump.

3. Connect the fuel pressure adapter in line between the fuel hose and the pump output port.

4. Connect a pressure gauge to the adapter.

5. Start the engine a measure the fuel pressure. Replace the fuel pump if the fuel pressure is less than the specified test pressure (**Table 1**).

FUEL PUMP RELAY

The fuel pump relay in an integral part of the relay unit. Refer to *Relay Unit* in Chapter Nine.

AIR FILTER HOUSING

Air filter service is in Chapter Three.
Refer to **Figure 20**.

Removal

1. Securely support the motorcycle on a level surface.

2. Remove the cover bolts (A, **Figure 21**) and pull the air filter cover (B) from the housing. Discard the cover O-ring.

3. Remove the air filter element (**Figure 22**).

4. Remove the air filter housing bolts (A, **Figure 23**).

5. Tilt the air filter housing out, and lift the housing until its post disengages from the damper in the air-filter-housing bracket.

6. Disconnect the crankcase breather hose (**Figure 24**) from the port on the housing, and remove the housing. Remove and discard the two O-rings from the throttle body.

7. If necessary, remove the air filter housing bracket bolts, and remove the bracket.

Installation

1. If removed, install the air filter housing bracket. Tighten the air filter housing bracket bolts to 10 N•m (89 in.-lb.).

2. Lubricate two new O-rings with lithium-soap grease, and install them onto the throttle body.

3. Connect the crankcase breather hose (**Figure 24**) to its fitting, and push housing down so its post engages the damper in the housing bracket.

4. Press the housing in so the housing output fittings mate with the throttle body intake ports.

5. Install the air filter housing bolts (A, **Figure 23**), and tighten them to 4 N•m (35 in.-lb.).

6. Install the air filter element so the filter's post (**Figure 25**) slides into the cylinder (B, **Figure 23**) in the housing.

7. Install the air filter cover with a new O-ring. Tighten the cover bolts (A, **Figure 21**) securely.

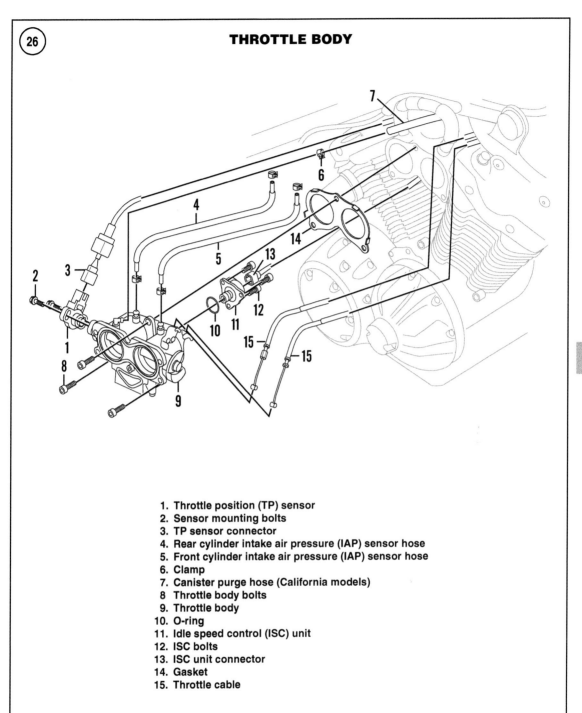

26 THROTTLE BODY

1. Throttle position (TP) sensor
2. Sensor mounting bolts
3. TP sensor connector
4. Rear cylinder intake air pressure (IAP) sensor hose
5. Front cylinder intake air pressure (IAP) sensor hose
6. Clamp
7. Canister purge hose (California models)
8. Throttle body bolts
9. Throttle body
10. O-ring
11. Idle speed control (ISC) unit
12. ISC bolts
13. ISC unit connector
14. Gasket
15. Throttle cable

Inspection

1. Wipe out the interior of the housing and cover.

2. Inspect the air filter housing, input port and output ports for cracks or damage. If any damage is noted, replace the housing to avoid the possibility of unfiltered air entering the engine.

3. Inspect the air filter cover for cracks or damage. Replace the cover as needed.

THROTTLE BODY

Removal/Installation

Refer to **Figure 26**.

1. Securely support the motorcycle on a level surface.

2. Remove the rider's seat and the left engine cover (Chapter Fifteen).

3. Remove the fuel tank and air filter housing as described in this chapter.

4. Loosen the locknut (A, **Figure 27**), remove the return cable (B) from the bracket, and disengage the cable end from the throttle wheel.

5. Repeat Step 4, and disengage the pull cable (C, **Figure 27**) from the throttle wheel.

6. Disconnect the throttle position (TP) sensor connector (A, **Figure 28**).

7. Disconnect the front-cylinder IAP sensor hose (B, **Figure 28**) and the rear-cylinder IAP sensor hose (C) from their respective fittings on the throttle body. Note that the rear-cylinder hose is marked with a white dot; the front-cylinder hose with a yellow dot.

8. On California models disconnect the canister purge hose (A, **Figure 29**) from its fitting on the throttle body.

9. Remove the throttle body bolts (B, **Figure 29** and A, **Figure 30**), and disengage the throttle body from the intake manifold.

10. Disconnect the connector (B, **Figure 30**) from the idle speed control (ISC) unit, and remove the throttle body.

11. Remove and discard the gasket (**Figure 31**).

12. If necessary, remove the ISC bolts (A, **Figure 32**), and remove the ISC unit (B) from the throttle body. Discard the ISC O-ring.

CAUTION
Do not disassemble the throttle body. It cannot be serviced.

13. Installation is the reverse of removal.
   a. If removed, install the ISC unit with a new O-ring. Lubricate the O-ring with lithium-soap grease. Tighten the ISC bolts (A, **Figure 32**) securely.
   b. Install a new gasket (**Figure 31**) onto the intake manifold. The side with the pins must face the manifold.
   c. Tighten the throttle body bolts (B, **Figure 29** and A, **Figure 30**) to 10 N•m (89 in.-lb.).

THROTTLE POSITION (TP) SENSOR

Removal/Installation

1. Securely support the motorcycle on a level surface.
2. Remove the rider's seat (Chapter Fifteen).
3. Remove the fuel tank and air filter housing as described in this chapter.
4. Place a mark across the TP sensor and throttle body so the sensor can be reinstalled in its original position.
5. Disconnect the TP sensor connector (A, **Figure 28**).

NOTE
The TP sensor can be replaced with the throttle body installed. The throttle

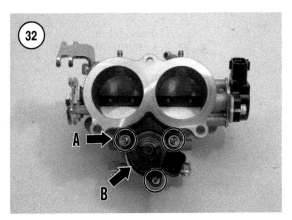

body is removed in this procedure for photographic clarity.

6. Remove the mounting bolts (**Figure 33**), and pull the sensor from the throttle shaft. Note how the sensor engages the throttle shaft.

7. Installation is the reverse of removal.

   a. Fit the TP sensor onto the throttle body so the sensor engages the throttle shaft as noted during removal.

   b. Align the mark made during removal on the TP sensor with the mark on the throttle body.

   c. Tighten the mounting bolts securely.

   d. Adjust the TP sensor as described in this section.

Adjustment

A multimeter (Yamaha 88 part No. YU-A1927), the digital circuit tester (Yamaha part No. 90890-03174), or an equivalent digital meter is needed for this adjustment.

1. Check the idle speed. If it is out of specification, adjust the idle speed as described in *Throttle Valve Synchronization* in Chapter Three.

2. Remove the fuel tank and air filter housing as described in this chapter.

3. Back probe the TP sensor connector (A, **Figure 28**), and connect a digital voltmeter positive test probe to the yellow terminal in the sensor connector. Connect the negative test probe to the connector's black/blue terminal.

4. Turn the main switch on. Measure the output voltage while the throttle is closed. Output voltage should be within the specified range (**Table 2**).

5. If necessary, loosen the TP mounting bolts (D, **Figure 28**). Rotate the sensor around the throttle shaft until the output voltage is within specification. Tighten the bolts securely.

Resistance Test

1. Remove the TP sensor as described in this section.

2. Connect the multimeter positive test probe to the blue terminal in the TP sensor. Connect the negative test probe to the sensor's black/blue terminal.

3. Measure the sensor's resistance. The sensor is faulty if its maximum resistance is outside the range specified in **Table 2**.

INTAKE MANIFOLD

Refer to **Figure 34**.

Removal

1. Remove the throttle body as described in this chapter.

2. Remove the left engine cover (Chapter Fifteen).

3. Remove the finished cover (Chapter Four) from the left side of each cylinder head.

4. Drain the coolant (Chapter Three).

5. Turn out the bracket bolts (A, **Figure 35**), and remove the left engine cover bracket (B).

6. Loosen the hose clamp, and disconnect the thermostat inlet hose (A, **Figure 36**) from output fitting in the rear cylinder head. Be prepared to catch residual coolant that leaks from the hose.

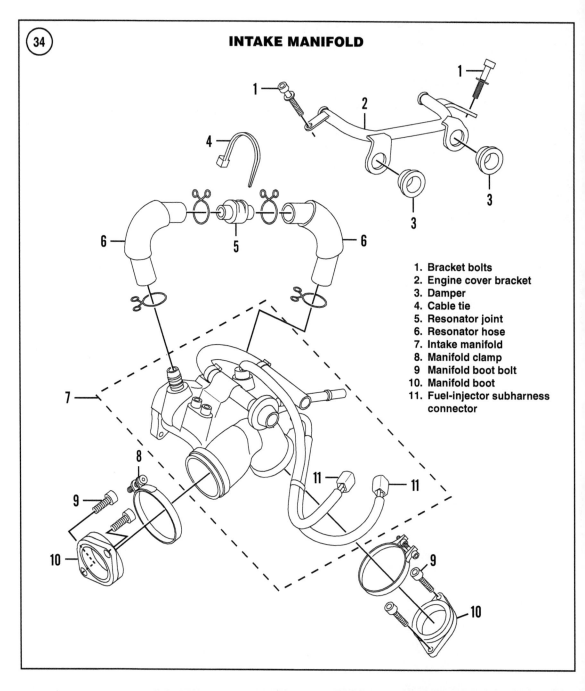

INTAKE MANIFOLD

1. Bracket bolts
2. Engine cover bracket
3. Damper
4. Cable tie
5. Resonator joint
6. Resonator hose
7. Intake manifold
8. Manifold clamp
9 Manifold boot bolt
10. Manifold boot
11. Fuel-injector subharness connector

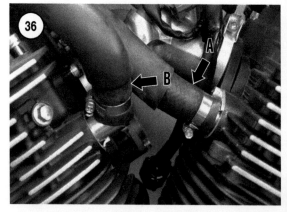

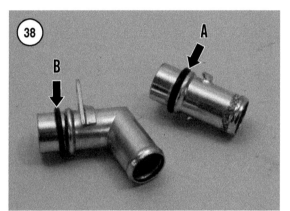

7. Repeat Step 5 and disconnect the hose (B, **Figure 36**) from the front cylinder head fitting.

8. Remove the output fitting bolt (A, **Figure 37**), and pull the output fitting from the rear cylinder head. Discard the fitting O-ring (A, **Figure 38**).

9. Repeat Step 7, and remove the output fitting from the front cylinder head (B, **Figure 37**). Discard the fitting O-ring (B, **Figure 38**).

10. Remove the spark plug cap from each spark plug.

11. Remove the ignition coil bracket bolts (**Figure 39**) so the ignition coils can be moved out of the way.

12. Separate the halves of the 8-pin (A, **Figure 40**) and 4-pin (B) fuel injector subharness connectors.

13. Disconnect the fuel hose (C, **Figure 40**) from the fuel rail.

14. Disconnect each end of the resonator hose (A, **Figure 41**) from its fitting on the intake manifold body. Clip the cable tie (B, **Figure 41**) that secures the right handlebar switch cable to the resonator joint, and remove the resonator hose assembly.

15. Loosen the screw (A, **Figure 42**) on each intake manifold clamp.

16. Remove each bolt (B, **Figure 42**) from the manifold boot on the rear cylinder head.

NOTE
Manifold removal can be difficult. Note how it is removed from between the cylinders to make installation easier.

17. Manipulate the intake manifold as necessary, and remove the rear cylinder manifold boot (C, **Figure 42**) from the motorcycle.

18. Manipulate the manifold enough to disconnect its output port from the front cylinder manifold boot, and remove the intake manifold from the left side.

19. If necessary, remove the manifold boot from the front cylinder head.

Installation

1. If removed, install the manifold boot onto the front cylinder head by performing the following:

   a. Apply engine oil to the mating surfaces of the manifold boot and the cylinder head intake port.

   b. Set the manifold boot onto the front cylinder head intake port so the indexing tab (A, **Figure 43**) on the boot (B) faces up.

   c. Install the manifold boot bolts (B, **Figure 42**), and tighten the bolts to 10 N•m (89 in.-lb.).

2. Slip a manifold clamp onto each output port on the intake manifold.

3. From the left side of the motorcycle, set the intake manifold between the cylinders. Seat the manifold's front cylinder output port into the manifold boot on the front cylinder head. Make sure the port is completely seated in the boot.

4. Repeat Step 1, and install the manifold boot onto the rear cylinder head (C, **Figure 42**).

5. Press the manifold's rear output port into the rear-cylinder. Make sure the port is completely seated in the boot, and that the tab on the manifold's port (A, **Figure 44**) sits against the tab on the manifold boot (B).

6. Slip the clamp over each manifold boot. Tighten each manifold clamp screw (A, **Figure 42**) to 4 N•m (35 in.-lb.).

7. Connect the fuel hose (C, **Figure 40**) to the fuel rail. Make sure the hose connector locks onto the fuel rail fitting.

8. Connect the halves of the 8-pin (A, **Figure 40**) and 4-pin (B) fuel-injector subharness connectors.

9. Move the ignition coil bracket into place, and install the bracket bolts (**Figure 39**). Tighten the ignition coil bracket bolts to 7 N•m (62 in.-lb.).

10. Connect the spark plug lead to each spark plug.

11. Connect each resonator hose to the fittings (A, **Figure 41**) on the intake manifold. Secure the right handlebar switch wire to the resonator joint to the manifold with a new cable tie (B, **Figure 41**).

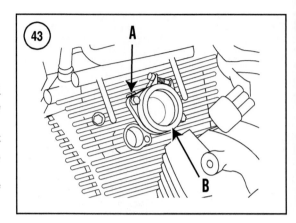

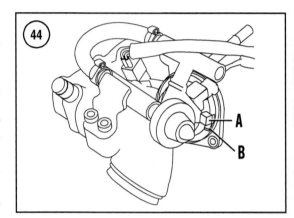

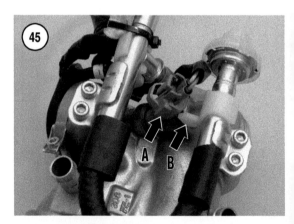

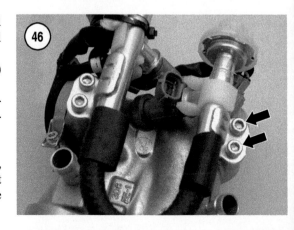

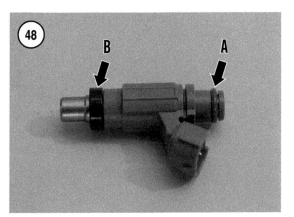

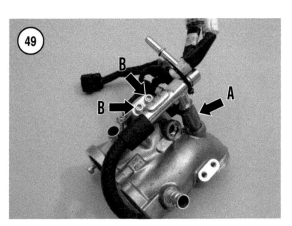

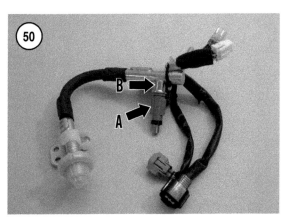

12. Install a new O-ring onto the rear cylinder head output fitting (A, **Figure 38**).

13. Press the output fitting into the port in the rear head, and install the cylinder head output fitting bolt (A, **Figure 37**). Tighten the bolt to 10 N•m.

14. Connect the thermostat inlet hose (A, **Figure 36**) to the rear cylinder head fitting, and securely tighten the clamp.

15. Repeat Steps 12-14 and install the front cylinder head output fitting (B, **Figure 37**) and its hose (B, **Figure 36**).

16. Install the finished cover onto each cylinder head (Chapter Four).

17. Install the left engine cover (Chapter Fifteen).

18. Install the throttle body (this chapter).

19. Add coolant (Chapter Three).

20. Start the engine and check for coolant leaks.

Disassembly

1. Disconnect the fuel injector connector (A, **Figure 45**). Label the connector and its injector either front or rear. Note that the injector is centered between the arms of the holder (B, **Figure 45**).

2. Remove the fuel rail bolts (**Figure 46**), and lift the fuel rail. The injector may come out with the fuel rail or it may remain in the intake manifold fitting.

3. Pull the fuel injector (**Figure 47**) from its port in the intake manifold or on the fuel rail.

4. Remove and discard the injector's O-ring (A, **Figure 48**) and gasket (B).

5. Repeat for the remaining injector (A, **Figure 49**).

Assembly

1. Lubricate a new O-ring with lithium-soap grease, and install the O-ring (A, **Figure 48**) onto the injector.

2. Press the fuel injector (A, **Figure 50**) into its port (B) on the fuel rail until it bottoms. Make sure the injector is centered between arms of the holder (B, **Figure 45**).

3. Lubricate a new gasket (B, **Figure 48**) with lithium-soap grease, and seat the gasket in the intake manifold port.

CAUTION
Do not tear the gasket when installing the fuel injectors.

4. Position the fuel rail over the intake manifold so the fuel injector aligns with its gasket, and gently press the rail straight into the manifold until the injector bottoms (A, **Figure 49**).

5. Install the fuel rail bolts (B, **Figure 49**). Tighten them to 10 N•m (89 in.-lb.).

6. Repeat Steps 1-5, and install the remaining fuel injector.

Inspection

1. Inspect each fuel injector (**Figure 48**) for damage.
2. Check the electrical terminals in the fuel injector and the subharness for corrosion or damage.
3. Inspect the injector nozzle for carbon buildup or damage.
4. Repeat for the other fuel injector.
5. Inspect the fuel injector ports in the fuel rail (B, **Figure 50**) and intake manifold (**Figure 51**) for contamination. Clean as needed.
6. Replace any part that is worn or damaged.

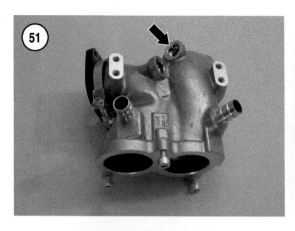

FUEL INJECTOR

Remove, install and inspect the fuel injectors as described in *Intake Manifold* in this chapter.

AIR TEMPERATURE (AT) SENSOR

Removal/Installation

1. Securely support the motorcycle on a level surface.
2. Remove the bolt, and remove the sensor (A, **Figure 52**) from its mount on the left side of the lower fork bridge.
3. Disconnect the AT sensor connector (B, **Figure 52**), and remove the sensor.
4. Installation is the reverse of removal. Tighten the AT sensor bolt to 7 N•m (62 in.-lb.).

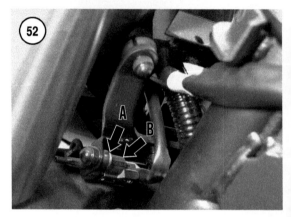

Resistance Test

1. Remove the AT sensor as described in this section.
2. Fill a beaker or pan with water, and place it on a stove or hot plate.

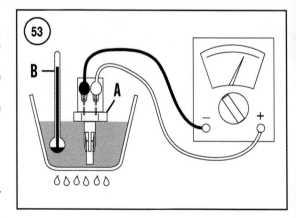

> *NOTE*
> *The AT sensor (A, **Figure 53**) and thermometer (B) must not touch the container sides or bottom. If either does, it will result in a false reading.*

3. Place a thermometer in the pan of water. Use a cooking or candy thermometer that is rated higher than the test temperature.
4. Mount the AT sensor so its sensing tip and the threaded portion of the body are submerged as shown in A, **Figure 53**.

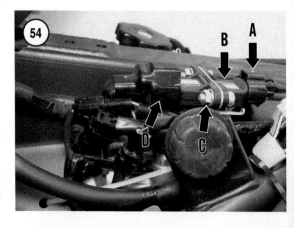

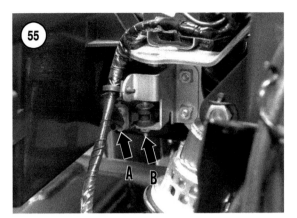

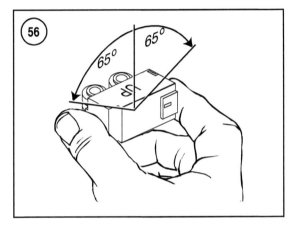

5. Attach an ohmmeter to the AT sensor terminals. Gradually heat the water, and let it cool down to 80° C (176° F). Note the resistance of the AT sensor when the water temperature cools to the specified value.

6. Replace the AT sensor if the reading is outside the specified range at the given temperature (**Table 2**).

INTAKE AIR PRESSURE (IAP) SENSOR

Removal/Installation

1. Remove the fuel tank as described in this chapter.

2. Remove the left engine cover (Chapter Fifteen).

3. Roll back the boot, and disconnect the connector (A, **Figure 54**) from the IAP sensor (B). Label the connector and the sensor.

4. Remove the nut (C, **Figure 54**) from each sensor bolt, and remove the sensor from the bracket. Disconnect the hose from the bottom of the sensor. Label the hose.

5. If the remaining cylinder's sensor (D, **Figure 54**) is not being serviced, remount it so it will not be damaged. Finger-tighten the nuts and bolts.

6. Installation is the reverse of removal.

    a. Connect the correct hose and connector to each sensor.

    b. Tighten the IAP sensor nut/bolt to 10 N•m (89 in.-lb.).

Output Voltage Test

1. Remove the fuel tank as described in this chapter.

2. Remove the left engine cover (Chapter Fifteen).

3. Back probe the harness side of the relevant IAP sensor connector (A, **Figure 54**). Connect the voltmeter positive test probe to the pink terminal (front cylinder) or to the pink/white terminal (rear cylinder) in the IAP sensor connector.

4. Connect the negative test probe to the black/blue terminal in the connector.

5. Turn the main switch on, and measure the output voltage. It should be within the range specified in **Table 2**.

LEAN ANGLE SENSOR

Removal/Installation

1. Remove the battery box (Chapter Nine).

2. Disconnect the lean angle sensor connector (A, **Figure 55**).

3. Remove the mounting nuts and bolts (B, **Figure 55**), and pull the sensor from the mount.

4. Installation is the reverse of removal. Tighten mounting hardware securely.

Output Voltage Test

1. Remove the lean angle sensor as described in this section.

2. Reconnect the sensor connector (A, **Figure 55**).

3. Back probe the connector and connect a voltmeter positive test probe to the yellow/green terminal in the connector. Connect the negative test probe to the connector's black/blue terminal.

4. Position the sensor so the side marked UP faces up.

5. Hold the sensor parallel to the floor, turn on the main switch and record the voltage.

6. Tilt the sensor 65° (**Figure 56**), and record the voltage.

7. Replace the sensor if each reading is not within specification (**Table 2**).

OXYGEN (O₂) SENSOR

Removal/Installation

1. Remove the rear cylinder exhaust pipe as described in this chapter.

2. Remove the oxygen sensor (A, **Figure 57**) from the exhaust pipe.

3. Installation is the reverse of removal. Tighten the oxygen sensor to 44 N•m (32.5 ft.-lb.).

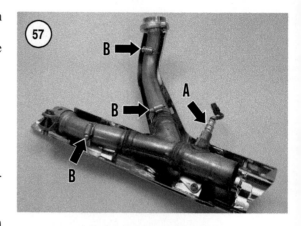

ELECTRONIC CONTROL UNIT (ECU)

Removal/Installation

1. Securely support the motorcycle on a level surface.

2. Remove the rear seat (Chapter Fifteen).

3. Remove the tool tray as described in *Battery* in Chapter Nine.

4. Lift the ECU (**Figure 58**) from its mount next to the battery.

5. Disconnect the large connector (A, **Figure 59**) and the small connector (B) from the ECU, and remove the ECU.

6. Installation is the reverse of removal. Make sure each connector securely mates with its ECU mate.

THROTTLE CABLE

Removal/Installation

1. Securely support the motorcycle on a level surface.

2. Remove the frame neck covers, fuel tank and air filter housing as described in this chapter.

3. Note how the throttle cables (**Figure 60**) are routed through the holders on the upper fork bridge and along the main frame backbone. The new cable must be rerouted along the same path.

4. Loosen the locknut (A, **Figure 61**), remove the return cable (B) from the throttle body bracket, and disengage the cable end from the throttle wheel.

5. Loosen the other locknut and disengage the pull cable (C, **Figure 61**) from the throttle wheel.

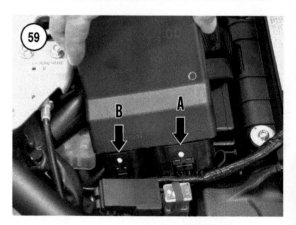

6. Remove the front brake master cylinder (Chapter Fourteen). Suspend the master cylinder from the motorcycle. Keep it upright so air cannot enter the brake like.

7. Remove the clamp screw (A, **Figure 62**) from the pull cable clamp.

8. Remove the mounting screws (B, **Figure 62**) and separate the halves of the right handlebar switch assembly.

9. Disengage the ends (A, **Figure 63**) of both the pull and return cables from the throttle drum. Remove each cable from the switch housing.

NOTE
The piece of string in the next step is used to pull the new throttle cable

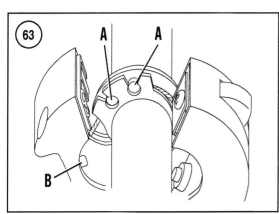

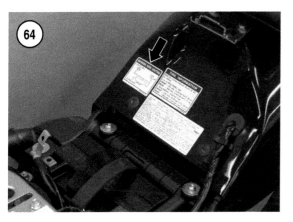

through the frame so the cable will be properly routed.

10. Tie a piece of heavy string or cord to the cable ends at the throttle body. Wrap this end with tape. Tie the other end of the string to the frame.

11. Starting at the handlebar, carefully pull the throttle cable along the frame and through the holders on the fork bridge. Make sure the attached string follows the same path as the throttle cable.

12. Untie the string from the old cable, and tie it to the throttle body ends of the new cables.

13. Pull the string back through the frame, routing the new cable through the same path as the old.

14. Remove the string, and lubricate the ends of the new cable with lithium-soap grease.

15. At the throttle body, connect the return cable end (B, **Figure 61**) to the throttle wheel. Fit the cable into the bracket, and secure it in place with the locknut (A, **Figure 61**).

16. At the throttle body connect the pull cable (C, **Figure 61**) to the throttle wheel. Fit the cable to the bracket and secure it in place with the locknut.

17. At the handlebar, lubricate the ends of the new cable with lithium-soap grease. Feed the cables through their ports in the rear half of the switch housing, and connect the cable ends (A, **Figure 63**) to the throttle grip. Make sure the cables rests in the grooves of the throttle drum.

18. Reinstall the handlebar switch onto the handlebar, and install the screws (B, **Figure 62**). The pin (B, **Figure 63**) on the switch housing must engage the hole in the handlebar, and the outboard edge of the switch must engage the slot in the throttle grip assembly.

19. Set the cable clamp into place on the housing, and install clamp screw (A, **Figure 62**).

20. Operate the throttle grip. Check that the throttle linkage operates correctly without binding.

21. Adjust throttle cable free play as described in Chapter Three.

22. Reinstall the frame neck covers, the air filter housing and fuel tank as described in this chapter.

23. Start the engine. Turn the handlebar from side to side without operating the throttle. If the engine speed increases as the handlebar is turned, the throttle cable is routed incorrectly. Recheck the cable routing.

EVAPORATIVE EMISSIONS CONTROL SYSTEM (CALIFORNIA MODELS)

All California models are equipped with an evaporative emission control system, which consists of a charcoal canister, rollover valve, assorted hoses and modified throttle body and fuel tank. A schematic of the EVAP system is on the label affixed to the rear fender (**Figure 64**).

The evaporative emission control system captures fumes from the fuel tank and stores them in a charcoal canister. When the motorcycle is ridden at high speed, the vapors pass through a purge hose to the throttle body and are burned. A gravity-operated rollover valve, which sits in line between the fuel tank and charcoal canister, assures that the fumes remain in the canister until they can be safely burned.

Maintenance

Maintenance to the evaporative emissions control system consists of checking that the canister is securely mounted and inspecting the condition and routing of the hoses. Service to the emission control system is limited to replacement of damaged parts. Do not attempt to modify or remove the emissions control system.

1. The main switch must remain off during EVAP service.
2. Make sure all hoses are attached and that they are not damaged or pinched.
3. Replace any worn or damaged parts immediately.
4. There is no replacement interval for the canister provided that it is not damaged or contaminated.
5. When purchasing replacement parts (throttle body and fuel tank), buy parts made for California models. Parts sold for non-California models will not work with the emissions control system.

Rollover Valve Test

1. Remove the fuel tank and frame neck covers as described in this chapter.
2. Remove the finished covers from the front cylinder (Chapter Four).
3. Disconnect the hose (A, **Figure 65**) from each end of the rollover valve. Label each hose and fitting on the rollover valve.
4. Remove the mounting screw (B, **Figure 65**), and remove the rollover valve.
5. Test the rollover valve by performing the following:
   a. Hold the rollover valve with the large end facing up as shown in **Figure 66**.
   b. Blow into the A end of the valve. Air should flow from the B end.
   c. Hold the valve in the same position and blow into the B end. Air should not flow from the A end.
   d. Replace the rollover valve if it fails either portion of this test.
6. Install by reversing these removal steps.
   a. Position the rollover valve so its B end (**Figure 66**) faces down.

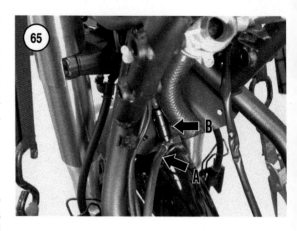

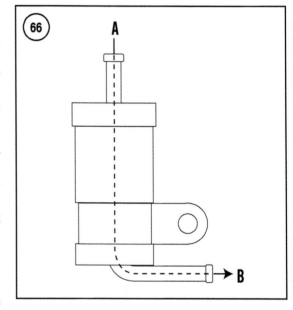

b. Make sure the hose clamps are tight.

Canister
Removal/Installation

1. Securely support the motorcycle on a level surface.

NOTE
The charcoal canister mounts to the bracket on the shift pedal/floorboard assembly.

2. Disconnect the purge hose (A, **Figure 67**) and breather hose (B) from their respective canister fittings. Label each hose and its fitting.
3. Remove each canister bolt (C, **Figure 67**) and its washer, and lower the canister from the mounting bracket. Account for the collar and damper installed with each mount.
4. Install by reversing these removal steps. Note the following:

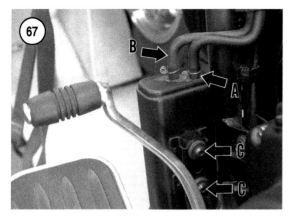

a. Connected each hose to the correct fitting on the EVAP canister.

b. Fit the charcoal canister onto its mount. Install each canister bolt with its washer. Make sure a damper and collar are in place on each mount. Tighten the canister bolts to 7 N•m (62 in.-lb.).

EXHAUST SYSTEM

Refer to **Figure 68**.

Removal

1. Securely support the motorcycle on a level surface.
2. Remove the coolant reservoir cap cover (Chapter Ten).
3. Disconnect the halves of the O_2 sensor connector (**Figure 69**).
4. Loosen the muffler clamp bolt (**Figure 70**).
5. Remove the muffler mounting bolts (**Figure 71**) from the inboard side of the muffler bracket, and slide the muffler from the rear-cylinder exhaust pipe. Discard the muffler gasket.
6. Loosen the clamp bolt (**Figure 72**) on the rear cylinder exhaust pipe.
7. Remove the header nuts (**Figure 73**) from the rear exhaust pipe.
8. Disengage the rear exhaust pipe from the rear-cylinder exhaust port (A, **Figure 74**). Pull the pipe assembly rearward, and disengage the rear pipe assembly from the front exhaust pipe. Discard the rear-cylinder exhaust gasket (B, **Figure 74**) and the exhaust pipe gasket.
9. Repeat Step 8, and remove the front exhaust pipe (A, **Figure 75**). Discard the exhaust gasket.
10. If necessary, remove the muffler bracket bolts (A, **Figure 76**), and lower the bracket (B) from the frame.

11. If necessary, remove the pipe guard from the either front, upper-rear or lower-rear exhaust pipes by performing the following:
   a. Note the location of each exhaust-pipe-guard clamp (B, **Figure 57**).
   b. Loosen the exhaust-pipe-guard clamp screw until the band releases the clamp fitting. Remove and discard the clamp.
   c. Repeat substep b for each remaining exhaust-pipe-guard clamp.
   d. Remove the guard from the exhaust pipe.
12. If necessary, disassemble the upper or lower exhaust pipe guard by performing the following:
   a. Remove each exhaust pipe guard bolt from the inboard side of the guard. Account for the washer and grommet installed with each bolt.
   b. Separate the inner guard from the outer guard.

Installation

1. If necessary, assemble the upper- or lower-exhaust-pipe guard by performing the following:
   a. Fit the inner guard against the outer guard.
   b. Install each bolt with a washer and grommet.
   c. Tighten the exhaust pipe guard bolts to 7 N•m (62 in.-lb.).
2. If necessary, install a guard on the front, upper-rear or lower-rear exhaust pipes by performing the following.
   a. Set the guard in place on the exhaust pipe.
   b. Wrap the band of a new clamp around the assembly, feed the band into the clamp fitting, and tighten the clamp screw (B, **Figure 57**).
   c. Repeat for each remaining clamp. Position the clamps in the locations noted during removal.
   d. Tighten the exhaust-pipe-guard clamp screws to 6 N•m (53 in.-lb.).
3. If removed, install the muffler bracket by performing the following:
   a. Fit the muffler bracket into place on the frame.
   b. Install the muffler bracket bolts (A, **Figure 76**). Tighten the bolts to 53 N•m (39 ft.-lb.).
4. Verify all exhaust header studs are tightened to 15 N•m (11 ft.-lb.).
5. Install a new exhaust gasket into the front-cylinder exhaust port.
6. Fit the front exhaust pipe (A, **Figure 75**) onto front cylinder exhaust port studs. Install and finger-tighten the header nuts (B, **Figure 75**).
7. Install a new exhaust gasket (B, **Figure 74**) into the rear-cylinder exhaust port, and install a new exhaust pipe gasket into the lower exhaust pipe fitting.
8. Fit the rear exhaust pipe into the rear-cylinder exhaust port (A, **Figure 74**), and slide the rear pipe assembly forward until the lower exhaust pipe is seated on the front exhaust pipe.

8

EXHAUST SYSTEM

(68)

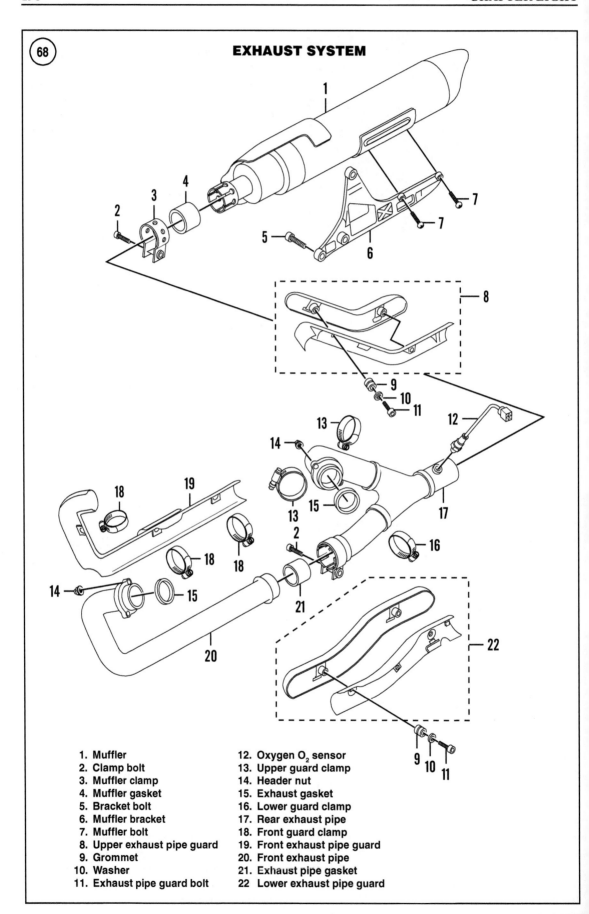

1. Muffler
2. Clamp bolt
3. Muffler clamp
4. Muffler gasket
5. Bracket bolt
6. Muffler bracket
7. Muffler bolt
8. Upper exhaust pipe guard
9. Grommet
10. Washer
11. Exhaust pipe guard bolt
12. Oxygen O_2 sensor
13. Upper guard clamp
14. Header nut
15. Exhaust gasket
16. Lower guard clamp
17. Rear exhaust pipe
18. Front guard clamp
19. Front exhaust pipe guard
20. Front exhaust pipe
21. Exhaust pipe gasket
22 Lower exhaust pipe guard

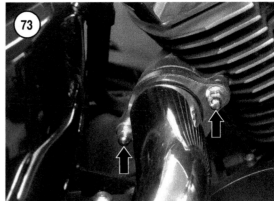

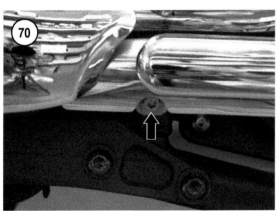

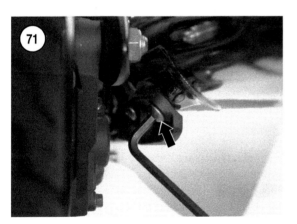

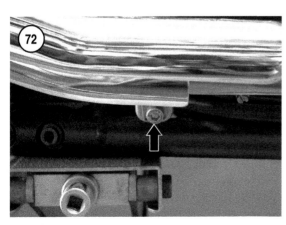

9 Install and finger-tighten the rear-cylinder header nuts (**Figure 73**).

10. Install a new muffler gasket into the muffler fitting.

11. Slide the muffler onto the rear exhaust pipe until the muffler is seated on the pipe.

12. Install and finger-tighten the muffler bolts (**Figure 71**).

13. Tighten the fasteners to the specification in the given order:

    a. Tighten the front header nuts (B, **Figure 75**) and then the rear header nuts (**Figure 73**) to 20 N•m (15 ft.-lb.).

b. Tighten the exhaust pipe clamp bolt (**Figure 72**) and then the muffler clamp bolt (**Figure 70**) to 12 N•m (106 in.-lb.).

c. Tighten the muffler bolts (**Figure 71**) to 35 N•m (26 ft.-lb.).

14. Connect the halves of the oxygen sensor (**Figure 69**).

15. Install the coolant reservoir cap cover (Chapter Ten).

ON-BOARD DIAGNOSTIC SYSTEM

NOTE
Most motorcycle dealerships and parts suppliers will not accept the return of any electrical part. Consider any test results carefully before replacing a component that tests only slightly out of specification, especially resistance.

The on-board diagnostic system monitors various sensors and actuators in the air/fuel, ignition and electrical systems. When it detects an error in a monitored component, the diagnostic system sets a trouble code and alerts the rider by turning on the engine trouble warning light in the meter assembly.

After the engine is stopped and the main switch turned on, a two-digit trouble code is displayed in the clock LCD portion of the meter assembly. **Figure 77** lists the trouble codes, the type of malfunction each code identifies, the likely cause(s) of the problem and any related diagnostic code. Once a trouble code is set, it remains stored in the engine control unit (ECU) until the problem has been corrected. Stored codes are erased by reinstating the ECU.

Under normal operating conditions, the engine trouble warning light turns on 1.4 seconds after the main switch is turned on, and it turns on while the starter button is pressed. If the warning light does not turn on under these conditions, the LED may be burned out. Inspect the meter assembly (Chapter Nine).

Fail-Safe Operation

Usually when an error is detected, the ECU sets the affected component to a preset value so the motorcycle can still operate. Even though, the motorcycle continues to run with a stored trouble code, perform the relevant troubleshooting procedures and eliminate the problem as soon as possible. If the problem cannot be solved, take the motorcycle to a dealership as soon as possible.

However, the motorcycle cannot operate when trouble codes 12, 19, 30, 41, 50, Er-1, Er-2, Er-3 or Er-4 have been set. In these instances, the ECU alerts the rider that the engine is inoperable by flashing the engine trouble warning light when the starter button is pressed.

Diagnostic Mode

In addition to performing self-diagnosis, the on-board diagnostic system lets a technician test various sensors and actuators. This is done by switching to the diagnostic mode and entering a diagnostic code.

When the diagnostic code for a sensor is entered, the system activates the sensor and displays the sensor's output in the meter assembly. For example, the diagnostic code for a coolant temperature sensor is *06*. When this code is entered, the meter assembly displays the coolant temperature. The state of the coolant temperature sensor can be determined by comparing the displayed temperature to the actual coolant temperature measured by the technician.

When the code for an actuator is entered, the ECU operates the actuator for a certain period of time. For example, the diagnostic code for front cylinder fuel injector (No. 1) is *36*. When this code is entered, the ECU operates the front cylinder fuel injector five times at one second intervals. By listening to the injector, a technician can confirm that the sensor is operational.

Refer to **Figure 78** and **Figure 79** for the various diagnostic codes, any data that is displayed in the meter assembly, as well as any action required to test the sensor or actuator.

Entering diagnostic mode

1. Turn the main switch off.
2. Turn the engine stop switch to run.
3. Partially remove the fuel tank to gain access to the fuel pump connector.
4. Disconnect the fuel pump connector (**Figure 80**).

(77) TROUBLE CODES

Trouble code	Malfunction	Probable cause	Related diagnostic code	Trouble-shooting chart
12	ECU does not receive normal signals from the crankshaft position (CKP) sensor.	Open or short circuit in wiring harness. Defective crankshaft position (CKP) sensor. Timing rotor malfunction. Improperly installed sensor. ECU malfunction.	None	**Figure 82**
13	Open or short detected in front cylinder intake air pressure (IAP) sensor circuit.	Open or short circuit in wiring harness. Defective front cylinder intake air pressure (IAP) sensor. ECU malfunction.	03	**Figure 83**
14	Front cylinder intake air pressure (IAP) sensor hose fault.	Detached, clogged, pinched or kinked intake air pressure (IAP) sensor hose. ECU malfunction.	03	**Figure 84**
15	Open or short detected in the throttle position (TP) sensor circuit.	Open or short circuit in wiring harness. Defective or improperly installed throttle position (TP) sensor. ECU malfunction.	01	**Figure 85**
19	Open detected in the blue/black wire to the ECU.	Open in the wiring harness. ECU malfunction.	20	**Figure 86**
21	Short or open detected in the coolant temperature (CT) sensor circuit.	Short or open in the wiring harness. Defective or improperly installed coolant temperature (CT) sensor. ECU malfunction.	06	**Figure 87**
22	Open or short detected in the air temperature (AT) sensor circuit.	Open or short in the wiring harness. Defective or improperly installed air temperature (AT) sensor. ECU malfunction.	05	**Figure 88**
24	Abnormal signal received from oxygen (O_2) sensor.	Open or short in the wiring harness. Defective or improperly installed oxygen (O_2) sensor. ECU malfunction.	None	**Figure 89**
25	Open or short in the rear cylinder intake air pressure (IAP) sensor circuit.	Open or short in the wiring harness. Defective rear cylinder intake air pressure (IAP) sensor. ECU malfunction.	04	**Figure 90**
26	Rear cylinder intake air pressure (IAP) sensor hose fault.	Detached, clogged, pinched or kinked intake air pressure (IAP) sensor hose. ECU malfunction.	04	**Figure 91**
30	Motorcycle overturned.	Motorcycle has fallen. ECU malfunction.	08	**Figure 92**
33	Malfunction detected in the primary coil lead of the front cylinder ignition coil.	Open or short in the wiring harness. Front cylinder ignition coil fault. ECU malfunction. Ignition cutoff circuit malfunction.	30	**Figure 93**

(continued)

8

(77) (continued) TROUBLE CODES

Trouble code	Malfunction	Probable cause	Related diagnostic code	Trouble-shooting chart
34	Malfunction detected in the primary coil lead of the rear cylinder ignition coil.	Open or short in the wiring harness. Rear cylinder ignition coil fault. ECU malfunction. Ignition cutoff circuit malfunction.	31	**Figure 94**
37	Engine idle speed high.	Open or short in the wiring harnessor subharness. Throttle body malfunction. Throttle cable malfunction. ISC valve stuck fully open. ECU malfunction.	54	**Figure 95**
41	Short or open detected in the lean angle sensor circuit.	Short or open in the wiring harness. Defective lean angle sensor. ECU malfunction.	08	**Figure 96**
42	The ECU does not receive normal signals from the speed sensor or a short or open detected in the neutral switch circuit.	Open or short in the wiring harness. Speed sensor malfunction. Defective transmission gear. Neutral switch malfunction. Defective shift drum. ECU malfunction.	07, 21	**Figure 97**
43	The ECU cannot monitor battery voltage.	Open or short in the wiring harness. ECU malfunction.	09	**Figure 98**
44	An error is detected while reading or writing CO adjustment values to the EEPROM.	ECU malfunction.	60	**Figure 99**
46	The ECU detects abnormal power supply to the fuel injection system.	Charging system malfunction.	None	**Figure 100**
50	Faulty ECU memory. When this malfunction is detected, a trouble code may not be displayed in the meter.	ECU malfunction. The ECU is not properly reading the program or writing data to its internal memory.	None	**Figure 101**
Er-1	No signal received from the ECU.	Open or short in the wiring harness. Defective ECU connector. Meter malfunction. ECU malfunction.	None	**Figure 102**
Er-2	No signal received from the ECU within a specified period.	Improper connection in the wiring harness. Meter malfunction. ECU malfunction.	None	**Figure 102**
Er-3	Data from the ECU cannot be received correctly.	Improper connection in the wiring harness. Meter malfunction. ECU malfunction.	None	**Figure 102**
Er-4	Non-registered data received from the meter.	Improper connection in the wiring harness. Meter malfunction. ECU malfunction.	None	**Figure 102**

ACTUATOR DIAGNOSTIC CODES

Diagnostic code	Item	System actuation	Test action
30	Front cylinder ignition coil	One second after the engine stop switch has been turned from off to on, the diagnostic system actuates front cylinder ignition coil 5 times at 1 second intervals, and it turns on the engine trouble warning light.	Use a spark tester to confirm that the ignition coil is firing. Refer to *Spark Test* in *Engine Will Not Start* in Chapter Two.
31	Rear cylinder ignition coil	One second after the engine stop switch has been turned from off to on, the diagnostic system actuates rear cylinder ignition coil 5 times at 1 second intervals, and it turns on the engine trouble warning light.	Use a spark tester to confirm that the ignition coil is firing. Refer to *Spark Test* in *Engine Will Not Start* in Chapter Two.
36	Front cylinder fuel injector	One second after the engine stop switch has been turned from off to on, the diagnostic system actuates the front cylinder fuel injector 5 times at 1 second intervals, and it turns on the engine trouble warning light.	Listen to the fuel injector to confirm that it is operating.
37	Rear cylinder fuel injector	One second after the engine stop switch has been turned from off to on, the diagnostic system actuates rear cylinder fuel injector 5 times at 1 second intervals, and it turns on the engine trouble warning light.	Listen to the fuel injector to confirm that it is operating.
50	Fuel pump relay (in the relay unit)	One second after the engine stop switch has been turned from off to on, the diagnostic system actuates the fuel pump relay 5 times at 1 second intervals, and it turns on the engine trouble warning light. The light is off when the relay is on; the light is on when the relay is off.	Listen to the relay unit to confirm it is operating.
51	Radiator fan relay	One second after the engine stop switch has been turned from off to on, the diagnostic system actuates radiator fan relay for 5 cycles (2 seconds on followed by 3 seconds off). The engine trouble warning light and the radiator fan are on when the relay turns on. They turn off when the relay turns off.	Listen to the radiator fan relay to confirm it is operating.
52	Headlight relay	One second after the engine stop switch has been turned from off to on, the diagnostic system actuates headlight relay for 5 cycles (2 seconds on followed by 3 seconds off). The engine trouble warning light and headlight turn on when the relay is on.	Listen to the headlight relay to confirm it is operating.
54	Idle speed control (ISC) valve	On second after the engine stop switch has been turned from off to on, the diagnostic system actuates the ISC unit. The ISC valve turns to its fully closed position and then moves to the standby position. The operation is completed within approximately 12 seconds.	The ISC unit vibrates during operation. Place a hand on the unit to confirm its operation.

8

SENSOR DIAGNOSTIC CODES

Diagnostic code	Item	Test action	Meter display
01	Throttle angle	Manually move the throttle to the fully opened and fully closed position. The meter displays the throttle angle of each position.	Fully closed: 12-22° Fully open: 87-107°
03	Pressure difference between the atmospheric pressure and the front cylinder intake air pressure	Turn the engine stop switch off and then on. Operate the starter – without starting the engine. If the displayed value changes, the sensor is good.	The meter displays the front cylinder intake air pressure.
04	Pressure difference between the atmospheric pressure and the rear cylinder intake air pressure	Turn the engine stop switch off and then on. Operate the starter – without starting the engine. If the displayed value changes, the sensor is good.	The meter displays the rear cylinder intake air pressure.
05	Air temperature	Measure the temperature as close to the air temperature sensor as possible. The AT sensor is good if the measured temperature equals value displayed in the meter.	The meter displays the air temperature.
06	Coolant temperature	Measure the coolant temperature at a point close to the coolant temperature sensor.	The coolant temperature sensor is good if the measured temperature equals the value displayed in the meter. The meter displays the temperature of the engine coolant.
07	Vehicle speed pulse	Rotate the rear wheel and note the meter. The displayed number should increase as the rear wheel is rotated.	The meter displays the number of pulses generated when the rear wheel is turned. This number is cumulative and increase sequentially from 0 to 999. It resets to 0 once 999 is reached.
08	Lean angle sensor	Displays the voltage generated by the lean angle sensor. Note the voltage when the motorcycle is held upright and when it is leaned more the 65°.	Upright: 0.4-1.4 volts Overturned: 3.7-4.4 volts
09	Fuel system voltage	Turn the engine stop switch off and then on. The system displays the value of the fuel system supply voltage (battery voltage). Measure battery voltage and compare the displayed value to the measured value.	Approximately 12 volts.
20	Sidestand switch	Displays the on/off status of the sidestand switch when the transmission is in gear. Manually move the sidestand to the indicated positions and note the display.	Stand retracted: on Stand extended: off

(continued)

79 (continued)

Diagnostic code	Item	Test action	Meter display
21	Neutral switch	Displays the on/off status of the neutral switch. Switch the transmission to the indicated setting and note the display.	Transmission in neutral: on Transmission in gear: off
60	EEPROM fault	The meter displays a cylinder fault code to identify the portion of the EEPROM that is faulty.	00 = No fault 01 = Fault in cylinder No. 1 (front) 02 = Fault in cylinder No. 2 (rear) If a fault exists in both cylinders, the display alternates between 01 and 02 every two seconds.
61	Trouble-code history	Sequentially displays the trouble codes that have occurred once and been corrected. If multiple codes are stored, the different codes are displayed at two second intervals. Once all stored codes are displayed, process is repeated.	Displays codes 12-70 sequentially. 00 = No codes stored in history
62	Trouble-code history erasure	Displays the total number of trouble codes (up to 25) that have been stored. The trouble codes are erased from history when the engine stop switch is turned from off to run.	Displays stored total (1-25). 00 is displayed when no trouble codes are stored.
70	Control number	The meter displays the program control number (00-255).	

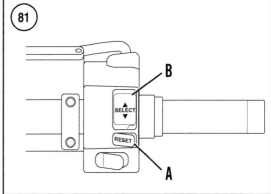

NOTE
In Step 4, all portions of the meter display go blank except for the clock and trip displays.

5. Press and hold the RESET switch (A, **Figure 81**) and the up side of the SELECT switch (B). While still holding both switches, turn the main switch on and continue to hold the switches until *dIAG* appears in the clock display. This may take 8 seconds or more.

6. Simultaneously press and hold the RESET switch and the up side of the SELECT switch until *d01* ap-

pears in the clock display. This may take 2 seconds or more.

7. Turn the engine stop switch off.

8. Press the SELECT and RESET switches to display a particular diagnostic code. Pressing the up side of the SELECT switch toggles upward through the diagnostic codes (01-70). Pressing the down side of the SELECT switch toggles downward through the diagnostic codes (70-01). To rapidly scroll through the codes, press and hold the up or down side of the SELECT switch for one second. Release the switch when the desired diagnostic code is displayed in the clock display.

TROUBLE CODE 12: ECU DOES NOT RECEIVE NORMAL SIGNALS FROM THE CRANKSHAFT POSITION (CKP) SENSOR

Inspection item/probable cause	Operation and repair
Sensor installation	Check the CKP sensor for correct installation (Chapter Nine). Tighten the mounting screws as necessary.
Electrical connector	Inspect the CKP sensor connector and the ECU connectors for loose or corroded terminals. Check the locking condition of each connector. Repair or replace a connector as necessary.
Open or short in the wiring	Check the continuity on each indicated wire between the CKP sensor connector and the ECU connector. 1. Gray 2. Black/blue Also check for a short on each wire. Repair a defective wire.
Defective CKP sensor	Perform the CKP sensor resistance test (Chapter Nine). Replace the sensor if it is out of specification.
ECU REINSTATEMENT METHOD AFTER THE PROBLEM IS CORRECTED	Crank the engine.

a. To test a sensor, use the SELECT and RESET buttons to displays the sensor's diagnostic code. The ECU activates that sensor, and the meter assembly displays the sensor's output. The sensor is good if the meter displays the information indicated in **Figure 79**.

b. To test an actuator, use the SELECT and RESET buttons to display the actuator's diagnostic code. Initiate the test by turning the engine stop switch from off to on. If the engine stop switch is already on, turn it off and then turn it back on. An actuator is good if it operates as described in **Figure 78**.

9. Turn the main switch off to exit the diagnostic mode.

Troubleshooting

Whenever the engine does not operate normally, check the engine trouble warning light. If the light is on or flashing, a trouble code has been set. Perform the procedures in *Engine Trouble Warning Light On* as described in this section. If the light is not on or flashing, perform the procedures in *Engine Trouble Warning Light Not On* as described in this section.

Note that two sets of codes are used during troubleshooting: a trouble code and a diagnostic code.

A trouble code indicated that the on-board diagnostic system has detected a particular error. During troubleshooting, locate the troubleshooting chart for a particular trouble code and perform the indicated tests.

A diagnostic code initiates a test. Once the system is switched to diagnostic mode, entering a diagnostic code tests a particular sensor or actuator to gather information during troubleshooting.

Engine trouble warning light on

Perform the following when the trouble warning light turns on or flashes.

1. Turn the main switch on, and record the trouble code displayed in the meter assembly.

2. Refer to **Figure 77** to determine the malfunction and likely causes related to that trouble code. Also locate the troubleshooting chart for this trouble code (**Figure 82-102**).

3. Turn to the indicated troubleshooting chart, and perform the test procedures in the listed order until the problem is resolved.

4. Once a fault has been corrected, reinstate the ECU by performing the ECU reinstatement action given at the end of the troubleshooting chart. This also erases the trouble code from memory.

TROUBLE CODE 13: OPEN OR SHORT DETECTED IN THE FRONT CYLINDER INTAKE AIR PRESSURE (IAP) SENSOR

Inspection item/probable cause	Operation and repair
Electrical connector	Inspect the front cylinder IAP sensor connector and the ECU connectors for loose or corroded terminals. Check the locking condition of each connector. Repair or replace a connector as necessary.
Open or short in the wiring	Check the continuity on each indicated wire between the front cylinder IAP sensor connector and the ECU connector. 1. Black/blue 2. Pink 3. Blue Also check for a short on each wire. Repair any defective wire.
Defective front-cylinder IAP sensor	1. Switch to the diagnostic mode, and enter diagnostic code 03. Refer to the *Sensor Diagnostic Codes* (**Figure 79**), and perform the indicated action. 2. Perform the IAP sensor output voltage test as described in this chapter. 3. Replace the sensor if it fails either test.
ECU REINSTATEMENT METHOD AFTER THE PROBLEM IS CORRECTED	Turn the main switch on.

Engine trouble warning light not on

Perform the following if the engine is not operating normally and the trouble warning light is *not* on or flashing.

1. Switch the system to diagnostic mode as described in this section.

2. Check each of the following components by entering the relevant diagnostic code. Perform any action indicated in **Figure 78** or **Figure 79**.

a. Throttle position (TP) sensor – diagnostic code 01.

b. Front cylinder ignition coil – diagnostic code 30.

c. Rear cylinder ignition coil – diagnostic code 31.

d. Front cylinder fuel injector – diagnostic code 36.

e. Rear cylinder fuel injector – diagnostic code 37.

3. Note the following:

a. When checking the throttle position (TP) sensor (diagnostic code 01), the displayed specification should be within the indicated range when the throttle is fully opened and when fully closed.

b. When checking an actuator (diagnostic codes 30, 31, 36 and 37), make sure the device operates as described in the **Figure 78**.

4. Repair or replace any faulty component.

5. If all of the above components operate or are within specification, the fuel injection system is most likely operating correctly. Check the engine for a mechanical problem.

8

Figures 84-102 are on the following pages.

TROUBLE CODE 14: FRONT CYLINDER INTAKE AIR PRESSURE (IAP) SENSOR HOSE CLOGGED OR DISCONNECTED

Inspection item/probable cause	Operation and repair
Detached, kinked or clogged hose	Inspect the hose on the front cylinder IAP sensor. Reconnect, repair or replace the hose.
Sensor Installation	Make sure the sensor is securely mounted. Tighten the screws as necessary.
Electrical connector	Inspect the front cylinder IAP sensor connector and the ECU connectors for loose or corroded terminals. Check the locking condition of each connector. Repair or replace a connector as necessary.
Defective front-cylinder IAP sensor	1. Switch to the diagnostic mode, and enter diagnostic code 03. Refer to *Sensor Diagnostic Codes* (**Figure 79**), and perform the indicated action. 2. Perform the IAP sensor output voltage test as described in this chapter. 3. Replace the sensor if it fails either test.
ECU REINSTATEMENT METHOD AFTER THE PROBLEM IS CORRECTED	Start the engine and run it at idle.

TROUBLE CODE 15: OPEN OR SHORT DETECTED IN THE THROTTLE POSITION (TP) SENSOR

Inspection item/probable cause	Operation and repair
Sensor installation	Check the TP sensor for correct installation. Tighten the mounting screws as necessary.
Electrical connector	Inspect the TP sensor connector and the ECU connectors for loose or corroded terminals. Check the locking condition of each connector. Repair or replace a connector as necessary.
Open or short in the wiring	Check the continuity on each indicated wire between the TP sensor connector and the ECU connector. 1. Blue 2. Yellow 3. Black/blue Also check for a short on each wire. Repair any defective wire.
Open in the TP sensor	Backprobe the TP sensor connector and connect a digital voltmeter's positive test probe to the yellow terminal; connect the negative test probe to the black/blue terminal. Turn on the main switch, and measure the voltage. The sensor has an open if voltage equals 5 volts; replace the sensor.
Defective TP sensor	1. Switch to the diagnostic mode, and enter diagnostic code 01. Refer to *Sensor Diagnostic Codes* (**Figure 79**), and perform the indicated action. 2. Perform the TP sensor resistance test as described in this chapter. 3. Replace the sensor if it fails either test.
ECU REINSTATEMENT METHOD AFTER THE PROBLEM IS CORRECTED	Turn the main switch on.

TROUBLE CODE 19: A BREAK OR DISCONNECT OF THE BLUE/BLACK WIRE OF THE ECU IS DETECTED

Inspection item/probable cause	Operation and repair
Diagnostic Test/ECU connector	1. Switch to the diagnostic mode, and enter diagnostic code 20. Refer to *Sensor Diagnostic Codes* (**Figure 79**), and perform the indicated action. 2. Inspect the ECU connector for loose or corroded terminals. Check the locking condition of the connector. Repair or replace the connector as necessary.
Open or short in the wiring	Check the continuity on the blue/black wire between the ECU connector and the ignition switch. Also check for a short on the wire. Repair the wire if defective.
Defective sidestand switch	Check the continuity of the sidestand switch (Chapter Nine). Replace the sidestand switch if it fails the continuity test.
ECU REINSTATEMENT METHOD AFTER THE PROBLEM IS CORRECTED	If the transmission is in gear, retract the sidestand. If the transmission is in neutral, reconnect the wiring.

8

TROUBLE CODE 21: OPEN OR SHORT DETECTED IN THE COOLANT TEMPERATURE (CT) SENSOR

Inspection item/probable cause	Operation and repair
Sensor installation	Check the CT sensor for correct installation (Chapter Ten). If necessary, tighten the CT sensor to 18 N•m (13 ft.-lb.).
Electrical connector	Inspect the CT sensor connector and the ECU connectors for loose or corroded terminals. Check the locking condition of each connector. Repair or replace a connector as necessary.
Open or short in the wiring	Check the continuity on each indicated wire between the ECU connector and the CT sensor connector. 1. Black/blue 2. Green/white Also check for a short on each wire. Repair any defective wire.
Defective CT sensor	1. Switch to the diagnostic mode, and enter diagnostic code 06. Refer to *Sensor Diagnostic Codes* (**Figure 79**), and perform the indicated action. 2. Perform the CT sensor resistance test (Chapter Ten). 3. Replace the CT sensor if it fails either test.
ECU REINSTATEMENT METHOD AFTER THE PROBLEM IS CORRECTED	Turn the main switch on.

TROUBLE CODE 22: OPEN OR SHORT DETECTED
IN THE AIR TEMPERATURE (AT) SENSOR

Inspection item/probable cause	Operation and repair
Sensor installation	Check the AT sensor for correct installation as described in this chapter. Tighten the sensor as necessary.
Electrical connector	Inspect the AT sensor connector and the ECU connector for loose or corroded terminals. Check the locking condition of each connector. Repair or replace a connector as necessary.
Open or short in the wiring	Check the continuity on each indicated wire between the ECU connector and the AT sensor connector: 1. Brown/white 2. Black/blue Also check for a short on each wire. Repair any defective wire.
Defective CT sensor	1. Switch to the diagnostic mode, and enter diagnostic code 05. Refer to *Sensor Diagnostic Codes* (**Figure 79**), and perform the indicated action. 2. Perform the AT sensor resistance test as described in this chapter. 3. Replace the AT sensor if it fails either test.
ECU REINSTATEMENT METHOD AFTER THE PROBLEM IS CORRECTED	Turn the main switch on.

TROUBLE CODE 24: ABNORMAL SIGNAL
FROM THE OXYGEN (O_2) SENSOR

Inspection item/probable cause	Operation and repair
Sensor installation	Check the O_2 sensor for correct installation as described in this chapter. If necessary, tighten the oxygen sensor to 44 N•m (32.5 ft.-lb.).
Electrical connector	Inspect the oxygen sensor connector and the ECU connectors for loose or corroded terminals. Check the locking condition of each connector. Repair or replace a connector as necessary.
Open or short in the wiring	Check the continuity on each indicated wire between the ECU connector and the harness side of the oxygen sensor connector. 1. Gray/white 2. Red/white 3. Gray/black 4. Black/blue Also check for a short on each wire. Repair any defective wire.
Check the fuel pressure	Perform the fuel pressure test as described in *Fuel Pump* in this chapter. Replace the fuel pump if the pressure is out of specification.
Defective oxygen sensor	Replace the O_2 sensor as described in this chapter.
ECU REINSTATEMENT METHOD AFTER THE PROBLEM IS CORRECTED	Start the engine, and run it at idle.

TROUBLE CODE 25: OPEN OR SHORT DETECTED IN THE REAR CYLINDER INTAKE AIR PRESSURE (IAP) SENSOR

Inspection item/probable cause	Operation and repair
Electrical connector	Inspect the IAP sensor connector and the ECU connectors for loose or corroded terminals. Check the locking condition of each connector. Repair or replace a connector as necessary.
Open or short in the wiring	Check the continuity on each indicated wire between the rear cylinder IAP sensor connector and the ECU connector: 1. Black/blue 2. Pink/white 3. Blue Also check for a short on each wire. Repair any defective wire.
Defective rear-cylinder IAP sensor	1. Switch to the diagnostic mode, and enter diagnostic code 04. Refer to *Sensor Diagnostic Codes* (**Figure 79**), and perform the indicated action. 2. Perform the IAP sensor output voltage test as described in this chapter. 3. Replace the IAP sensor if it fails either test.
ECU REINSTATEMENT METHOD AFTER THE PROBLEM IS CORRECTED	Turn the main switch on.

8

TROUBLE CODE 26: REAR CYLINDER INTAKE AIR PRESSURE (IAP) SENSOR HOSE CLOGGED OR DISCONNECTED

Inspection item/probable cause	Operation and repair
Detached, kinked or clogged hose	Inspect the hose on the rear cylinder IAP sensor. Reconnect, repair or replace the hose.
Sensor installation	Make sure the sensor is securely mounted. Tighten the screws as necessary.
Electrical connector	Inspect the rear cylinder IAP sensor connector and the ECU connectors for loose or corroded terminals. Check the locking condition of each connector. Repair or replace a connector as necessary.
Defective rear-cylinder IAP sensor	1. Switch to the diagnostic mode, and enter diagnostic code 04. Refer to *Sensor Diagnostic Codes* (**Figure 79**), and perform the indicated action. 2. Perform the IAP sensor output voltage test as described in this chapter. 3. Replace the sensor if it fails either test.
ECU REINSTATEMENT METHOD AFTER THE PROBLEM IS CORRECTED	Start the engine and run it at idle.

TROUBLE CODE 30: MOTORCYCLE OVERTURNED

Inspection item/probable cause	Operation and repair
The motorcycle has fallen	Raise the motorcycle to an upright position.
Sensor installation	Make sure the lean angle sensor is securely installed.
Electrical connector	Inspect the lean angle sensor connector and the ECU connectors for loose or corroded terminals. Check the locking condition of each connector. Repair or replace a connector as necessary.
Defective sensor	1. Switch to the diagnostic mode, and enter diagnostic code 08. Refer to *Sensor Diagnostic Codes* (**Figure 79**), and perform the indicated action. 2. Perform the lean angle sensor output voltage test as described in this chapter. 3. Replace the sensor if it fails either test.
ECU REINSTATEMENT METHOD AFTER THE PROBLEM IS CORRECTED	Turn the main switch on. To start the engine, the main switch must be turned off and then on.

TROUBLE CODE 33: MALFUNCTION DETECTED IN THE PRIMARY LEAD OF THE FRONT CYLINDER IGNTION COIL

Inspection item/probable cause	Operation and repair
Electrical connector	Inspect the front cylinder ignition coil connector (primary side) and the ECU connectors for loose or corroded terminals. Check the locking condition of each connector. Repair or replace a connector as necessary.
Open or short in the wiring	1. Check the continuity on the orange wire between the front cylinder ignition coil connector and the ECU connector. 2. Check the continuity on the black/red wire between the front cylinder ignition coil connector and the right handlebar switch connector. 3. Also check for a short on each wire. 4. Repair any defective wire.
Defective front-cylinder ignition coil	1. Switch to the diagnostic mode, and enter diagnostic code 30. Refer to *Actuator Diagnostic Codes* (**Figure 78**), and perform the indicated action. 2. Check the continuity of the primary and secondary coils. 3. Perform the ignition coil resistance test (Chapter Nine). 4. Replace the ignition coil if it fails any test.
ECU REINSTATEMENT METHOD AFTER THE PROBLEM IS CORRECTED	Start the engine and run it at idle.

TROUBLE CODE 34: MALFUNCTION DETECTED IN THE PRIMARY LEAD OF THE REAR CYLINDER IGNITION COIL

Inspection item/probable cause	Operation and repair
Electrical connector	Inspect the rear cylinder ignition coil connectors (primary side) and the ECU connector for loose or corroded terminals. Check the locking condition of each connector. Repair or replace a connector as necessary.
Open or short in the wiring	1. Check the continuity on the gray/red wire between the ignition coil connector and the ECU connector. 2. Check the continuity on the black/red wire between the ignition coil connector and the right handlebar switch connector. 3. Also check for a short on each wire. 4. Repair any defective wire.
Defective rear-cylinder ignition coil	1. Switch to the diagnostic mode, and enter diagnostic code 31. Refer to *Actuator Diagnostic Codes* (**Figure 78**), and perform the indicated action. 2. Check the continuity of the primary and secondary coils. 3. Perform the ignition coil resistance test (Chapter Nine). 4. Replace the ignition coil if it fails any test.
ECU REINSTATEMENT METHOD AFTER THE PROBLEM IS CORRECTED	Start the engine and run it at idle.

8

TROUBLE CODE 37: ENGINE IDLE SPEED IS HIGH

Inspection item/probable cause	Operation and repair
Throttle valve does not fully close	Inspect the throttle valves as described in *Throttle Body* in this chapter. Check and adjust throttle cable free play (Chapter Three).
ISC valve is stuck fully open due to poor electrical connection	1. Check that the idle speed control (ISC) unit connector is securely connected to the ISC unit. 2. Check that the ISC subharness connector is securely connected to its harness mate.
ISC valve stuck open because it does not close when the main switch is turned off	Confirm ISC unit operation by placing a hand on the ISC unit and turning the main switch off. Vibration should be felt as the valve closes.
ISC valve not operating correctly	1. Switch to the diagnostic mode, and enter diagnostic code 54. Refer to *Actuator Diagnostic Codes* (**Figure 78**), and perform the indicated action. The ISC valve should move to the fully closed position and then open to the standby position. The ISC unit faulty if this does not occur. 2. If the ISC valve closes and opens to the standby position, start the engine. If the error occurs again, replace the throttle body as described in this chapter.
ECU REINSTATEMENT METHOD AFTER THE PROBLEM IS CORRECTED	Turn the main switch on and then off. The ISC valve returns to its original position. The ECU will be reinstated if the engine idles within specification once the engine is started.

TROUBLE CODE 41: OPEN OR SHORT DETECTED IN THE LEAN ANGLE SENSOR

Inspection item/probable cause	Operation and repair
Electrical connector	Inspect the lean angle sensor connector and the ECU connector for loose or corroded terminals. Check the locking condition of each connector. Repair or replace a connector as necessary.
Open or short in the wiring	Check the continuity of each indicated wire between the lean angle sensor connector and the ECU connector. 1. Blue 2. Yellow/green 3. Black/blue Also check for a short on each wire. Repair any defective wire.
Defective lean angle sensor	1. Switch to the diagnostic mode, and enter diagnostic code 08. Refer to *Sensor Diagnostic Codes* (**Figure 79**), and perform the indicated action. 2. Perform the lean angle sensor output voltage test as described in this chapter. 3. Replace the lean angle sensor it fails either test.
ECU REINSTATEMENT METHOD AFTER THE PROBLEM IS CORRECTED	Start the engine and run it at idle.

TROUBLE CODE 42: ABNORMAL SIGNAL RECEIVED FROM THE SPEED SENSOR OR OPEN CIRCUIT DETECTED IN THE NEUTRAL SWTICH

Inspection item/probable cause	Operation and repair
Speed Sensor Check	
Speed sensor or ECU connector	Inspect the speed sensor connector and the ECU connectors for loose or corroded terminals. Check the locking condition of each connector. Repair or replace a connector as necessary.
Open or short in speed sensor wiring	Check the continuity of each indicated wire between the speed sensor connector and the ECU connector. 1. Blue 2. White/yellow 3. Black/blue Also check for a short on each wire. Repair any defective wire.
Broken tooth on transmission gear	Inspect the primary drive gear that the speed sensor monitors (Chapter Six). Replace the gear as needed.
Defective speed sensor	1. Switch to the diagnostic mode, and enter diagnostic code 07. Refer to *Sensor Diagnostic Codes* (**Figure 79**), and perform the indicated action. 2. Perform the speed sensor voltage test (Chapter Nine). 3. Replace the speed sensor if it fails either test.

(continued)

AIR/FUEL, EMISSIONS AND EXHAUST SYSTEMS

97 (continued)

Inspection item/probable cause (continued)	Operation and repair
Neutral Switch Check	
Neutral switch or ECU connector	Inspect the neutral switch connector and the ECU connectors for loose or corroded terminals. Check the locking condition of each connector. Repair or replace a connector as necessary.
Open in the neutral switch wiring	1. Check the continuity of the sky blue wire between the neutral switch connector and the relay unit connector. 2. Check the continuity of the blue/yellow wire between the relay unit connector and the ignition switch connector. 3. Check the continuity of the blue/black wire between the ignition switch connector and the ECU connector. 4. Repair any defective wire.
Defective shift drum	Inspect the neutral post on the shift drum. Replace the shift drum as needed (Chapter Seven).
Defective neutral switch	1. Switch to the diagnostic mode, and enter diagnostic code 21. Refer to *Sensor Diagnostic Codes* (**Figure 79**), and perform the indicated action. 2. Check the continuity of the neutral switch (Chapter Nine). 3. Replace the neutral switch if it fails either test.
ECU REINSTATEMENT METHOD AFTER THE PROBLEM IS CORRECTED	Start the engine, and ride the motorcycle at a speed of 12-19 mph (20-30 km/h).

98

TROUBLE CODE 43: ECU DETECTS ABNORMAL VOLTAGE SUPPLIED TO THE FUEL SYSTEM

Inspection item/probable cause	Operation and repair
Electrical connector	Inspect the relay unit connector and the ECU connectors for loose or corroded terminals. Check the locking condition of each connector. Repair or replace a connector as necessary.
Open or short in the wiring	1. Check the continuity of each indicated wire between the relay unit connector and the ECU connector. a. Blue/red b. Red/blue 2. Check the continuity of the red wire between the relay unit connector and the starter relay connector. 3. Check the continuity of the blue/white wire between the relay unit connector and the diode 2 connector. 4. On 2007-2009 models, check the continuity of the black/red wire between the diode 2 connector and the right handlebar switch connector. 5. Also check for a short on each wire. 6. Repair any defective wire
Defective fuel pump relay in the relay unit.	1. Switch to the diagnostic mode, and enter diagnostic code 09. Refer to *Sensor Diagnostic Codes* (**Figure 79**), and perform the indicated action. 2. Perform the relay unit fuel pump relay test (Chapter Nine). 3. The fuel pump relay is faulty if it fails either test. Replace the relay unit (Chapter Nine). 4. If the fuel pump relay is within specification, replace the ECU.
ECU REINSTATEMENT METHOD AFTER THE PROBLEM IS CORRECTED	Start the engine and run it at idle.

TROUBLE CODE 44: ERROR DETECTED WHILE READING OR WRITING CO ADJUSTMENT VALUES TO THE EEPROM

Inspection item/probable cause	Operation and repair
Defective ECU	1. Switch to the diagnostic mode, and enter diagnostic code 60. Refer to *Sensor Diagnostic Codes* (**Figure 79**), and perform the indicated action. The ECU is faulty if a cylinder fault code is displayed. Take the motorcycle to a dealership for a known-good-unit test before replacing the ECU.
ECU REINSTATEMENT METHOD AFTER THE PROBLEM IS CORRECTED	Turn the main switch on.

TROUBLE CODE 46: POWER SUPPLY TO THE FUEL INJECTION SYSTEM IS NOT NORMAL

Inspection item/probable cause	Operation and repair
Electrical connector	Inspect the ECU connector for loose or corroded terminals. Check the locking condition of each connector. Repair or replace the connector as necessary.
Faulty battery	Check the battery state of charge (Chapter Nine). Recharge or replace the battery as needed.
Defective stator	Perform the stator resistance test (Chapter Nine). Replace the stator if it is out of specification.
Defective voltage regulator/rectifier	Perform the charging voltage test in *Voltage Regulator/Rectifier* in Chapter Nine. Replace the voltage regulator/rectifier if charging voltage is out of specification.
Open or short in the wiring	1. Check the continuity of the red wire between the battery and the main fuse. 2. Check the continuity of the wire between the main fuse and the ignition switch connector. (Check black/red to red). 3. Check the continuity of the brown wire between the ignition switch connector and the ignition fuse. 4. Check the continuity of the red/white wire between the ignition fuse and the ECU connector. 5. Also check for a short on each wire indicated in Steps 1-4. 6. Repair any defective wire.
ECU REINSTATEMENT METHOD AFTER THE PROBLEM IS CORRECTED	Start the engine and run it at idle.

TROUBLE CODE 50: FAULTY ECU MEMORY

Inspection item/probable cause	Operation and repair
Defective ECU	Replace the ECU. Take the motorcycle to a dealership for a known-good-unit test before replacing the ECU.
ECU REINSTATEMENT METHOD AFTER THE PROBLEM IS CORRECTED	Turn the main switch on.

TROUBLE CODES ER-1, ER-2, ER-3 OR ER-4

Note:
Perform the following tests when the meter displays any of the following trouble codes.
Er-1: No signal received from the ECU.
Er-2: No signal received from the ECU within a specified time.
Er-3: Data from the ECU received incorrectly.
Er-4: Non-registered data received from the ECU.

Inspection item/probable cause	Operation and repair
Electrical connector	Inspect the ECU connectors and the meter assembly connector for loose or corroded terminals. Check the locking condition of each connector. Repair or replace a connector as necessary.
Open or short in the wiring	Check the continuity of the yellow/blue wire between the ECU connector and the meter assembly connector. Also check for a short on the wire. Repair a defective wire.
Meter assembly malfunction	Replace the meter assembly (Chapter Nine).
ECU malfunction	Take the motorcycle to a dealership for a known-good-unit test before replacing the ECU.
ECU REINSTATEMENT METHOD AFTER THE PROBLEM IS CORRECTED	Turn the main switch on.

Tables 1-3 are on the following pages.

Table 1 FUEL SYSTEM SPECIFICATIONS

Item	Specification
Throttle body type	Mikuni ACW40
Throttle body ID mark	
2007 models	
U.S. and Canada models	3D81 00
California models	3D82 10
2008 models	
U.S. and Canada models	3D81 20
California models	3D82 30
Throttle valve size	No. 40
Engine idle speed	950-1050 rpm
Intake vacuum pressure	32.0-37.3 kPa (9.4-11.0 in. Hg)
Fuel injector model	NIKK INP-284
Fuel pump	
Test pressure	324 (47 psi)
Throttle cable free play (at throttle grip flange)	4.0-6.0 mm (0.16-0.24 in.)

Table 2 FUEL SYSTEM ELECTRICAL SPECIFICATIONS

Item	Specification
Air temperature (AT) sensor resistance	290-390 ohms @ 80° C (176° F)
Fuel level sender resistance	830-1720 ohms @ 25° C (77° F)
Lean angle sensor output voltage	
Less than 65°	0.4-1.4 volts
More than 65°	3.7-4.4 volts
Throttle position sensor	
Resistance	
2007 models	4.0-6.0 k ohms @ 20° C (68° F)
2008-2010 models	3.1-5.7 k ohms @ 20° C (68° F)
Output voltage (throttle closed)	0.63-0.73 volts
Intake air pressure (IAP) sensor output voltage	3.75-4.25 volts

Table 3 AIR/FUEL AND EXHAUST SYSTEM TORQUE SPECIFICATIONS

Item	N•m	in.-lb.	ft.-lb.
Air filter housing bracket bolt	10	89	–
Air filter housing bolt	4	35	–
Air temperature (AT) sensor bolt	7	62	–
Canister bolts (California models)	7	62	–
Cylinder head output fitting bolt	10	89	–
Exhaust system			
Exhaust header nut	20	–	15
Exhaust header stud	15	–	11
Exhaust pipe clamp bolt	12	106	–
Exhaust pipe guard bolt	7	62	–
Exhaust-pipe-guard clamp screw	6	53	–
Manifold clamp screw	4	35	–
Manifold boot bolt	10	89	–
Muffler bracket bolt	53	–	39
Muffler bolt	35	–	26
Muffler clamp bolt	12	106	–
Fuel level sender bolts	8	71	–
(continued)			

Table 3 AIR/FUEL AND EXHAUST SYSTEM TORQUE SPECIFICATIONS (continued)

Item	N•m	in.-lb.	ft.-lb.
Fuel pump bolt	6	53	–
Fuel rail bolts	10	89	–
Fuel tank bolts	23	–	17
Fuel valve screws	7	62	–
Ignition coil bracket bolts	7	62	–
Intake air pressure (IAP) sensor nut/bolt	10	89	–
Left engine cover bolt	10	89	–
Oxygen (O_2) sensor	44	–	32.5
Subtank bolts	10	89	–
Subtank bracket bolts	7	62	–
Throttle body bolts	10	89	–
*Refer to text.			

8

CHAPTER NINE

ELECTRICAL SYSTEM

This chapter contains service and test procedures for electrical system components. Fuel and cooling system electrical service are in Chapter Eight and Chapter Ten respectively. Refer to Chapter Three for spark plug service. Refer to Chapter Eight for the on-board diagnostic system.

Before working on any part of the electrical system, check the appropriate wiring diagram at the end of this manual. Also refer to *Electrical Testing* in Chapter Two. **Tables 1-4** are at the end of this chapter.

ELECTRICAL COMPONENT REPLACEMENT

Most motorcycle dealerships and parts suppliers will not accept the return of any electrical part. If the exact cause of an electrical system malfunction cannot be determined, have a dealership retest the specific system to verify test results. If a new electrical component is installed and the system still does not work, the unit, in all likelihood, cannot be returned for a refund.

ELECTRICAL CONNECTORS

Many electrical problems can be traced to damaged wiring, contaminated connectors or corroded terminals. Connectors can be serviced by disconnecting them and cleaning the terminals with electrical contact cleaner.

To prevent corrosion or contamination, pack electrical connectors with dielectric grease when reconnecting them. Dielectric grease does not interfere with current flow, and it seals and waterproofs electrical connectors. Only use this compound or an equivalent sealant designed for electrical use. Other materials may interfere with the current flow. Do not use silicone sealant.

Electrical connectors may not always be found in their original locations. To avoid errors, follow the electrical cable from the specific component to where it connects to the wiring harness or to another component. Refer to the wiring diagram for that particular model, and check the wire colors to confirm a connector has been correctly identified.

BATTERY

Warning

Always wear safety glasses when servicing the battery. Even though the battery is sealed, electrolyte could leak from a cracked battery case. Electrolyte is very corrosive and can cause severe burns as well as permanent injury. If electrolyte spills onto clothing or skin, immediately neutralize the electrolyte with a solution of baking soda and water. Flush the area with plenty of clean water.

The battery is a sealed, maintenance-free battery type. The battery electrolyte cannot be serviced.

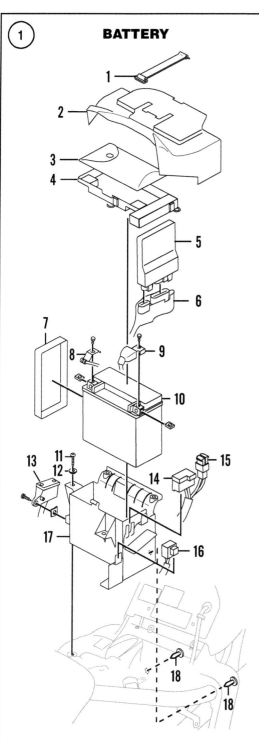

BATTERY

1. Strap
2. Battery cover
3. Tool kit
4. Tool tray
5. ECU
6. ECU connectors
7. Battery band
8. Negative cable
9. Positive cable
10. Battery
11. Battery box bolt
12. Collar
13. Rear brake
    master cylinder
    reservoir
14. Fuse box
15. Main fuse
16. Relay unit
17. Battery box
18. Trim clip

Never attempt to remove the sealing cap from the top of a maintenance free battery. It should never be removed.

When replacing the battery, use a maintenance-free type. Do not install a conventional lead-acid battery.

To prevent accidental shorts during electrical service, always disconnect the negative cable from the battery before beginning work.

Safety Precautions

1. Do not smoke or permit any open flame near a battery being changed or one that has been recently changed.
2. Do not disconnect live circuits at the battery. A spark usually occurs when a live circuit is broken.
3. Exercise caution when connecting or disconnecting a battery charger. Turn the power switch off before making or breaking connections.
4. Keep children and pets away from the charging equipment and the battery.

Removal/Installation

Refer to **Figure 1**.
1. Turn the ignition switch off.
2. Remove the rider's seat and the right side cover (Chapter Fifteen).
3. Remove the rubber cover from the battery.
4. Release the strap (A, **Figure 2**), and lift the tool tray from the battery. Note that the left side of the tray (B, **Figure 2**) sits atop and captures the ECU.

CAUTION
When removing the battery, always disconnect the negative cable first, and then disconnect the positive cable.

5. Make sure the main switch is off. Disconnect the negative cable from the negative terminal (A, **Figure 3**).

6. Remove the red protective cover (B, **Figure 3**), and disconnect the positive cable from the positive terminal.

7. Lift the battery from the battery box. If the battery is being replaced, remove the band from the battery, and install it on the new battery.

8. Inspect the battery box for wear or deterioration. Replace if necessary.

9. Install the battery by reversing the removal steps. Note to the following:

   a. Install the battery so its terminals face forward.

> *CAUTION*
> *Make sure each electrical cable is connected to the correct terminal. Connecting the cables backwards reverses the polarity and may damage the ignition system.*

   b. First connect the positive cable to the positive terminal (B, **Figure 3**), and then connect the negative cable to the negative terminal (A).

   c. Coat the battery connections with dielectric grease to retard corrosion.

   d. Install the red protective cap back over the positive terminal.

   e. Makes sure the left side of the tool tray (B, **Figure 2**) engages the ECU as noted during removal.

Inspection/Testing

Check the state of charge in a maintenance free battery by measuring its open circuit voltage. This is the voltage measured across the battery terminals once the battery has been disconnected from the motorcycle.

1. Remove the battery as described in this section. Do not clean the battery while it is mounted in the frame.

2. Set the battery on a stack of newspapers or shop cloths to protect the workbench surface.

3. Inspect the battery pads in the battery box for contamination or damage. Clean the pads and compartment with a solution of baking soda and water.

4. Check the battery case for cracks or other damage. If the battery case is warped, discolored or has a raised top, the battery has been overcharging or overheating.

5. Check the battery terminals and bolts for corrosion or damage. Clean parts thoroughly with a solution of baking soda and water. Replace severely corroded or damaged parts.

6. If corroded, clean the top of the battery with a stiff bristle brush using the baking soda and water solution.

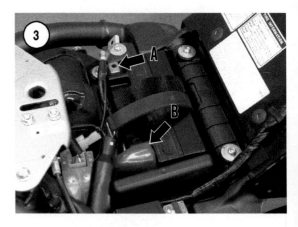

7. Check the cable terminals for corrosion and damage. If corrosion is minor, clean the cable terminals with a stiff wire brush. Replace severely worn or damaged cables.

8. Check the state of charge by measuring the battery's open circuit voltage as described in this section.

Open Circuit Voltage

Measure the open circuit voltage when battery temperature is 20° C (68° F). Use a digital voltmeter. Wait 30-minutes after operating the motorcycle before measuring open circuit voltage.

1. Remove the battery from the motorcycle as described in this section.

2. Connect a voltmeter across the battery terminals (**Figure 4**), and measure the voltage.

   a. The battery is fully charged if the open circuit voltage is 12.8 volts or greater.

   b. Charge the battery if the open circuit voltage is 12.7 volts or less.

   c. Replace the battery if the open circuit voltage is 12.0 volts or less.

Charging

A digital voltmeter and a charger with an adjustable amperage output are required when charging a maintenance free battery. If this equipment is not available, have the battery charged by a shop with the proper equipment. Excessive voltage and amperage from an unregulated charger can damage the battery and shorten its service life.

A battery self-discharges approximately one percent of its given capacity each day. If a battery not in use (without any loads connected) loses its charge within a week after charging, the battery is defective.

If the motorcycle is not used for long periods of time, an automatic battery charger with variable volt-

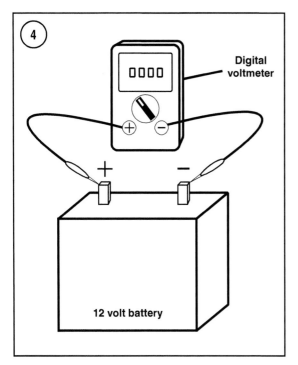

age and amperage outputs is recommended for optimum battery service life.

WARNING
During charging, highly explosive hydrogen gas is released from the battery. Charge the battery in a well-ventilated area away from open flames, including appliance pilot lights. Do not allow smoking in the area. Never check the charge of the battery by arcing across the terminals. The resulting spark can ignite the hydrogen.

CAUTION
Always disconnect the battery cables from the battery. If a battery is charged with the cables connected, the charger may damage the diodes within the voltage regulator/rectifier.

1. Remove the battery from the motorcycle as described in this section.
2. Set the battery on a stack of newspapers or shop cloths to protect the surface of the workbench.
3. Connect the positive charger lead to the positive battery terminal; connect the negative charger lead to the negative terminal.
4. Set the charger to 12 volts. If the output of the charger is variable, select the low setting.

CAUTION
Never set the battery charger to more than 4 amps. The battery will be dam-

aged if the charge rate exceeds 4 amps.

5. The charging time depends upon the discharged condition of the battery. Use the charging amperage and length of time suggested on the battery label. Normally, a battery should be charged at a slow rate of 1/10th its rated capacity.
6. Turn the charger on.
7. After the battery has been charged for the predetermined time, turn the charger off and disconnect the leads.
8. Wait 30 minutes, and then measure the open circuit voltage as described in this section.
   a. If the battery voltage is greater than 12.8 volts, the battery is fully charged.
   b. If the battery voltage is 12.7 volts or less, the battery is undercharged and requires additional charging. If the voltage is less than 12.0 volts, replace the battery.
9. If the battery remains stable for one hour, the battery is charged.
10. Install the battery into the motorcycle as described in this section.

Replacement

When replacing a battery, make sure the new battery is charged completely before installing it in the motorcycle. Failure to do so causes permanent damage and reduces the service life of the battery. Charging a new battery after it has been used does not bring its charge back to 100 percent. When purchasing a new battery from a dealership or parts store, verify its charge status. If necessary, have the store perform the initial or booster charge to bring the battery up to 100 percent charge before picking up the battery.

NOTE
Recycle the old battery. Most motorcycle dealerships will accept an old battery in trade when a new battery is purchased. Never place an old battery in the household trash. Most jurisdictions prohibit the disposal of any acid or lead (heavy metal) contents in landfills.

BATTERY BOX

Removal/Installation

Refer to **Figure 1**.
1. Remove the right side side cover and the rear fender (Chapter Fifteen).
2. Remove the battery as described in this chapter.

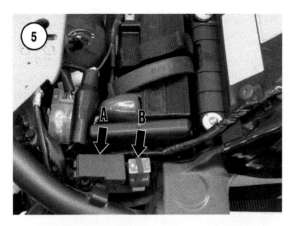

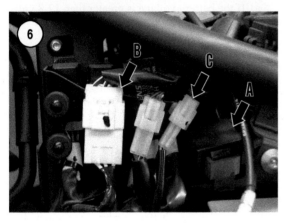

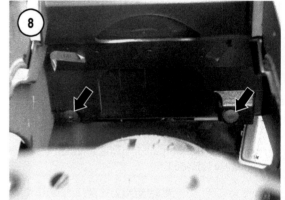

3. Remove the ECU (Chapter Eight).

4. Remove the fuse box (A, **Figure 5**), main fuse (B, **Figure 5**) and the relay unit (A, **Figure 6**) from their tangs on the battery box.

5. Remove the reservoir bolt (**Figure 7**) and separate the rear brake master cylinder reservoir from the battery box.

6. Remove the mudguard trim clips (**Figure 8**).

7. Remove the battery box bolts (**Figure 9**), and lift the battery box from the frame. Account for the collar installed with each bolt.

8. Installation is the reverse of removal. Note the following:

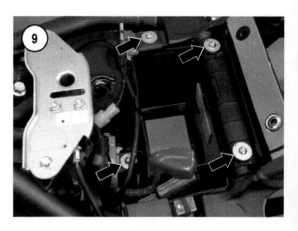

  a. The fuse box, main fuse and relay unit must securely engage the mounting tangs on the battery box.
  b. Tighten the battery box bolts (**Figure 9**) to 7 N•m (62 in.-lb.).
  c. Make sure each ECU connector securely connects to its mate on the ECU.

CHARGING SYSTEM

The charging system consists of the battery, main fuse, alternator and the regulator/rectifier assembly.

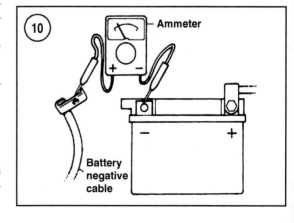

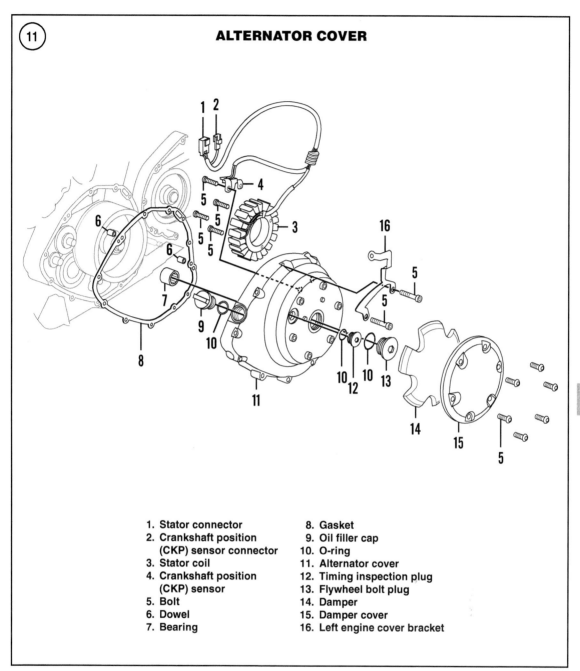

ALTERNATOR COVER

1. Stator connector
2. Crankshaft position (CKP) sensor connector
3. Stator coil
4. Crankshaft position (CKP) sensor
5. Bolt
6. Dowel
7. Bearing
8. Gasket
9. Oil filler cap
10. O-ring
11. Alternator cover
12. Timing inspection plug
13. Flywheel bolt plug
14. Damper
15. Damper cover
16. Left engine cover bracket

Troubleshooting

Refer to the *Electrical Troubleshooting* in Chapter Two.

Current Draw Test

1. Turn the main switch off.
2. Disconnect the negative cable from the battery as described in this chapter.
3. Connect an ammeter between the battery negative lead and the negative terminal of the battery (**Figure 10**).

4. The ammeter should read less than 0.1 mA. If the amperage is greater, there is a voltage drain in the system that will discharge the battery.

STATOR ASSEMBLY

Removal/Installation

The stator assembly includes the stator coil and the crankshaft position (CKP) sensor. The stator coil and CKP sensor are not available separately.

Refer to **Figure 11**.

1. Remove the alternator cover (Chapter Five).

2. Remove the wire clamp bolts and lift the wire clamp (A, **Figure 12**) from the alternator cover. Note that the left wire clamp bolt also secures the CKP sensor in place.

3. Remove the remaining CKP sensor bolt and release the CKP sensor (B, **Figure 12**).

4. Remove the stator bolts, and release the stator (C, **Figure 12**).from the cover.

5. Pry the wire grommet (D, **Figure 12**) from the cover.

6. Note how the stator assembly cable is routed through the cover, and remove the stator assembly and its cable.

7. Installation is the reverse of removal.
   a. Route the cable along the same path noted during removal.
   b. Apply threadlocking compound to the threads of the stator bolts, CKP sensor bolt, and wire clamp bolts. Tighten the bolts to 10 N•m (89 in.-lb.).
   c. Seat the grommet (D, **Figure 12**) in the cover. Apply sealant to the top of the grommet once it is seated.
   d. Reinstall the alternator cover (Chapter Five).

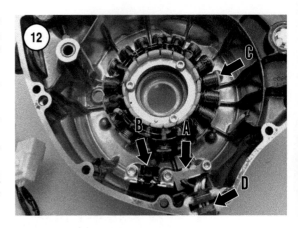

Stator Coil Resistance Test

In order to get accurate resistance measurements, the stator assembly must be warm (minimum temperature is 20° C [68° F]). If necessary, start the engine and let it warm up to normal operating temperature.

1. Remove the left side cover (Chapter Fifteen).

2. Separate the halves of the stator connector (B, **Figure 6**).

3. Connect the ohmmeter test probes to a pair of terminals in the stator side of the connector.

4. Check the reading on the meter, and record the resistance for that pair of terminals.

5. Repeat Step 3 and Step 4 and measure the resistance between each of the remaining terminal pairs. Take a total of three readings. Refer to **Figure 13**.

6. The stator is faulty and must be replaced if any resistance is outside the specified range (**Table 1**).

7. Use the ohmmeter to check the continuity between each terminal in the stator side of the connector and ground. If any reading indicates continuity, one or more of the stator wires is shorted to ground. Replace the stator assembly.

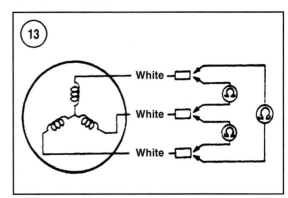

VOLTAGE REGULATOR/RECTIFIER

The voltage rectifier converts the alternating current generated by the alternator into direct current. The voltage regulator maintains the voltage to the battery and additional electrical loads (lights, igni-

tion, etc.) at a constant voltage regardless of variations in engine speed and load.

Removal/Installation

The voltage regulator/rectifier mounts to the left side of the frame.

1. Securely support the motorcycle on a level surface.

2. Disconnect the negative cable from the battery as described in this chapter.

3. Remove the cover screws (A, **Figure 14**). Pull the rear of the cover (B, **Figure 14**) until it disengages from the grommet, and remove the cover.

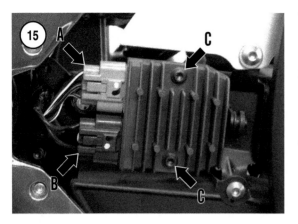

4. Disconnect the gray (A, **Figure 15**) and black connectors (B) from their mates on the regulator/rectifier. Label the connectors and their mates.

5. Remove the regulator/rectifier bolts (C, **Figure 15**), and remove the regulator/rectifier from the frame.

6. Install by reversing these removal steps while noting the following:

   a. Tighten the voltage regulator/rectifier bolts and the cover bolts to 7 N•m (62 in.-lb.).

   b. Apply a dielectric compound to the electrical connector before reconnecting it.

   c. Connect the gray (A, **Figure 15**) and black connectors (B) to their original mates on the regulator/rectifier.

Charging Voltage Test

Use a 20 DC voltmeter to perform this test.

1. Connect a shop tachometer to the spark plug lead on the front cylinder according to the manufacturer's instructions.

2. Remove the cover (B, **Figure 14**) from the regulator rectifier.

3. Back probe the black regulator/rectifier connector (B, **Figure 15**) and connect the voltmeter positive test probe to the regulator/rectifier-connector's

black/red terminal. Connect the negative test probe to the connector's black terminal.

4. Start the engine and increase engine speed to approximately 5,000 rpm. The measured voltage should equal the charging voltage specified in **Table 1**.

5. If the charging voltage is out of specification, check the stator coil resistance as described in *Stator Assembly* in this chapter.

IGNITION SYSTEM

Ignition timing and advance are maintained without adjustment. Ignition timing inspection procedures given in Chapter Three can be used to determine if the ignition system is operating properly.

Precautions

Certain measures must be taken to protect the transistorized ignition system. Instantaneous damage to the semiconductors in the system will occur if the following precautions are not observed.

1. Never connect the battery backwards. If the battery polarity is incorrect, the voltage regulator, alternator and ECU will be damaged.

2. Do not disconnect the battery while the engine is running. The resultant voltage surge will damage the voltage regulator and possibly burn out the lights.

3. Keep all connections between the various units clean and tight. Be sure that the wiring connectors are firmly pushed together.

4. Do not substitute another type of ignition coil or battery.

5. Each solid state unit is mounted on a rubber vibration isolator. Be sure that the isolators are in place when replacing any units.

SPARK PLUG CAP

Resistance Test

1. Remove the finished covers from the cylinder heads (Chapter Four).

2. Disconnect the spark plug cap (**Figure 16**) from the spark plug, and remove the cap from the spark plug lead.

3. Measure the resistance between each end of the cap as shown in **Figure 17**.

4. Replace the spark plug cap if the resistance exceeds the specification in **Table 1**.

5. Repeat this test for the other spark plug cap.

IGNITION COIL

The ignition coil is a transformer that develops the high voltage required to jump the spark plug gap. Regular maintenance involves keeping the electrical connections clean and tight.

The models in this manual have two ignition coils mounted to a bracket on the frame main bone (**Figure 18**). The upper coil is the rear cylinder coil; the lower, the front cylinder coil. Occasionally check to see that the coils and bracket are mounted securely.

Removal/Installation

1. Remove the fuel tank (Chapter Eight).
2. Remove the finished covers (Chapter Four).
3. Disconnect the negative cable from the battery as described in this chapter.
4. Disconnect the spark plug cap (**Figure 16**) from the relevant spark plug.

> *NOTE*
> *Note how the ignition coil's secondary lead is routed through the frame. It will have to be rerouted along the same path during installation.*

5. Disconnect the two primary-coil spade connectors (A, **Figure 18**) from the terminals on the ignition coil. Label each connector and its related terminal.
6. Remove the ignition coil bolts (B, **Figure 18**), and remove the coil.
7. Install by reversing the removal steps. Note the following:
   a. Tighten the ignition coil bolts to 7 N•m (62 in.-lb.).
   b. Connect the primary coil connectors (A, **Figure 18**) to their original terminals.

Resistance Test

The ignition coils must be at a minimum temperature of 20° C (68° F) during this test. If necessary, start the engine and let it warm up to normal operating temperature. If the motorcycle will not start, heat the coils with a portable hair dryer.

1. Securely support the motorcycle on level ground.
2. Remove the fuel tank (Chapter Eight).
3. Remove the finished covers (Chapter Four).
4. Disconnect the negative cable from the battery as described in this chapter.
5. Disconnect the spark plug cap (**Figure 16**) from the relevant spark plug.
6. Disconnect the two primary-coil spade connectors (A, **Figure 18**) from the terminals on the ignition coil.

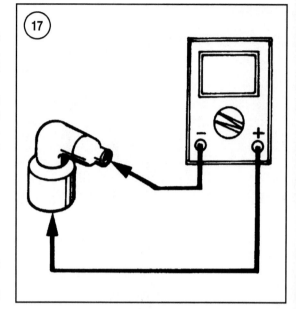

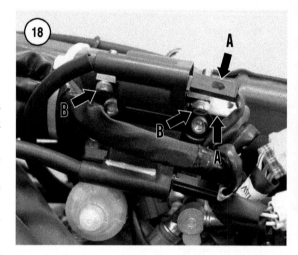

7. Measure the primary coil resistance by performing the following:
   a. Connect the ohmmeter positive test probe to the black/red terminal on the ignition coil. Connect the negative test probe to the orange terminal (front cylinder coil) or to the gray/red terminal (rear cylinder coil). Refer to A, **Figure 19**.
   b. Replace the ignition coil if the primary resistance is out of specification (**Table 1**).
8. Measure the secondary coil resistance by performing the following:
   a. Connect the ohmmeter positive test probe to the coil's black/red terminal. Connect the negative test probe to the spark plug lead (B, **Figure 19**).
   b. Replace the ignition coil if the secondary coil resistance is out of specification (**Table 1**).
9. Repeat this test for the other ignition coil.

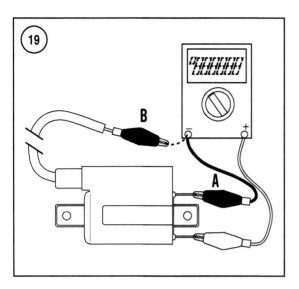

CRANKSHAFT POSITION (CKP) SENSOR

Removal/Installation

The CKP sensor is an integral part of the stator assembly. Remove the stator assembly as described in this chapter.

Resistance Test

1. Remove the left side cover (Chapter Fourteen).
2. Separate the halves of the CKP connector (C, **Figure 6**).
3. Connect the ohmmeter positive test probe to the gray terminal in the sensor side of the connector; connect the negative test probe to the sensor's black terminal.
4. Replace the stator assembly as described in this chapter if the CKP sensor resistance is out of specification (**Table 1**).

STARTING SYSTEM

When the starter button is pressed under the correct conditions, control current flows through the starter relay coil, which energizes the relay. The starter relay contacts close, and load current flows directly from the battery to the starter.

The starter only operates when the transmission is in neutral or when the clutch lever is pulled in while the sidestand is up. The starting circuit cutoff relay prevents the flow of control current to the starter relay unless one of these conditions has been met. The starting circuit cutoff relay is energized and the contacts close only when the neutral switch is closed (the transmission is in neutral) or when both the clutch switch and sidestand switch are closed (when the clutch lever is pulled in and the sidestand is up).

CAUTION
Do not operate the starter for more than 5 seconds at a time. Let it cool approximately 10 seconds, and then use it again.

Troubleshooting

Refer to *Electrical Troubleshooting* in Chapter Two.

STARTER

Operational Test

1. Securely support the motorcycle on a level surface, and shift it into neutral. Block the front wheel so it cannot roll in either direction.
2. Turn the main switch off, and disconnect the negative cable from the battery as described in this chapter.

WARNING
Once the battery positive lead is disconnected, make sure it cannot touch any metal on the motorcycle. This will result in a short.

3. Disconnect the electrical lead (B, **Figure 3**) from the positive battery terminal. Wrap the cable end with electrical tape, and secure the lead safely out of the way.
4. Reconnect the negative cable (A, **Figure 3**) to the battery.

WARNING
The test in the next step will probably produce sparks. Make sure no flammable gas or fluid is in the vicinity. Also make sure the jumper wire is as large as the battery cable. A smaller wire could melt.

5. Pull the boot back from the starter terminal (A, **Figure 20**).
6. Apply battery voltage directly to the starter by connecting a jumper from the battery positive terminal to the starter terminal. The starter should operate.
7. If the starter does not operate, repair or replace the starter as described in this section.

Removal/Installation

1. Securely support the motorcycle on a level surface.
2. Make sure the main switch is off.
3. Disconnect the negative cable from the battery as described in this chapter.

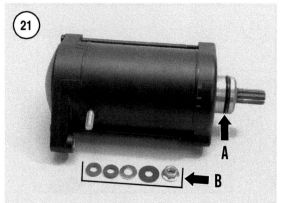

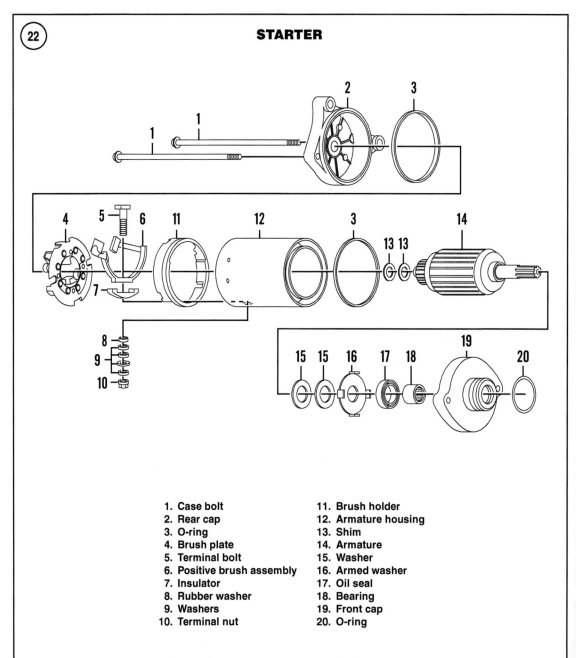

STARTER

1. Case bolt
2. Rear cap
3. O-ring
4. Brush plate
5. Terminal bolt
6. Positive brush assembly
7. Insulator
8. Rubber washer
9. Washers
10. Terminal nut
11. Brush holder
12. Armature housing
13. Shim
14. Armature
15. Washer
16. Armed washer
17. Oil seal
18. Bearing
19. Front cap
20. O-ring

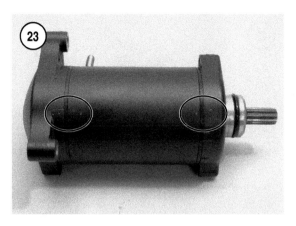

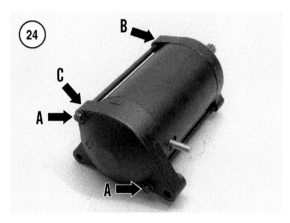

4. Pull back the rubber boot, and disconnect the cable from the starter terminal (A, **Figure 20**).

5. Remove the starter bolts (B, **Figure 20**). Pull the starter toward the right and remove it.

6. Remove and discard the O-ring (A, **Figure 21**).

7. Install by reversing these removal steps while noting the following:

   a. Install a new O-ring. Lubricate the O-ring with lithium-soap grease.

   b. Tighten the starter bolts (B, **Figure 20**) and the starter terminal nut (A) to 10 N•m (89 in.-lb.).

   c. Make sure the electrical connector is free of corrosion and is tight.

Disassembly

Refer to **Figure 22**.

1. If still installed, remove and discard the O-ring (A, **Figure 21**) from the front cap.

NOTE
The precise number and order of washers may vary. Record the quantity and type of washers during removal. Label each component as it is removed. Washers must be reinstalled in the same order to insulate the positive brush assembly from the housing.

2. Remove the nut from the terminal bolt. Remove the large fiber washer, steel washer, and two small fiber washers. Refer to B, **Figure 21**.

3. Note the indexing marks on the armature housing and on each cap (**Figure 23**). If these marks are not clearly visible, mark each end of the housing and each cap.

4. Remove the case bolts (A, **Figure 24**) from the housing.

5. Pull the front cap (B, **Figure 24**) from the armature shaft. Account for the armed washer (**Figure 25**). It may come out with the front cap or it may remain on the armature shaft.

NOTE
Record the quantity, type and thickness of the shims and washer used on both ends of the armature shaft. These shims and washers must be installed in their original order and positions.

6. Remove the armed washer (**Figure 25**) and washers (**Figure 26**) from the armature shaft. Store them in a labeled plastic bag.

7. Pull the rear cap (C, **Figure 24**) from the armature housing. Remove the shims (**Figure 27**) from the commutator end of the armature. Store them in a labeled plastic bag.

8. Pull the armature (A, **Figure 28**) from the front end of the armature housing. Discard the O-ring from each end of the housing.

9. Lift the brush plate (B, **Figure 28**) from the housing.

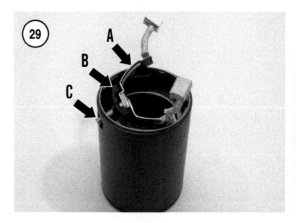

10. Remove the positive brush assembly (A, **Figure 29**) and the insulator (B) from the housing. Remove and discard the rubber washer (A, **Figure 30**).

11. Lift the brush holder (**Figure 31**) from the armature housing.

> *CAUTION*
> *Do not immerse the armature coil or armature housing in solvent. The insulation could be damaged. Wipe the windings with a cloth lightly moistened in solvent, and dry the windings with compressed air.*

12. Clean all grease, dirt and carbon from the components.

13. Inspect the starter as described in this section.

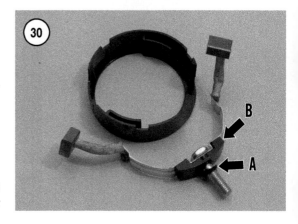

Assembly

1. Make sure the insulator (B, **Figure 30**) is in place on the terminal bolt, and install a new rubber washer (A).

2. Set the brush holder (**Figure 31**) into the rear of the armature housing.

3. Insert the terminal bolt (C, **Figure 29**) through the hole in the armature housing, and seat the positive brush assembly (A) into the brush holder.

4. Prepare the brush plate for installation by performing the following:

    a. Cut four 1.5 in. strips from a cable tie.

    b. Pull back the brush spring, and insert a strip (A, **Figure 32**) between the brush holder and the spring.

    c. Repeat substep b for each holder in the brush plate.

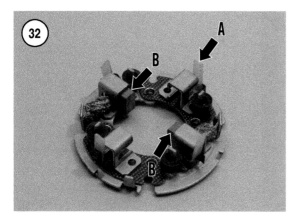

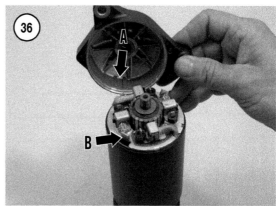

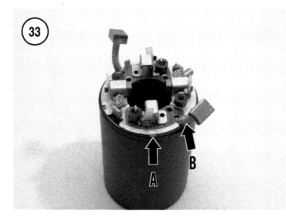

d. Press each negative brush (B, **Figure 32**) in its holder.

5. Install the brush plate so the plate's indexing tab (A, **Figure 33**) engages the cutout in the armature housing. Make sure each positive brush wire (B, **Figure 33**) sits in a cutout in the brush plate.

6. Press each positive brush into its holder in the brush plate (**Figure 34**).

7. Insert the armature into the housing until the armature bottoms against the brush holder. Make sure the commutator sits between the brushes in the plate. Refer to **Figure 35**. Exercise caution so the commutator is not damaged.

8. Pull the cable tie (**Figure 35**) from each brush holder so the spring presses the brush against the commutator.

9. Lubricate two new O-rings with lithium-soap grease, and seat an O-ring onto each end of the armature housing.

10. Install the shims (**Figure 27**) onto the commutator end of the armature. Reinstall the same number of shims removed during disassembly.

11. Install the end cap so the cap's slot (A, **Figure 36**) engages the tab (B) on the brush plate.

12. Install the correct number of washers onto the armature shaft (**Figure 26**) as noted during disassembly.

13. Seat the armed washer (**Figure 25**) into the front cap, and fit the cap (B, **Figure 24**) onto the armature housing. Make sure the indexing marks (**Figure 23**) noted during disassembly align.

14. Install the case bolts (A, **Figure 24**), and tighten them securely.

NOTE
The precise number and order of washers may vary. Install the washers in the order noted during disassembly.

15. Install the two small fiber washers, a steel washer and the large fiber washer, the steel washer and the nut. Tighten the terminal nut to 10 N•m (89 in.-lb.).

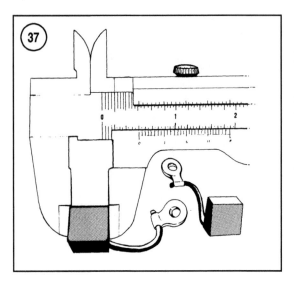

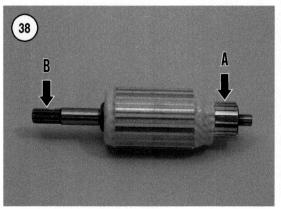

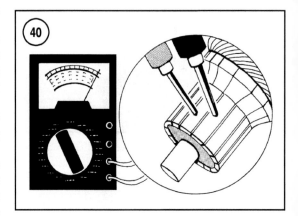

16. Lubricate a new front cover O-ring with lithium soap grease, and install it onto the front cover (A, **Figure 21**).

17. Clean all dirt and other contaminants from the mounting lugs. The lug areas service as part of the ground circuit for the starter so there must be good contact between the lugs and the crankcase.

Inspection

Replace the starter if any component is defective, worn to the service limit or out of specification.

1. Pull the spring away from each brush and pull the brush out of its holder in the brush plate. Measure the length of each brush (**Figure 37**). Replace the brush set, if the length of any brush is less than the wear limit listed in **Table 1**.

2. Use a spring gauge to measure the spring pressure of each brush spring. Replace the brush set if a spring pressure is outside the range specified in **Table 1**.

3. Inspect the commutator (A, **Figure 38**). The mica in a good commutator sits below the surface of the copper bars. Measure the mica undercut, the distance between the top of the mica and the top of the adjacent copper bars (**Figure 39**). If the mica undercut is less than the specification in **Table 1** have the commutator serviced by a dealership or electrical repair shop.

4. Inspect the commutator copper bars for discoloration. A pair of discolored bars indicates grounded armature coils.

5. Measure the diameter of the commutator. Replace the starter if the commutator diameter is less than the wear limit specified in **Table 1**.

6. Use an ohmmeter and perform the following:
   a. Check the continuity between the commutator bars (**Figure 40**). There should be continuity between pairs of bars.

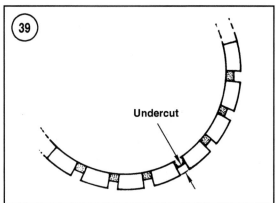

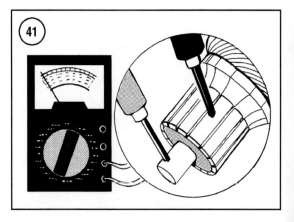

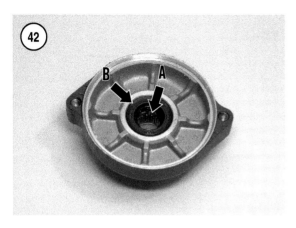

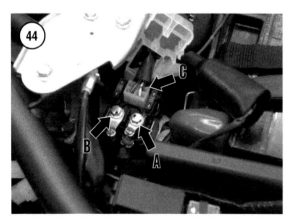

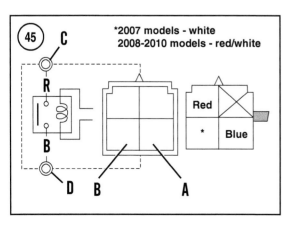

b. Check the continuity between the commutator bars and the armature shaft (**Figure 41**). There should be *no* continuity (infinite resistance).

7. Inspect the bearing (A, **Figure 42**) and oil seal (B) in the front cap for wear or damage.

8. Inspect the bushing (**Figure 43**) in the rear cap for wear or damage.

9. Inspect the armature shaft (B, **Figure 38**) for broken, cracked or excessively worn teeth.

10. Clean all dirt and contaminants from the mounting lugs of the rear cap. The lugs ground the starter so there must be good contact between the starter lugs and the crankcase.

STARTER RELAY

Removal/Installation

1. Securely support the motorcycle on a level surface.

2. Make sure the main switch is turned off. Disconnect the negative cable from the battery as described in this chapter.

3. If necessary, remove the seat bracket (Chapter Fifteen).

4. Press the lock arms on the starter relay cover and remove the cover.

5. Remove the terminal bolt, and disconnect the red battery lead (A, **Figure 44**) from the relay's positive terminal.

6. Remove the terminal bolt, and disconnect black starter lead (B, **Figure 44**), from the relay's negative terminal.

7. Disconnect the starter relay connector (C, **Figure 44**).

8. Remove the relay from its mounting tangs.

9. Installation is the reverse of removal. Pay attention to the following:

   a. Install the relay in the rubber mount.
   b. Make sure all connections are free of corrosion and are tight.
   c. Tighten the starter relay terminal bolts (A and B, **Figure 44**) to 7 N•m (62 in.-lb.).

Continuity Test

1. Securely support the motorcycle on a level surface.

2. Remove the starter relay as described in this section.

3. Use jumper wires to connect the positive battery terminal to the white (2007 models) or red/white (2008-2010 models) terminal (A, **Figure 45**) in the relay; connect the negative battery terminal to the blue terminal (B).

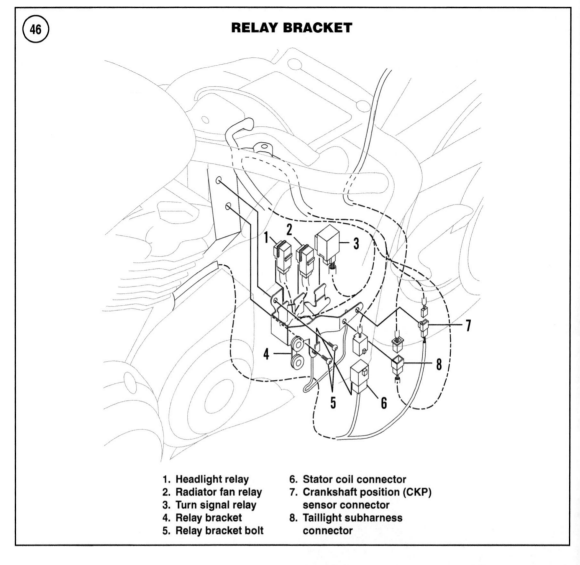

RELAY BRACKET

1. Headlight relay
2. Radiator fan relay
3. Turn signal relay
4. Relay bracket
5. Relay bracket bolt
6. Stator coil connector
7. Crankshaft position (CKP) sensor connector
8. Taillight subharness connector

4. Connect the ohmmeter positive test probe to the red battery terminal (C, **Figure 45**) in the relay; connect the negative test probe to the black starter terminal (D). The relay should have continuity.

5. Replace the starter relay if it fails this test.

RELAY BRACKET

Refer to **Figure 46**.

1. Disconnect the negative cable from the battery as described in this chapter.

2. Remove the left side cover (Chapter Fifteen).

3. Lift the stator coil connector (A, **Figure 47**) from its mounting tang, and disconnect the halves of the connector.

4. Release the taillight subharness connector (B, **Figure 47**) and the CKP connector (C) from their mounts on the relay bracket. Disconnect the halves of each connector.

5. Remove the turn signal relay (A, **Figure 48**), the radiator fan relay (B), and the headlight relay (C) from their respective tangs on the relay bracket.

6. Note how the wires are routed, then secure the wires safely out of the way.

7. Remove the relay bracket bolts (D, **Figure 48**), and lower the bracket from the frame.

8. Installation is the reverse of removal.

   a. Tighten the relay bracket bolts to 7 N•m (62 in.-lb.).

   b. Reconnect the halves of each connector, and securely mount each relay or connector onto its original tang.

RELAY UNIT

The relay unit is an integrated unit that includes the starting circuit cutoff relay (SCCR), the fuel pump relay, and several diodes. Replace the relay unit if any one of its components parts is out of specification.

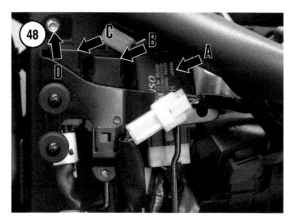

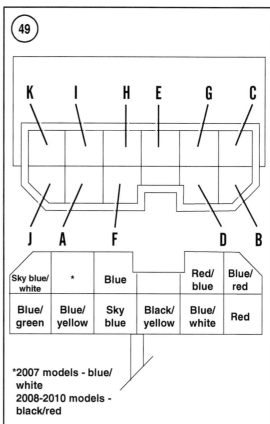

Sky blue/ white	*	Blue		Red/ blue	Blue/ red
Blue/ green	Blue/ yellow	Sky blue	Black/ yellow	Blue/ white	Red

*2007 models - blue/ white
2008-2010 models - black/red

9

NOTE
*The relay unit on 2007 models uses two blue/white terminals (A and G, **Figure 49**). Connect the battery or multimeter to the correct terminals during any test.*

Removal/Installation

1. Remove the rider's seat and the left side cover (Chapter Fifteen).
2. Disconnect the negative cable from the battery as described in this chapter.
3. Lift the relay unit (D, **Figure 47**) from its mounting tang in front of the battery case.
4. Disconnect the relay connector and remove the relay.
5. Installation is the reverse of removal. Make sure the relay's damper is securely mounted to its tang.

Fuel Pump Relay Test

1. Remove the relay unit as described in this section.
2A. On 2007 models, connect the positive battery terminal to the first blue/white terminal in the relay unit (A, **Figure 49**). Connect the negative battery terminal to the unit's blue/red terminal (B, **Figure 49**).

2B. On 2008-2010 models, connect the positive battery terminal to the black/red terminal in the relay unit (A, **Figure 49**). Connect the negative battery terminal to the unit's black/red terminal (B, **Figure 49**).
3. Connect the multimeter positive test probe to the red terminal in the relay unit (C, **Figure 49**). Connect the multimeter negative test probe to the unit's red/blue terminal (D, **Figure 49**).
4. The relay should have continuity.

SCCR Test

1. Remove the relay unit as described in this section.
2A. On 2007 models, connect the positive battery terminal to the first blue/white terminal in the relay (A, **Figure 49**). Connect the negative battery terminal to the relay's black/yellow terminal (E, **Figure 49**).
2B. On 2008-2010 models, connect the positive battery terminal to the black/red terminal in the relay (A, **Figure 49**). Connect the negative battery terminal to the relay's black/yellow terminal (E, **Figure 49**).
3. Connect the multimeter positive test probe to the blue terminal in the relay (F, **Figure 49**). Connect the multimeter negative test probe to the relays other blue/white terminal (G, **Figure 49**).
4. The relay should have continuity.

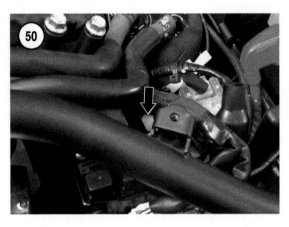

Relay Unit Test

1. Remove the relay unit as described in this section.
2. Connect a multimeter positive test probe to the sky blue terminal in the relay unit (H, **Figure 49**). Connect the negative test probe to the unit's black/yellow terminal (E, **Figure 49**). The meter should indicate continuity.
3. Reverse the connections in Step 2. The meter should indicate no continuity.
4. Connect a multimeter positive test probe to the sky blue terminal in the relay unit (H, **Figure 49**). Connect the negative test probe to the unit's blue/yellow terminal (I, **Figure 49**). The meter should indicate continuity.
5. Reverse the connections in Step 4. The meter should indicate no continuity.
6. Connect a multimeter positive test probe to the sky blue terminal in the relay unit (H, **Figure 49**). Connect the negative test probe to the unit's sky blue/white terminal (J, **Figure 49**). The meter should indicate continuity.
7. Reverse the connections in Step 6. The meter should indicate no continuity.
8. Connect a multimeter positive test probe to the blue/green terminal in the relay unit (K, **Figure 49**). Connect the negative test probe to the unit's blue/yellow terminal (I, **Figure 49**). The meter should indicate continuity.
9. Reverse the connections in Step 8. The meter should indicate no continuity.
10. The relay unit is faulty if it fails any portion of this test.

DIODE 1

Removal/Installation

1. Remove the rider's seat and seat bracket (Chapter Fifteen).
2. Disconnect the negative cable from the battery as described in this chapter.

3. Pull the diode (**Figure 50**) from its position in front of the seat bracket mount on the left side.
4. Disconnect the connector from diode 1, and remove diode 1.
5. Installation is the reverse of removal. Tighten the seat bracket bolts to 7 N•m (62 in.-lb.).

Continuity Test

The diode has two red/white terminals.
1. Disconnect the connector from diode 1.
2. Check the continuity in one direction by performing the following:
   a. Connect a multimeter positive test probe to the white terminal in diode 1. Connect the negative test probe to first red/white terminal in diode 1. The meter should indicate continuity.
   b. With the multimeter positive test probe still connected to the white terminal in diode 1, move the negative test probe to second red/white terminal. The meter should indicate continuity.
3. Check the continuity in the opposite direction by performing the following:
   a. Connect the negative test probe to the white terminal in diode 1. Connect the positive test probe to the first red/white terminal in the diode. The meter should indicate no continuity.
   b. With the multimeter negative test probe still connected to the white terminal, connect the positive test probe to the second red/white terminal. The meter should indicate no continuity.
4. Replace diode 1 if it fails either portion of this test.

DIODE 2 (2007-2009 MODELS)

Removal/Installation

1. Remove the left side cover (Chapter Fifteen).

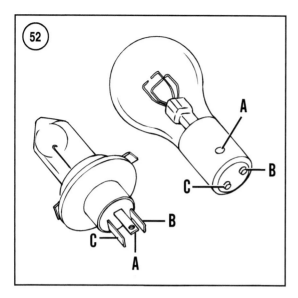

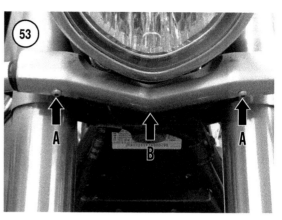

2. Disconnect the negative cable from the battery as described in this chapter.
3. Disconnect the connector (**Figure 51**) from diode 2, and remove diode 2.
4. Installation is the reverse of removal.

Continuity Test

1. Disconnect the connector (**Figure 51**) from diode 2.
2. Connect a multimeter positive test probe to the blue/white terminal in diode 2. Connect the negative test probe to the black/red terminal. The meter should indicate continuity.
3. Reverse the connections in Step 2. The meter should indicate no continuity.
4. Replace diode 2 if it fails either portion of this test.

LIGHT BULBS

Bulb Continuity Test

Refer to **Figure 52**.
On bulbs with two terminals, use an ohmmeter to check the continuity across the two terminals. Replace a bulb that does not have continuity.
On headlight, turn signal, tail/brake light bulbs and other bulbs with three terminals, check the continuity by performing the following:
1. Connect the ohmmeter's negative test probe to the A terminal; connect the positive test probe to the B terminal. The bulb should have continuity.
2. Keep the negative test probe connected to the A terminal, and move the positive test probe to the C terminal. The bulb should have continuity.
3. Replace the bulb if it fails either portion of this test.

Socket Continuity Test

1. Install a known good bulb into the affected socket.
2. Disconnect the socket connector from its harness mate.
3. Check the continuity across the terminals in the socket side of the connector. The socket should have continuity. Replace a socket if the test indicates no continuity.

HEADLIGHT

Lens Assembly Removal/Installation

WARNING
If the headlight has just burned out or just has just been turned off, the bulb will be hot. Do not touch the bulb until it cools.

CAUTION
All models are equipped with a quartz-halogen bulb. Do not touch the bulb glass with your fingers. Traces of oil on the bulb drastically reduces the life of the bulb. Clean any traces of oil from the bulb with a cloth moistened in alcohol or lacquer thinner.

1. Remove the mounting screws (A, **Figure 53**) and pull turn signal cover (B) from the lower fork bridge.
2. Remove the mounting screws from the top (**Figure 54**) and each side of the headlight housing (A, **Figure 55**).
3. Pull the lens assembly forward until it disengages from the headlight housing.
4. Disconnect the headlight connector (**Figure 56**) from the bulb, and remove the lens assembly.

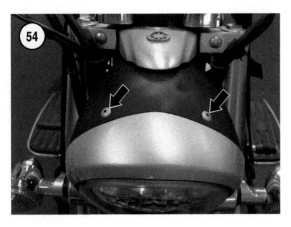

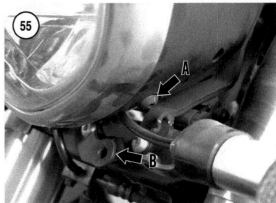

5. Installation is the reverse of removal. Make sure the post on the turn signal cover engages the grommet (B, **Figure 55**).

Bulb Removal/Installation

1. Remove the lens assembly as described in this section.

2. Pull the boot (**Figure 57**) from the lens assembly. Note where the boot's tabs are positioned in the assembly.

3. Release the securing clip (A, **Figure 58**), and remove the bulb (B) from the lens assembly.

4. Install the bulb by reversing the removal steps; note the following:

   a. Fit the bulb into the lens assembly so the bulb's tabs engage the slots (C, **Figure 58**) in the assembly.

   b. Make sure the electrical connector is free of corrosion and is tightly pushed onto the bulb terminals.

Housing and Bracket Removal/Installation

Refer to **Figure 59**.

1. On XVS13CT models, remove the windshield assembly (Chapter Fifteen).

2. Remove the lens assembly as described in this section.

> *NOTE*
> *Note how the wires are routed through the holes in the headlight housing and bundled together. Lens assembly installation can be difficult if the wires are not properly routed and bundled.*

3. Open the left and right bundles. The right bundle (A, **Figure 60**) contains the main switch connectors; the left (B) holds the meter assembly connectors and turn signal connectors.

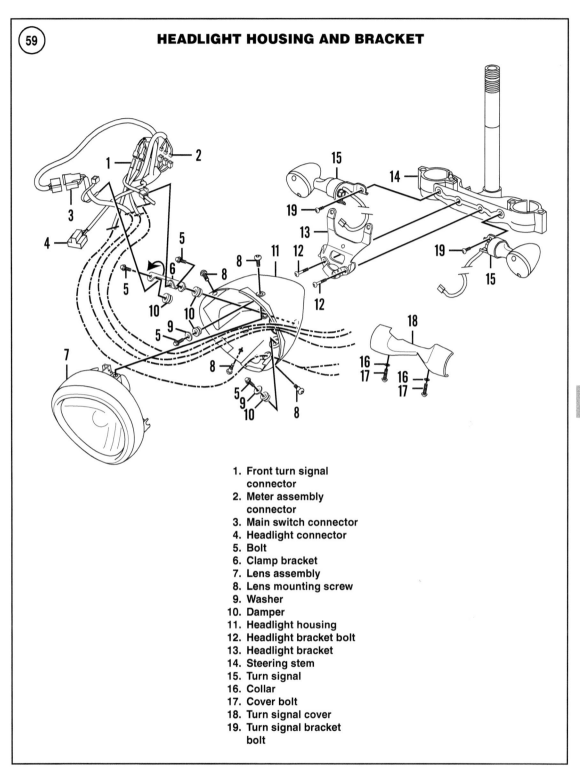

HEADLIGHT HOUSING AND BRACKET

1. Front turn signal
   connector
2. Meter assembly
   connector
3. Main switch connector
4. Headlight connector
5. Bolt
6. Clamp bracket
7. Lens assembly
8. Lens mounting screw
9. Washer
10. Damper
11. Headlight housing
12. Headlight bracket bolt
13. Headlight bracket
14. Steering stem
15. Turn signal
16. Collar
17. Cover bolt
18. Turn signal cover
19. Turn signal bracket
    bolt

4. Release the cable ties that secure the wires within the headlight housing. Note the location of each cable tie.

5. Separate the halves of each connector. Label the connector halves.

6. Feed the wire and connectors through the openings in the headlight housing. Note that the device side of the turn signal wires are routed through the small hole at the front of the housing (C, **Figure 60**).

NOTE
Account for the washer and collar installed with each headlight housing bolt.

7. Remove the upper headlight housing bolt (A, **Figure 61**). Note that this bolt secures the main switch cover to the headlight housing.

8. Remove the middle headlight housing bolts (B, **Figure 61**), and remove the cable-tie bracket installed beneath these bolts.

9. Remove the lower headlight housing bolt (C, **Figure 61**), and remove the housing from the motorcycle.

10. If necessary, remove the bracket bolts (A, **Figure 62**), and remove the headlight bracket (B) from the lower fork bridge.

11. Installation is the reverse of removal. Note the following:

   a. Tighten the headlight bracket bolts (A, **Figure 62**) to 23 N•m (17 ft.-lb.).

   b. Tighten the headlight housing bolts (A, B and C, **Figure 61**) to 7 N•m (62 in.-lb.).

   c. Route the wires as noted during removal.

   d. Make sure the electrical connectors are free of corrosion and pushed tightly together.

   e. Adjust the headlight as described in this section.

Headlight Adjustment

1. Vertical adjustment:

   a. Insert a screwdriver through the hole on the left side of the housing (**Figure 63**) until the screwdriver engages the adjuster.

   b. To raise the beam, turn the vertical adjuster clockwise when viewed from the left side. To lower the beam, turn the adjuster counterclockwise.

2. Horizontal adjustment:

   a. Insert a screwdriver through the hole on the right side of the housing (**Figure 64**) until the screwdriver engages the adjuster.

   b. To adjust the beam to the left, turn the horizontal adjuster clockwise when viewed from the right side. To adjust the beam to the right, turn the adjuster counterclockwise.

HEADLIGHT RELAY

Removal/Installation

1. Remove the left side cover (Chapter Fifteen).

2. Lift the headlight relay (C, **Figure 48**) from its mounting tang on the relay bracket.

3. Disconnect the headlight relay connector, and remove the relay.

4. Installation is the reverse of removal. The relay's damper must securely engage the relay bracket mounting tang.

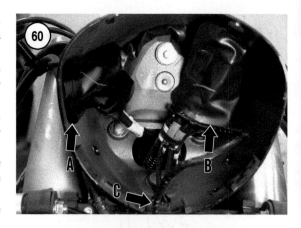

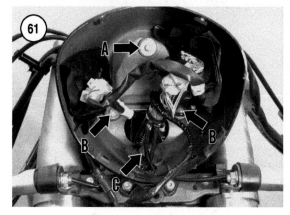

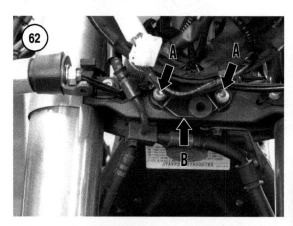

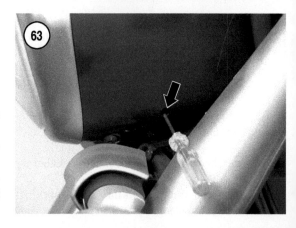

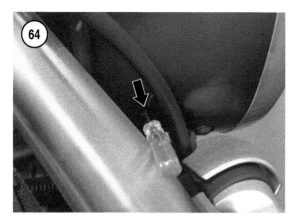

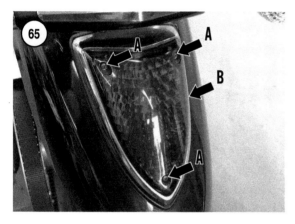

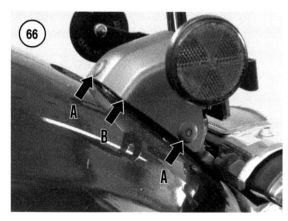

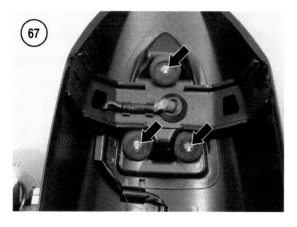

Continuity Test

1. Remove the headlight relay as described in this section.

CAUTION
The jumper wire must be the same gauge as the battery cable.

2. Use a jumper wire to connect the positive battery terminal to the brown terminal in the relay. Connect the negative battery terminal to the yellow/black terminal in the relay.

3. Connect an ohmmeter positive test probe to the red/yellow terminal in the relay. Connect the negative test probe to the relay's green/blue terminal.

4. The meter should indicate continuity.

TAIL/BRAKE LIGHT ASSEMBLY

Bulb
Removal/Installation

1. Remove the screws (A, **Figure 65**) and pull the lens (B) from the tail/brake light assembly. Account for the lens gasket. Replace the gasket if damaged.

2. Press the bulb slightly into the socket, turn the bulb counterclockwise, and remove it.

3. Press the new bulb into the socket until the bulb bottoms, and turn it clockwise to lock it in position.

4. Make sure the gasket is in place, and reinstall the lens. Tighten the screws (A, **Figure 65**) securely. Do not overtighten the lens screws. This will crack the lens.

Assembly
Removal/Installation

1. Remove the rear fender (Chapter Fifteen).

2. Remove the taillight lens and bulb as described in this section.

3. Remove the trim clips (A, **Figure 66**), and remove the cover (B) from the fender. The taillight connector mounts beneath this cover.

4. Disconnect the halves of the tail/brake light connector.

5. Remove the nut and washer (**Figure 67**) from each assembly stud. Account for the spacer and damper on each stud.

6. Remove the tail/brake light assembly from the fender. Account for the grommet in each fender mount.

7. Installation is the reverse of removal.

   a. Make sure a grommet is in place in each fender mount.

   b. Install a damper, spacer washer and nut onto each assembly stud.

c. Make sure the electrical connectors are free of corrosion and are securely mated to each other.

LICENSE PLATE LIGHT

Bulb Removal/Installation

1. Remove the bolts (A, **Figure 68**) and lift the bracket cover (B) from the turn signal bracket.
2. Turn the socket (A, **Figure 69**) counterclockwise and remove it from the license-plate-light housing.
3. Pull the bulb from the socket.
4. Installation is the reverse of removal.
   a. Press and new bulb into the socket.
   b. Press the socket into the housing and turn the socket clockwise to lock it in place.

Housing Removal/Installation

1. Remove the bolts (A, **Figure 68**) and lift the bracket cover (B) from the turn signal bracket.
2. Turn the socket (A, **Figure 69**) counterclockwise and remove it from the light housing.
3. Pull the license-plate-light housing (B, **Figure 69**) from the cover. Account for the damper behind the housing.
4. Installation is the reverse of removal. Make sure the housing damper is in place.

TURN SIGNAL ASSEMBLY

Refer to **Figure 70**.

Bulb Removal/Installation

1. Remove the screws (A, **Figure 71**) from the lens. Account for the washer on each screw.
2. Remove the lens (B, **Figure 71**) and gasket from the housing. Account for the inner lens on front turn signal assemblies.
3. Wash the lens with a mild detergent.
4. Press the bulb (**Figure 72**) slightly into the socket and turn the bulb counterclockwise. Remove it. Install the new bulb, and turn it clockwise to lock it in place.
5. Install the lens. Tighten the screws (A, **Figure 71**) securely. Make sure the gasket is in place. Do not overtighten the lens screws. This will crack the lens.

Assembly Removal/Installation

1A. If servicing a front turn signal unit
   a. Remove the headlight lens assembly as described in this chapter.

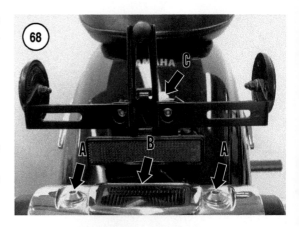

   b. Disconnect the relevant turn signal connectors.
1B. If servicing a rear turn signal unit, perform the following:
   a. Remove the bolts (A, **Figure 68**) and lift the bracket cover (B) from the turn signal bracket.
   b. Disconnect the halves of the relevant turn signal connector (C, **Figure 68**).
2. Remove the nut (**Figure 73**) from the turn signal mounting stud.
3. Remove the turn signal assembly from its bracket. Feed the wire through the hole in the bracket.
4. Installation is the reverse of removal.
   a. Feed the connector and wire through the turn signal bracket, and fit the turn signal stud through the bracket mount.
   b. Tighten the turn signal nut to 11 N•m (97 in.-lb.).
   c. Make sure the electrical connectors are free of corrosion and are securely.

TURN SIGNAL RELAY

Removal/Installation

1. Remove the left side cover (Chapter Fifteen).
2. Lift the turn signal relay (A, **Figure 48**) from its mounting tang on the relay bracket.

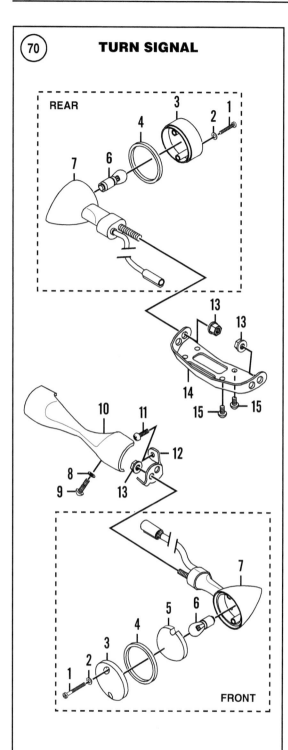

70 **TURN SIGNAL**

REAR

FRONT

1. Lens screw
2. Washer
3. Lens
4. Gasket
5. Inner lens
6. Bulb
7. Turn signal assembly
8. Collar
9. Cover bolt
10. Front turn signal cover
11. Bracket bolt
12. Front turn signal bracket
13. Mounting nut
14. Rear turn signal bracket
15. Bracket bolt

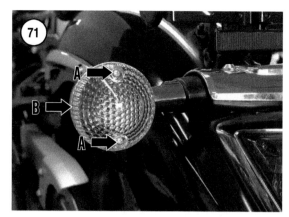

3. Disconnect the turn signal relay connector, and remove the relay.

4. Installation is the reverse of removal. The relay's damper must securely engage the relay bracket mounting tang.

Voltage Test

Refer to **Table 1**.

1. Remove the turn signal relay as described in this section.

2. Check the input voltage by performing the following:

a. Set a voltmeter to the DV 20 volt range.

b. Connect the voltmeter positive test probe to the brown terminal in the harness side of the relay connector. Connect the voltmeter negative test probe to a good ground.

c. Turn the main switch ON, and check the voltage on the meter. It should read battery voltage. If it does not, repair the wiring between the main switch and the turn signal relay.

3. Check the output voltage from the relay by performing the following:

a. Reconnect the connector to the relay.

b. Set a voltmeter to the DV 20 volt range.

c. Back probe the turn signal relay, and connect the voltmeter positive test probe to the brown/white terminal the relay connector. Connect the voltmeter negative test lead to a good ground.

d. Turn the main switch ON, and turn the flasher switch on (either left or right).

e. Repeats substep c and substep d with the positive test probe connected to the yellow/red terminal in the relay connector.

f. Repeats substep c and substep d with the positive test probe connected to the white terminal in the relay connector.

g. Output voltage should equal battery voltage during each portion of this test

h. Replace the relay if output voltage is less than battery voltage during any portion of this test.

METER ASSEMBLY

Removal/Installation

Refer to **Figure 74**.

1. Securely support the motorcycle on a level surface.

2. Disconnect the negative cable from the battery as described in this chapter.

3. Remove the lens assembly from the headlight housing as described in this chapter.

4. Open the right bundle (B, **Figure 60**) in the headlight housing. Separate the halves of all the meter assembly connectors.

5. Cover the fuel tank with a tarp or blanket.

6. Remove the cover screws (A and B, **Figure 75**), and lift the cover (C) from the meter assembly. Account for the collar installed with each screw.

7. Remove the bracket bolts (A, **Figure 76**), and remove the meter assembly cover bracket (B).

8. Remove the meter assembly bolts (**Figure 77**).

9. Lift the meter assembly (**Figure 78**) from the upper fork bridge. Pull the meter assembly lead (**Figure 79**) from the hole in the headlight housing and remove the meter assembly to the bench. Note how

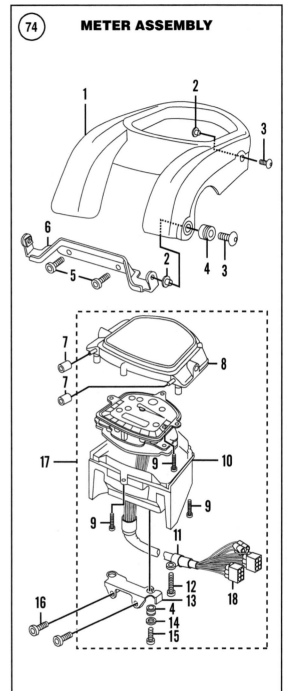

74   **METER ASSEMBLY**

1. Meter cover	11. Clamp
2. Collar	12. Clamp screw
3. Cover screw	13. Meter assembly
4. Damper	bracket
5. Bracket bolt	14. Washer
6. Meter assembly	15. Meter assembly
cover bracket	bracket bolt
7. Hose	16. Meter assembly bolt
8. Case cover	17. Meter assembly
9. Case screw	18. Meter assembly
10. Case	connectors

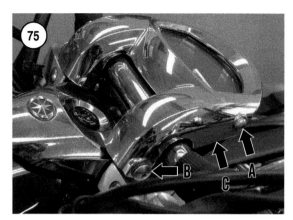

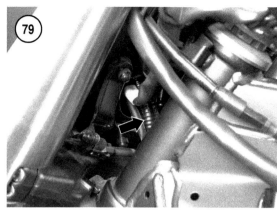

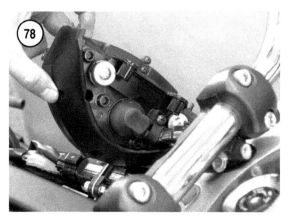

the meter assembly lead is routed through the motorcycle.

10. Installation is the reverse of removal.

   a. Apply threadlocking compound to the threads of the meter assembly bolts, and tighten the bolts to 23 N•m (17 ft-lb.).

   b. Tighten the meter assembly bracket bolts (A, **Figure 76**) to 7 N•m (62 in.-lb.)

   c. Make sure a damper is installed in each of the forward cover mounts, and tighten each meter assembly cover screw (B, **Figure 75**) to 7 N•m (62 in.-lb.).

Indicator Lights

The meter assembly includes the following indicator lights: neutral indicator, oil level warning light, fuel level warning light, turn signal indicator light, high beam indicator, coolant temperature warning light, and the engine trouble warning light. Each of these indicator lights as well as the meter illumination lights are LEDs.

Whenever the main switch is turned on the fuel level warning light, oil level warning light, coolant temperature warning light and the engine trouble warning light should turn on for a few seconds and then go out. If one or more of these LEDs does not light, the LED may be burned out or the circuit may be damaged. Take the unit to a dealership for further testing.

HORN

Removal/Installation

The horn sits on the right frame downtube.

1. Disconnect each connector (A, **Figure 80**) from its spade terminal on the back of the horn.

2. Remove the horn nut and washer (B, **Figure 80**), and remove the horn.

3. Installation is the reverse of removal.

Test

1. Disconnect each connector (A, **Figure 80**) from its spade connectors.
2. Connect an ohmmeter positive test probe to terminal A, **Figure 81**. Connect the negative test probe to terminal B, **Figure 81**.
3. The resistance should be within specification (**Table 1**). Replace the horn as needed.

Adjustment

1. Remove the horn as described in this section.
2. Use jumpers to connect the battery directly to the terminals on the back of the horn.
3. Turn the adjuster (C, **Figure 81**) clockwise or counterclockwise until the desired sound is obtained.
4. Install the horn.

SPEED SENSOR

Removal/Installation

1. Remove the riders seat (Chapter Fifteen).
2. Remove the engine pulley and the pulley housing (Chapter Seven).
3. Disconnect the halves of the speed sensor connector (**Figure 82**).
4. Release any cable ties or holders that secure the speed sensor wire to the frame. Note the location of these ties, and note how the speed sensor wire is routed along the motorcycle.
5. Disconnect the crankcase breather hose (A, **Figure 83**) from its crankcase fitting, and remove the heat shield (B).
6. Remove the speed sensor bolt (A, **Figure 84**), and lift the sensor (B) from the crankcase. Discard the speed sensor O-ring.
7. Installation is the reverse of removal. Note the following:
   a. Lubricate a new O-ring with lithium-soap grease, and install it onto the speed sensor.
   b. Tighten the speed sensor bolt to 10 N•m (89 in.-lb.).

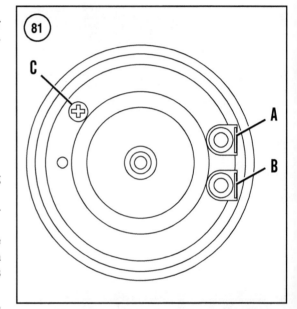

Voltage Test

1. Securely support the motorcycle on a level surface with the rear wheel off the ground.
2. Check the wiring in the speed sensor circuit. All connections and grounds must be clean and tight.
3. Remove the rider's seat (Chapter Fifteen).
4. Back probe the speed sensor connector (**Figure 82**), and connect a voltmeter positive test probe to the white/yellow terminal in the harness side of the

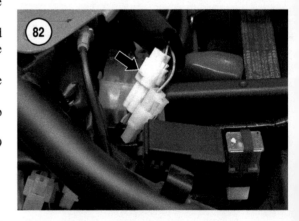

connector. Connect the negative test probe to the sensor's black/blue terminal.
5. Turn the main switch ON and slowly rotate the rear wheel.
6. The speed sensor should cycle from 0.6 to 4.8 volts with each full rotation of the wheel. Replace the sensor if its output voltage is out of specification.

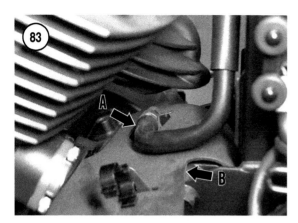

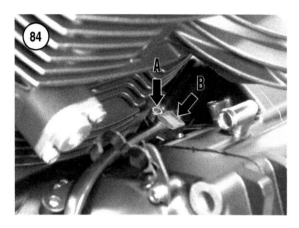

CAUTION
Do not attempt to start the engine with the battery negative cable disconnected. This will damage the wiring harness.

4. When separating connector halves, pull the housings and not the wires.

5. After locating a defective circuit, check the terminals to make sure they are clean and properly connected. Check all wires going into a connector housing to make sure each wire is properly positioned and that the wire end is not loose.

6. To properly connect connectors, push them together until they click into place.

7. When replacing a handlebar switch assembly, route the cables correctly so they will not be crimped when the handlebar is turned from side to side.

8. Note the routing of all wires and the cable ties and holders used to secure them in place. Always secure wires in their original location.

Continuity Diagrams

Test switches for continuity with an ohmmeter or a test light by following the continuity diagrams included with the wiring diagrams in this manual.

To test a particular switch perform the following:

1. Turn to the wiring diagram for a particular model, and locate the continuity diagram for the switch to be tested. For example, refer to **Figure 85**. The line shows which terminals should show continuity when the switch is activated.

2. Disconnect the switch connector, and check continuity at the terminals on the switch side of the connector. If a connector mates directly to the switch (like in the front brake light switch), check the continuity at the terminals on the switch.

3. Set the switch to each of its operating positions and compare the results with the appropriate switch continuity diagram.

Button position		
	P	B
Push	•———|———•	
Off		

SWITCHES

Precautions

When testing switches, note the following:

1. First check the fuses in the relevant circuit as described in this chapter.

2. Check the battery as described in this chapter. Charge the battery to the correct state of charge, if required.

3. Disconnect the negative cable from the battery if the switch connectors are not disconnected from the circuit.

LEFT HANDLEBAR SWITCH

The left handlebar switch housing includes the headlight dimmer switch, turn signal switch and the horn switch. If any of these switches is faulty, replace the left handlebar switch.

Removal/Installation

1. Remove the fuel tank and frame neck covers (Chapter Eight).

2. Disconnect the halves of the 5-pin (A, **Figure 86**) and the 6-pin (B) left handlebar switch connectors.

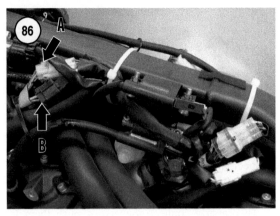

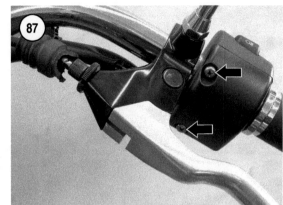

3. Disconnect the clutch switch connector.

4. Note how the handlebar switch cable is routed along the handlebar and through the fork legs. Release any clamps or cable ties that secure the switch cable to the motorcycle.

5. Remove the screws (**Figure 87**) and separate the housing halves from the handlebar.

6. Installation is the reverse of these steps. Note the following:

    a. Position the switch assembly so the line formed by the switch half mating surfaces aligns with the index mark on the handlebar (A, **Figure 88**).

    b. The gap between the switch assembly and the handlebar grip (B, **Figure 88**) must be less than 3 mm (0.12 in.).

    c. Make sure all terminals are free of corrosion, and apply a dielectric grease to each electrical connector prior to reconnecting it.

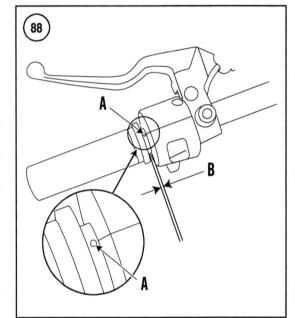

RIGHT HANDLEBAR SWITCH

The right handlebar switch housing includes the select switch, the reset switch, the engine stop switch and the start switch. If any one of these switches is faulty, replace the right handlebar switch.

Removal/Installation

1. Remove the fuel tank and frame neck covers (Chapter Eight).

2. Separate the halves of the 4-pin (A, **Figure 89**) and 8-pin (B) the right handlebar switch connectors.

3. Disconnect the brake switch connectors (A, **Figure 90**).

4. Remove the cable ties that secure the handlebar switch cable to the motorcycle. Note how the cable is routed. It must be rerouted along the same path.

5. Remove the clamp screw (B, **Figure 90**) from the pull cable clamp.

6. Remove the mounting screws (C, **Figure 90**) and separate the halves of the right handlebar switch assembly.

7. Disengage the ends (A, **Figure 91**) of both the pull and return cables from the throttle drum. Remove each cable from the switch housing.

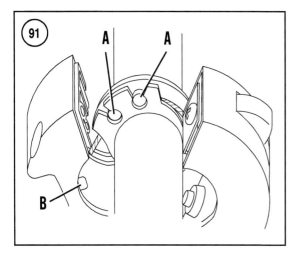

8. Installation is the reverse of removal. Note the following:

    a. Apply lithium-soap grease to the ends of the pull and return cables (A, **Figure 91**).

    b. The pin (B, **Figure 91**) on the switch housing must engage the hole in the handlebar, and the outboard edge of the switch must engage the slot in the throttle grip assembly.

    c. Make sure all terminals are free of corrosion, and apply a dielectric grease to the electrical connectors before reconnecting them.

    d. Use cable ties to secure the handlebar switch cable to the places noted during removal.

    e. Tighten the pull cable mounting screw.

    f. Adjust the throttle cable free play as described in Chapter Three.

OIL LEVEL SWITCH

Removal/Installation

1. Drain the engine oil (Chapter Three).
2. Remove the fuel tank and the frame neck cover (Chapter Eight).
3. Follow the wire from the oil level switch in the bottom of the crankcase to the oil level switch connector (A, **Figure 92**). Separate the halves of the connector, and release any holder or cable tie that secures the wire in place.
4. Place a drain pan beneath the oil pan.
5. Remove the oil level switch bolts, and lower the oil level switch (**Figure 93**) from the oil pan. Discard the O-ring.
6. Installation is the reverse of removal.

    a. Install a new oil level switch O-ring.

    b. Tighten the oil level switch bolts to 10 N•m (89 in.-lb.).

Resistance Test

1. Remove the oil level switch as described in this section.
2. Connect the ohmmeter's positive test probe to the terminal in the switch side of the connector (A, **Figure 94**); connect the negative test probe to the switch base (B).
3. Hold the switch in its upright position (**Figure 94**), and measure the resistance.
4. Hold the switch in the inverted position, and measure the resistance.
5. Replace the oil level switch if either resistance is outside the specified range (**Table 1**).

Oil Level Warning Light Test

The self-diagnostic system uses the oil level warning light to indicate the status of the oil level switch circuit.

1. Turn the main switch on and watch the oil level warning light.

2. The light should turn on for a few seconds and then turn off.

3A. Replace the meter assembly as described in this chapter with a known good assembly if the oil level warning light does not turn on as described in Step 2. Retest using the known good assembly.

3B. If the oil level warning light flashes ten times, goes out for 2.5 seconds and then repeats this cycle; the self-diagnostic system has detected an error in the oil level switch. Replace the switch.

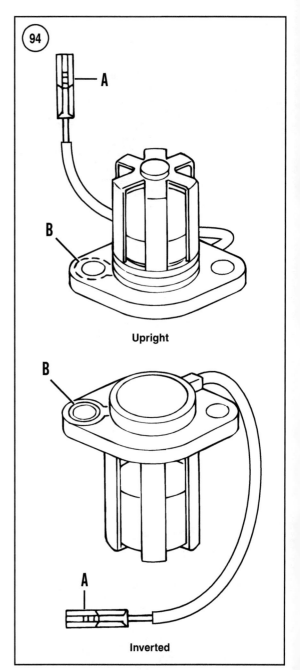

Upright

Inverted

MAIN SWITCH

Removal

1. Remove the fuel tank and frame neck covers (Chapter Eight).

2. On XVS13CT models, remove the windshield bracket from each side (Chapter Fifteen).

3. Remove the handlebar assembly (Chapter Twelve).

4. Remove the lens assembly from the headlight housing as described in this chapter.

5. Separate the halves of each main switch connector (A, **Figure 95**). Feed the main switch cable through the hole in the headlight housing. Note the routing of the wiring.

6. Remove the upper headlight housing bolt (B, **Figure 95**). Account for the washer and collar installed with this bolt. Note that this bolt turns into a nut on the main switch cover.

7. Remove the steering stem nut (A, **Figure 96**) and washer.

8. Loosen the clamp bolt (B, **Figure 96**) on each side of the upper fork bridge.

9. Lift the upper fork bridge from the fork legs, and set it on a rag placed across the frame.

10. Use a bolt extractor to remove the shear bolts (A, **Figure 97**), and move the main switch (B) from beneath the upper fork bridge.

Installation

1. Set the main switch into place, and install new shear bolts (A, **Figure 97**). Tighten each bolt until its head shears off.

2. Lower the upper fork bridge onto the fork legs. Route the main switch cable along the path noted during removal, and feed the cable through the hole in the headlight housing.

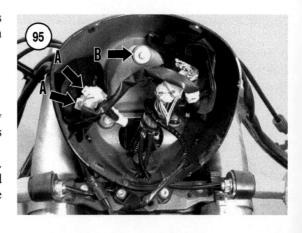

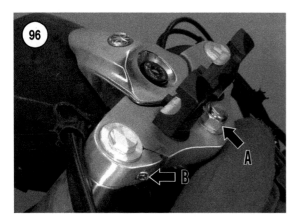

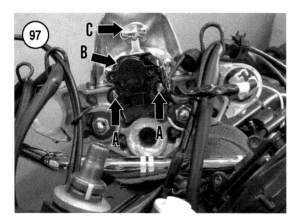

3. Install the steering head nut (A, **Figure 96**) and washer. Tighten the nut to 110 N•m (81 ft.-lb.).
4. Check that the upper edge of the upper fork bridge aligns with the top of each fork tube. If necessary, adjust the height of a fork leg as described in Chapter Twelve.
5. Tighten the upper fork bridge clamp bolts (B, **Figure 96**) to 23 N•m (17 ft.-lb.).
6. Install the headlight housing bolt (B, **Figure 95**) with its collar and washer. Turn it into the nut on the main switch cover (C, **Figure 97**), and tighten the headlight housing bolt to 7 N•m (62 in.-lb.).
7. Connect the halves of the main switch connectors (A, **Figure 95**).
8. Complete assembly by reversing Steps 1-4 in *Removal* in this section.

NEUTRAL SWITCH

Removal/Installation

The neutral switch sits in the left side of the crankcase.
1. Securely support the motorcycle on level ground, and shift the transmission into neutral.
2. Remove the engine pulley cover and pulley (Chapter Seven).
3. Disconnect the neutral switch connector (A, **Figure 98**).
4. Remove and remove the neutral switch (B, **Figure 98**) and its gasket from the crankcase. Discard the gasket.
5. Install by reversing these removal steps. Note the following:
   a. Install a new neutral switch gasket.
   b. Tighten the neutral switch to 20 N•m (15 ft.-lb.).

SIDESTAND SWITCH

Removal/Installation

1. Remove the fuel tank and frame neck covers (Chapter Eight).
2. Separate the halves of the sidestand switch connector (B, **Figure 92**).
3. Follow the sidestand switch wire, and disconnect any holders or cable ties that secure it in place. Note how the wire is routed along the frame. The new switch wire must be rerouted along the same path.
4. Remove the sidestand switch bolts (A, **Figure 99**), and remove the sidestand switch (B) from the sidestand bracket.
5. Installation is the reverse of these steps.
   a. Tighten the sidestand switch bolts to 4 N•m (35 in.-lb.).

b. Route the sidestand switch wire along its original path. Secure it at the points noted during removal.

CLUTCH SWITCH

Removal/Installation

The clutch switch mounts beneath the clutch lever.
1. Disconnect the connector from the clutch switch.
2. Remove the switch screw, and remove the switch.
3. Install the switch by reversing this procedure. Apply threadlocking compound to the threads of the clutch switch screws, and tighten the screws to 7 N•m (62 in.-lb.).

BRAKE LIGHT SWITCH

Front Switch
Removal/Installation

The front brake light switch mounts beneath the front brake master cylinder.
1. Disconnect the front brake switch connectors (A, **Figure 90**).
2. Remove the switch mounting screw, and remove the switch.
3. Install by reversing this procedure. Check the switch operation. The brake light should come on when the front brake lever is applied.

Rear Switch
Removal/Installation

The rear brake light switch mounts to the brake pedal/footrest bracket.
1. Remove the fuel tank and frame neck covers (Chapter Eight).
2. Separate the halves of the rear-brake-switch connector (**Figure 100**).
3. Follow the wire to the brake light switch. Release any holders or cable ties that secure the wire to the motorcycle.
4. Disconnect the spring (A, **Figure 101**) from the boss on the brake pedal, and lift the switch (B) from its mount.
5. Installation is the reverse of removal.
  a. Route the cable along its original path, and secure it to the motorcycle as noted during removal.
  b. Adjust the rear brake light switch as described in Chapter Three.

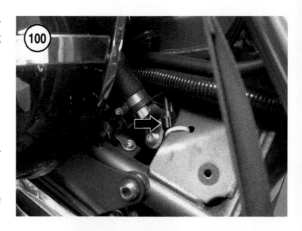

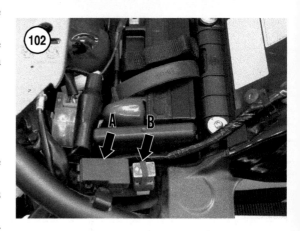

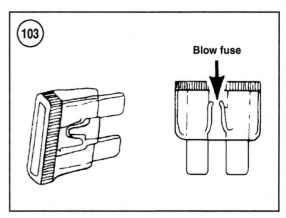

Blow fuse

FUSES

CAUTION
Whenever a fuse blows, determine the reason for the failure before replacing the fuse. Usually, the trouble is a short in the wiring. This may be caused by worn-through insulation or a disconnected wire shorting to ground. Never substitute metal foil or wire for a fuse. Do not use a higher amperage fuse than specified. An overload could result in an electrical fire and damage the wiring harness and or bike.

Removal/Installation

The fuse box (A, **Figure 102**) and the 50-amp main fuse (B) mount onto the left side of the battery box. Fuses other than the main fuse sit in the fuse box. The fuses, and their amperage rating, are listed in **Table 3**.

1. Remove the seat (Chapter Fifteen).
2. Remove the battery cover as described in this chapter.
3. Remove the fuse box cover and open the box.
4. Remove the suspected fuse by pulling it out of the holder with needlenose pliers.
5. Install a new fuse and reinstall the fuse box cover.

Testing

1. Remove the suspected fuse as described in this section.
2. Visually inspect the fuse (**Figure 103**). Replace a fuse with a blown or cracked element.
3. If necessary, check the continuity across the two spade connectors. Replace a fuse that does not have continuity (low resistance).
4. A replacement fuse must have the same amperage rating as the original.

9

Table 1 ELECTRICAL SYSTEM SPECIFICATIONS

Item	Specification
Cylinder numbering (front to rear)	1-2
Battery	
Model	YTX20L-BS
Capacity	12 volt, 18.0 amp hour
Stator coil resistance	0.112-0.168 ohms @ 20° C (68° F)
Regulator/rectifier	
Charging voltage	14 volts @ 5000 rpm
Regulated voltage	14.2-14.8 volts
Rectifier capacity	50.0 amp
Rectifier withstand voltage	40.0 volt
Ignition system type	Transistorized coil ignition (digital)
Crankshaft position (CKP) sensor resistance	248-372 ohms @ 20° C (68° F)
Ignition coil	
Primary coil resistance	2.16-2.64 ohms @ 20° C (68° F)
Secondary coil resistance	8.64-12.96 k ohms @ 20° C (68° F)
(continued)	

Table 1 ELECTRICAL SYSTEM SPECIFICATIONS (continued)

Item	Specification
Spark plug cap resistance	10.0 k ohms @ 20° C (68° F)
Speed sensor	0.6-4.8 volts
Starter	
Brush length	12.5 mm (0.49 in.)
Brush length wear limit	5.0 mm (0.20 in.)
Brush spring pressure	7.65-9.10.01 N (780-1021 gf [27.54-36.03 oz.])
Commutator diameter	28 mm (1.10 in.)
Commutator diameter wear limit	27 mm (1.06 in.)
Mica undercut	0.7 mm (0.03 in.)
Horn	
Coil resistance	1.01-1.11 ohms @ 20° C (68° F)
Turn signal relay	
Frequency	75-95 cycles/min
Wattage	21 (23) W x 2 + LED
Input voltage	12 volts
Output voltage	12 volts
Oil level switch resistance	
Upright position	484-536 ohms @ 20° C (72° F)
Inverted position	114-126 ohms @ 20° C (72° F)

Table 2 BULB SPECIFICATION

Item	Watt (Quantity)
Headlight (high/low beam)	60/55 W (1)
Tail/brake light	5/21 W (1)
Front turn signal	21/5 W (2)
Rear turn signal	21 W (2)
License plate	5 W (1)
Meter lights	LED
Indicator lights	LED

Table 3 FUSES

Item	Amperage
Main	50 A
Headlight	20 A
Taillight	10 A
Signal system	10 A
Ignition	15 A
Radiator fan	20 A
Fuel injection system	10 A
Backup fuse (odometer and clock)	10 A
Reserve fuses	20, 15 and 10 A (1 each)

Table 4 ELECTRICAL SYSTEM TORQUE SPECIFICATIONS

Item	N•m	in.-lb.	ft.-lb.
Alternator cover bolt	10	89	–
Battery box bolts	7	62	–
Clutch switch*	7	62	–
Crankshaft position (CKP) sensor bolt*	10	89	–
Damper cover bolt	7	62	–
Flywheel bolt	90	–	66
Front turn signal bracket bolt	23	–	17
Handlebar clamp bolt	28	–	20.5
Headlight bracket bolts	23	–	17

(continued)

Table 4 ELECTRICAL SYSTEM TORQUE SPECIFICATIONS (continued)

Item	N•m	in.-lb.	ft.-lb.
Headlight housing bolts	7	62	–
Ignition coil bolts	7	62	–
Ignition coil bracket bolt	7	62	–
Meter assembly bolts*	23	–	17
Meter assembly bracket bolts	7	62	–
Meter assembly cover screws	7	62	–
Neutral switch	20	–	15
Oil level switch bolt	10	89	–
Relay bracket bolts	7	62	–
Seat bracket bolts	7	62	–
Sidestand switch bolt	4	35	–
Speed sensor bolt	10	89	–
Starter bolts	10	89	–
Starter relay terminal bolt	7	62	–
Starter terminal nut	10	89	–
Stator coil bolts*	10	89	–
Stator wire clamp bolt*	10	89	–
Steering head nut	110	–	81
Timing inspection plug	6	53	–
Turn signal nut	11	97	–
Upper fork bridge clamp bolt	23	–	17
Voltage regulator/rectifier bolt	7	62	–
Voltage regulator/rectifier cover bolt	7	62	–

*Refer to text.

9

CHAPTER TEN

COOLING SYSTEM

Table 1 and Table 2 are at the end of this chapter.

COOLING SYSTEM PRECAUTIONS

WARNING
Antifreeze is toxic and should never be poured into storm sewers, septic systems, or onto the ground. Place used antifreeze in the original container and dispose of it according to local regulations. Do not store coolant where it is accessible to children or pets.

WARNING
Do not remove the radiator cap when the engine is hot. The coolant is very hot and under pressure. Severe scalding could result if the coolant contacts skin.

WARNING
The radiator fan and fan relay are connected directly to the battery. Whenever the engine is warm or hot, the fan may start even with the main switch turned off. Never work around the fan or touch the fan until the engine is completely cool.

CAUTION
Drain and flush the cooling system at the intervals specified in Chapter Three. Refill with a mixture of ethylene glycol antifreeze (formulated for aluminum engines) and distilled water mixed in a one-to-one ratio. Do not reuse the old coolant since it deteriorates with use. Do not operate the cooling system with only distilled water even in climates where antifreeze protection is not required. Doing so will promote internal engine corrosion.

COOLING SYSTEM INSPECTION

The pressurized cooling system consists of the radiator, water pump, thermostat, radiator fan and coolant reservoir.

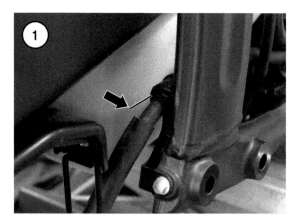

The coolant reservoir sits inside the rear frame member on the right side. Keep the coolant level in the reservoir at the full mark (**Figure 1**).

1. Check the coolant level when the engine is cold and the motorcycle upright.
2. If the level is low, remove the reservoir cap (**Figure 2**), and add coolant to the reservoir.
3. Check the coolant hoses and clamps for looseness or damage.
4. Start the engine and let it idle. If steam is observed at the muffler, a head gasket might be damaged. If enough coolant leaks into the cylinder, it could cause hydrolock and thus prevent engine cranking.
5. Check for coolant in the engine oil. If the oil on the dipstick is foamy or milky-looking, coolant is in the oil. It can quickly cause severe damage. Correct the problem immediately.

CAUTION
If the engine oil is contaminated with coolant, change the oil and filter after performing the repair.

6. Check the radiator for clogged or damaged fins. Refer radiator repair to a dealership or a radiator repair shop.
7. Check all coolant hoses for cracks or damage. Replace all questionable parts. Make sure the hose

clamps are tight but not so tight that they cut the hoses. Refer to *Hoses and Hose Clamps* in this chapter.
8. When troubleshooting the cooling system for loss of coolant, pressure test the system as described in Chapter Three.

HOSES AND HOSE CLAMPS

Hoses deteriorate with age. Replace them at the intervals specified in Chapter Three or whenever they show signs of cracking or if they are leaking. The spray of hot coolant from a cracked hose can injure the rider and passenger. Loss of coolant can also cause the engine to overheat and cause damage.

Whenever any component of the cooling system is removed, inspect the hoses and clamps to determine if replacement is necessary.

Inspection

1. With the engine cold, check the cooling hoses for brittleness, hardness or cracks. Replace hoses in this condition.
2. With the engine hot, examine the hoses for swelling along the entire hose length. Replace hoses that appear swollen.
3. Check the area around each hose clamp. Signs of rust around clamps indicate possible leaks from a damaged or over-tightened clamp.

Removal/Installation

Replace hoses when the engine is cold.
1. Drain the cooling system as described in Chapter Three.
2. Loosen the clamps on the hose to be replaced. Slide the clamps along the hose and out of the way.

CAUTION
Do not apply excessive force to a hose when attempting to remove it. Many of the hose fittings are fragile and can be easily damaged.

3. Twist the hose end to break the seal, and remove the hose from the hose fitting. If the hose has been on for some time, it may have become fused to the fitting. If so, insert a small screwdriver or pick tool between the hose and joint. While working the tool around the joint, carefully pry the hose loose.
4. Examine the hose fittings for cracks or other damage. Repair or replace parts as required. Remove rust and corrosion with a wire brush.
5. Inspect the hose clamps and replace them if necessary.

10

6. Slide the hose clamp over the outside of the hose, and then install the hose onto the fitting. Make sure the hose clears all obstructions and is routed properly.

> *NOTE*
> *If it is difficult to install a hose on a fitting, apply some antifreeze into the end of the hose. This usually aids installation.*

7. With the hose positioned correctly on the fitting, slide the clamp back away from end of the hose slightly. Tighten the clamp securely but not so much that the hose is damaged.

> *NOTE*
> *If installing coolant hoses onto the engine while it is removed from the frame, check the position of the hose clamp(s) to make sure it can be loosened during engine installation.*

8. Refill the cooling system as described in Chapter Three. Start the engine and check for leaks. Retighten the hose clamps as necessary.

COOLANT RESERVOIR CAP COVER

Removal/Installation

1. Securely support the motorcycle on a level surface.
2. Remove each coolant-reservoir-cap cover bolt (A, **Figure 3**), and remove the coolant-reservoir-cap cover (B). Account for the washer on each bolt.
3. Remove the cap cover.
4. Installation is the reverse of removal. Tighten the coolant-reservoir-cap cover bolts (A, **Figure 3**) to specification (**Table 2**).

COOLANT RESERVOIR COVER

Removal/Installation

1. Securely support the motorcycle on a level surface.
2. Remove the coolant reservoir cap cover as described in this chapter.
3. Remove the muffler and rear cylinder exhaust pipe (Chapter Eight).
4. Remove each coolant reservoir cover bolt (A, **Figure 4**) along with its washer. Lower the reservoir cover (B, **Figure 4**) from the frame. Account for the damper and collar installed on the lower front cover mount.
5. Installation is the reverse of removal. Tighten the coolant reservoir cover bolts (A, **Figure 4**) to 7 N•m (62 in.-lb.).

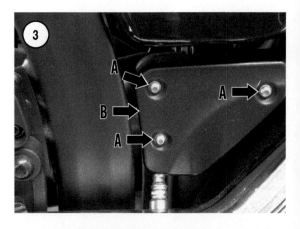

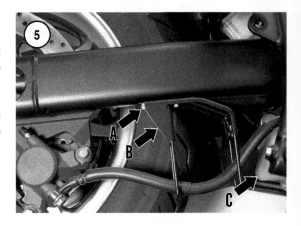

COOLANT RESERVOIR

Removal/Installation

1. Remove the coolant reservoir cover as described in this chapter.
2A. On 2007-2009 models, remove the mounting bolts (A, **Figure 5**), and lower the rear brake hose guide (B) from the swing arm.
2B. On 2010 models, lower the rear brake hose from the bracket on the swing arm.
3. Remove the cap (A, **Figure 6**) from the reservoir, and remove the reservoir bolt (B).

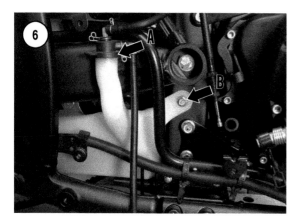

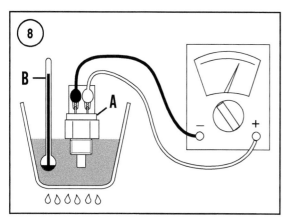

4. Lift the reservoir until its locating knobs disengage from the support bracket.
5. Pull the reservoir rearward (C, **Figure 5**), and remove it from the frame. Move the rear brake hose as necessary.
6. Installation is the reverse of removal.
   a. Press the reservoir onto the support bracket until the locating knobs engages the mounts in the bracket.
   b. Tighten the reservoir bolt (B, **Figure 6**) to 7 N•m (62 in.-lb.).
   c. Tighten the rear brake hose guide bolts (A, **Figure 5**) to 7 N•m (62 in.-lb.).

COOLANT TEMPERATURE (CT) SENSOR

Removal/Installation

1. Remove the rider's seat and left engine cover (Chapter Fifteen).
2. Remove the fuel tank and frame neck covers (Chapter Eight).
3. Disconnect the negative cable from the battery (Chapter Nine).
4. Disconnect the CT sensor connector (A, **Figure 7**).
5. Unscrew the sensor (B, **Figure 7**), and remove it from the thermostat housing. Discard the sensor gasket.
6. Installation is the reverse or removal.
   a. Install a new sensor gasket.
   b. Tighten the coolant temperature sensor to 18 N•m (13 ft.-lb.).

Resistance Test

1. Remove the coolant temperature sensor as described in this section.
2. Fill a beaker or pan with water, and place it on a stove or hot plate.

NOTE
The coolant temperature sensor (A, Figure 8) and thermometer (B) must not touch the container sides or bottom. If either does, it will result in a false reading.

3. Place a thermometer in the pan of water. Use a cooking or candy thermometer that is rated higher than the test temperature.
4. Mount the sensor so its sensing tip and the threaded portion of the body are submerged as shown in **Figure 8**.
5. Attach an ohmmeter to the sensor terminals as shown (**Figure 8**). Gradually heat the water, and let it cool down to 80° C (176° F). Note the resistance of the coolant temperature sensor.
6. Replace the sensor if the reading is outside the specified range (**Table 1**).

THERMOSTAT HOUSING

Refer to **Figure 9** and **Figure 10**.

Removal/Installation

The thermostat housing mounts between the frame members directly behind the steering head. Even

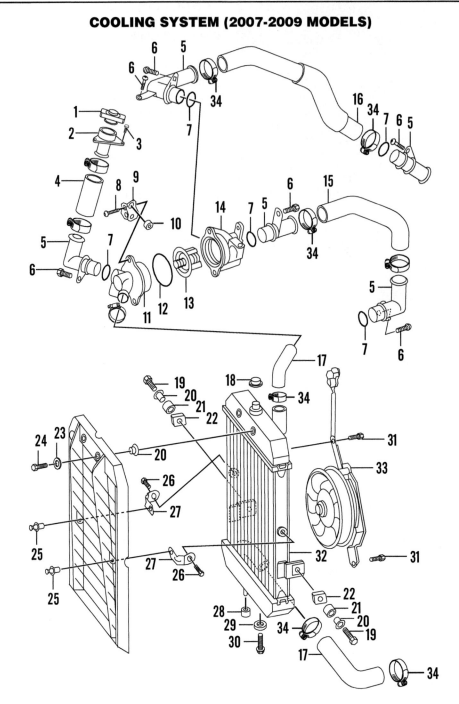

COOLING SYSTEM (2007-2009 MODELS)

1. Radiator cap
2. Filler neck
3. Filler neck bolts
4. Filler neck hose
5. Hose fitting
6. Hose fitting bolt
7. O-ring
8. Thermostat cover bolt
9. Thermostat bracket
10. Grommet
11. Thermostat cover
12. O-ring
13. Thermostat
14. Thermostat housing
15. Front cylinder
    thermostat hose
16. Rear cylinder
    thermostat hose
17. Radiator hose
18. Grommet
19. Radiator bolt
20. Collar
21. Damper
22. Special nut
23. Washer
24. Radiator cover bolt
25. Trim clip
26. Radiator cover bracket bolt
27. Radiator cover bracket
28. Grommet
29. Washer
30. Drain bolt
31. Radiator fan bolt
32. Radiator
33. Radiator fan
34. Clamp

COOLING SYSTEM (2010 MODELS)

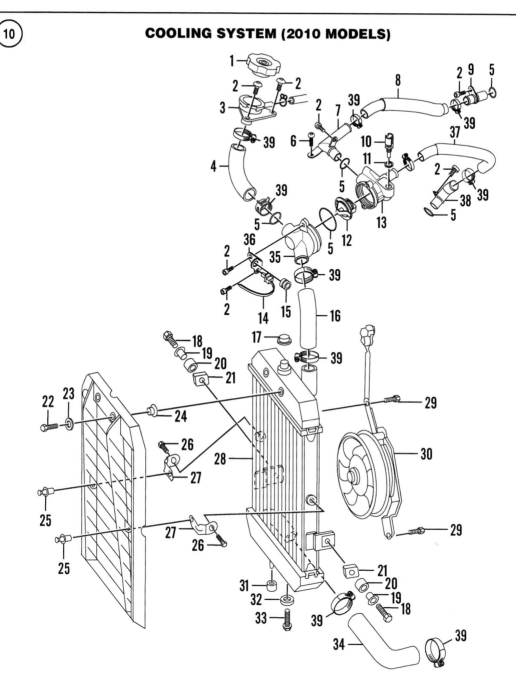

1. Radiator cap
2. Bolt
3. Filler neck
4. Filler neck hose
5. O-ring
6. Hose fitting bolt
7. Hose fitting
8. Rear cylinder thermostat hose
9. Hose fitting
10. Coolant temperature sensor
11. O-ring
12. Thermostat
13. Thermostat housing
14. Cable strap
15. Grommet
16. Radiator hose
17. Grommet
18. Radiator bolt
19. Collar
20. Damper
21. Special nut
22. Radiator cover bolt
23. Washer
24. Collar
25. Trim clip
26. Radiator cover bracket bolt
27. Radiator cover bracket
28. Radiator
29. Radiator fan bolt
30. Fan
31. Grommet
32. Washer
33. Drain bolt
34. Radiator hose
35. Thermostat cover
36. Thermostat bracket
37. Front cylinder inlet hose
38. Hose fitting
39. Clamp

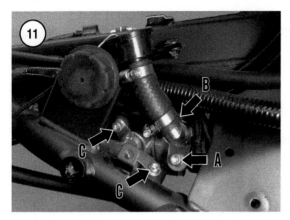

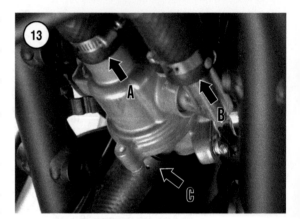

though there is little room to work, the housing can be removed while the engine is in the frame.

1. Remove the fuel tank, frame neck cover and exhaust system (Chapter Eight).

2. Remove the rider's seat and left engine cover (Chapter Fifteen).

3. Remove the finished covers from the front cylinder (Chapter Four).

4. Remove the radiator as described in this chapter.

5. Disconnect the coolant reservoir hose from the its fitting on the filler neck.

6. Remove the fitting bolt (A, **Figure 11**), and remove the filler neck assembly and its fitting from the thermostat housing. Discard the fitting O-ring. If necessary, loosen the clamps and remove the filler neck hose (B, **Figure 11**).

7. Loosen the hose clamp, and disconnect the thermostat inlet hose (A, **Figure 12**) from output fitting in the rear cylinder head. Be prepared to catch residual coolant that dribbles from the hose. Repeat this procedure, and disconnect the thermostat inlet hose (B, **Figure 12**) from the front cylinder-head fitting.

8. Loosen the hose clamp, disconnect the front-cylinder thermostat inlet hose (A, **Figure 13**) from it fitting on the thermostat housing. Repeat this procedure and disconnect the rear-cylinder thermostat inlet hose (B, **Figure 13**) from its fitting.

9. Release the clamp, and disconnect the radiator hose (C, **Figure 13**) from its fitting on the thermostat cover.

10. Disconnect the coolant temperature (CT) sensor connector (A, **Figure 14**).

11. Remove the bolts (C, **Figure 11**) securing the hanging bracket to the frame.

12. Unhook the thermostat hanging bracket from frame post (B, **Figure 14**) on the left side.

13. Remove the thermostat housing by moving it between the cylinder head and the frame tube on the right side. If difficulty is encountered, remove the CT sensor and the thermostat cover bolt (A, **Figure 15**) that secures the hanger bracket (B) to the cover.

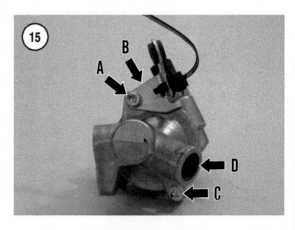

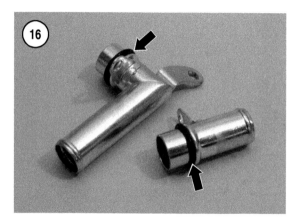

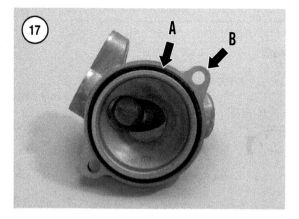

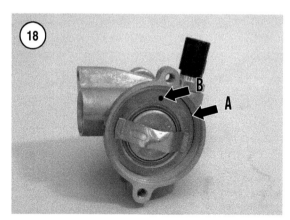

10

14. Installation is the reverse of removal.
   a. Install a new O-ring (**Figure 16**) onto each hose fitting.
   b. Apply threadlocking compound to the threads of each hose fitting bolt, and tighten the bolt to 10 N•m (89 in.-lb.).

Disassembly/Assembly

1. Remove the cover bolt (A, **Figure 15**), and remove the hanger bracket (B) from the thermostat cover. Note how the tang on the hanger bracket engages the cover.
2. Remove the remaining cover bolt (C, **Figure 15**), and remove the thermostat cover (D) from the housing. Discard the cover O-ring (A, **Figure 17**).
3. Remove the thermostat (A, **Figure 18**) from the housing.
4. Installation is the reverse of removal.
   a. Seat the thermostat in its housing so its breather hole (B, **Figure 18**) faces up.
   b. Install a new thermostat cover O-ring (A, **Figure 17**).
   c. Install the hanger bracket (B, **Figure 15**) so its tang engages the thermostat cover as noted during removal.
   d. Tighten the thermostat cover bolts (A and C, **Figure 15**) to 10 N•m (89 in.-lb.).

Inspection

1. Inspect the thermostat cover (B, **Figure 17**), housing (**Figure 19**) and hose fittings (**Figure 16**) for corrosion or contaminants. Clean as necessary.
2. Make sure all ports are clear.
3. Inspect the cover, housing and hose fittings for cracks or other signs of damage.
4. Check all hoses for cracks or signs of deterioration.
5. Test the thermostat as described in this section.

Thermostat Test

1. Remove and disassemble the thermostat housing as described in this section.
2. Fill a beaker or pan with water, and place it on a stove or hot plate.
3. Suspend the thermostat so it is submerged as shown in **Figure 20**.

NOTE
*The thermometer (A, **Figure 20**) and the thermostat (B) must not touch the container sides or bottom. If either does, the test will yield false results.*

4. Place a thermometer in the pan of water. Use a cooking or candy thermometer that is rated higher than the test temperature.

NOTE
Thermostat operation may be slow. It may take 3-5 minutes for the thermostat to operate properly.

5. Gradually heat and gently stir the water until it reaches the opening temperature listed in **Table 1**. At this temperature, the thermostat valve should start to open. Once the water temperature reaches the specified fully open temperature, the valve should be fully opened.
6. Measure the valve lift.
7. If the valve fails to operate at the specified temperature or if valve lift is less than the specified value **Table 1**, replace the thermostat because it cannot be serviced. The replacement thermostat must have the same temperature rating as the original.

RADIATOR

Refer to **Figure 9** and **Figure 10**.

Removal/Installation

1. Remove the rider's seat (Chapter Fifteen).
2. Remove the fuel tank (Chapter Eight).
3. Drain the coolant (Chapter Three).
4. Separate the halves of the radiator fan connector (**Figure 21**).
5. Release the hose clamp, and disconnect the radiator inlet hose (**Figure 22**) and outlet hose (A, **Figure 23**) from their respective fittings.
6. Remove the radiator bolt (B, **Figure 23**) from each side of the radiator. Account for the collar and damper installed with each bolt.
7. Lower the radiator so is post disengages from the mount on the frame, and remove the radiator. Account for the grommet on the radiator upper post.
8. Install the radiator by reversing these removal steps.
   a. Fit the radiator between the frame members so its upper post engages the frame mount. Make sure the grommet is in place on the post or in the frame mount.
   b. Install the damper and collar with each radiator bolt (B, **Figure 23**), and tighten the bolts to 7 N•m (62 in.-lb.).
   c. Make sure all electrical connectors are free of corrosion and securely connected to their mates.
   d. Refill the cooling system with the recommended type and quantity of coolant as described in Chapter Three.
   e. Check the hoses for leaks.

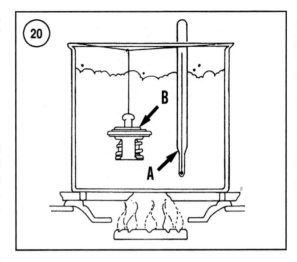

Inspection

1. Remove the bolts (A, **Figure 24**) from the top of the shroud.
2. Remove the trim clips (B, **Figure 24**) and remove the shroud (C) from the radiator.
3. Wash the exterior of the radiator (A, **Figure 25**) with a water hose on low pressure. Spray both the front and the back to remove all dirt and debris. Use a whiskbroom or stiff paintbrush to remove any stubborn debris.

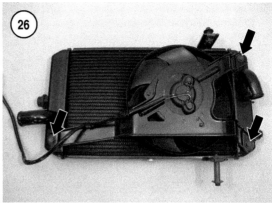

7. To prevent oxidation to the radiator, touch up any area where the black paint is worn off. Use good quality spray paint. Do not apply heavy coats as this cuts down on the cooling efficiency of the radiator.

8. Inspect the radiator cap seal for deterioration or damage. Check the spring for damage. Pressure test the radiator cap as described in *Cooling System* in Chapter Three.

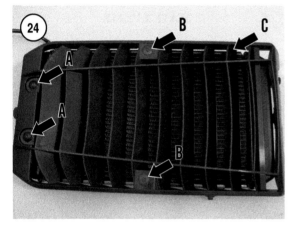

RADIATOR FAN

Removal/Installation

1. Remove the radiator as described in this chapter.
2. Remove the radiator fan bolts (**Figure 26**), and then remove the fan assembly from the radiator.
3. Install by reversing these removal steps. Apply threadlocking compound to the radiator fan bolts, and tighten the bolts securely.

Operational Test

1. Remove the fuel tank (Chapter Eight).
2. Separate the halves of the radiator fan connector (**Figure 21**).
3. Use jumpers to connect the positive battery terminal to the black/white terminal in the fan side of the radiator fan connector; connect the negative battery terminal to the black terminal in the connector's fan side.
4. The fan motor should run freely with no grinding or excessive noise.
5. Replace the radiator fan if it does not operate correctly.

RADIATOR FAN RELAY

Removal/Installation

1. Remove the side cover from the left side (Chapter Fifteen).

CAUTION
Do not press too hard on the cooling fins and tubes. Damage could cause a leak.

4. Carefully straighten out any bent cooling fins with a broad-tipped screwdriver.
5. Check for cracks or coolant leaks (usually a moss-green colored residue) at the filler neck, hose fittings and the tank seams (B, **Figure 25**).
6. Check the mounting bracket and radiator mounts for cracks or damage.

10

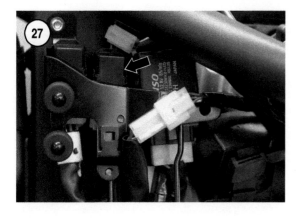

2. Lift the radiator fan relay (**Figure 27**) from its tang on the relay bracket.
3. Disconnect the radiator fan relay connector, and remove the relay.
4. Installation is the reverse of removal.

Test

1. Remove the radiator fan relay as described in this section.
2. Use jumpers to connect the battery positive terminal to the red/white terminal in the relay. Connect the negative battery terminal to the relay's green/yellow terminal.
3. Connect an ohmmeter positive test probe to the brown/white terminal in the relay. Connect the negative test probe to the relay's blue terminal.
4. The meter should indicate continuity. Replace the relay if it fails this test.

WATER PUMP

Service and inspect the water pump as described in *Oil/Water Pump* in Chapter Five.

Table 1 COOLING SYSTEM SPECIFICATIONS

Item	Specification
Coolant temperature sensor resistance	290-354 ohms 80° C (176° F)
Coolant quantities	
Total system capacity	2.10 L (2.22 qt.)
Radiator capacity	0.55 L (0.58 qt.)
Reservoir capacity (to the FULL level line)	0.45 L (0.48 qt.)
Coolant temperature	90-100° C (194-212° F)
Radiator Core	
Width	197.0 mm (7.76 in.)
Height	320.0 mm (12.60 in.)
Depth	22.0 mm (0.87 in.)
Radiator cap opening pressure	93.3-122.7 kPa (13.5-17.8 psi)
Valve relief pressure	4.9 kPa (0.7 psi)
Thermostat opening temperature	80.5-83.5° C (176.9-182.3° F)
Thermostat full open temperature	95.0° C (203.0° F)
Thermostat valve lift (full open)	8.0 mm (0.31 in.)
Water pump	
Impeller shaft tilt service limit	0.15 mm (0.006 in.)

Table 2 COOLING SYSTEM TORQUE SPECIFICATIONS

Item	N•m	in.-lb.	ft.-lb.
Coolant drain bolt	2	18	–
Coolant reservoir bolt	7	62	–
Coolant-reservoir-cap cover bolts	4	35	–
Coolant reservoir cover bolts	7	62	–
2007-2009 models	7	62	–
2010 models	10	89	–
Coolant temperature sensor	18	–	13
Filler neck bolt	10	89	–
Hose fitting bolt*	10	89	–
Radiator bolts	7	62	–
Radiator pipe bolt	10	89	–
Rear brake hose guide bolts	7	62	–
Thermostat cover bolts	10	89	–

*Refer to text.

CHAPTER ELEVEN

WHEELS AND TIRES

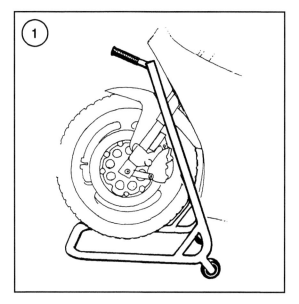

This chapter covers the tires and wheels including the wheel pulley.

Table 1 and **Table 2** are at the end of this chapter.

MOTORCYCLE STAND

Many procedures in this chapter require that the motorcycle be supported with a wheel off the ground.

A motorcycle front end stand (**Figure 1**) or swing arm stand does this safely and effectively. Before purchasing or using a stand, check the manufacturer's instructions to make sure the stand will work on the motorcycle. If the stand or motorcycle requires modification or adjustment, perform the required service before lifting the motorcycle.

An adjustable centerstand can also be used to support the motorcycle with a wheel off the ground. Again, check the manufacturer's instructions and perform any necessary modifications before supporting the motorcycle.

When using a motorcycle stand, have an assistant standing by. Some means to tie down one end of the motorcycle is also needed. Regardless of how the motorcycle is supported, make sure it is stable and secure before walking away from it.

BRAKE ROTOR PROTECTION

Be careful when removing, handling and installing a wheel. Brake rotors are relatively thin in order to dissipate heat and to minimize unsprung weight. A rotor can withstand tremendous rotational loads, but it can be damaged when subjected to side impact loads.

11

Protect the rotor when servicing a wheel. Never set a wheel down on the brake rotor. It may be bent or scratched. When a wheel must be placed on its side, support the wheel on wooden blocks (**Figure 2**). Position the blocks along the outer circumference of the wheel so the rotor lies between the blocks and does not rest on them.

WHEEL INSPECTION

1. Remove the wheel as described in this chapter.
2. Inspect the oil seals (A, **Figure 3**) for excessive wear, hardness, cracks or other damage. If necessary, replace the seals as described in *Front Hub* or *Rear Hub* in this chapter.
3. Inspect the bearings by performing the following.

   a. Turn each bearing inner race (B, **Figure 3**) by hand. Each bearing must turn smoothly with no traces of drag or excessive noise. Some axial play (side-to-side) is normal (**Figure 4**), but radial play (up and down) must be negligible.
   b. Check a sealed bearing's outer seal for buckling or other damage that would admit dirt into the bearing.
   c. On a non-sealed bearing, check the balls for evidence of wear, pitting or excessive heat (bluish tint).
   d. Check the bearing fit in the hub by trying to move the bearing laterally with your hand. The bearing should fit tightly in the bore. Loose bearings allow the wheel to wobble. If a bearing is loose, the bearing bore in the hub is probably worn or damaged.
   e. Replace questionable bearings as described in *Front Wheel Bearing* or *Rear Wheel Bearing* in this chapter. Ensure a perfect match by comparing the old bearing to the new one.
4. Remove any corrosion from the axle (**Figure 5**) or collars with a piece of fine emery cloth.

> *WARNING*
> *Do not attempt to straighten a bent axle.*

5. Check axle runout by rolling the axle along a surface plate or a piece of glass. If the axle is not straight, replace it.
6. Install the wheel on a truing stand. Check wheel runout by performing the following:
   a. Measure the radial (up and down) runout of the wheel rim with a dial indicator as shown in **Figure 6**.
   b. Measure the axial (side-to-side) runout of the wheel rim with a dial indicator as shown in **Figure 6**.

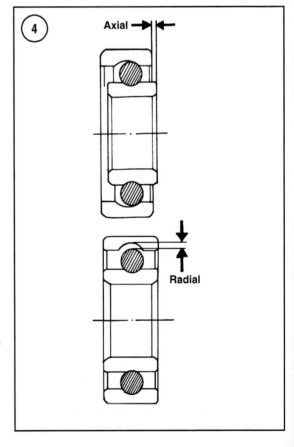

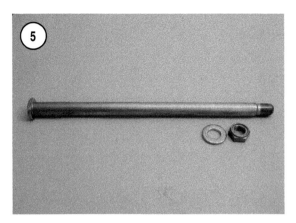

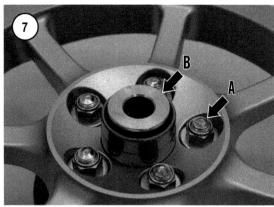

10. On the rear wheel check the tightness of the wheel pulley nuts (A, **Figure 7**). If a nut is loose, tighten it to 95 N•m (70 ft.-lb.).

11. Inspect the wheel rim for dents, bending or cracks. Check the rim and rim sealing surface (cast wheels) for scratches that are deeper than 0.5 mm (0.01 in.). If any of these conditions are present, replace the wheel.

FRONT WHEEL

Refer to **Figure 8**.

Removal

1. Securely support the motorcycle with the front wheel off the ground.

2. Check the wheel bearings by performing these preliminary tests:

   a. Hold the wheel along its side (hands 180° apart), and try to rock it back and forth. If any play is noticed at the axle, the wheel bearings are worn or damaged.

   b. While an assistant applies the brake, rock the wheel again. On wheels with severely worn bearings, play will be detected even though the wheel is locked in position.

   c. Spin the wheel and listen for excessive wheel bearing noise. Grinding or catching noises indicate worn bearings.

   d. If either bearing is worn or damage, replace both wheel bearings as a set. Refer to *Front Wheel Bearing* in this chapter.

NOTE
If the brake lever is applied while the calipers are off the front wheel, both calipers must be disassembled to reseat the caliper pistons, and the brakes must be bled. A wooden block between the brake lever and the handlebar prevents the accidental application of the front brakes. Refer to Chapter Fourteen.

7. If the wheel runout is out of specification (**Table 1**), inspect the wheel bearings as described earlier in this section.

   a. If the wheel bearings are in good condition, the wheel must be replaced.

   b. If either wheel bearing is worn, disassemble the hub and replace both bearings as a set as described in this chapter.

8. Check the tightness of the brake disc bolts (C, **Figure 3**). If a bolt is loose, remove and reinstall the bolts with a threadlocking compound. Clean any old threadlocking compound from the threads, and tighten the brake disc bolts to 23 N•m (17 ft.-lb.).

9. Inspect the brake discs, and measure the brake disc runout as described in Chapter Fourteen. If the runout is excessive, measure the wheel runout. If wheel runout is within specification, replace the brake disc. Refer to the procedure in Chapter Fourteen.

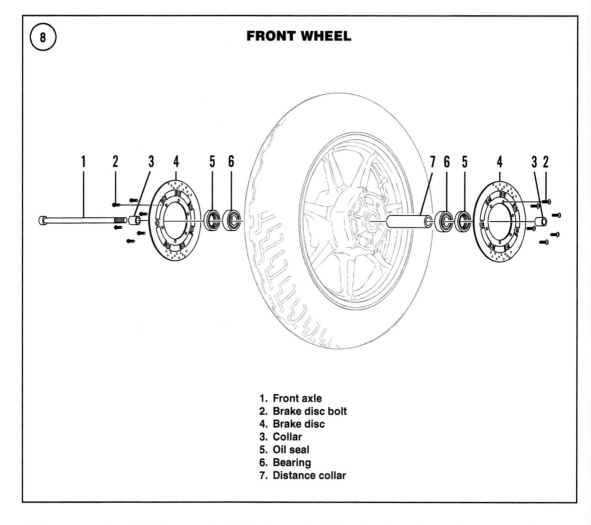

FRONT WHEEL

⑧

1. Front axle
2. Brake disc bolt
4. Brake disc
3. Collar
5. Oil seal
6. Bearing
7. Distance collar

3. Insert a wooden block between the brake lever and the handlebar grip. Use a rubber band to hold the block in place.

4. Remove the reflector nut and washer. Pull the reflector from its bracket on each side.

5. Remove the brake calipers by performing the following:

    a. Remove the front caliper bracket bolts (**Figure 9**). Rotate the caliper from the brake disc, and suspend the caliper so it does not hang from the brake hose. Note how the brake hose is routed.

    b. Repeat for the other caliper.

6. Loosen the clamp bolt (A, **Figure 10**) on the right fork leg.

7. Remove the front axle (B, **Figure 10**).

8. Roll the wheel from between the fork legs. Account for the collar (A, **Figure 11**) on each side of the hub.

CAUTION
Do not lay a wheel on the brake disc.
*Refer to **Brake Rotor Protection** in this chapter.*

9. If the wheel must be set down on its side, place wooden blocks (**Figure 2**) beneath the tire.

10. Inspect the wheel as described in this chapter. If either wheel bearing is questionable, replace both bearings as a set as described in this chapter.

Installation

1. Make sure the axle and the axle bearing surfaces of the fork sliders are free of burrs and nicks.

2. Apply a light coat of lithium-soap grease to the front axle and to the lips of the oil seal (B, **Figure 11**) in each side of the hub.

3. Insert a collar (A, **Figure 11**) into each oil seal.

4. Roll the wheel into place between the fork legs. Make sure the rotation arrow on the wheel points in the direction of forward rotation.

5. Insert the front axle (B, **Figure 10**) through right fork leg and hub, and turn the axle into the left fork leg. Tighten the axle securely, but do not torque it to specification at this time.

6. Remove the motorcycle support, and lower the front wheel to the floor. Pump the fork several times

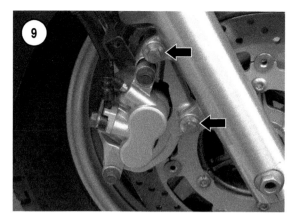

to align the suspension. Make sure the fork moves smoothly.

7. Tighten the front axle (B, **Figure 10**) to 59 N•m (43.5 ft.-lb.), and then tighten the front axle clamp bolt (A) to 20 N•m (15 ft.-lb.).

8. Install each brake caliper by performing the following:

   a. Lower the caliper onto the brake disc. Be careful not to damage the leading edge of the brake pads during installation.

   b. Install the front caliper bracket bolts (**Figure 9**), and tighten them to 40 N•m (30 ft.-lb.).

   c. Route the brake hose along the path noted during removal.

   d. Install the reflector onto each side.

9. After the wheel is completely installed, rotate it several times to make sure it turns freely. Apply the front brake as many times as necessary to ensure the brake pads properly engage the brake discs.

FRONT HUB

Refer to **Figure 8**.

Disassembly/Assembly

1. Remove the front wheel as described in this chapter.

2. Remove the collar (A, **Figure 11**) from each side of the hub.

> *CAUTION*
> *Do not lay a wheel on the brake disc. Refer to **Brake Rotor Protection** in this chapter.*

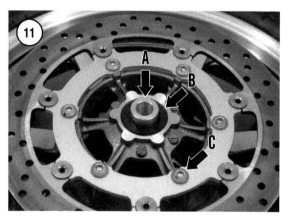

3. Use wooden blocks to support the wheel. Place the tire on the blocks so the brake disc will not be damaged (**Figure 2**).

> *NOTE*
> *The hub can be serviced with the brake disc in place. Nonetheless, consider removing the brake disc so it will not be damaged.*

4. Remove the brake disc bolts (C, **Figure 11**), and lift the brake disc from the hub. Repeat this on the opposite side.

5. Pry the oil seal (**Figure 12**) from the each side of the hub. Place a shop rag beneath the pry tool so the hub will not be damaged.

6. Inspect the bearings as described in *Wheel Inspection* in this chapter. If necessary, remove and replace the front bearings as described in this chapter.

7. Pack the lips of a new oil seal with lithium-soap grease. Drive the seal into the hub with seal driver

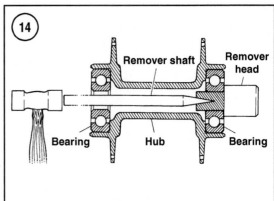

or a large diameter socket (**Figure 13**) seated on the outer portion of the seal. Drive the seal until it seats against the bearing or when the outer surface is flush with the hub.

8. Repeat for the oil seal on the opposite side of the hub.

9. If removed, install the brake disc. Apply thread-locking compound to the threads of the brake disc bolts (C, **Figure 11**), and tighten the front brake disc bolts to 23 N•m (17 ft.-lb.).

10. Install the front wheel as described in this chapter.

FRONT WHEEL BEARING

Removal

The following procedure describes the use of the Motion Pro wheel bearing remover. This split-collet tool can be ordered through most motorcycle deal-erships. The tool can be purchased as a set or individual pieces can be purchased separately.

1. Select the correct size remover head and insert it into the inner race of one bearing (**Figure 14**).

2. From the opposite side of the hub, insert the remover shaft through the hub bore and into the slot in the backside of the remover head. Position the hub with the remover head resting against a solid surface. Strike the remover shaft to force it into the slot in the remover head. This tightens the remover head against the bearing's inner race.

3. Reposition the wheel. Strike the end of the remover shaft with a hammer and drive the bearing (**Figure 15**) out of the hub. Slide the bearing and tool assembly out of the hub.

4. Tap the remover head to release it from the bearing.

5. Remove the distance collar. Note how the collar is positioned in the hub. It will have to be reinstalled with the same orientation during assembly.

6. Repeat this procedure and remove the bearing from the other side.

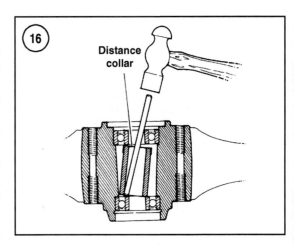

7. If the special tool or its equivalent is not available, remove the bearings by performing the following:

   a. Using a long drift and hammer, tilt the distance collar away from one side of the hub (**Figure 16**) and then drive the opposite bearing out of the hub.

   b. Remove the distance collar.

   c. Turn the wheel over and use the drift to drive the remaining bearing from the hub.

8. Clean the hub and distance collar with solvent. Dry them with compressed air.

9. Install new bearings as described in this section.

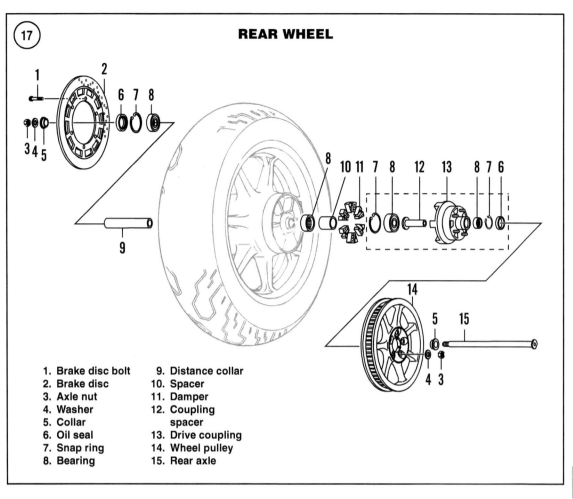

REAR WHEEL

1. Brake disc bolt
2. Brake disc
3. Axle nut
4. Washer
5. Collar
6. Oil seal
7. Snap ring
8. Bearing
9. Distance collar
10. Spacer
11. Damper
12. Coupling spacer
13. Drive coupling
14. Wheel pulley
15. Rear axle

Installation

1. Place the bearings in a freezer overnight. This will ease installation.

2. Blow any dirt or foreign matter out of the hub before installing the bearing.

3. Pack the open side of each bearing with grease.

4. Position a bearing with the manufacturer's marks facing out, and place the bearing squarely on the bore opening on the left side of the hub. Select a bearing driver or socket (**Figure 13**) with an outside diameter that matches (or is slightly smaller than) the outside diameter of the bearing. Drive the bearing into the bore until it bottoms.

5. Turn the hub over. Install the distance collar and center it against the left bearing's inner race.

6. Place the right bearing (manufacturer's marks facing out) squarely against the bore opening. Using the same socket or bearing driver (**Figure 13**), drive the bearing partway into the bore. Stop and check the distance collar. It must still be centered within the bearing. If it is not, install the axle partway through the hub and center the distance collar. Remove the axle and continue installing the bearing until it bottoms.

7. Reassemble the hub as described in this chapter.

REAR WHEEL

Refer to **Figure 17**.

Removal

1. Securely support the motorcycle on a level surface with the rear wheel off the ground.

2. Remove the muffler as described in *Exhaust System* in Chapter Eight.

3. Remove the rear fender (Chapter Fifteen).

4. Remove the rear caliper bolts (A. **Figure 18**) and lower the rear brake caliper from the disc. Suspend the caliper so it does not hang from the brake hose. Note how the brake hose is routed.

5. Remove the brake pads from the caliper bracket as described in Chapter Fourteen.

6. Loosen the drive belt adjuster locknut (A, **Figure 19**) and turn the adjuster (B) into the swing arm. Repeat on the adjuster in the other side of the swing arm.

7. Loosen the axle nut (C, **Figure 19**).

8. Push the wheel forward, and remove the drive belt (**Figure 20**) from the wheel pulley.

> *NOTE*
> *The left and right belt pullers are not identical. Label each puller so it can be reinstalled on the correct side.*

9. Remove the axle nut (C, **Figure 19**), washer (D) and the right belt puller (E).

10. Support the wheel. Remove the axle (A, **Figure 21**) and the left belt puller (B) from the left side. Lower the wheel to the floor.

11. Roll wheel rearward until the caliper bracket (B, **Figure 18**) can be lowered from the swing arm.

> *NOTE*
> *The collars are not identical. The collar in the right side of the hub is black (**Figure 22**); the left collar is silver (B, **Figure 7**). If these colors are not distinct, mark each collar so it can be reinstalled in its original location during assembly.*

12. Roll the wheel from between the swing arm, and remove the wheel. Account for the collar in each side of the hub.

13. Inspect the rear wheel as described in this chapter.

14. If necessary, disassemble the hub as described in this chapter.

Installation

1. Apply a coat of lithium-soap grease to the rear axle (**Figure 5**), bearings and oil seals.

2. If removed, install each collar (**Figure 22** and B, **Figure 7**) into its original location in the hub.

3. Position the wheel between the swing arm and roll the wheel forward.

4. Fit the caliper bracket onto the swing arm so the bracket arm (A, **Figure 23**) slides along the indexing boss on the swing arm (**Figure 24**).

5. Roll the rear wheel into position in the swing arm, and fit the drive belt onto the wheel pulley. Make sure the mount in the caliper bracket (B, **Figure 23**) aligns with the collar in the right side of the hub.

6. Set the left chain puller (B, **Figure 21**) into the left side of the swing arm so the puller's raised sides sit vertically.

7. Insert the rear axle from the left side. It must pass through the belt puller and left side of the swing arm, the hub, brake caliper bracket and emerge from the right side of the swing arm.

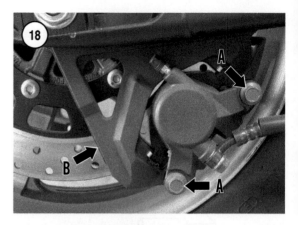

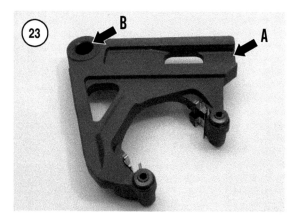

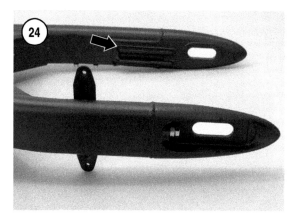

8. Rotate the axle head so its flats engage the raised sides of the left belt puller, and seat the axle within the puller. Refer to A, **Figure 21**.

9. Install the right belt puller (E, **Figure 19**) into the swing arm so its flat side faces the swing arm.

10. Install the washer (D, **Figure 19**) and axle nut (C) onto the end of the axle.

11. Adjust the drive belt as described in Chapter Three.

12. Tighten the rear axle nut to 150 N•m (111 ft.-lb.).

13. Install the brake pads into the caliper bracket as described in Chapter Fourteen.

14. Fit the caliper over the brake disc, and seat it against on the caliper bracket.

15. Tighten the rear caliper bolts (A, **Figure 18**) to 27 N•m (20 ft.-lb.).

REAR HUB

Preliminary Inspection

CAUTION
Do not remove the wheel bearings for inspection purposes. The bearings are damaged during removal and cannot be reused. Remove wheel bearings only if they must be replaced.

1. Remove the rear wheel as described in this chapter.

2. Insert the axle through the hub, and turn the axle by hand. Each bearing should turn smoothly without noise or excessive play.

3. Inspect the rear wheel as described in *Wheel Inspection* in this chapter.

Disassembly/Assembly

Refer to **Figure 17**.

1. Remove the rear wheel as described in this chapter. If still in place, remove the collar from the left (B, **Figure 7**) and right sides (**Figure 22**) of the hub. Note the differences in the collars.

2. Set the wheel on wooden blocks (**Figure 2**) to protect the brake disc.

3. Pry the oil seal from the right side of the hub (A, **Figure 25**) and from the outboard side of the drive hub assembly (A, **Figure 26**). Place a shop rag beneath the pry tool so the hub will not be damaged.

NOTE
If the drive hub assembly is difficult to remove from the hub, tap against the backside of the pulley (from the opposite side of the wheel through the wheel

spokes) with the wooden handle of a hammer. Tap evenly around the perimeter of the pulley until the coupling assembly is free of the hub and the rubber dampers.

4. Grasp the wheel pulley (B, **Figure 26**). Pull the pulley/drive hub assembly straight up and remove it from the hub.

5. Remove the spacer (A, **Figure 27**) from the left side of the hub.

6. Inspect the wheel bearings and the drive coupling bearing as described in *Wheel Inspection* in this chapter. If necessary, remove and replace the rear wheel bearings as described in this chapter.

7. Inspect the rear hub as described in this section.

8. If removed, install the drive coupling by performing the following.

   a. Make sure the dampers (A, **Figure 28**) are properly seated within the rear hub.

   b. Seat the spacer (A, **Figure 27**) in the hub.

   c. Set the drive coupling onto the hub so the coupling spines (A, **Figure 29**) align with the spaces (B, **Figure 27**) between the rubber dampers, and install the drive coupling into the hub. Press the coupling onto the hub until the coupling bottoms.

9. Pack the lips of a new oil seal with lithium-soap grease. Drive the seal with a seal driver (**Figure 30**) or a large diameter socket squarely seated on the outer portion of the seal. Drive the seal until it seats against the bearing or when the outer surface is flush with the hub or drive coupling. Repeat this step on the opposite side.

10. Install the correct collar into the oil seal in the left (B, **Figure 7**) and right sides (**Figure 22**) sides of the hub.

Inspection

1. Inspect the rear hub bearings and drive coupling bearing as described in *Wheel Inspection* in this chapter. If necessary, remove and replace the bearings as described in *Rear Wheel Bearing* in this chapter.

2. Check the oil seal (A, **Figure 25** and A, **Figure 26**) for damage. If any seal is damaged, replace the oil seals as a set.

3. Inspect the drive coupling by performing the following:

   a. Remove the rubber dampers (A, **Figure 28**) and inspect them for cracks, wear or deterioration. If any damage is found, replace all the dampers as a complete set.

   b. Inspect the damper bosses (B, **Figure 28**) in the rear hub. Check for cracks or wear. If any damage is visible, replace the rear wheel.

   c. Inspect the drive coupling splines (A, **Figure 29**) for cracks or damage, replace if necessary.

CAUTION
If the wheel pulley requires replacement, also replace the engine pulley and the drive chain. Never install a new drive chain over worn sprockets or a worn drive chain over new sprockets. The old parts will wear out the new part prematurely.

4. Inspect the wheel pulley teeth (**Figure 31**) for broken or worn teeth. If the teeth are visibly worn

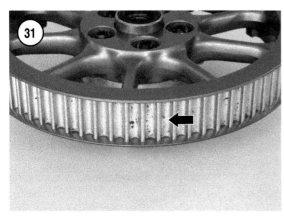

replace the wheel sprocket as described in this chapter, drive belt (Chapter Thirteen) and engine pulley (Chapter Seven).

REAR WHEEL BEARING

Refer to **Figure 17**.

Removal

A ball bearing is installed in the inboard side of the drive coupling (B, **Figure 29**) and in the right side

of the rear hub (B, **Figure 25**). A needle bearing (C, **Figure 26**) is used in the outboard side of the drive coupling and the left side of the rear hub (C, **Figure 28**).

1. If still installed, remove the drive coupling from the hub as described in this chapter.
2. Set the wheel on wooden blocks so the brake disc side faces up.
3. Remove the oil seal (A, **Figure 25**) and snap ring from the hub. Discard the snap ring.
4A. Use the collet-style tool (**Figure 14**) to remove the ball bearing (B, **Figure 25**) from the right side of the hub as described in *Front Bearing* in this chapter.
4B. If the special tool is unavailable, remove the ball bearing by performing the following:
    a. Set the wheel on wooden blocks so the left side faces up.
    b. Insert a drift through the needle bearing.
    c. Use the drift to tap against the right bearing's outer race until the bearing is driven from the hub (**Figure 16**).
5. Once the ball bearing is out, remove the distance collar from the hub.
6. Set the wheel on wooden blocks so the right side of the hub faces up.
7. Insert a drift from the right side of the hub, and drive the needle bearing (C, **Figure 28**) from the hub.
8. Pry the oil seal (A, **Figure 26**) from the drive coupling.
9. Remove the snap ring (C, **Figure 29**) from each side of the drive coupling. Discard each snap ring.
10. Remove the drive coupling ball and needle bearings by repeating Steps 4-7. Once the ball bearing has been removed from the drive coupling, remove the coupling spacer instead of the distance collar mentioned in Step 5.

Installation

Wheel hub

1. Place the bearings in a freezer overnight. This will ease installation.
2. Blow any dirt or foreign matter out of the hub before installing the bearing.
3. Squarely seat the needle bearing in the left side of the hub so the side with the manufacturers marks faces out.
4. Select an appropriately sized bearing driver or socket and drive the needle bearing (C, **Figure 28**) into the bore until it bottoms.
5. Turn the wheel over. Install the distance collar, and center it against the bearing inner race.
6. Pack the open side of the ball bearing with grease.

11

7. Position the bearing with the manufacturer's marks facing out, and place the bearing squarely onto the bore in the right side of the hub.

8. Select an appropriately sized bearing driver or socket and drive the bearing (B, **Figure 25**) partway into the bore. Stop and check the distance collar. It must still be centered within the bearing. If it is not, install the axle partway through the hub and center the collar. Remove the axle, and continue installing the bearing until it bottoms.

9. Install a new snap ring so it completely sits within the groove in the hub bore.

10. Pack the lips of a new oil seal with lithium-soap grease. Place the seal squarely onto the bore opening so the manufacturer's marks face out.

11. Using the same bearing driver or socket used in Step 8, drive the oil seal (A, **Figure 25**) into the bore until the seal is flush with the hub.

Drive coupling

1. Place the bearings in a freezer overnight. This will ease installation.

2. Blow any dirt or foreign matter out of the coupling before installing the bearings.

3. Squarely seat the needle bearing in the left side of the coupling so the side with the manufacturers marks faces out.

4. Select an appropriately sized bearing driver or socket and drive the bearing (C, **Figure 26**) into the bore until the bearing bottoms.

5. Install a new snap ring into the groove in the left side of the coupling. Make sure it seats correctly.

6. Turn the coupling over and install the coupling spacer.

7. Pack the open side of the ball bearing with grease.

8. Position the ball bearing with the manufacturer's marks facing out, and place the bearing squarely onto the bore opening in the right side of the coupling.

9. Select an appropriately sized bearing driver or socket and drive the bearing (B, **Figure 29**) into the bore until the bearing bottoms.

10. Install a new snap ring (C, **Figure 29**) so it completely sits within the groove in the coupling bore.

11. Turn the coupling over so the left side faces up.

12. Pack the lips of a new oil seal with lithium-soap grease. Place the seal squarely onto the bore opening so the manufacturer's marks face out.

13. Using an appropriately sized bearing driver or socket and drive the seal (A, **Figure 26**) into the bore until the seal is flush with the coupling.

WHEEL PULLEY

Refer to **Figure 17**.

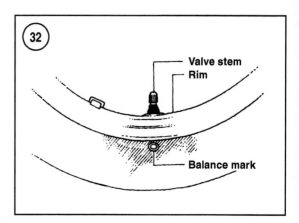

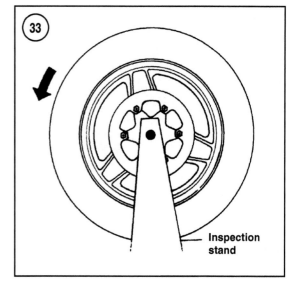

Removal/Assembly

1. Remove the rear wheel as described in this chapter.

2. Remove each wheel pulley nut and its washer (D, **Figure 26**). Discard the self-locking nuts.

3. Install by reversing these removal steps while noting the following:

   a. Clean the wheel pulley and hub mating surfaces.

   b. Install new self-locking wheel pulley nuts (D, **Figure 26**).

   c. Following a crisscross pattern, evenly snug down the pulley nuts in two-to-three steps.

> *CAUTION*
> *On a new motorcycle or after a new wheel pulley has been installed, check the torque on the wheel pulley nuts after ten minutes of riding and after each ten-minute riding period until the nuts have seated and remain tight. Failure to keep the pulley nuts correctly tightened will damage the rear hub.*

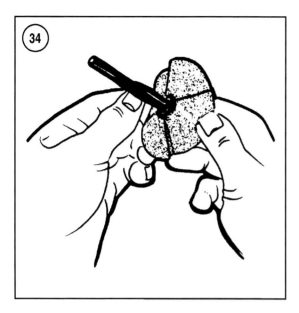

d. Tighten the wheel pulley nuts to 95 N•m (70 ft.-lb.).

WHEEL BALANCE

An unbalanced wheel is unsafe. Depending upon the degree of unbalance and the speed of the motorcycle, a rider may experience anything from a mild vibration to a violent shimmy that may result in loss of control.

Before balancing a wheel, thoroughly clean the wheel assembly. Makes sure the wheel bearings are in good condition and properly lubricated. The wheel must rotate freely. Also check the balance mark on the tire (**Figure 32**). It must align with the valve stem. If it does not, break the tire loose from the rim and align it before balancing the wheel. Refer to *Tubeless Tires* in this chapter.

NOTE
When balancing the wheels, do so with the brake disc(s) attached. These rotate with the wheel and affect the balance.

1. Remove the wheel as described in this chapter.
2. Make sure the valve stem and the valve cap are tight.
3. Mount the wheel on a stand such as the one shown in **Figure 33** so it can rotate freely.
4. Check the wheel runout as described in *Wheel Inspection* in this chapter. Do not try to balance a wheel with excessive runout.
5. Remove any balance weights mounted on the wheel.
6. Give the wheel a spin, and let it coast to a stop. Mark the tire at the highest point (12 o'clock). This is the wheel's lightest point.

7. Spin the wheel several more times. If the wheel keeps coming to rest at the same point, it is out of balance. If the wheel stops at different points each time, the wheel is balanced.

NOTE
Adhesive test weights are available from motorcycle dealers. These are adhesive-backed weights that can be cut to the desired length and attached directly to the rim.

8. Loosely attach a balance weight (or tape a test weight) at the upper or light side (12 o'clock) of the wheel.
9. Rotate the wheel 1/4 turn (3 o'clock). Release the wheel and note the following:
   a. If the wheel does not rotate (if it stays at the 3 o'clock position), the correct balance weight was installed. The wheel is balanced.
   b. If the wheel rotates and the weighted portion goes up, replace the weight with the next heavier size.
   c. If the wheel rotates and the weighted portion goes down, replace the weight with the next lighter size.
   d. Repeat this step until the wheel remains at rest after being rotated 1/4 turn. Rotate the wheel another 1/4 turn, another 1/4 turn, and another to see if the wheel is correctly balanced.
10. Remove the test weight, and install the correct weight onto the rim according to the weight manufacturer's directions.

TUBELESS TIRES

WARNING
Do not install an inner tube inside a tubeless tire. The tube will cause abnormal heat buildup in the tire.

Tubeless tires have the word *TUBELESS* molded in the tire sidewall and the rims have *TUBELESS* cast on them.

When a tubeless tire is flat, take it to a motorcycle dealership or tire specialist for repair. Punctured tubeless tires should be removed from the rim to inspect the inside of the tire and to apply a combination plug/patch from the inside (**Figure 34**). Do not rely on a plug or cord repair applied from outside the tire. They might be acceptable on a car, but they are dangerous on a motorcycle.

After repairing a tubeless tire, do not exceed 50 mph (80 kph) for the first 24 hours. Never race on a repaired tubeless tire. The patch could work loose due to tire flex and heat.

11

Repair

1. Remove the tire from the rim as described in this section.
2. Inspect the rim inner flange. Smooth any scratches on the sealing surface with emery cloth. If a scratch is deeper than 0.5 mm (0.020 in.), the wheel should be replaced.
3. Inspect the tire inside and out. Replace a tire if any of the following is found:
   a. A puncture larger than 3 mm (1/8 in.) diameter.
   b. A punctured or damaged sidewall.
   c. More than 2 punctures in the tire.
4. Apply the plug/patch, following the instructions supplied with the patch kit.

Removal

The wheels can easily be damaged during tire removal. Special care must be taken with tire irons to avoid scratching and gouging the outer rim surface. Protect the rim by using rim protectors or scraps of leather between the tire iron and the rim. The stock cast wheels are designed for use with tubeless tires.

When removing a tubeless tire, take care not to damage the tire beads, inner liner of the tire or the wheel rim flange. Use tire levers or flat-handled tire irons (**Figure 35**) with rounded ends.

> *NOTE*
> *While removing a tire, support the wheel on two blocks of wood so the brake disc does not contact the floor.*

1. Place a balance mark opposite the valve stem (**Figure 32**) on the tire sidewall so the tire can be reinstalled in the same position for easier balancing.
2. Remove the valve core to deflate the tire.

> *CAUTION*
> *The inner rim and tire bead are sealing surfaces on a tubeless tire. Do not scratch the inside of the rim or damage the tire bead.*

> *NOTE*
> *Removal of tubeless tires from their rims can be very difficult because of the exceptionally tight bead/rim seal. Breaking the bead seal may require the use of a bead breaker (**Figure 36**). If breaking the seal is difficult, take the tire to a motorcycle dealership to avoid damaging the wheel.*

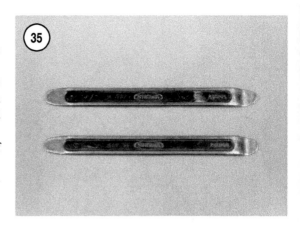

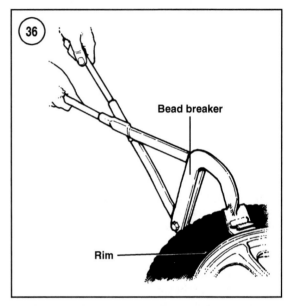

3. Press the entire bead on both sides of the tire into the center of the rim.
4. Lubricate the beads with soapy water.

> *NOTE*
> *Use rim protectors or insert scraps of leather between the tire irons and the rim to protect the rim from damage.*

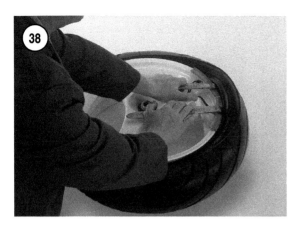

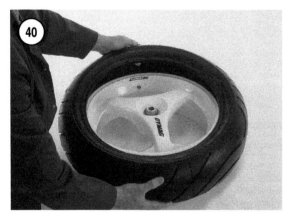

5. Insert the tire iron under the bead next to the valve stem (**Figure 37**). Force the bead on the opposite side of the tire into the center of the rim and pry the bead over the rim with the tire iron.

6. Insert a second tire iron next to the first to hold the bead over the rim (**Figure 38**). Work around the tire with the first tool prying the bead over the rim.

NOTE
Step 7 is required only if it is necessary to completely remove the tire from the rim.

7. Set the wheel on its edge. Insert a tire tool between the second bead and the same side of the rim that the first bead was pried over (**Figure 39**). Force the bead on the opposite side from the tool into the center of the rim. Pry the second bead off the rim, working around the wheel with two tire irons as with the first.

8. Inspect the valve stem seal. Because rubber deteriorates with age, it is advisable to replace the valve stem when replacing a tire.

Installation

1. Inspect the tire for any damage, especially inside.

2. A new tire may have balancing rubbers inside. These are not patches and should not be disturbed.

3. Manufacturers place a colored spot near the bead that indicates a lighter point on the tire. Install the tires so this balance mark (either the manufacturer's or the one made during removal) sits opposite the valve stem (**Figure 32**).

4. Most tires have directional arrows on the sidewall that indicate the direction of rotation. Install the tire so the arrow points in the direction of forward rotation.

5. Lubricate both beads of the tire with soapy water.

6. Place the backside of the tire into the center of the rim. The lower bead should go into the center of the rim and the upper bead outside. Work around the tire in both directions (**Figure 40**).

7. Starting at the side opposite the valve stem, press the upper bead into the rim (**Figure 41**). Pry the bead into the rim on both sides of the initial point with a tire tool, working around the rim to the valve (**Figure 42**).

8. Check the bead on both sides of the tire for an even fit around the rim.

WARNING
Never exceed 56 psi (385 kPa) inflation pressure as the tire could burst causing injury. Never stand directly over the tire while inflating it.

11

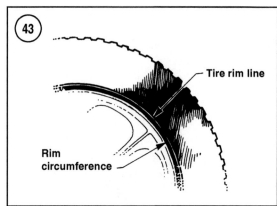

Tire rim line

Rim circumference

9. Place an inflatable band around the circumference of the tire. Slowly inflate the band until the tire beads are pressed against the rim. Inflate the tire enough to seat it against the rim. Deflate and remove the band.

10. After inflating the tire, check to see that the beads are fully seated and that the tire rim lines are the same distance from the rim all the way around the tire (**Figure 43**). If the beads will not seat, deflate the tire, re-lubricate the rim and beads with soapy water, and re-inflate the tire.

11. Inflate the tire to the required pressure. Refer to tire inflation pressure specifications listed in **Table 1**. Screw on the valve stem cap.

12. Balance the wheel assembly as described in this chapter.

Table 1 WHEEL AND TIRE SPECIFICATIONS

Item	Specification
Front Wheel	
Wheel size	16M/C × MT3.00
Wheel material	Aluminum
Wheel travel	135.0 mm (5.31 in.)
Radial runout limit	1.0 mm (0.04 in.)
Lateral runout limit	0.5 mm (0.02 in.)
Front Tire	
Type	Tubeless
Size	130/90-16M/C 67H
Model	
Dunlop	D404F X
Bridgestone	EXEDRA G721
Wear limit	1.0 mm (0.04 in.)
Rear Wheel	
Wheel size	16M/C × MT4.50
Wheel material	Aluminum
Wheel travel	110.0 mm (4.331 in.)
Radial runout limit	1.0 mm (0.04 in.)
Lateral runout limit	0.5 mm (0.02 in.)

(continued)

Table 1 WHEEL AND TIRE SPECIFICATIONS (continued)

Item	Specification
Rear Tire	
Type	Tubeless
Size	170/70B 16M/C 75H
Model	
Dunlop	K555
Bridgestone	EXEDRA G722 G
Wear limit	1.0 mm (0.04 in.)
Tire inflation pressure (cold)[1]	
Front	250 kPa (36 psi)
Rear	280 kPa (41 psi)
Maximum load[2]	
XVS13A models	210 kg (463 lb.)
XVS13CT models	190 kg (419 lb.)

1. Tire inflation pressures apply to original equipment tires only. Aftermarket tires may require different pressures. Refer to the tire manufacturer's specifications.
2. Load equals the total weight of rider, passenger, accessories and all cargo.

Table 2 WHEEL TORQUE SPECIFICATIONS

Item	N•m	in.-lb.	ft.-lb.
Brake disc bolts*	23	–	17
Drive belt adjuster locknut	16	–	12
Front brake caliper bracket bolts	40	–	30
Front axle	59	–	43.5
Front axle clamp bolt	20	–	15
Muffler bolts	35	–	26
Rear axle nut	150	–	111
Rear brake caliper bolts	27	–	20
Wheel pulley nuts*	95	–	70

*Refer to text.

11

CHAPTER TWELVE

FRONT SUSPENSION AND STEERING

This chapter covers the handlebar, front fork and steering components.

Table 1 and **Table 2** are at the end of this chapter.

HANDLEBAR

Removal

1. Securely support the motorcycle on a level surface.
2. Remove the fuel tank (Chapter Eight).

CAUTION
Cover the front fender and frame with plastic to protect them from accidental brake fluid spills. Brake fluid will damage most finishes. Immediately wash spilled brake fluid with soapy water and rinse the area thoroughly.

3. Cover the front fender and frame to protect them.
4. Remove the cover screws (A and B, **Figure 1**), and lift the cover (C) from the meter assembly. Account for the collar installed with each screw.
5. Remove the bracket bolts (A, **Figure 2**), and remove the meter assembly cover bracket (B).
6A. If the handlebar is being replaced, continue with Step 7.
6B. If the handlebar is not being replaced, proceed to Step 14.
7. Remove all cable ties that secure cables to the handlebar. Note the location of all ties and the routing of all cables and wiring.
8. Remove the front brake master cylinder (Chapter Fourteen). Secure the master cylinder to the motor-cycle. Keep the master-cylinder reservoir upright. This prevents brake fluid spills, and it helps keep air out of the brake system. Do not disconnect the hydraulic brake line.
9. Remove the right and left handlebar switches (Chapter Nine).
10. Remove the cap from the right handlebar weight (A, **Figure 3**). Remove the weight from the handlebar end.
11. Slide the throttle grip assembly (B, **Figure 3**) from the handlebar.
12. Remove the left handlebar grip by performing the following:
   a. Remove the cap from the left handlebar weight (A, **Figure 4**), and remove the weight from the handlebar end.
   b. Insert a thin-bladed screwdriver under the hand grip (B, **Figure 4**).
   c. Spray electrical contact cleaner under the hand grip. Quickly twist the grip to break its seal, and remove the grip.
13. Remove the clutch lever by performing the following:
   a. Slide the clutch lever boot (A, **Figure 5**) away from the adjuster, and loosen the clutch cable locknut (B). Rotate the adjuster (C, **Figure 5**) to provide maximum slack in the cable, and disconnect the cable end from the clutch hand lever.
   b. Disconnect the electrical lead from the clutch switch.
   c. Loosen the clutch lever clamp bolt (C, **Figure 4**), and slide the clutch lever assembly from the handlebar.

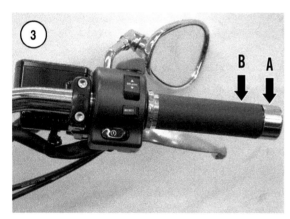

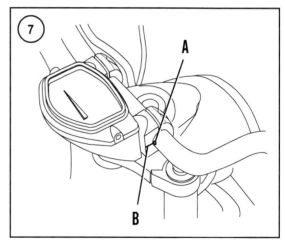

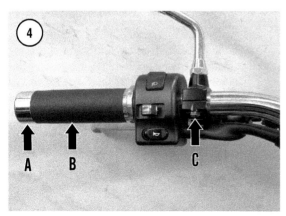

14. Loosen and remove the handlebar clamp bolts (A, **Figure 6**), and remove each handlebar clamp (B).

15. Lift the handlebar from the handlebar holder. If the handlebar is not being replaced, lay it across the tarp protecting the frame.

Installation

1. Position the handlebar against the holder so the punch mark on the handlebar (A, **Figure 7**) aligns with the line (B) on the holder.

2. Fit each handlebar clamp (B, **Figure 6**) into position, and install the clamp bolts (A).

3. Tighten the handlebar clamp bolts to 28 N•m (21 ft.-lb.). Tighten each lower clamp bolt first and then the upper clamp bolts.

4. Fit and meter assembly cover bracket (B, **Figure 2**) into place, and install the cover bracket bolts (A). Tighten the to 7 N•m (62 in.-lb.).

5. Make sure a damper is in place in each forward mount of the meter assembly cover. Set the cover into place (C, **Figure 1**) and install the cover screws (A and B, **Figure 1**). Tighten the front meter assembly cover screws (B, **Figure 1**) to 7 N•m (62 in.-lb.) and tighten the rear screws (A) securely.

6. Install the clutch lever assembly by performing the following:

   a. Slide the clutch lever assembly onto the handlebar. Position the clutch lever assembly (A, **Figure 8**) so the gap in the clamp aligns with the index mark (B) on the handlebar.

   b. Tighten the clutch lever clamp bolt (C, **Figure 4**) to 7 N•m (62 in.-lb.).

   c. Lubricate the clutch cable end with lithium-soap grease, and connect the cable end to the clutch lever.

   d. Fit the cable through the slot in the clutch adjuster and locknut, and turn the adjuster so the slots no longer align.

   e. Connect the clutch switch connector to the switch.

7. Install the left handlebar switch (Chapter Nine). Make sure the line formed by the mating surfaces of the switch halves aligns with the dot (A, **Figure 9**) on the handlebar.

8. Install a new left handlebar grip by performing the following:

   a. Apply a thin layer of rubber adhesive to the end of the handlebar.

   b. Slide the hand grip (B, **Figure 4**) onto the handlebar so the gap between the grip and the left handlebar switch is less than 3 mm (0.12 in.) (B, **Figure 9**). Reposition the switch and clutch lever as necessary.

   c. Wipe away excess adhesive.

   d. Install the handlebar weight (A, **Figure 4**) into the left end of the handlebar. Tighten the weight to 23 N•m (17 ft.-lb.) and install the end cap.

WARNING
Do not ride with a loose hand grip.

   e. Check the hand grip after 10 minutes to make sure it is tight.

9. Slide the throttle grip assembly (B, **Figure 3**) on the right end of the handlebar. Lubricate the throttle drip assembly with lithium-soap grease.

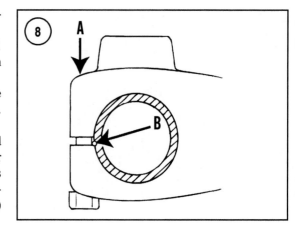

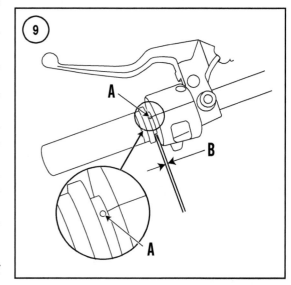

10. Install the right handlebar weight (A, **Figure 3**) into the end of the handlebar. Tighten the weight to 23 N•m (17 ft.-lb.) and install the end cap.

11. Install the right handlebar switch (Chapter Nine).

12. Install the front brake master cylinder (Chapter 14).

13. Adjust the clutch cable free play and throttle cable free play (Chapter Three).

Inspection

Check the handlebar along the entire mounting area for cracks or damage. Replace a bent or damaged handlebar immediately. If the bike is involved in a crash, examine the handlebar, steering stem and front fork legs carefully.

HANDLEBAR HOLDER

Removal/Installation

1. Remove the meter assembly (Chapter Nine).

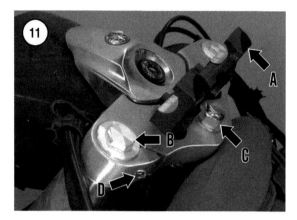

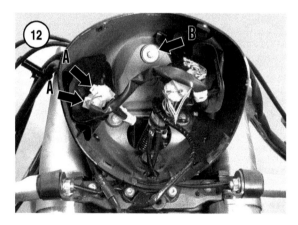

2. Remove the handlebar as described in this chapter.

NOTE
The upper fork bridge is shown removed for photographic clarity. The handlebar holder can be removed while the fork bridge is in place.

3. Remove each handlebar holder nut (A, **Figure 10**). Note that the nuts also secure the cable guide (B, **Figure 10**) to the bottom of the fork bridge.
4. Lift the handlebar holder (A, **Figure 11**) from the upper fork bridge. Account for the washer and damper installed in each mount.

5. Installation is the reverse of removal.
  a. Make sure the washer and damper is in place on each mount in the upper fork bridge.
  b. Fit the cable guide (B, **Figure 10**) over the handlebar holder studs before installing the nuts (A).
  c. Tighten the handlebar holder nuts to 32 N•m (23 ft.-lb.).

FRONT FORK

Service Methods

The following section describes complete removal and service for the front fork. Fork adjustments are addressed in Chapter Three.

To prevent damaging a front fork component during service, note the following:
1. Avoid rounding off the shoulders on the fork cap bolts by using a 6-point socket.
2. Do not overtighten the handlebar and fork bridge clamp bolts, which could damage the fork bridge threads and fork tubes. Tighten all clamp bolts to specification (**Table 2**).
3. The fork sliders are easily scratched. Handle them carefully during all service procedures.
4. When holding the fork tubes in a vise, protect the tubes with soft jaws, and do not overtighten the vise.
5. Before concluding that a major problem exists with the front fork, drain the fork oil and refill the fork legs with the proper type and quantity of fork oil as described in this chapter. If the problem still exists, such as poor damping, leaks around the seals or a tendency to bottom or top out, follow the service procedures in this section.
6. To simplify fork service and to prevent the mixing of parts, service each fork leg individually.

Removal

1. Securely support the motorcycle with a front end stand.
2. On XVS13CT models, remove the windshield assembly and the windshield bracket (Chapter Fifteen).
3. Remove the fuel tank so it will not be scratched (Chapter Eight).
4. Remove the front wheel (Chapter Eleven).
5. Remove the front fender (Chapter Fifteen).
6. Remove the meter assembly (Chapter Nine).
7. Remove the handlebar (this chapter). Lay the handlebar across the tarp protecting the frame.
8. Separate the halves of each 2-pin main switch connectors (A, **Figure 12**). Feed the main switch cable through the hole in the housing.

9. Remove the upper headlight housing bolt (B, **Figure 12**). Account for the washer and collar installed with this bolt. Note that this bolt turns into a nut on the main switch cover.

10. If a fork leg will be serviced, perform the following:

  a. Set an oil pan beneath the fork leg. Loosen the Allen bolt at the bottom of the fork leg just enough to break it loose. If the bolts is loosened too much, oil will dribble from the bottom of the leg.

  b. Use a 6-point socket to loosen the cap nut (B, **Figure 11**) on the relevant fork tube.

11. Note that the upper edge of the tube aligns with the top of the upper fork bridge (**Figure 13**). The fork leg must be reinstalled to the same height during assembly.

12. Remove the steering head nut (C, **Figure 11**) and its washer.

13. Loosen the clamp bolt (D, **Figure 11**) on each side of the upper fork bridge.

14. Lift the upper fork bridge from the fork tubes. Set the upper fork bridge across the tarp protecting the frame.

15. Slide the upper fork cover (**Figure 14**) and the cover spacer from the fork tube.

16. Loosen the clamp bolts (**Figure 15**) on the lower fork bridge. Rotate the fork leg, and lower it from the lower fork bridge and the lower fork cover.

17. If necessary, remove the fork cover bolts (A, **Figure 16**), and remove the lower fork cover (B).

Installation

1. If removed, install the lower fork onto the fork leg and let it rest against the slider.

2. Slide the fork leg through its mount in the lower fork bridge. Tighten the lower fork bridge clamp bolts (**Figure 15**) to hold the leg in place.

3. Set the upper fork bridge into place on the fork legs.

4. Install the washer and steering head nut (C, **Figure 11**). Tighten the nut to 110 N•m (81 ft.-lb.).

5. Loosen the lower fork bridge clamp bolts (**Figure 15**), and adjust the fork leg until the edge of the fork tube aligns with the top of the upper fork bridge (**Figure 13**). Tighten the lower fork bridge clamp bolts (**Figure 15**) to specification (**Table 2**).

6. Remove the steering head nut and its washer. Remove the upper fork bridge.

7. Set the lower fork cover (B, **Figure 16**) against the lower fork bridge, and install the fork cover bolts (A). Tighten the bolts to 18 N•m (13 ft.-lb.).

8. Slide the upper cover (**Figure 14**) and its spacer down the fork leg, and seat the cover on the spacer.

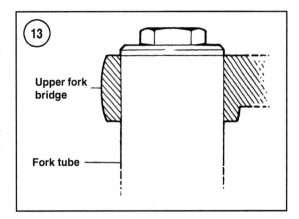

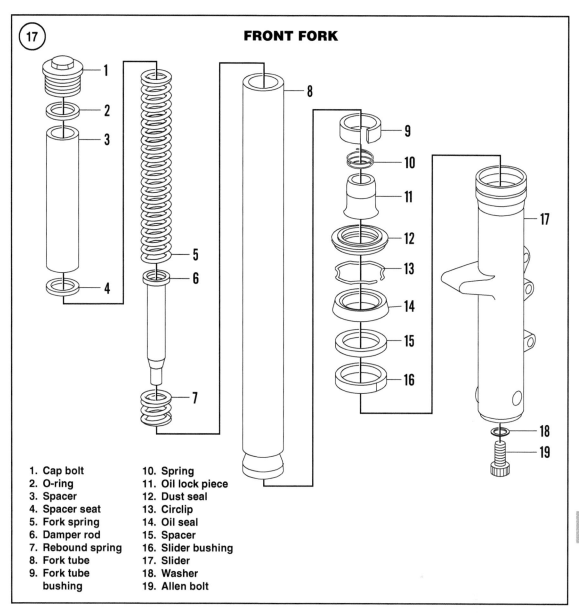

FRONT FORK

1. Cap bolt
2. O-ring
3. Spacer
4. Spacer seat
5. Fork spring
6. Damper rod
7. Rebound spring
8. Fork tube
9. Fork tube bushing
10. Spring
11. Oil lock piece
12. Dust seal
13. Circlip
14. Oil seal
15. Spacer
16. Slider bushing
17. Slider
18. Washer
19. Allen bolt

9. Set the upper fork bridge into place on the fork legs. Insert the main switch wires through the hole in the headlight housing.

10. Install the washer and steering head nut (C, **Figure 11**). Tighten the nut to 110 N•m (81 ft.-lb.).

11. If the fork leg was serviced, tighten the cap bolt (B, **Figure 11**) to 23 N•m (17 ft.-lb.).

12. Tighten the upper fork bridge clamp bolts (D, **Figure 11**) to 23 N•m (17 ft.-lb.).

13. Install the upper headlight housing bolt (B, **Figure 12**) with its washer and collar. Turn the bolt into the nut on the main switch cover, and tighten the headlight housing bolt to 7 N•m (62 in.-lb.).

14. Connect the halves of each 2-pin main switch connectors (A, **Figure 12**). Wrap the connectors in their bundle.

15. Complete the assembly by reversing Steps 2-7.

Disassembly

A damper rod holder (Yamaha part No. 90890-01426); T-handle (Yamaha part No: YM-01326 or 90890-01326) and fork seal driver (Yamaha part No. YM-01442 or 90809-01442) or equivalent tools are need to service the fork legs.

NOTE
The fork leg Allen bolt can be removed without using the damper rod holder and T-handle. However, the Allen bolt cannot be tightened to the torque speci-fication without these tools.

Refer to **Figure 17**.

1. Secure the fork vertically in a vise with soft jaws.

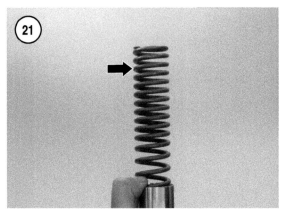

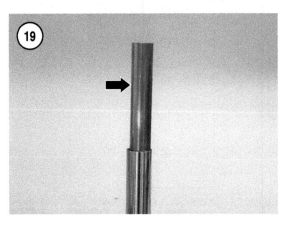

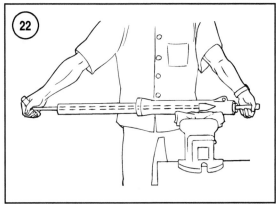

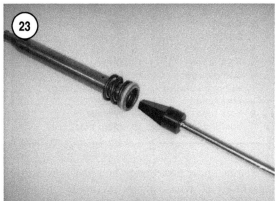

2. Remove the cap bolt (**Figure 18**) from the fork tube.

3. Remove the spacer (**Figure 19**), seat (**Figure 20**) and the fork spring (**Figure 21**).

4. Remove the fork leg from the vise. Invert the leg and pour the oil from the fork leg.

5. Secure the slider horizontally in a vise (**Figure 22**).

6. Install the damper rod holder onto the T-handle. Insert the tool into the fork tube so the rod holder engages the damper rod (**Figure 23**). Hold the damper rod, and remove the Allen bolt and its washer from the bottom of the slider (**Figure 24**).

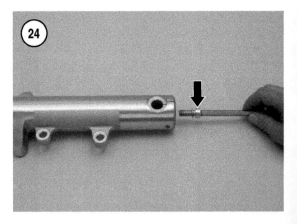

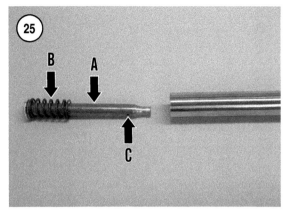

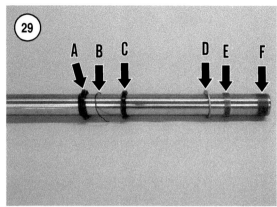

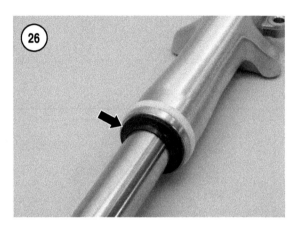

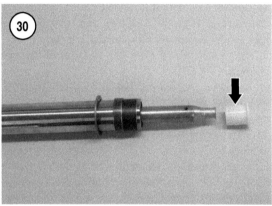

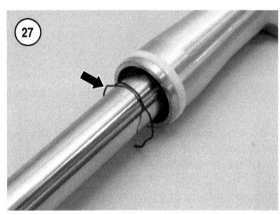

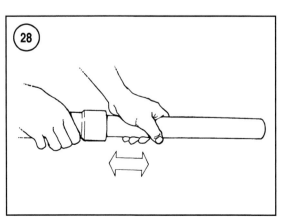

7. Remove the damper rod (A, **Figure 25**) and its spring (B) from the fork leg.

8. Pry the dust seal (**Figure 26**) from the slider, and slide the seal up the fork leg.

9. Remove the circlip (**Figure 27**) from its groove in the slider.

10. There is an interference fit between the slider bushing and the fork tube bushing. To remove the fork tube from the slider, firmly grasp the fork tube, pull hard on the fork tube using quick in-and-out stokes, and remove the tube from the slider (**Figure 28**).

11. Slide the dust seal (A, **Figure 29**), circlip (B), oil seal (C), spacer (D) and slider bushing (E) from the fork tube.

12. Remove the oil lock piece (**Figure 30**) from the slider.

13. Inspect all parts as described in this section.

Assembly

1. Coat all parts with SAE 10W fork oil before installation.

2. If removed, install a new fork tube bushing (F, **Figure 29**) as described in *Inspection* in this section.

3. Slide the rebound spring (B, **Figure 25**) onto the damper rod (A).

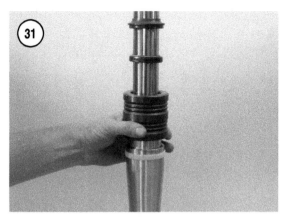

4. Insert the damper rod into the fork tube until the rod emerges from the fork tube end. Install the oil lock piece (**Figure 30**) onto the damper rod.

5. Install the fork tube into the slider until the tube bottoms.

6. Install the damper rod holder onto the T-handle. Insert the tool into the fork tube so the rod holder engages the damper rod (**Figure 23**).

7. Slide a new copper washer onto the Allen bolt (**Figure 24**).

8. Apply threadlocking compound to the threads of the Allen bolt. Insert the Allen bolt through the bottom of the slider and thread it into the oil lock piece.

9. Hold the damper rod with the special tool (**Figure 22**), and tighten the Allen bolt to 30 N•m (22 ft.-lb.).

10. Slide a new slider bushing (E, **Figure 29**) and spacer (D) down the fork tube.

NOTE
Use the Yamaha fork seal driver and adapter to install the slider bushing and washer in the next step. If these tools unavailable, use a universal oil seal driver or a piece of galvanized pipe and a hammer. If both ends of the pipe are threaded, wrap one end with duct tape to prevent the threads from damaging the interior of the slider.

11. Drive the slider bushing and spacer into place (**Figure 31**) until the bushing bottoms in the slider.

CAUTION
The plastic wrap installed in the next step protects the oil seal and dust seal so they will not be torn during installation.

12. Wrap the end of the fork tube with plastic wrap. Liberally coat the plastic wrap with fork oil.

13. Lubricate the lips of the oil seal with fork oil, and install the oil seal (C, **Figure 29**) onto the fork tube. The side with the manufacturer's marks must faces up, away from the fork slider.

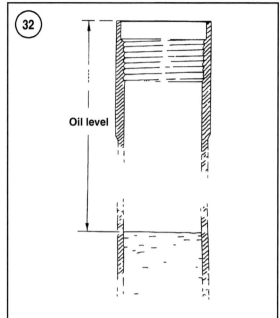

Oil level

14. Use the same tool used in Step 11, and drive the oil seal into the slider until the circlip groove in the slider can be seen above the top of the oil seal.

15. Slide the circlip (**Figure 27**) down the fork tube, and seat the clip into the groove in the slider. Make sure the clip is completely seated in the slider groove.

16. Lubricate a new dust seal with fork oil. Slide the seal down the fork tube, and install it into the fork slider.

17. Tap the dust seal (**Figure 26**) into the slider.

18. Secure the fork leg upright in a vise, and fill the fork leg with the correct quantity of SAE 10W fork oil. Refer to **Table 1** for the specified quantity.

19. Slowly pump the fork tube up and down several times to distribute the fork oil.

20. Compress the fork completely and measure the fluid level after the fork oil settles. Use an oil level gauge to measure the fluid level from the top of the fork tube (**Figure 32**). If necessary, add or remove

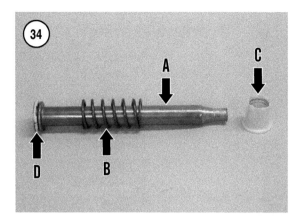

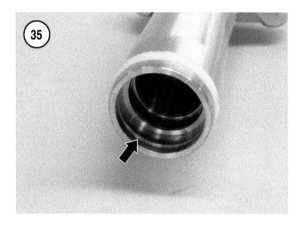

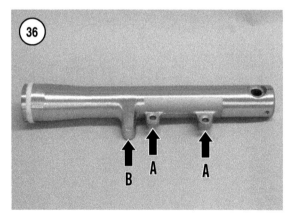

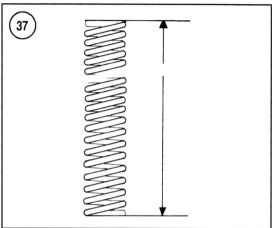

oil to set the fluid level to the value specified in **Table 1**.

21. Pull the fork tube out of the slider until it is fully extended.

22. Install the fork spring (**Figure 21**) into the fork tube so the closer wound coils face up.

23. Install the seat (**Figure 20**) onto the top of the fork spring. Make sure it is seated correctly.

24. Install the spacer (**Figure 19**).

25. Lubricate a new O-ring (**Figure 33**) with lithium-soap grease, and install it onto the fork cap.

26. Install the fork cap while pushing down on the spring. Start the bolt slowly, do not cross-thread it.

Tighten the fork cap as tightly as possible. The cap bolt will be tightened to specification once the fork is installed on the motorcycle.

27. Install the fork leg as described in this section.

Inspection

1. Thoroughly clean all parts in solvent and dry them with compressed air.

2. Blow out the oil holes (C, **Figure 25**) in the damper rod with compressed air. Clean them if necessary.

3. Check the damper rod assembly for:
   a. Bent, cracked or damaged damper rod (A, **Figure 34**).
   b. Excessively worn rebound spring (B, **Figure 34**).
   c. Damaged oil lock piece (C, **Figure 34**).
   d. Excessively worn or damaged piston or piston ring (D, **Figure 34**).
   e. Replace any worn part.

4. Check the fork tube for straightness and for signs of wear or scratches. Replace if bent or severely scratched.

5. Check the fork tube for chrome flaking or creasing. This condition will damage the oil seal. Replace the fork tube if necessary.

6. Check the seal area of the slider bore (**Figure 35**) for dents, scratches or other damage that would allow oil leakage. Replace the slider if necessary.

7. Check the slider for dents or exterior damage that may cause the upper fork tube to hang up during riding. Replace if necessary. Check for cracks or damage to the brake caliper (A, **Figure 36**) and fender mounting bosses (B).

8. Inspect the front axle threads in the slider for damage. If damage is slight, chase the threads with a metric tap. If damage is excessive, replace the slider.

9. Measure the uncompressed length of the fork spring (**Figure 37**). If the spring is not within specification (**Table 1**), replace it.

12

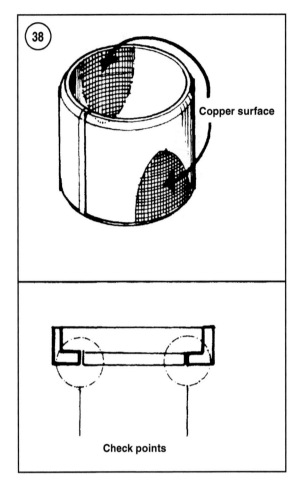

Copper surface

Check points

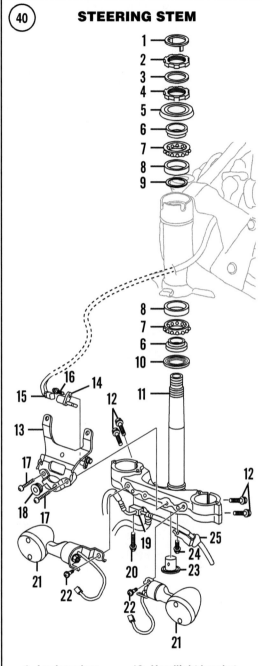

STEERING STEM

1. Lockwasher
2. Locking ring nut
3. Rubber washer
4. Adjusting ring nut
5. Bearing cap
6. Inner race
7. Bearing
8. Outer race
9. Washer
10. Dust seal
11. Steering head
12. Lower bridge clamp bolt
13. Headlight bracket
14. Air temperature (AT) sensor
15. Connector
16. Bolt
17. Headlight bracket bolt
18. Grommet
19. Brake hose union
20. Union bolt
21. Turn signal assembly
22. Turn signal bracket bolt
23. Collar
24. Guide bolt
25. Brake hose guide

10. Inspect the fork tube slider bushing (F, **Figure 29**). If it is scratched or scored, it must be replaced. If the Teflon coating is worn off so that the copper base material is showing on approximately 3/4 of the total surface (**Figure 38**), the bushing must be replaced.

  a. To replace the fork tube bushing, open the bushing slot with a screwdriver (**Figure 39**) and slide the bushing off the fork tube.

  b. Lubricate the new bushing with fork oil, open its slot and slide the bushing onto the fork tube groove.

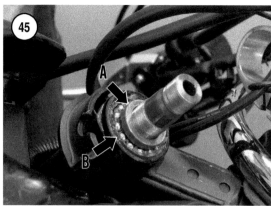

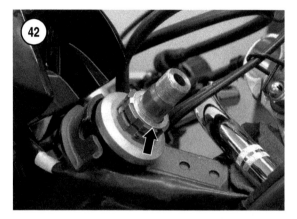

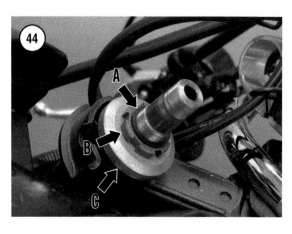

11. Replace the fork cap O-ring (**Figure 33**). Lubricate the O-ring with fork oil before installation.
12. Replace any parts that is worn or damaged.

STEERING STEM

Disassembly/Removal

The ring nut wrench (Yamaha part No. YU-33975 or 90890-01403) or an equivalent tool, is needed to disassemble and reassembly the steering head.

Refer to **Figure 40**.

1. Securely support the motorcycle on a level surface.
2. Remove the each fork leg as described in this chapter.
3. Remove the air temperature (AT) sensor (Chapter Eight).
4. If necessary, remove the headlight bracket (Chapter Nine).
5. Remove the brake hose guide bolt (A, **Figure 41**), and release the front brake hose guide from the lower fork bridge.
6. Remove the brake hose union bolt (B, **Figure 41**), and separate the brake hose union from the lower fork bridge. Use a bungee cord or wire to suspend the union from the motorcycle.
7. Remove the turn signal bracket bolt (C, **Figure 41**), and remove the turn signal assembly from each side of the lower fork bridge.
8. Lift the lockwasher (**Figure 42**) from the top of the ring nuts.
9. Remove the locking ring nut (**Figure 43**), and then the rubber washer (A, **Figure 44**).
10. Hold onto the lower end of the steering stem assembly. Loosen and remove the adjusting ring nut (B, **Figure 44**), and then remove the bearing cap (C).
11. Remove the upper bearing inner race (A, **Figure 45**) and the bearing (B) from the steering head.
12. Lower the steering stem assembly down and out of the steering head.

12

Assembly/Installation

1. Liberally apply lithium-soap grease to the bearings and races.

2. If removed, install the lower bearing (A, **Figure 46**) onto the steering stem.

3. Slide the steering stem up through the frame steering head.

4. Install the upper bearing (B, **Figure 45**) and the bearing inner race (A).

5. Install the bearing cap (C, **Figure 44**) and the adjusting ring nut (B).

6. Adjust the steering head bearings by performing the following:

    a. Set a torque wrench at a right angle to the ring nut wrench (**Figure 47**).

    b. Seat the bearings within the steering head by tightening the adjusting ring nut to (B, **Figure 44**) 52 N•m (38 ft.-lb.).

    c. Loosen the adjusting ring nut one turn.

    d. Tighten the adjusting ring nut to 18 N•m (13 ft.-lb.).

7. Inspect the steering head as described in Chapter Three. If any binding or looseness is noted, disassemble and inspect the steering head as described in this section.

8. Install the rubber washer (A **Figure 44**) and the locking ring nut (**Figure 43**) Tighten the locking ring nut finger-tight. Check the slots on the locking ring. They should align with those on the adjusting ring nut. If they do not, tighten the locking ring nut until alignment is achieved. If necessary, hold the adjusting ring nut so it does not move while the slots are aligned.

9. Install the lockwasher (**Figure 42**) so its fingers are seated in the ring nut slots.

10. Install the upper fork bridge onto the steering stem shaft. Loosely install the washer and the steering head nut (**Figure 48**).

11. Temporarily insert each fork leg through the lower and upper fork bridges. Tighten the lower fork bridge clamp bolts (**Figure 49**) just enough to hold the fork legs in position.

12. Tighten the steering head nut (**Figure 48**) to 110 N•m (81 ft.-lb.).

13. Turn the steering stem by hand to make sure it turns freely and does not bind. If the steering stem is too tight, the bearings can be damaged; if the steering stem is too loose, the steering will become unstable. Repeat Steps 6-9 if necessary.

14. Remove the fork legs and upper fork bridge.

15. Install each turn signal assembly by performing the following:

    a. Fit a turn signal assembly into place so the tang of the turn signal bracket sits in the hole in the lower fork bridge.

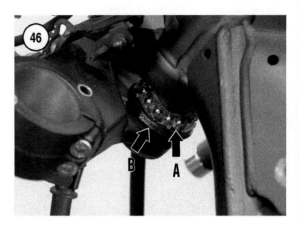

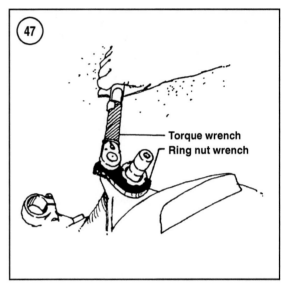

Torque wrench
Ring nut wrench

    b. Apply threadlocking compound to the threads of the turn signal bracket bolt (C, **Figure 41**), and tighten the bolt to 23 N•m (17 ft.-lb.).

16. Install the brake hose union into place under the fork bridge.

    a. Set the brake hose union into position against the bottom of the lower fork bridge.

    b. Make sure the notch on the fork bridge engages the cutout in the brake hose union.

    c. Apply threadlocking compound to the threads of the union bolt (B, **Figure 41**), and tighten the bolt to 10 N•m (89 in.-lb.).

17. Fit the brake hose guide onto the bottom of the lower fork bridge to the tang on the guide engages the hole in the fork bridge. Apply threadlocking compound to the threads of the guide bolt (A, **Figure 41**), and tighten the brake hose guide bolt to 10 N•m (89 in.-lb.).

18. Install the headlight bracket (Chapter Nine).

19. Properly install the fork legs and upper fork bridge as described in *Front Fork* in this chapter.

20. Install the air temperature (AT) sensor (Chapter Eight).

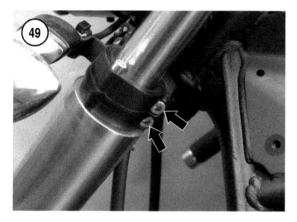

Inspection

1. Clean the upper and lower bearings in a bearing degreaser. Thoroughly dry both bearings with compressed air. Make sure all solvent is removed.
2. Wipe the old grease from the outer races located in the steering head, and then clean the outer races with a rag soaked in solvent. Thoroughly dry the races with a lint-free cloth. Check the races for pitting, galling and corrosion. If any of these conditions exist, replace the races as described in this chapter.
3. If any race is worn or damaged, replace the race and bearing as an assembly. Follow the procedure described in this chapter.
4. Check the welds around the steering head for cracks or damage. If any damage is found, refer repairs to the dealership.
5. Check the bearings for pitting, scratches or discoloration indicating wear or corrosion. Replace the bearings as described in this chapter if any ball is less than perfect.
6. If the bearings are in good condition, pack them thoroughly with lithium-soap grease. To pack the bearings, spread some grease in the palm of your hand and scrape the open side of the bearing cage across your palm until the bearing is completely full of grease.

7. Thoroughly clean all mounting parts in solvent. Dry them completely.
8. Inspect the ring nuts and their threads for wear or damage. If necessary, clean the threads with an appropriate size metric tap or replace the nut(s). If the threads are damaged, inspect the appropriate steering stem thread(s) for damage. If necessary, clean the threads with an appropriate size metric die.
9. Check the underside of the steering head nut for damage. Replace the nut as necessary.
10. Inspect the steering stem and the lower fork bridge for cracks or other damage. Make sure the fork bridge clamping areas are free of burrs and that the bolt holes are in good condition.
11. Inspect the upper fork bridge for cracks or other damage. Check both the upper and lower surface of the fork bridge. Make sure the fork bridge clamping areas are free of burrs and that the bolt holes are in good condition.

STEERING HEAD BEARING RACES

Removal/Installation

Do not remove the upper and lower bearing outer races unless they will be replaced. These races are pressed into place and are damaged during removal. Never reuse an outer race that has been removed. If either outer race is removed, replace both the outer races along with the bearings and inner races at the same time.

CAUTION
If any binding is observed when removing or installing the bearing races, stop and release all tension from the bearing race. Check the tool alignment to make sure the bearing race is moving evenly in its mounting bore. Otherwise, the bearing race may gouge the frame mounting bore and cause permanent damage.

CAUTION
If removal is difficult, do not chance damage to the steering head or new bearing races. Have a dealership perform this procedure.

1. Chill the new bearing outer races in a freezer overnight to shrink the outer diameter of the race as much as possible.
2. Remove the steering stem as described in this chapter.
3. Insert a brass or aluminum drift into the steering head and tap the lower race out from the steering

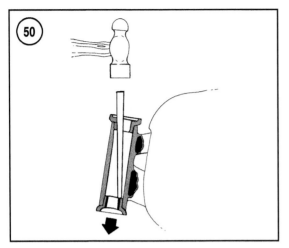

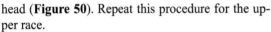

head (**Figure 50**). Repeat this procedure for the upper race.

4. Clean the race seats in the steering head. Check for cracks or other damage.

5. Insert the new upper race into the steering head with the cupped side facing out and square the race with the race bore.

> *CAUTION*
> *To avoid damage to the races and to the race seats in the steering head, install the races as described in the following.*

> *CAUTION*
> *When installing the bearing outer races with the threaded rod or similar tool, do not let the rod or tool contact the face of the bearing race. It could damage the race.*

6. To install the upper race, insert the puller rod through the bottom of the steering head. Seat the lower plate against the steering head.

7. At the top of the steering stem, slide the driver down and seat it squarely on top of the bearing race. Install the nut onto the rod (**Figure 51**).

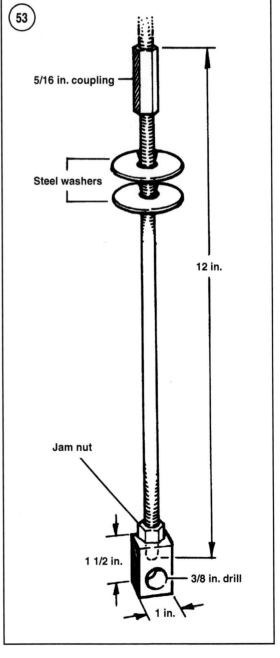

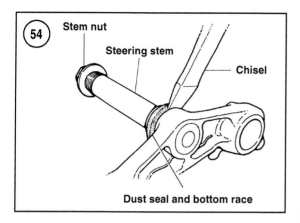

54 Stem nut

Steering stem

Chisel

Dust seal and bottom race

8. Hold the threaded rod to prevent it from turning and tighten the nut with a wrench. Continue to tighten the nut until the race is completely drawn into the steering head. Remove the puller assembly and inspect the bearing race. It should be bottomed in the steering head as shown in **Figure 52**.

9. Turn the special tool over and repeat this procedure for the lower bearing race.

10. If the special tool is unavailable, assemble a puller as shown in **Figure 53**. The block mounted at the bottom of the threaded rod is used as a T-handle to hold tool the stationary when the bearing race is being installed from the opposite end. The hole drilled through the block must be large enough to accept a suitable rod for a T-handle. If the handle is not available, hold the bottom of the rod with two nuts locked together. Two or more thick washers are also required. The outside diameter of these washers must be greater than the outside diameter of the bearing races.

STEERING STEM BEARING

Removal/Installation

Do not remove the lower bearing inner race (B, **Figure 46**) from the steering stem unless the race is going to be replaced. Never reuse a lower bearing inner race that has been removed. It is no longer true and will damage the rest of the bearing assembly if reused.

CAUTION
Replacing the lower bearing inner race can be difficult. If there is any doubt about one's ability to remove and install an inner race, have a dealership perform this service.

1. Install the steering stem nut onto the top of the steering stem to protect the threads.

2. Loosen the lower bearing inner race from the shoulder at the base of the steering stem with a chisel as shown in **Figure 54**. To prevent binding, make several passes around the perimeter of the bearing. Discard the lower race and dust seal.

3. Clean the steering stem with solvent and dry it thoroughly.

4. Position the new dust seal and new lower bearing inner race onto the steering stem until it stops on the raised shoulder. Align the inner race with the machined shoulder on the steering stem.

CAUTION
Select a driver or piece of pipe that matches the inside diameter of the inner race. The tool must only drive against the inner circumference of the race. The tool must not touch any portion of the race's bearing-contact-face during installation. This will damage the inner race, and it will have to be replaced.

5. Lower the tool over the steering stem until the tool sits on the inner circumference of the bearing inner race.

6. Drive the inner race onto the steering stem until it bottoms.

12

Table 1 FRONT SUSPENSION SPECIFICATIONS

Item	
Fork oil	
Viscosity	SAE 10W fork oil
Capacity per leg	490.0 cc (16.57 oz.)
Oil level (measured from top of the fully	
compressed fork tube with the fork spring removed)	105.0 mm (4.13 in.)
Front fork travel	135.0 mm (5.31 in.)
(continued)	

Table 1 FRONT SUSPENSION SPECIFICATIONS (continued)

Item	
Fork spring	
Free length	345.5 mm (13.60 in.)
Wear limit	339.4 mm (13.36 in.)
Installed length	339.4 mm (13.36 in.)
Spacer length	183 mm (7.20 in.)

Table 2 FRONT SUSPENSION AND STEERING TORQUE SPECIFICATIONS

Item	N•m	in.-lb.	ft.-lb.
Brake hose guide bolt*	10	89	–
Brake hose union bolt*	10	89	–
Clutch lever clamp bolt	7	62	–
Fork bottom Allen bolt*	30	–	22
Fork cap bolt	23	–	17
Fork cover bolts	18	–	13
Front axle	59	–	43.5
Front axle clamp bolt	20	–	15
Front caliper bracket bolt	40	–	30
Front brake master cylinder clamp bolt	10	89	–
Handlebar clamp bolts*	28	–	21
Handlebar holder nut	32	–	24
Handlebar weight	23	–	17
Headlight bracket bolt	23	–	17
Headlight housing bolt	7	62	–
Lower fork bridge clamp bolt			
2007-2009 models	23	–	17
2010 models	45	–	32
Lower fork cover bolts	18	–	13
Meter assembly cover bracket bolts	7	62	–
Meter assembly cover screws	7	62	–
Steering head nut	110	–	81
Steering stem adjuster ring nut*		–	
Initial	52	–	38
Final	18	–	13
Turn signal bracket bolt*	23	–	17
Upper fork bridge clamp bolts	23	–	17

*Refer to text.

CHAPTER THIRTEEN

REAR SUSPENSION AND DRIVE BELT

This chapter covers procedures for servicing the rear shock absorber, suspension linkage, swing arm and the drive belt.

Refer to *Rear Suspension* in Chapter Three for shock absorber spring preload adjustment procedures.

Table 1 and **Table 2** are at the end of this chapter.

SHOCK ABSORBER AND SUSPENSION LINKAGE

Refer to **Figure 1**.

Removal/Installation

1. Securely support the motorcycle with the rear wheel off the ground.
2. Remove both the side covers (Chapter Fifteen).
3. Remove the muffler, rear cylinder exhaust pipe and the subtank (Chapter Eight).
4. Remove the coolant reservoir (Chapter Ten).
5. Remove the battery box and relay bracket (Chapter Nine).
6. Remove the rear wheel (Chapter Eleven).
7. Remove the nut and washer from the upper (A, **Figure 2**) and lower (B) the suspension arm bolts.
8. Pull the suspension arm bolts (A, **Figure 3**), and remove each suspension arm (B) from the swing arm. Mark each nut, bolt and suspension arm so they can be reinstalled in their original position.
9. Remove the nut and washer (**Figure 4**) from the shock absorber lower bolt.
10. Pull the shock lower bolt (C, **Figure 3**), and lower the suspension lever (A, **Figure 5**) from the shock mount.
11. Remove the cap (**Figure 6**) from the upper shock absorber nut. Do not lose this cap. It assures that electrical wires cannot rub against the edges of the nut during operation.
12. Remove the nut (**Figure 7**) from the upper shock bolt.
13. Pull the upper shock absorber bolt (**Figure 8**), and remove the shock absorber from the motorcycle. Note that the bolts flats rest against the flats of the lock plate on the frame.
14. Remove the nut (B, **Figure 5**) from the suspension lever bolt.
15. Pull the suspension lever bolt (A, **Figure 9**), and remove the suspension lever (B) from its frame mount. Account for the collar (C, **Figure 9**). It can remain behind in the frame mount.
16. Inspect the components as described in this section.
17. Installation is the reverse of removal. Note to the following:

13

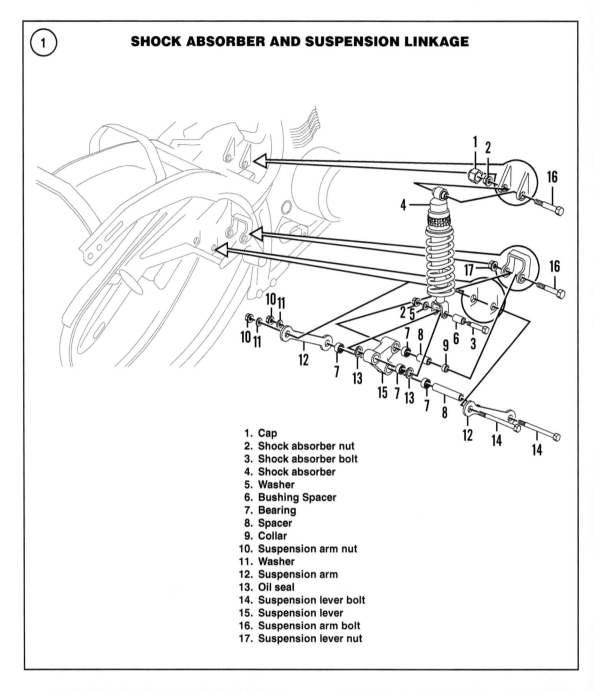

① SHOCK ABSORBER AND SUSPENSION LINKAGE

1. Cap
2. Shock absorber nut
3. Shock absorber bolt
4. Shock absorber
5. Washer
6. Bushing Spacer
7. Bearing
8. Spacer
9. Collar
10. Suspension arm nut
11. Washer
12. Suspension arm
13. Oil seal
14. Suspension lever bolt
15. Suspension lever
16. Suspension arm bolt
17. Suspension lever nut

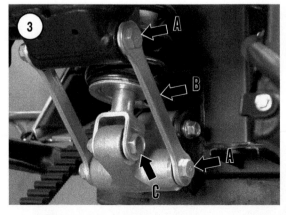

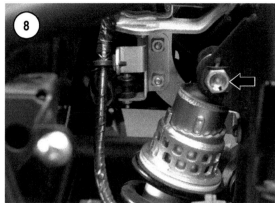

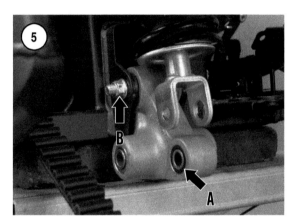

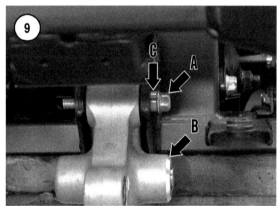

13

a. Install all bolts from the right side and nuts from the left.
b. Make sure the collar (**Figure 10**) is in place on the suspension lever bolt, and that the collar sits in the right side of the frame mount (C, **Figure 9**).
c. Tighten the suspension lever nut to specification (**Table 2**).
d. Tighten each shock absorber nut to 48 N•m (35 ft.-lb.). Fit the cap (**Figure 6**) onto the upper shock absorber nut.
e. Install each suspension arm in its original position.

f. Tighten each suspension arm nut to 59 N•m (43.5 ft.-lb.).

Shock Absorber Inspection

1. Clean and dry the hardware and the mounts on the shock absorber.
2. Inspect the damper housing (A, **Figure 11**) for dents, damage or oil leaks.
3. Inspect the shock spring (B, **Figure 11**) and retainer for cracks or other signs of fatigue.
4. Inspect the bushing (**Figure 12**) in the upper mount for wear or damage.
5. Inspect the lower mount (C, **Figure 11**) for elongation, cracks or other damage.
6. If any part of the shock absorber is worn or damaged, replace the shock absorber. Replacement parts are unavailable.
7. Replace the mounting hardware as necessary.

Suspension Linkage Inspection

1. Clean and dry the hardware, spacers and mounts.
2. Inspect the suspension arms (**Figure 13**) for dents or other damage. Also inspect the mounts for cranks or elongation.
3. Remove the spacer (A, **Figure 14**) from each mount in the suspension lever.
4. Remove and discard the oil seal (B, **Figure 14**) from each side of the suspension-lever rear mount.
5. Inspect the needle bearings by performing the following:
   a. Wipe excess grease from each bearing (C, **Figure 14**), and inspect the needles for pitting, wear or other damage.
   b. Insert the collar into its bearing, and turn the collar by hand. The bearing should turn smoothly without binding or excessive noise.
   c. If any bearing is worn or damaged, replace it as described in *Needle Bearing Removal/ Installation* in this section.
   d. Two bearings are used in the middle suspension-arm mount. If either bearing in this mount is worn, replace both bearings as a set. Install each bearing in the middle mount so the bearing sits flush with the outside edge of the bearing bore.
   e. When installing a needle bearing into the front or rear mount, press the bearing into place so it sits 4.5 mm (0.18 in.) below the edge of the suspension lever (**Figure 15**).
6. Check the spacers (A, **Figure 14**) for scoring or excessive wear. Replace spacers as necessary.
7. Install new the oil seals (B, **Figure 14**) into each side of the rear mount. Pack the lips of the oil seal with lithium-soap grease.

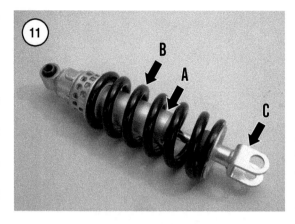

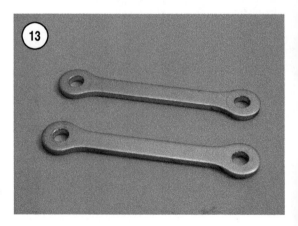

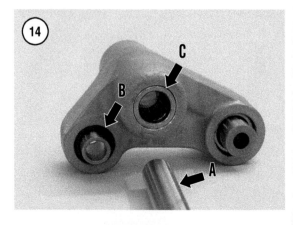

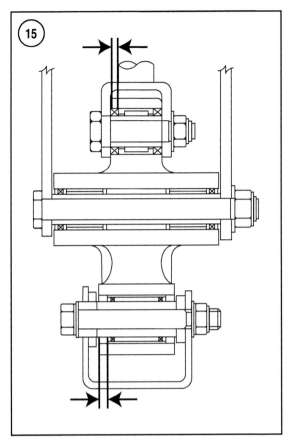

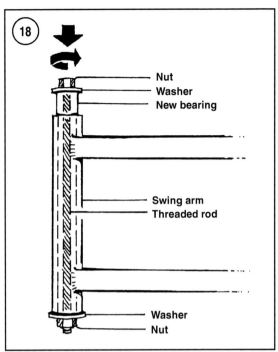

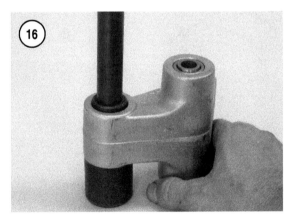

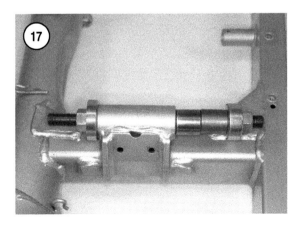

NOTE
A different length spacer is used in each mount in the suspension lever. Install each spacer in the proper mount.

8. Lubricate each spacer (A, **Figure 14**) with lithium-soap grease, and install the spacer into its correct mount in the suspension lever.

9. Replace the mounting hardware as necessary.

Needle Bearing Removal/Installation

1. Use a blind bearing remover to remove each bearing (C, **Figure 14**) from the middle mount on the suspension lever. Follow the instructions from the tool's manufacturer.

2. Use a hydraulic press to remove the needle bearing from the front and rear suspension-lever mounts. Support the suspension lever in the press, and use a driver that matches the diameter of the needle bearing (**Figure 16**).

3. Thoroughly clean and dry the bearing bore.

4. Pack the new bearing with lithium-soap grease.

5. Use a swing arm bearing installer (**Figure 17**, [Motion Pro part No. 08-0213]), to install the new bearings. If necessary, follow the tool manufacturer's instructions.

6. If a special tool is not available, one can be fabricated from a socket, three large washers, a threaded rod and two nuts. Assemble the washers threaded rod, bearing and nuts as shown in **Figure 18**.

7. Hold the lower nut with a wrench, and turn the upper nut to press the bearing into the bearing bore.

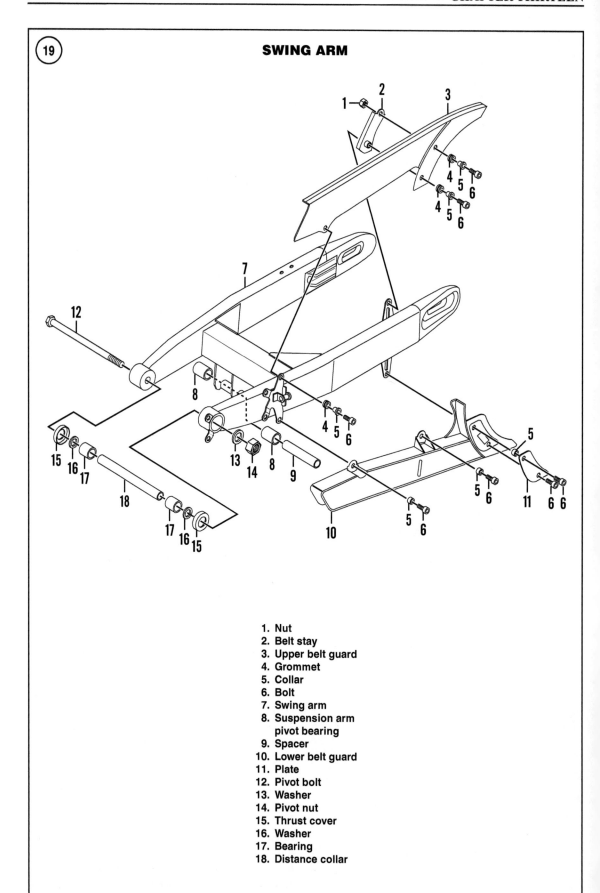

SWING ARM

1. Nut
2. Belt stay
3. Upper belt guard
4. Grommet
5. Collar
6. Bolt
7. Swing arm
8. Suspension arm
   pivot bearing
9. Spacer
10. Lower belt guard
11. Plate
12. Pivot bolt
13. Washer
14. Pivot nut
15. Thrust cover
16. Washer
17. Bearing
18. Distance collar

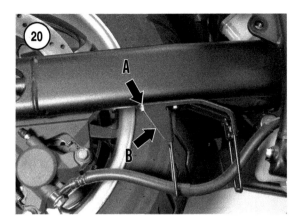

Turn the nut slowly, and watch the bearing carefully. Make sure it does not turn sideways.

8. Position a bearing in its bore as described in *Swing Arm* in this chapter or in *Suspension Linkage Inspection* in this section.

Shock Absorber Disposal

The gas must be released before a shock absorber is discarded in the trash. To do so, drill a 2-3 mm (0.08-0.12 in.) hole through the shock absorber at a point 15-20 mm (0.59-0.79 in.) from the upper end of the cylinder (the end with the preload adjuster).

SWING ARM

Refer to **Figure 19**.

Removal

1. Securely support the motorcycle on level ground.
2. Remove the muffler, rear exhaust pipe, and muffler bracket (Chapter Eight).
3. Remove the shock absorber and suspension linkage as described in this chapter.
4. Check the swing arm bearings by performing the following:
   a. Grasp both ends of the swing arm and move it up and down. The swing arm should move smoothly with no abnormal noise from the bearings. If any binding or noise is noted, the bearings are worn and must be replaced as described in this section.
   b. Try to move the swing arm from side to side in a horizontal arc. If more than a slight amount of movement is felt, the bearings are worn and must be replaced as described in this section.
5. Note the location of any clamps or cable ties that secure wires to the swing arm. Release the wires from the clamps, and suspend the rear brake caliper safely out of the way.
6. Remove the bolts (A, **Figure 20**), and lower the rear brake hose guide (B) from the swing arm. Note the location of any ties or holders securing the brake lines and hoses.
7. Remove the voltage regulator/rectifier (Chapter Nine).
8. Remove the upper and lower drive belt guides as described in this chapter.
9. Remove the pivot nut (**Figure 21**) and washer.
10. Pull the pivot bolt (**Figure 22**) from the right side, and remove the swing arm from the frame.
11. Remove the thrust cover (**Figure 23**) and washer from each side of the frame pivot. Remove the washer (A, **Figure 24**) from the thrust cover (B).

13

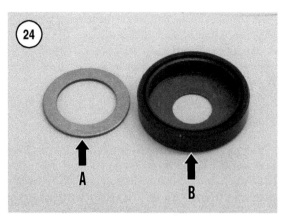

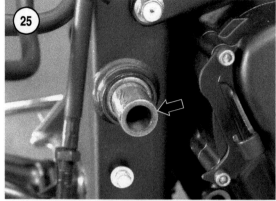

12. Remove the distance collar (**Figure 25**) from the frame pivot.

13. Inspect the swing arm as described below in this chapter.

Installation

1. Apply lithium-soap grease to the bearing (**Figure 26**) in the frame pivot on each side.

2. Lubricate the distance collar (**Figure 25**) with lithium-soap grease, and install the collar into the pivot bearings.

3. Lubricate the thrust cover washer (B, **Figure 24**) with lithium-soap grease. Fit a washer into the thrust cover (A, **Figure 24**), and install the thrust cover (**Figure 23**) onto the frame pivot.

4. Repeat Step 3 and install the thrust cover onto the other frame pivot.

5. Lubricate the pivot bolt (**Figure 27**) with lithium-soap grease.

6. Raise the swing arm into position so its pivots align with the frame pivots.

7. Insert the pivot bolt (**Figure 22**) from the right side until the bolt emerges from the left side of the swing arm.

8. Install the washer and pivot nut (**Figure 21**). Tighten the pivot nut to 85 N•m (63 ft.-lb.).

9. Install the lower and upper drive belt guides, the suspension linkage and the shock absorber as described in this chapter.

10. Install the rear brake guide (B, **Figure 20**) onto the swing arm. Tighten the bolts (A, **Figure 20**) to 7 N•m 62 ft.-lb.).

11. Reinstall the any removed components.

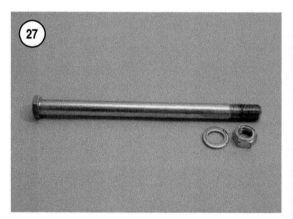

Inspection

1. Check the pivot bolt (**Figure 27**) for straightness. A bent bolt restricts the movement of the swing arm.

2. Inspect the pivot bolt threads. Clean and dress the threads as necessary.

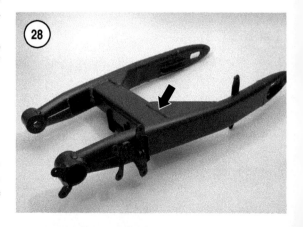

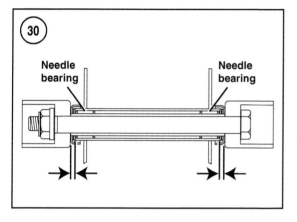

Needle
bearing

Needle
bearing

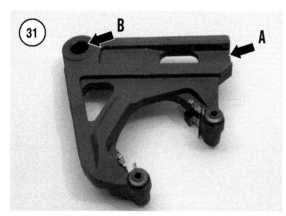

B

A

A

B

D

C

3. Check all welds (**Figure 28**) on the swing arm for cracks or fractures.

4. Remove the collar (**Figure 29**) from the suspension arm pivot on the swing arm.

5. Check the needle bearings in the suspension arm pivot by performing the following.

    a. Turn each bearing with a finger. A bearing should turn smoothly without excessive play or noise.

    b. Use a lint-free cloth to remove surface grease from the bearings.

    c. Check the bearing rollers for evidence of wear, pitting or rust.

    d. If either bearing is damaged, replace both bearings. Refer to *Needle Bearing Removal/ Installation* in *Shock Absorber and Suspension Linkage* in this chapter. Install each suspension arm pivot bearing until its outside edge is flush with the outside edge of the bearing bore.

6. Repeat Step 5 and inspect the needle bearing in each side of the frame pivot (**Figure 26**). If either bearing is damaged, replace both bearings. Refer to *Needle Bearing Removal/Installation* in *Shock Absorber and Suspension Linkage* in this chapter. Install each frame pivot bearing so its outside edge is installed to a depth of 0-1 mm (0-0.04 in.) from the outside edge of the frame bore (**Figure 30**).

7. Inspect each thrust cover (B, **Figure 24**) and washer (A).

8. Inspect the caliper bracket (A, **Figure 31**) for cracks or other signs of damage. Replace the bracket it if necessary.

9. Inspect the mounting hole (B, **Figure 31**) on the caliper bracket. If elongated or damaged, replace the bracket.

DRIVE BELT GUIDE

Removal/Installation

1. Remove the upper drive belt guide (A, **Figure 32**) by performing the following:

    a. Remove the drive-belt-guide bolts (B, **Figure 32**). Account for the collar and grommet installed with the bolt.

    b. Remove the lower rear drive-belt-guide bolt and its washer. Account for the grommet installed with the bolt.

    c. Lift the upper guide from the swing arm.

2. Remove the lower drive belt guide (C, **Figure 32**) by performing the following:

    a. Remove each drive belt guide bolt (D, **Figure 32**) along with its collar.

    b. Remove the lower guide from the swing arm.

3. Installation is the reverse of removal. Apply threadlocking compound to the threads of the belt guide bolts, and tighten the bolts to 7 N•m (62 in.-lb.).

13

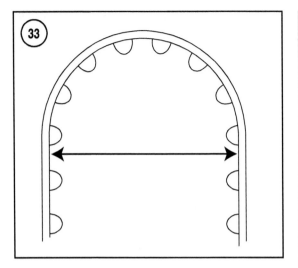

DRIVE BELT

CAUTION
When handling a used or new belt, never bend it sharply or wrap the belt in a loop smaller than 127mm (5 in.). Refer to **Figure 33***. This will weaken or break belt fibers and cause premature failure.*

Removal/Installation

CAUTION
If the existing drive belt will be reused, it must be installed so it travels in the same direction. Mark the belt during removal.

1. Remove the rear wheel (Chapter Ten).
2. Remove the swing arm as described in this chapter.
3. Remove the engine pulley (Chapter Seven).
4. Draw an arrow on the top of the belt to indicate the direction of forward rotation.
5. Remove the pulley from between the belt runs, and remove the drive belt.
6. Installation is the reverse of removal.
   a. Reinstall an existing drive belt so it travels in the direction noted during removal. A new belt can be installed in either direction.
   b. Adjust the drive belt tension as (Chapter Three).

Inspection

1. Wipe the drive belt with a clean cloth.
2. Wash the drive belt in a bath of mild detergent and water. Use a soft brush to remove any dirt.

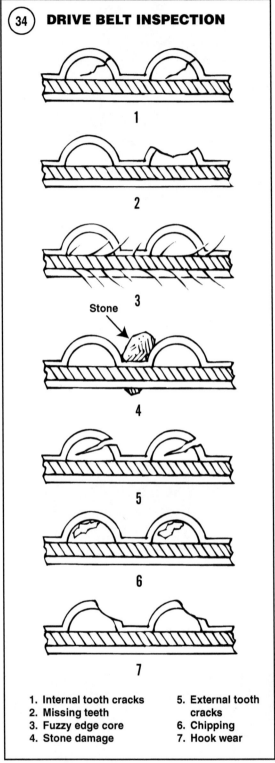

DRIVE BELT INSPECTION

1. Internal tooth cracks
2. Missing teeth
3. Fuzzy edge core
4. Stone damage
5. External tooth cracks
6. Chipping
7. Hook wear

3. Rinse the belt with plenty of clean water, and dry it thoroughly.
4. Inspect the drive belt and teeth for severe wear, damage or oil contamination. Refer to **Figure 34** for various types of drive belt wear or damage. Replace a worn or damaged belt.

Table 1 REAR SUSPENSION AND DRIVE BELT SPECIFICATIONS

Item	New mm (in.)	Service limit mm (in.)
Drive belt deflection		
Motorcycle on the sidestand	5.0-7.0 (0.20-0.28)	–
Motorcycle on a suitable stand	4.0-6.0 (0.16-0.24)	–
Shock absorber travel	48.0 (1.89)	–
Shock spring free length	182 (7.17)	–
Shock spring installed length	166 (6.54)	–
Enclosed gas/air pressure	1200 kPa (174 psi)	–
Spring preload settings		
Standard	4	–
Minimum	1	–
Maximum	9	–
Swing arm end free play		
Radial	–	1.0 (0.04)
Axial	–	1.0 (0.04)

Table 2 REAR SUSPENSION AND DRIVE BELT TORQUE SPECIFICATIONS

Item	N•m	in.-lb.	ft.-lb.
Drive belt guide bolts*	7	62	–
Rear axle nut	150	–	111
Rear brake hose guide bolt	7	62	–
Shock absorber nut	48	–	35
Suspension arm nut	59	–	43.5
Suspension lever nut			
2007-2009 models	48	–	35
2010 models	32	–	23
Swing arm pivot nut	85	–	63
*Refer to text.			

13

BRAKES

The brake system consists of dual front disc brakes and a single rear disc brake.

Table 1 and **Table 2** are at the end of this chapter.

BRAKE SERVICE NOTES

WARNING
Do not use silicone based (DOT 5) brake fluid. Silicone-based fluid can damage the brake components leading to brake system failure.

WARNING
Never reuse brake fluid. Contaminated brake fluid can cause brake failure.

WARNING
Dispose of used brake fluid properly. Do not add brake fluid to engine oil to be recycled. Most recyclers will not accept oil that has been contaminated with other fluids (fork oil, brake fluid, or any other type of petroleum-based fluid).

WARNING
Whenever working on the brake system, do not inhale brake dust. It may contain asbestos, which can cause lung injury and cancer. Wear a face mask that meets requirements for trapping airborne particles, and wash hands and forearms thoroughly after completing the work.

WARNING
Do not use compressed air to clean any part of the brake system. This releases harmful brake pad dust. Use an aerosol brake cleaner to clean parts when servicing any component still installed on the motorcycle.

The brake system transmits hydraulic pressure from the master cylinder to the caliper. This pressure forces the brake pads against both sides of the brake disc and slows the motorcycle. As the pads wear, the pistons move out of the caliper bores and automatically adjust for pad wear. As this occurs, the fluid level in the master cylinder reservoir goes down. To compensate for this, occasionally add fluid. Refer to Chapter Three.

All tools and the work area must be clean during brake service. Caliper or master cylinder components can be damaged by even tiny particles of debris that enter the brake system. Do not use sharp tools inside the master cylinders, caliper cylinders or on the pistons. Sharp tools could damage these components and interfere with brake operation.

If there is any doubt about one's ability to service a brake component safely and correctly, take the job to a dealership.

Consider the following when servicing the front and rear brake systems.

1. Disc brake components rarely require disassembly. Do not disassemble them unless necessary.

2. When adding brake fluid, only use brake fluid clearly marked DOT 4 from a sealed container. Other grades of brake fluid may vaporize and cause brake failure.

3. Always use the same brand of brake fluid. One manufacturer's brake fluid may not be compatible

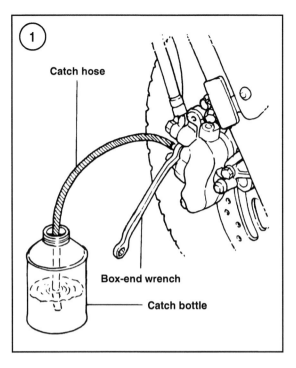

with another's. Do not mix different brands of brake fluids.

4. Brake fluid absorbs moisture, which greatly reduces its ability to perform correctly. Purchase brake fluid in small containers, and properly discard any small leftover quantities. Do not store brake fluid in a container with less than 1/4 of the fluid remaining. This small amount absorbs moisture very rapidly.

5. Use only DOT 4 brake fluid or isopropyl alcohol to wash parts. Never use petroleum-based solvents on the brake system's internal components. The seals will swell and distort. They will have to be replaced.

6. Whenever any brake banjo bolt or brake line nut is loosened, the system is opened and must be bled. If the brakes feel spongy, this usually means air has entered the system. For safe operation, refer to *Brake Bleeding* in this chapter.

7. Brake fluid damages most surfaces. To prevent brake fluid damage, note the following:
   a. Anticipate which parts are likely to come in contact with brake fluid. Cover the areas beneath these parts with plastic. Even a few drops of brake fluid can damage painted, plated or plastic surfaces.
   b. Keep a bucket of soap and water close to the motorcycle while working on the brake system. If brake fluid spills on any surface, immediately wash the area with soap and water and then rinse it thoroughly.
   c. To help control the flow of brake fluid when refilling the reservoirs, punch a small hole into the seal of a new container next to the edge of the pour spout.

BRAKE BLEEDING

General Bleeding Tips

Bleeding the brakes removes air from the brake system. Air in the brakes increases brake-lever or brake-pedal travel, and it makes the brakes feel soft or spongy. Under extreme circumstances, it can cause complete loss of brake pressure.

1. Clean the bleed valve and area around the valve before beginning. Make sure the opening in the valve is clear.

2. Use a box-end wrench to open and close the bleed valve. This prevents damage to the valve especially when the valve is rusted in place.

3. Replace a bleed valve with damaged threads or with a rounded hex head. A damaged valve is difficult to remove, and it cannot be properly tightened.

4. The catch hose (**Figure 1**) is the hose installed between the bleed valve and the catch bottle. Use a clear catch hose so the fluid can be seen as it leaves the bleed valve. Air bubbles in the catch hose indicate that air may be trapped in the brake system.

5. Open the bleed valve just enough to allow fluid to pass through the valve and into the catch bottle. If a bleed valve is too loose, air can be drawn into the system through the valve threads.

6. If air is suspected of entering through the valve threads, remove the bleed valve and apply Teflon tape to the valve threads. Make sure the Teflon tape does not cover the passage in the bleed valve. Reinstall the valve, and tighten it to 6 N•m (53 in.-lb.).

7. If the system is difficult to bleed, tap the banjo bolt on the master cylinder and caliper. This helps dislodge air bubbles that may be trapped at the hose connection. Also tap the brake hose union, located beneath the lower fork bridge, and any other hose connections in the brake line.

Bleeding the Brakes

The brakes can be bled manually or with a vacuum pump. Both methods are described here. Only use fresh DOT 4 brake fluid when bleeding the brakes. Do not reuse old brake fluid, and do not use DOT 5 (silicone based) brake fluid.

1. Check all banjo bolts in the system. They must be tight.

2. When bleeding the front brakes, turn the handlebars to level the front master cylinder.

3. Clean all dirt or foreign matter from the top of the master cylinder reservoir, and remove the top cover, diaphragm plate and the diaphragm from the reservoir.

4. Add DOT 4 brake fluid to the reservoir until the fluid level reaches the reservoir upper limit. Loosely

14

install the diaphragm and the cover. Leave them in place during bleeding to keep dirt out of the system and so brake fluid cannot spurt out of the reservoir.

5. Pump the brake lever or brake pedal a few times, and then release it. Remove the dust cap from the bleed valve on the caliper assembly.

6A. Perform the following when manually bleeding the brakes:

    a. Connect a length of clear tubing to the bleed valve (**Figure 1**, typical). Place the other end of the tube into a clean container. Fill the container with enough fresh DOT 4 brake fluid to keep the end submerged. The tube should be long enough so that its loop is higher than the bleed valve. This prevents air from being drawn into the caliper during bleeding.

    b. Apply the brake lever or pedal until it stops, and hold it in this position.

    c. Open the bleed valve with a box-end wrench. Let the brake lever or pedal move to the limit of its travel, and then close the bleed valve. Do not release the brake lever or pedal while the bleed valve is open.

    d. As brake fluid enters the system, the level in the reservoir drops. Add brake fluid as necessary to keep the fluid level 10 mm (3/8 in.) below the reservoir top so air will not be drawn into the system.

    e. Repeat substeps b-d until the brake fluid flowing from the hose is clear and free of air.

6B. Perform the following when vacuum bleeding the brakes:

    a. Assemble the vacuum tool following the manufacturer's instructions.

    b. Connect the pump's catch hose to the bleed valve on the brake caliper (**Figure 2**, typical).

    c. Keep an eye on the brake fluid level in the reservoir. It will drop rapidly. This is particularly true for the rear brake reservoir, which does not hold as much brake fluid as the front. Stop often and check the brake fluid level. Keep the level 10 mm (3/8 in.) from the top of the reservoir so air will not be drawn into the system.

    d. Operate the vacuum pump to create vacuum in the hose.

    e. Use a box-end wrench to open the bleed valve. The vacuum pump should pull fluid from the system. Close the bleed valve before the brake fluid stops flowing from the system or before the master cylinder reservoir runs empty. Add fluid to the reservoir as necessary.

    f. Operate the brake lever or brake pedal a few times, and release it.

    g. Repeat substeps c-f until the fluid leaving the bleed valve is clear and free of air bubbles.

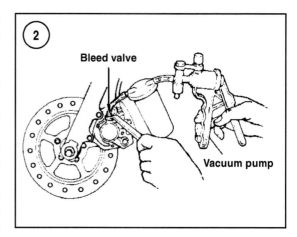

Bleed valve

Vacuum pump

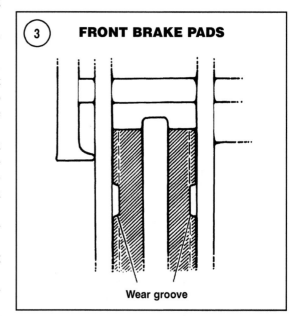

FRONT BRAKE PADS

Wear groove

7. Test the feel of the brake lever or pedal. It should feel firm and offer the same resistance each time it is operated. If the lever or pedal feels soft, air is still trapped in the system. Repeat the bleeding steps.

8. When bleeding is complete, disconnect the hose from the bleed valve. Tighten the bleed valve 6 N•m (53 in.-lb.).

9. When bleeding the front brakes, repeat Steps 1-8 at the other front caliper.

10. Add DOT 4 brake fluid to the master cylinder to correct the fluid level. Refer to Chapter Three.

11. Install the diaphragm, diaphragm plate and top cap. Be sure the cap is secured in place.

> *WARNING*
> *Do not ride the motorcycle until front and rear brakes as well as the brake light are working properly.*

12. Test ride the motorcycle slowly at first to make sure the brakes are operating properly.

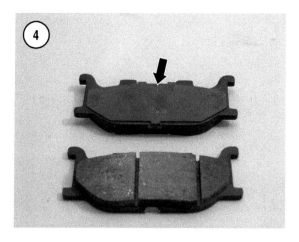

BRAKE FLUID DRAINING

Before disconnecting a brake hose, drain the brake fluid from the front or rear brakes as described below. Draining the system reduces the amount of fluid that can spill out when brake components are removed. Do not reuse brake fluid.

1. Remove the dust cap from the bleed valve. Remove all dirt from the valve and its outlet port.

2A. Perform the following to manually drain the brake fluid. An empty bottle, box-end wrench and a length of clear hose are needed.

   a. Connect a length of clear hose to the bleed valve on the caliper. Insert the other end into a container (**Figure 1**, typical).

   b. Apply the front brake lever or the rear brake pedal until it stops. Hold the lever or pedal in this position.

   c. Open the bleed valve with a box-end wrench, and let the lever or pedal move to the limit of its travel. Close the bleed valve, and release the lever or pedal.

   d. Repeat substep b and substep c until brake fluid stops flowing from the bleed valve.

2B. Perform the following to vacuum drain the brake fluid. A box-end wrench and hand-operated vacuum pump are needed.

   a. Connect the vacuum pump to the bleed valve on the brake caliper (**Figure 2**, typical).

   b. Operate the vacuum pump to create vacuum in the hose.

   c. Use a box-end wrench to open the bleed valve. The vacuum pump should pull fluid from the system.

   d. When fluid has stopped flowing through the hose, close the bleed valve.

   e. Repeat substeps b-d until brake fluid no longer flows from the bleed valve.

3. If draining the front brakes, repeat Step 1 and Step 2 on the other brake caliper.

4. Discard the brake fluid.

BRAKE PADS

Brake pad wear depends greatly upon riding habits and conditions. Periodically check the brake pads for wear. Check the pads more often when the wear indicator (**Figure 3**) approaches the edge of the brake disc. Refer to *Brake Pad Inspection* in *Brakes* in Chapter Three.

To maintain even brake pressure on the disc, always replace both pads in a caliper at the same time. When replacing the front brake pads, replace both pads in both front calipers at the same time. If any front brake pad is worn to the service limit (**Table 1**), replace all four front brake pads as a set.

Note that the brake hose does not need to be disconnected from the caliper during brake pad replacement. If the hose is removed, the brakes will have to be bled. Disconnect the hose only when servicing the brake caliper.

> *WARNING*
> *Use brake fluid clearly marked DOT 4 from a sealed container. Other types may vaporize and cause brake failure. Always use the same brand of brake fluid. Do not mix brake fluids from different manufacturers. They may not be compatible.*

> *CAUTION*
> *Check the pads more frequently when the wear indicator (**Figure 3**) approach the disc. On some pads, the wear lines are very close to the metal backing plate. If pad wear happens to be uneven, the backing plate may contact the disc and cause damage.*

Removal/Installation

Front brakes

> *CAUTION*
> *The inboard pad in the front caliper uses a shim (**Figure 4**), but the outboard pad does not. Note this when removing the brake pads. The shim must be installed on the same side of the caliper when the new pads are installed.*

1. Securely support the motorcycle on a level surface.

2. Remove the reflector and the brake hose holder from the reflector bracket.

14

3. Remove the caliper bolts (A, **Figure 5**), and lift the caliper (B) from the caliper bracket. Suspend the caliper so it does not hang from the brake hose. Note how the hose is routed.

4. Remove the outboard brake pad (**Figure 6**) from the caliper bracket, and the remove the inboard pad (**Figure 7**). Note the shim on the inboard pad. The shim must be installed on the new inboard pad.

5. Remove the pad spring (A, **Figure 8**) from the caliper and from each end caliper bracket (**Figure 9**). Discard the pad springs. New springs must be installed with new brake pads.

6. Inspect the brake pads as described in this section.

WARNING
The brake pads must be replaced as a set. If any pad requires replacement, replace both pads in both front calipers.

7. When new pads are installed in the caliper, the master cylinder brake fluid level rises as the caliper pistons are repositioned. Perform the following:

  a. Clean all debris from the top of the master cylinder.

  b. Remove the master cylinder cover, diaphragm plate and the diaphragm from the master cylinder.

  c. Install the old outboard pad into the caliper. Use the pad to slowly push the pistons (B, **Figure 8**) into the caliper until the pistons bottom. Constantly check the reservoir to make sure brake fluid does not overflow. Remove brake fluid if necessary.

  d. The pistons should move freely. If they do not, the caliper should be removed and serviced as described in this chapter.

CAUTION
When purchasing new pads, check that the friction compound of the new pads are compatible with the disc material. Remove any roughness from the backs of the new pads with a fine-cut file. Clean the pads with aerosol brake cleaner before installation.

8. Install new pad springs (**Figure 9**) onto the caliper bracket and into the caliper (A, **Figure 8**). Always use new pad springs when installing new brake pads.

9. Install the pad shim (**Figure 4**) onto the back of the inboard brake pad.

10. Install the inboard pad (**Figure 7**) and then outboard pad (**Figure 6**) into the caliper bracket with the friction material against the disc. The ears on each pad must straddle the pad springs in the bracket.

11. Lower the caliper (B, **Figure 5**) onto the caliper bracket.

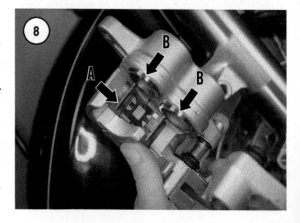

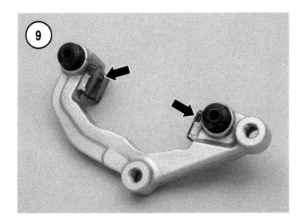

WARNING
Use just enough grease to lubricate the shaft of the caliper bolt. Excess grease could contaminate the brake pads. Do not get any grease on the bolt threads or on the brake pads.

12. Lubricate the shaft of the caliper bolts with silicone brake grease.

13. Install the caliper bolts (A, **Figure 5**), and secure the caliper to the caliper bracket.

14. Tighten the caliper bolts to 27 N•m (20 ft.-lb.).

15. Reinstall the brake hose holder and reflector. Tighten the brake hose holder bolt to 7 N•m (62 in.-lb.).

16. Repeat Steps 2-15 and replace the pads in the other front caliper.

17. Support the motorcycle with the front wheel off the ground. Spin the wheel and pump the brake lever until the pads are seated against the disc.

WARNING
Use brake fluid clearly marked DOT 4 from a sealed container. Other types may vaporize and cause brake failure. Always use the same brand of brake fluid. Do not intermix brake fluids. Many brands are not compatible with one another.

18. Refill the master cylinder reservoir, if necessary, to maintain the correct fluid level. Refer to Chapter Three. Install the diaphragm and top cover. Tighten the cover screws securely.

WARNING
Test ride the motorcycle and confirm that the brakes are operating correctly with full hydraulic advantage. If necessary, bleed the brake as described in this chapter.

14

19. Test ride the motorcycle slowly at first. Make sure the brakes are operating properly.

Rear brake

1. Securely support the motorcycle on a level surface.

2. Remove the rear caliper bolts (**Figure 10**), and lower the caliper from the brake disc. Suspend the caliper from so it does not hang from the brake hose. Note how the hose is routed.

3. Remove the outboard pad (**Figure 11**) and the inboard pad (**Figure 12**) from the caliper bracket.

4. Remove the pad spring (A, **Figure 13**) from each arm of the bracket. Note how each spring is seated in the caliper.

5. Inspect the brake pads as described in this section.

6. When new pads are installed in the caliper, the master cylinder brake fluid level rises as the caliper pistons are repositioned. Perform the following:

   a. Clean all dirt and foreign matter from the top of the master cylinder.

   b. Remove the master cylinder cover, diaphragm plate and the diaphragm from the master cylinder.

   c. Install the old outboard pad into the caliper. Use the pad to slowly push the piston into the caliper until the piston bottom. Constantly check the reservoir to make sure brake fluid does not overflow. Remove brake fluid if necessary.

   d. Remove the outboard pad.

   e. The pistons should move freely. If they do not move smoothly without sticking, the caliper should be removed and serviced as described in this chapter.

NOTE
When purchasing new pads, make sure the friction compound of the new pads are compatible with the disc material. Remove any roughness from the backs of the new pads with a fine-cut file. Clean the pads with aerosol brake cleaner before installation.

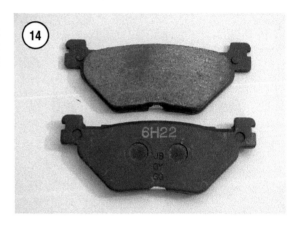

7. Seat new pad springs (A, **Figure 13**) in the caliper bracket. Always use new pad springs when installing new pads.

8. Install a new inboard pad (**Figure 12**), and then install the outboard pad (**Figure 11**) into the caliper bracket. Make sure the ears of each pad engage the pad springs.

9. Position the caliper onto the brake disc.

WARNING
Use just enough grease to lubricate the shaft of the caliper bolt. Excess grease could contaminate the brake pads. Do not get any grease on the bolt threads or on the brake pads.

10. Lubricate the shaft of the caliper bolts with silicone grease.

11. Install the rear caliper bolts (**Figure 10**). Tighten the bolts to 27 N•m (20 ft.-lb.).

12. Support the motorcycle with the rear wheel off the ground. Spin the wheel and pump the brake pedal until the pads are seated against the disc.

WARNING
Use brake fluid clearly marked DOT 4 from a sealed container. Other types may vaporize and cause brake failure. Always use the same brand of brake

fluid. Do not mix brake fluids. Many brands are not compatible with one another.

13. Check the fluid level in the master cylinder reservoir. Add brake fluid as necessary to correct the fluid level. Refer to Chapter Three. Install the diaphragm and top cover.

WARNING
Test ride the motorcycle and confirm that the brakes are operating correctly with full hydraulic advantage. If necessary, bleed the brake as described in this chapter.

14. Test ride the motorcycle slowly at first. Make sure the brakes are operating properly.

Inspection

1. Inspect the brake pads (front: **Figure 4**; rear: **Figure 14**) by performing the following:

   a. Inspect the friction material for light surface dirt, grease and oil contamination. Remove light contamination with sandpaper. If contamination has penetrated the surface, replace the brake pads.

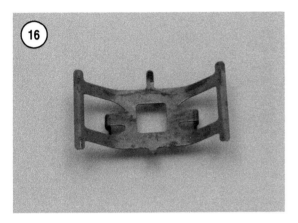

b. Inspect the brake pads for excessive wear or damage. Replace the brake pads if either pad is worn to the service limit (**Figure 15**).

c. Inspect the friction material for uneven wear, damage or contamination. Both pads should show approximately the same amount of wear. If the pads are wearing unevenly, the caliper may not be operating correctly. Inspect the caliper as described in this chapter.

d. If the brake pads appear okay, measure the thickness of the friction material with a vernier caliper. Replace both brake pads if the thickness on either pad equals or is less than the service limit (**Table 1**). When servicing the front brakes, replace both pads in both front calipers.

e. Inspect the metal plate on the back of each pad for corrosion and damage.

WARNING
Cleaning the brake disc is especially important if new pads are being installed. Many brake pad compounds are not compatible.

2. Use brake parts cleaner and a fine grade emery cloth to remove all road debris and brake pad residue from the brake disc surface.

3. Inspect the brake disc as described in this chapter.

4. Check the friction surface of the new pads for any foreign matter or manufacturing residue. If necessary, clean the pads with an aerosol brake cleaner.

5. Check the pad springs (front: **Figure 16** and **Figure 9**; rear: A, **Figure 13**) for wear or fatigue. Replace pad springs if they show any sign of damage or excessive wear.

6. Install new pad spring(s) whenever installing new brake pads.

FRONT CALIPER

Refer to **Figure 17**.

Removal

1. Securely support the motorcycle on level ground.

2. Remove the reflector and brake hose holder from the reflector bracket.

3A. Perform the following if the caliper will not be serviced.

   a. Remove the caliper brascket bolts (A, **Figure 18**).

   b. Rotate the caliper/bracket assembly (B, **Figure 18**) upward and off the brake disc.

   c. Suspend the caliper so it does not hang from the brake hose. Note how the brake hose is routed.

3B. Perform the following if the caliper will be serviced.

   a. Remove the front brake pads as described in Steps 1-6 of *Removal/Installation* in *Brake Pads* in this chapter.

   b. Fit the caliper back onto the caliper bracket, and install in the caliper bracket bolts (A, **Figure 18**).

   c. Insert a thin piece of wood or plastic between the brake disc and the pistons.

   d. Operate the brake lever, and press the pistons from their cylinders.

   e. Drain the brake fluid from the front brakes as described in this chapter.

CAUTION
Brake fluid destroys paint and finish. Immediately wash any spilled brake fluid from the motorcycle. Use soapy water, and rinse the area completely.

   f. Remove the banjo bolt (C, **Figure 18**), and disconnect the brake hose from the caliper. Note if the brake hose neck sits against the inboard or outboard side of indexing post. Discard the two copper washers.

   g. Seal the loose end of the brake hose in a plastic bag so brake fluid cannot leak onto the motorcycle.

14

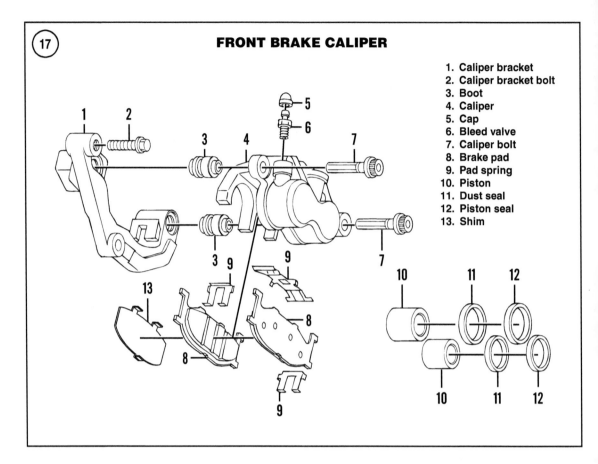

FRONT BRAKE CALIPER

1. Caliper bracket
2. Caliper bracket bolt
3. Boot
4. Caliper
5. Cap
6. Bleed valve
7. Caliper bolt
8. Brake pad
9. Pad spring
10. Piston
11. Dust seal
12. Piston seal
13. Shim

h. Remove the caliper bolts (D, **Figure 18**) and remove the caliper (B) from the caliper bracket.

i. Remove the caliper bracket bolts (A, **Figure 19**) and remove the caliper bracket (B) from the fork leg.

j. Disassemble and inspect the caliper as described in this section.

Installation

1A. If the caliper was not serviced, perform the following.

a. Lower the caliper/bracket assembly (B, **Figure 18**) onto the brake disc. Exercise caution so the leading edges of the brake pads are not damaged.

b. Fit the caliper bracket into place on the fork slider, and install the caliper bracket bolts (A, **Figure 18**). Tighten the caliper bracket bolts to 40 N•m (30 ft.-lb.).

1B. If the caliper was serviced, perform the following:

a. If removed, lubricate the boots (C, **Figure 19**) with silicone grease, and install them into the caliper bracket. Do not get grease on the brake pads or disc.

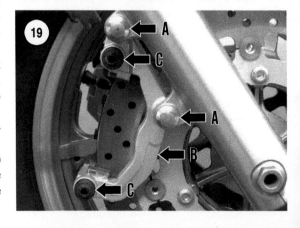

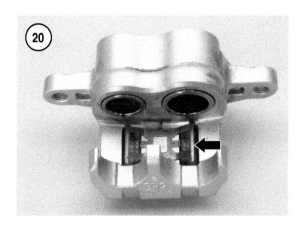

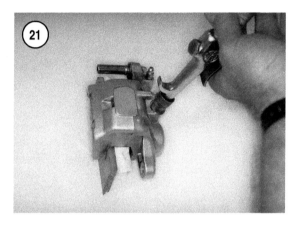

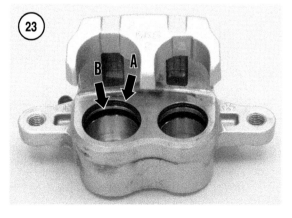

b. Fit the caliper bracket (B, **Figure 19**) into place on the fork slider, and install the caliper bracket bolts (A). Tighten the bolts to 40 N•m (30 ft.-lb.).

c. Install the front brake pads as described in Steps 8-16 of *Removal/Installation* in *Brake Pads* in this chapter.

d. Fit the brake hose onto the caliper port so the brake hose neck sits on the side of the indexing post noted during removal. Install a new copper washer onto each side of the brake hose fitting.

e. Install the banjo bolt (C, **Figure 18**). Tighten the bolt to 30 N•m (22 ft.-lb.).

f. Add brake fluid to the reservoir, and bleed the brakes as described in this chapter.

2. Install the brake hose holder and reflector onto the reflector bracket. Tighten the brake hose holder bolt to 7 N•m (62 in.-lb.).

Disassembly/Assembly

1. If still installed, remove the pad spring (**Figure 20**) from the caliper body and caliper bracket (**Figure 9**).

> *WARNING*
> *In the next step, the pistons may shoot out of the caliper body with considerable force. Keep fingers out of the way. Wear shop gloves, and apply air pressure gradually.*

2. Perform the following if the pistons were not dislodged from the cylinders during removal.

a. Pad the pistons with shop rags or wood blocks as shown in **Figure 21**.

b. Block the exposed housing fluid port holes on the caliper housing.

c. Apply compressed air through the caliper hose port and blow the pistons out of the caliper. Remove the pistons (**Figure 22**) from the caliper cylinders.

> *CAUTION*
> *In the following step, do not use a sharp tool to remove the dust and piston seals from the caliper cylinder. Sharp tools could damage the cylinder surface. The caliper will have to be replaced if the cylinder surface is damaged.*

3. Use a piece of plastic or wood to remove the dust seal (A, **Figure 23**) and the piston seal (B) from their grooves in each caliper cylinder. Discard both seals.

4. Clean all caliper parts, and inspect them as described in this section.

14

WARNING
Never reuse the old dust seals or piston seals. Very minor damage or age deterioration can make the seals useless.

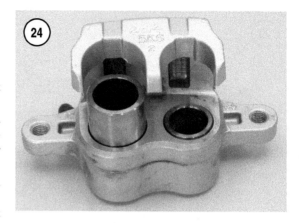

5. Coat the new dust seal with silicone grease. Coat the new piston seal with fresh DOT 4 brake fluid.
6. Install the new piston seal (B, **Figure 23**) and dust seal (A) into the grooves in the caliper cylinders. Make sure the seals are properly seated in their respective grooves.
7. Coat the pistons and caliper cylinders with fresh DOT 4 brake fluid.
8. Position each piston with the open end facing out toward the brake pads (**Figure 24**), and slide the pistons into the caliper cylinders. Push the pistons in until they bottom in the cylinders.
9. Install the caliper as described in this section.

Caliper Inspection Front and Rear

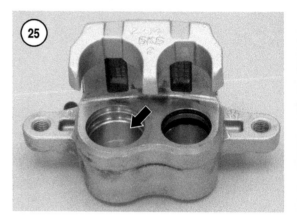

1. Clean all parts, except brake pads, with clean DOT 4 brake fluid. Place the cleaned parts on a lint-free cloth while performing the following inspection procedures.
2. Inspect the walls (**Figure 25**) in each cylinder for scratches, scoring or other damage. If rusty or corroded, replace the caliper assembly.
3. Inspect both seal grooves in each cylinder for damage. If damaged or corroded, replace the caliper assembly.
4. Measure the inside diameter of each cylinder bore with a bore gauge. Replace the brake caliper if the inside diameter of either bore is out of specification (**Table 1**).

5. Inspect the pistons (**Figure 26**) for scratches, scoring or other damage. If rusty or corroded, replace the pistons.
6. Inspect the caliper body for scratches or other signs of damage. Replace the caliper assembly if necessary.
7. Inspect the pad spring(s) (front caliper: **Figure 16** and A, **Figure 27**); rear caliper: A **Figure 13**). Replace a spring if it is cracked, worn or shows signs of fatigue.
8. Inspect the caliper bracket (front caliper: B, **Figure 27**; rear caliper B, **Figure 13**) for cracks or other signs of damage. Replace the caliper assembly if necessary.
9. Inspect the boots in the caliper bracket (front caliper: C, **Figure 19** and C, **Figure 27**; rear caliper C, **Figure 13**). Replace boots that are torn or becoming hard.
10. Inspect the mounting bolt holes (D, **Figure 27**) on the caliper bracket. If worn or damaged, replace the caliper assembly and inspect the corresponding bolt holes.

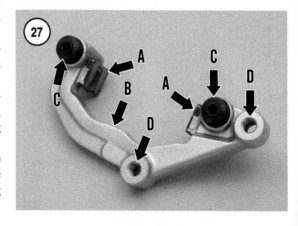

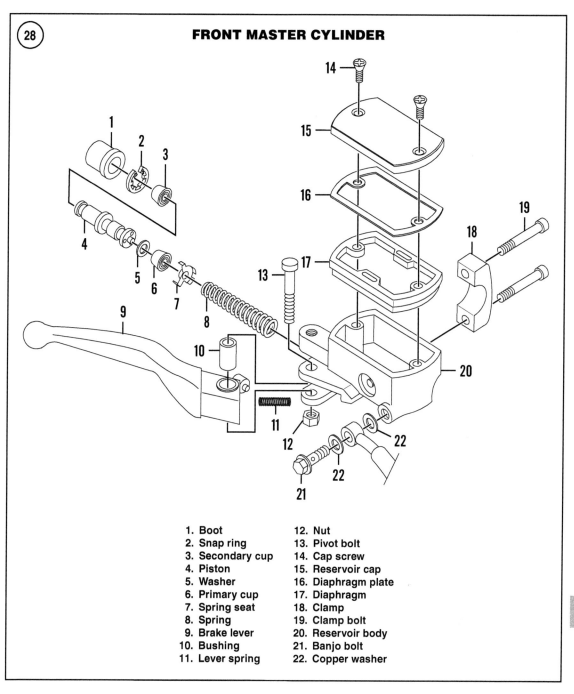

FRONT MASTER CYLINDER

28

1. Boot	12. Nut
2. Snap ring	13. Pivot bolt
3. Secondary cup	14. Cap screw
4. Piston	15. Reservoir cap
5. Washer	16. Diaphragm plate
6. Primary cup	17. Diaphragm
7. Spring seat	18. Clamp
8. Spring	19. Clamp bolt
9. Brake lever	20. Reservoir body
10. Bushing	21. Banjo bolt
11. Lever spring	22. Copper washer

11. Remove the bleed valve from the caliper body. Apply compressed air to the opening and make sure it is clear. If necessary, clean out the bleed valve with fresh brake fluid. Install the bleed valve finger-tight. It will be tightened to specification during brake bleeding.

12. Inspect the fluid opening in the base of each cylinder bore. Apply compressed air to the opening and make sure it is clear. Clean out the opening with fresh brake fluid if necessary.

13. Inspect the threads of the banjo bolt, caliper bolt, and caliper bracket bolt (front caliper). Clean up any minor thread damage. Replace the bolts and the caliper assembly if necessary.

FRONT MASTER CYLINDER

Refer to **Figure 28**.

Removal/Installation

1A. If the master cylinder will be serviced, perform the following:

14

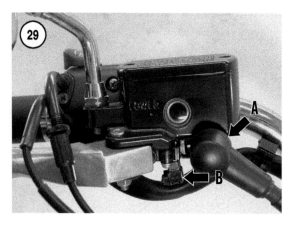

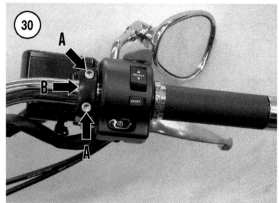

a. Drain the front brakes as described in this chapter.

b. Pull back the boot, (A, **Figure 29**), remove the banjo bolt and disconnect the brake hose from the master cylinder. Discard the copper washers.

c. Seal the loose end of the brake hose in a plastic bag so brake fluid cannot leak onto the motorcycle.

1B. If not servicing the master cylinder, proceed to Step 2. Make sure to keep the master cylinder upright so fluid does not leak.

2. Disconnect the electrical connectors from the front brake switch (B, **Figure 29**).

3. Remove two clamp bolts (A, **Figure 30**). Remove the clamp (B, **Figure 30**) and the master cylinder from the handlebar.

4. Install by reversing these removal steps. Note the following:

a. Position the master cylinder so the face of the clamp mating surface (A, **Figure 31**) aligns with the mark (B) on the handlebar.

b. Install the master cylinder clamp (B, **Figure 30**) so its "UP" stamp faces up.

c. Tighten the clamp bolts (A, **Figure 30**) to 10 N•m (89 in.-lb.) Tighten the upper clamp bolt first, then the lower bolt. There should be a gap at the lower part of the clamp after tightening.

d. Reconnect the electrical connectors to the front brake switch (B, **Figure 29**).

5. If the brake hose was disconnected from the master cylinder, perform the following:

a. Install the brake hose onto the master cylinder. Place a new copper washer on each side of the hose fitting, and tighten the banjo bolt to 30 N•m (22 ft.-lb.). Once installed, the hose must form a 30-50° angle with the master cylinder. Refer to **Figure 32**.

b. Add fresh DOT 4 brake fluid to the master cylinder, and bleed the brake system as described in this chapter.

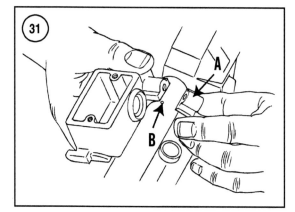

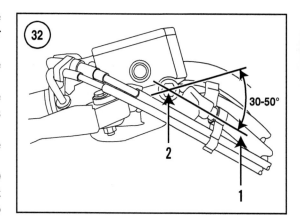

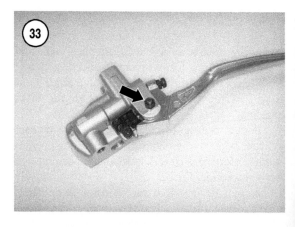

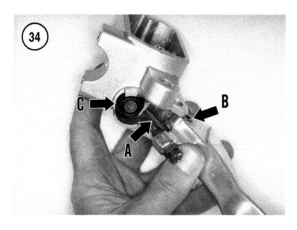

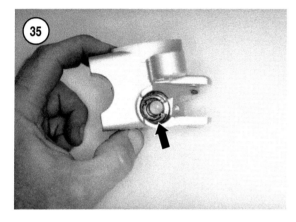

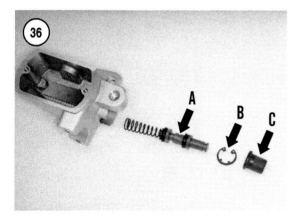

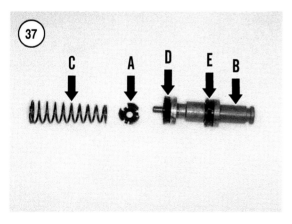

WARNING
Test ride the motorcycle to confirm that the brakes are operating properly. If necessary, bleed the brakes as described in this chapter.

6. Test ride the motorcycle slowly at first to make sure the brakes are operating properly.

Disassembly

1. Remove the master cylinder as described in this section.
2. Remove the reservoir cap, diaphragm plate and diaphragm. Pour out and discard any remaining brake fluid. Never reuse brake fluid.
3. Remove the nut (**Figure 33**) from the lever pivot bolt. Remove the bolt.
4. Pull the brake lever from the master cylinder. Account for the lever spring (A, **Figure 34**) and the bushing (B).
5. Remove the boot (C, **Figure 34**) from the master cylinder bore.
6. Remove the snap ring (**Figure 35**) from its groove in the cylinder bore, and then remove the piston assembly (A, **Figure 36**).

Assembly

1. If removed, install the spring seat (A, **Figure 37**) onto the piston (B), and fit the small end of the spring (C) onto the spring seat.

WARNING
When installing the piston assembly, do not allow the cups to turn inside out. This will damage the cups and allow brake fluid to leak within the cylinder bore.

2. Lubricate the piston assembly (A, **Figure 36**) with fresh brake fluid, and install the assembly into the cylinder bore. Be sure the piston assembly is oriented as shown in A, **Figure 36**.
3. Press the piston into the bore, and secure it in place with a new snap ring (B, **Figure 36**). The snap ring must be seated in the groove inside the cylinder bore as shown in **Figure 35**.
4. Lubricate the boot with fresh brake fluid. Position the boot so the end with the lip faces into the master cylinder bore, and carefully roll the boot over the piston so the boot seals the bore. Refer to **Figure 38**.
5. If removed, install the lever spring (A, **Figure 34**) and the bushing (B) into place on the brake lever. Lubricate the bushing with lithium-soap grease.

14

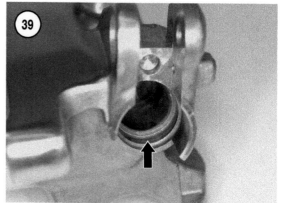

6. Slide the brake lever into place on the master cylinder body so the lever spring (A, **Figure 34**) engages the boss on the master cylinder body.

7. Install the brake lever bolt and tighten the nut (**Figure 33**) to 7 N•m (62 in.-lb.).

8. Install the diaphragm, diaphragm plate and cover after the master cylinder has been installed onto the handlebar as described in this section.

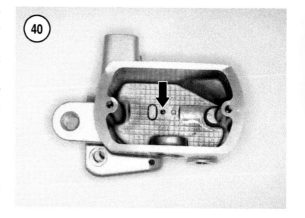

Inspection

1. Clean all parts in fresh DOT 4 brake fluid. Place the master cylinder components on a clean lint-free cloth for inspection.

2. Inspect the cylinder bore (**Figure 39**) and piston contact surfaces for scratches, wear or other signs of damage. Replace the master cylinder body if necessary.

3. Inspect the inside of the reservoir for scratches, wear or other signs of damage. Replace the master cylinder body if necessary.

4. Make sure the passage in the bottom of the brake fluid reservoir (**Figure 40**) is clear.

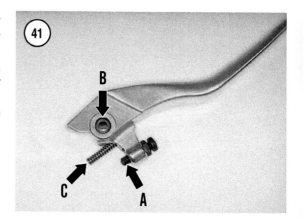

> *NOTE*
> *The spring (C, **Figure 37**), spring seat (A), primary cup (D), secondary cup (E) and piston (B) as well as the snap ring (B, **Figure 36**) and boot (C, **Figure 36**) are sold as the master cylinder kit. If any part is worn or damaged, replace the master cylinder kit.*

5. Check the end of the piston (B, **Figure 37**) for wear.

6. Check the primary cup (D, **Figure 37**) and secondary cup (E) on the piston for damage, softness or for swollen conditions.

7. Check the end of the adjuster screw (A, **Figure 41**) for signs of wear. Replace as necessary

8. Remove and inspect the brake lever bushing (B, **Figure 41**). Replace the bushing if it is worn or elongated.

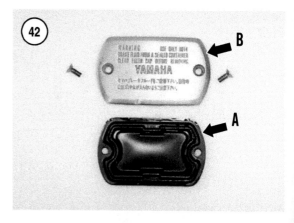

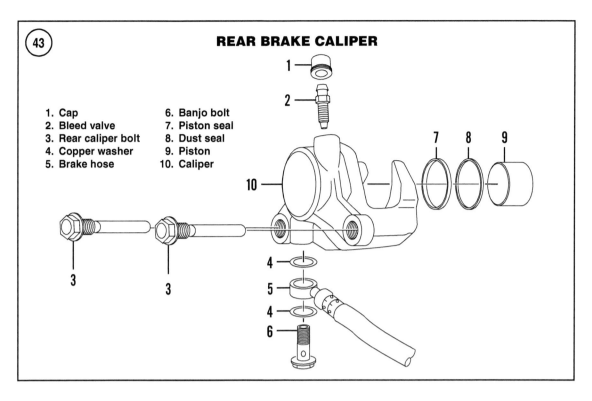

43 REAR BRAKE CALIPER

1. Cap
2. Bleed valve
3. Rear caliper bolt
4. Copper washer
5. Brake hose
6. Banjo bolt
7. Piston seal
8. Dust seal
9. Piston
10. Caliper

9. Remove the lever spring (C, **Figure 41**) from the hand lever. Replace the spring if it is worn or shows signs of fatigue.

10. Check the reservoir diaphragm (A, **Figure 42**) and cover (B) for damage and deterioration. Replace if necessary.

11. Inspect the threads in the master cylinder brake port. If the threads are damaged or partially stripped, replace the master cylinder body.

12. Measure the inside diameter of the master cylinder bore with a bore gauge. Replace the master cylinder if the inside diameter equals or exceeds the service limit listed in **Table 1**.

REAR BRAKE CALIPER

Refer to **Figure 43**.

Removal

1. Securely support the motorcycle on level ground.
2. Remove the caliper bolts (A, **Figure 44**), and lift the caliper from the disc and caliper bracket.

3A. If the caliper will not be serviced, suspend it so it does not hang from the brake hose. Note how the hose is routed.

3B. If the caliper will be serviced, perform the following:

   a. Remove the brake pads and pad springs as described in *Brake Pads* in this chapter.

   b. Seat the caliper onto the brake disc, and seat it against the caliper bracket. Install the caliper bolts (A, **Figure 44**) and tighten securely.

   c. Insert a thin piece of wood or plastic between the brake disc and the piston.

   d. Operate the brake pedal and drive the piston from the caliper cylinder.

   e. Drain the brake fluid from the rear brake as described in this chapter.

   f. Remove the banjo bolt (B, **Figure 44**), and separate the brake hose from the caliper. Discard the copper washers. Note how the brake hose neck sits against the outboard side of the caliper stop post.

   g. Seal the end of the brake hose in a plastic bag so brake fluid will not leak onto the motorcycle.

   h. Remove the caliper bolts (A, **Figure 44**), and remove the caliper from the caliper bracket.

14

Installation

1. If removed, install the pad springs and brake pads as described in *Brake Pads* in this chapter.

> *WARNING*
> *Use just enough grease to lubricate the shaft of the caliper bolt. Excess grease could contaminate the brake pads. Do not get any grease on the bolt threads or on the brake pads.*

2. Lubricate the shaft portion of the caliper bolts with silicone grease.
3. Slip the caliper over the brake pad, and seat the caliper on the caliper bracket.
4. Install the caliper bolts (A, **Figure 44**). Tighten rear caliper bolts to 27 N•m (20 ft.-lb.).
5. Perform the following if the brake hose was removed from the caliper.
  a. Secure the brake hose to the caliper with the banjo bolt (B, **Figure 44**). Place a new copper washer on each side of the brake hose fitting, and tighten the banjo bolt to 30 N•m (22 ft.-lb.). Seat the brake hose neck against the outboard side of the caliper stop post.
  b. Add brake fluid to the master cylinder, and bleed the brakes as described in this chapter.

Disassembly

Refer to **Figure 43**.
1. Remove the caliper as described in this section.
2. Remove the brake pads and pad springs as described in *Brake Pads* in this chapter.
3. If the piston was not removed from the cylinder during caliper removal, perform the following:
  a. Set the caliper on the bench with its inboard side facing down.
  b. Insert a piece of wood into the caliper.

> *WARNING*
> *In the next step, the piston may shoot out of the caliper body with considerable force. Keep your fingers out of the way. Wear shop gloves, and apply air pressure gradually.*

  c. Apply compressed air through the brake hose fitting and blow the piston out of its cylinder.
  d. Mark each piston so it can be installed into its original bore.
4. Remove the piston (A, **Figure 45**) from the caliper.

> *CAUTION*
> *In the following step, do not use a sharp tool to remove the dust and piston seals from the caliper cylinder. Sharp tools*

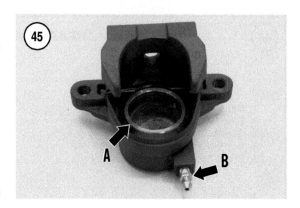

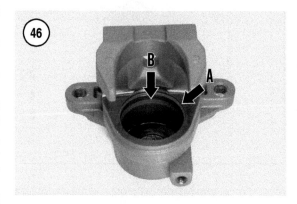

> *could damage the cylinder surface. The caliper will have to be replaced if the cylinder surface is damaged.*

5. Use a piece of plastic or wood to remove the dust seal (A, **Figure 46**) and the piston seal (B) from their grooves in each caliper cylinder. Discard all seals.
6. Clean all caliper parts, and inspect them as described in *Caliper Inspection* in *Front Caliper* in this chapter.

Assembly

> *WARNING*
> *Never reuse the old dust seals or piston seals. Very minor damage or age deterioration can make the seals useless.*

1. Coat the new dust seal silicone. Coat a new piston seal with fresh DOT-4 brake fluid.
2. Install the new piston seal (B, **Figure 46**) and dust seal (A) into their grooves in the caliper cylinder. Make sure the seals are properly seated in their respective grooves.
3. Coat the piston with DOT 4 brake fluid.

> *CAUTION*
> *Install each piston into its original cylinder. The outboard piston must be*

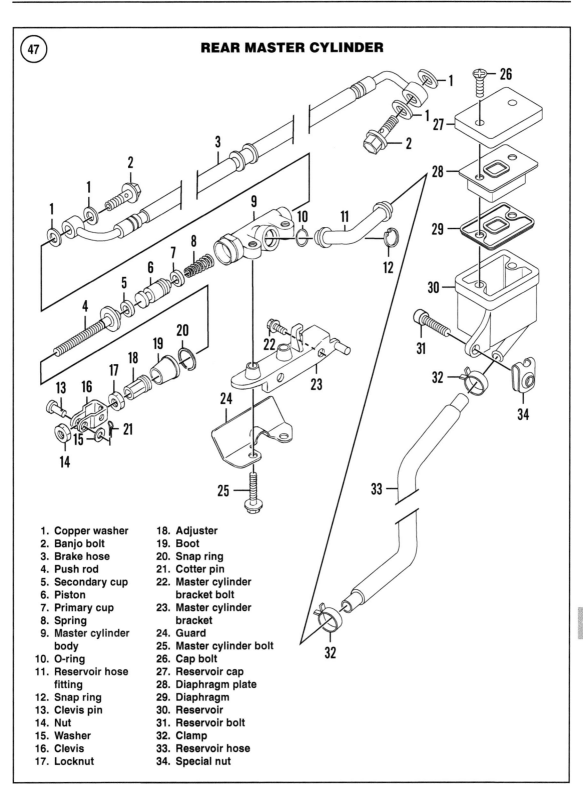

REAR MASTER CYLINDER

47

1. Copper washer
2. Banjo bolt
3. Brake hose
4. Push rod
5. Secondary cup
6. Piston
7. Primary cup
8. Spring
9. Master cylinder
   body
10. O-ring
11. Reservoir hose
    fitting
12. Snap ring
13. Clevis pin
14. Nut
15. Washer
16. Clevis
17. Locknut
18. Adjuster
19. Boot
20. Snap ring
21. Cotter pin
22. Master cylinder
    bracket bolt
23. Master cylinder
    bracket
24. Guard
25. Master cylinder bolt
26. Cap bolt
27. Reservoir cap
28. Diaphragm plate
29. Diaphragm
30. Reservoir
31. Reservoir bolt
32. Clamp
33. Reservoir hose
34. Special nut

installed in the outboard side of the caliper and vice versa.

4. Position the piston (A, **Figure 45**) with its open end up, and turn the piston into the cylinder. Press the piston into the cylinder until it bottoms.

5. If removed, install the bleed valve (B, **Figure 45**), and tighten it to 6 N•m (53 in.-lb.).

REAR BRAKE MASTER CYLINDER

Refer to **Figure 47**.

Removal

1. Securely support the motorcycle on a level surface.
2. Remove the right side cover (Chapter Fifteen).
3. Drain the fluid from the rear brake as described in this chapter.
4. Loosen the rear brake banjo bolt (A, **Figure 48**).
5. Remove the cotter pin (A, **Figure 49**) and washer from the inboard end of the clevis pin.
6. Pull the clevis pin (A, **Figure 50**), and separate the master cylinder clevis from the brake lever.
7. Remove the master cylinder bolts (B, **Figure 50**), and lower the guard (C) from the master cylinder bracket.
8. Lift the master cylinder (D, **Figure 50**) from the bracket.
9. Disconnect the brake and reservoir hoses from their respective ports by performing the following. Once removed, immediately seal each hose in a plastic bag so brake fluid will not leak onto the motorcycle.

   a. Remove the banjo bolt (A, **Figure 48**) and separate the brake hose from the master cylinder. Discard the copper washers. Note that the brake hose neck rests beneath the indexing post.
   b. Release the clamp, and disconnect the reservoir hose (B, **Figure 48**) from its port.

10. If necessary, remove the bracket bolts (E, **Figure 50**) and remove the master cylinder bracket from the frame.
11. Remove the reservoir bolt (**Figure 51**), and remove the reservoir (**Figure 52**) and its hose from behind the frame member. Note how the hose is routed. It must be rerouted along the same path.

Installation

1. Set the reservoir (**Figure 52**) into place behind the rear frame member, and install the reservoir bolt (**Figure 51**). Apply threadlocking compound to the bolt threads, and tighten the rear brake reservoir bolt to 7 N•m (62 in.-lb.). Reroute the reservoir hose along the path noted during removal.
2. If removed, fit the master cylinder bracket against the frame, and install the bracket bolt bolts (E, **Figure 50**). Tighten the rear master cylinder bracket bolts to 23 N•m (17 ft.-lb.).
3. Slide the reservoir hose (B, **Figure 48**) onto its master cylinder fitting. Secure the hose in place with the clamp.
4. Set the brake hose into place so the hose neck rests beneath the indexing post as noted during removal. Install a copper washer onto each side of the brake hose fitting, and install the banjo bolt (A, **Figure 48**). Finger-tighten the bolt.

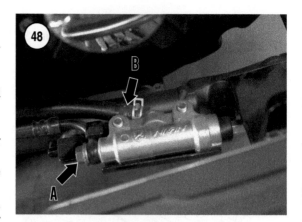
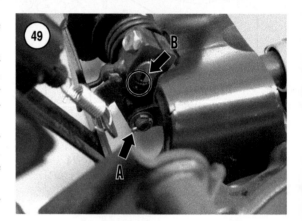
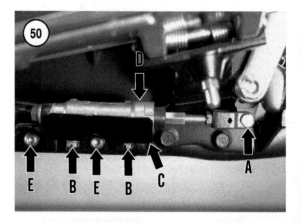
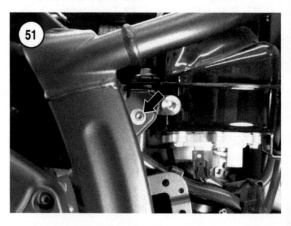

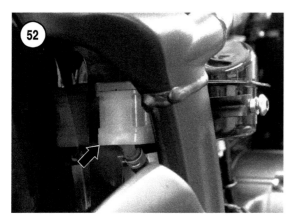

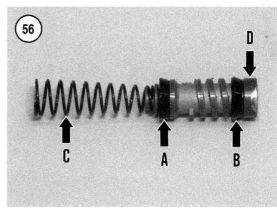

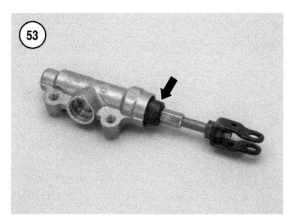

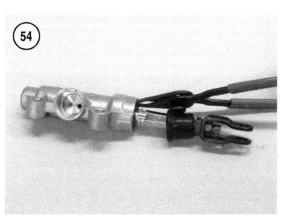

5. Set the master cylinder into place on the master cylinder bracket. Make sure the master cylinder clevis engages the brake pedal lever.

6. Position the guard (C, **Figure 50**) beneath the bracket, and install the master cylinder bolts (B). Tighten the bolts to 23 N•m (17 ft.-lb.).

7. Install the clevis pin (A, **Figure 50**), and secure the master cylinder clevis to the brake pedal lever.

8. Fit the washer onto the end of the clevis pin, and install a new cotter pin (A, **Figure 49**).

9. Tighten the banjo bolt (A, **Figure 48**) to the bolt to 30 N•m (22 ft.-lb.).

10. Add brake fluid and bleed the rear brake as described in this chapter.

11. If necessary, adjust the brake pedal height (Chapter Three).

Disassembly

1. Remove the rear brake master cylinder as described in this section.

2. Remove the snap ring (12, **Figure 47**), and disconnect the reservoir hose fitting (11) from the port on the master cylinder. Discard the O-ring (10, **Figure 47**).

3. Roll back the dust boot (**Figure 53**), and remove the snap ring (**Figure 54**) from its groove in the cylinder bore. Discard the snap ring.

4. Remove the pushrod assembly (A, **Figure 55**) and the piston assembly (B) from the cylinder bore. The spring should come out with the piston. If it does not, remove the spring from the cylinder bore.

5. Inspect the master cylinder and reservoir as described in this section.

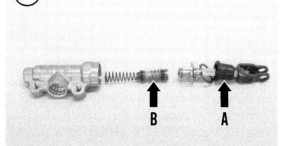

Assembly

1A. If reinstalling the piston, soak the piston in fresh DOT 4 brake fluid for at least 15 minutes to make the primary (A, **Figure 56**) and secondary cups (B) pliable. Coat the inside of the cylinder with fresh brake fluid prior to assembling the parts.

14

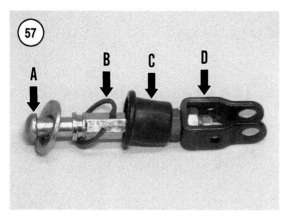

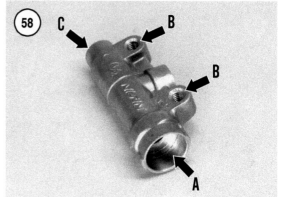

1B. If installing a new master cylinder kit, soak the new primary and secondary cups in brake fluid for at least 15 minutes. Roll the primary cup (A, **Figure 56**) onto the inboard end of the piston; roll the secondary cup (B) onto the outboard end.

2. If removed, fit the narrow end of the spring (C, **Figure 56**) onto the piston.

> *WARNING*
> *When installing the piston assembly, do not allow the cups to turn inside out. This will damage the cups and allow brake fluid to leak within the cylinder bore.*

3. Install the piston/spring assembly (B, **Figure 55**) into the master cylinder.

4. Place a dab of silicon grease onto the end of the pushrod (A, **Figure 57**), and slowly push the piston into the master cylinder with the pushrod assembly (A, **Figure 55**). Make sure the end of the push rod engages the seat in the piston.

5. Install a new snap ring (B, **Figure 57**) so it is completely seated in its groove in the master cylinder.

6. Check the operation of the master cylinder, and then slide the dust boot (**Figure 53**) into position. Make sure it is firmly seated against the master cylinder.

7. Lubricate a new O-ring (10, **Figure 47**) with DOT 4 brake fluid, and install the O-ring onto the reservoir hose fitting.

8. Press the reservoir hose fitting (11, **Figure 47**) into the master cylinder port, and install a new snap ring (12). Make sure the snap ring is completely seated within its groove.

9. Install the master cylinder as described in this section.

Inspection

> *NOTE*
> *The piston, cups, spring, pushrod, boot, circlip and adjuster are all replaced as*

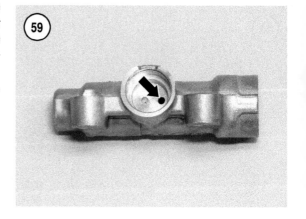

a kit. Individual parts are not available. If any of these parts are faulty, the master cylinder kit must be purchased.

1. Clean all parts in fresh DOT 4 brake fluid. Place the master cylinder components on a clean lint-free cloth for inspection.

2. Check the seat of the piston (D, **Figure 56**) where it contacts the pushrod for wear.

3. Check the primary cup (A, **Figure 56**) and secondary cup (B) for damage, softness or swelling.

4. Inspect the master piston and the spring (C, **Figure 56**) for damage or fatigue.

5. Inspect the end of the pushrod (A, **Figure 57**) where it contacts the piston for damage.

6. Inspect the pushrod dust boot (C, **Figure 57**) for tears or other signs of damage.

7. Inspect the clevis (D, **Figure 57**) and brake lever for cracks, bending or other signs of damage.

8. Inspect the cylinder bore (A, **Figure 58**) and piston contact surfaces for signs of wear or damage. If less than perfect, replace the master cylinder.

9. Inspect the threads master cylinder mounting bosses (B, **Figure 58**) and in the fluid outlet port (C). If the threads are damaged or partially stripped, replace the master cylinder assembly.

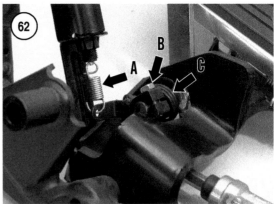

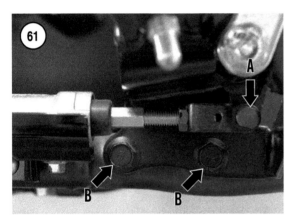

10. Make sure the passages in the inlet port (**Figure 59**) are clear.

11. Measure the master cylinder inside diameter with a bore gauge. If the inside diameter is out of specification (**Table 1**), replace the master cylinder body.

12. Inspect the reservoir diaphragm and cap for tears, cracks, or other signs of damage. Replace as necessary.

13. Inspect the reservoir and hose for cracks, wear or other signs of damage. Replace as necessary.

BRAKE PEDAL/FLOORBOARD ASSEMBLY

Removal

1. Securely support the motorcycle on a level surface.

2. Remove the frame neck covers (Chapter Eight).

3. Separate the halves of the rear brake light switch connector (**Figure 60**).

4. Remove the cable tie that secures the brake light switch wire to the frame downtube. Note the location of any cable ties.

5. Remove the cotter pin (A, **Figure 49**) and washer from the inboard end of the clevis pin.

6. Pull the clevis pin (A, **Figure 61**), and separate the master cylinder clevis from the brake pedal.

7. Remove the floorboard bracket bolts (B, **Figure 61**). Remove the brake pedal/floorboard assembly from the frame.

8. If necessary, remove the brake pedal by performing the following:

   a. Disengage the brake-light-switch spring (A, **Figure 62**) from the brake lever.
   b. Loosen the clamp bolt (B, **Figure 62**) on the brake lever.
   c. Note that the index mark on the brake lever aligns with the mark on the pedal shaft (B, **Figure 49**). If these marks are not visible, make new ones.
   d. Slide the brake lever from the brake pedal shaft. Note how the arms of the return spring engage the lever and the floorboard bracket.
   e. Remove the return spring (C, **Figure 62**) from the brake pedal shaft.
   f. Slide the brake pedal from the pivot in the footrest bracket.

Installation

1. If the brake pedal was removed, perform the following:

   a. Lubricate the brake pedal shaft with lithium-soap grease, and slide the pedal into the pivot.
   b. Install the return spring (C, **Figure 62**) and the brake lever. The indexing mark on the brake lever must aligns with the dot on the end of the brake pedal shaft (B, **Figure 49**). Make sure the arms of the return spring engage the bracket and brake lever as noted during removal.
   c. Tighten the brake lever clamp bolt (B, **Figure 62**) to 7 N•m (62 in.-lb.).
   d. Connect the brake-light-switch spring (A, **Figure 62**) to the brake lever.

2. Set the brake pedal/footrest assembly into place on the right side of the frame. Make sure the master cylinder clevis engages the brake lever.

14

3. Apply threadlocking compound to the threads of the floorboard bracket bolts (B, **Figure 61**), and tighten the bolts to 64 N•m (47 ft.-lb.).

4. Install the clevis pin (A, **Figure 61**) and secure the master cylinder clevis to the brake lever.

5. Fit the washer onto the end of the clevis pin, and install a new cotter pin (A, **Figure 49**).

6. Connect the halves of the rear brake light switch connector (**Figure 60**). Route the wire along its original path.

7. Use new cable ties to secure the brake switch wire to the frame downtube where noted during removal.

8. Adjust the brake pedal height and rear brake switch as described in Chapter Three.

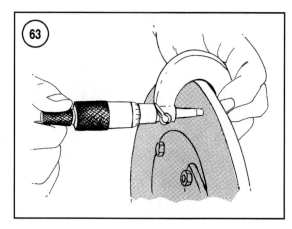

BRAKE DISC

The brake discs can be removed from the wheel hub once the wheel is removed from the motorcycle.

Inspection

A brake disc can be inspected while it is installed on the wheel. Small nicks and marks on the disc are not important. Radial scratches deep enough to snag a fingernail, however, reduce braking effectiveness and increase brake pad wear. If these grooves are evident and the brake pads are wearing rapidly, the disc should be replaced.

Do not machine a disc to compensate for any warp. Motorcycle brake discs are thin. Machining them only makes them thinner, causing them to warp quite rapidly. If a disc is warped, the brake pads may be dragging on the disc due to a faulty caliper and causing the disc to overheat. Overheating can also be caused when there is unequal pad pressure on the sides of the disc.

NOTE
Disc thickness can be measured with the wheel installed on the motorcycle.

1. Measure the thickness of the disc at several locations around the disc (**Figure 63**). The disc must be replaced if the thickness in any area is equal to or less than the service limit (**Table 1**).

2. Check the disc runout by performing the following:

    a. Make sure the disc mounting bolts are tight before running this check.

    b. When checking a front brake disc, mount a dial indicator so its plunger sits 2 mm (0.08 in.) from the outside diameter of the disc (**Figure 64**). When checking a rear brake disc, position the plunger 1.5 mm (0.06 in.) from the disc outside diameter.

    c. Slowly rotate the wheel, and watch the dial indicator. Replace the disc if runout is out of specification (**Table 1**).

3. Clean any rust or corrosion from the disc, and wipe it clean with lacquer thinner or aerosol brake cleaner. Never use oil-based solvents. They may leave an oil residue on the disc.

4. If unequal brake pad pressure is suspected, check the following:

    a. The floating caliper is binding on the caliper pins, which prevents the caliper from floating (side-to-side) on the disc.

    b. The brake caliper piston seals are worn or damaged.

    c. The master-cylinder relief port is plugged.

    d. The primary cup on the piston is worn or damaged.

Removal/Installation

1. Remove the front or rear wheel (Chapter Eleven).

CAUTION
Set the tire on two wooden blocks. Do not set the wheel down on the brake disc surface. It could be scratched or damaged.

NOTE
Insert a piece of wood or vinyl tube between the pads in the caliper(s). This way, if the brake lever or pedal is inadvertently applied, the pistons will not be forced out of the cylinders. If this does happen, the caliper(s) will have to be disassembled to reseat the pistons and the system will have to be bled as described in this chapter.

2. Remove the brake disc bolts (**Figure 65**).

3. Lift the brake disc from the hub.

4. Clean the threaded holes in the hub.

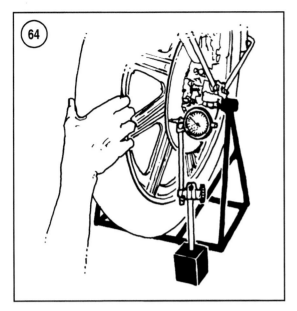

5. Clean the brake disc mounting surface on the hub.

6. Reverse the removal procedures to install the brake disc. Note the following:

    a. The brake disc bolts are made from a harder material than similar bolts used on the motorcycle. When replacing the bolts, always use standard Yamaha brake disc bolts. Never compromise, and use cheaper bolts. They will not properly secure the disc to the hub.

    b. Install a disc so its arrow points in the direction of forward wheel rotation.

    c. Apply small amount of threadlocking compound to the bolt threads.

    d. Evenly tighten the brake disc bolts in a crisscross pattern. Tighten the bolts to 23 N•m (17 ft.-lb.).

BRAKE HOSE

Check the brake hoses (front: **Figure 66**, rear: **Figure 47**) at the brake system inspection intervals in Chapter Three. Replace any brake hose that is cracked, bulging or shows signs of chafing, wear or other damage.

Removal/Installation

Front brake hose assembly

1. Cover areas of the motorcycle where brake fluid could spill.

2. Drain the brake fluid as described in this chapter.

3. Note how the brake hose is routed through the motorcycle. Make a drawing so the new hose can be routed along the same path as the original hose or pipe.

4. Remove the wheel (Chapter Eleven).

5. Remove the front fender (Chapter Fifteen).

6. Remove the headlight housing (Chapter Nine).

7. Remove the banjo bolts and disconnect the brake hose from each front caliper and from the master cylinder. Note the following:

    a. Once removed, immediately seal the hose end in a plastic bag so brake fluid will not leak onto the motorcycle.

    b. Discard the copper washers installed with each hose fitting.

    c. When disconnecting a brake hose from a caliper, note if the hose neck rests against the inboard or the outboard side of the indexing post.

8. Remove the brake hose guide bolt (A, **Figure 67**) and the brake hose union bolt (B).

9. Pull the brake hoses through of the guide beneath the upper fork bridge (**Figure 68**) and the guide on each fork leg.

10. Make sure that the hose assembly is free of any cable ties or holders, and remove the old hose assembly. Note the location of all cable ties and holders.

11. Installation is the reverse of removal. Note the following:

    a. Compare the new and hold hoses. Make sure they are the same.

    b. Route the new hose along the path noted during removal. Pass the hoses through all guides, and secure the hose to same point on the motorcycle noted during removal.

    c. Clean the banjo bolts and hose ends to remove any contamination.

    d. Make sure the notch on the lower fork bridge engages the cutout in the brake hose union. Apply threadlocking compound to the threads of the union bolt (B, **Figure 67**), and tighten the bolt to 10 N•m (89 in.-lb.).

    e. Fit the brake hose guide onto the bottom of the lower fork bridge so the tang on the guide engages the hole in the fork bridge. Apply thread-

14

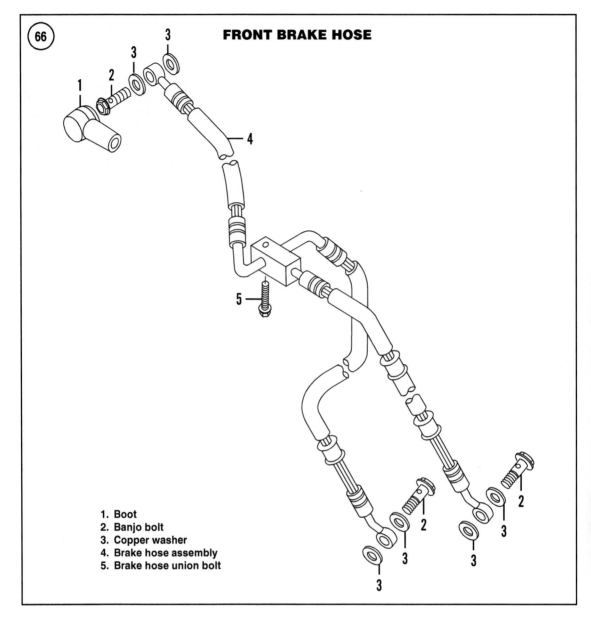

FRONT BRAKE HOSE

66

1. Boot
2. Banjo bolt
3. Copper washer
4. Brake hose assembly
5. Brake hose union bolt

locking compound to the threads of the guide bolt (A, **Figure 67**), and tighten the brake hose guide bolt to 10 N•m (89 in.-lb.).

f. Install a new copper washer onto each side of the hose fitting, and tighten the banjo bolt to 30 N•m (22 ft.-lb.).

g. When connecting a brake hose to a brake caliper, make sure the neck of the hose rests against the side of the indexing post as noted during removal.

h. Secure the hose to the master cylinder so the hose forms the angle shown in **Figure 32**.

i. Turn the handlebars from side to side to make sure the hose does not rub against any part or pull away from its brake component.

j. Refill the master cylinder and bleed the brakes as described in this chapter.

WARNING
Before riding the motorcycle, confirm that the brake lights work and that the front and rear brakes operate properly.

k. Slowly test ride the motorcycle to confirm that the brakes are operating properly.

Rear brake hose assembly

1. Remove the exhaust system (Chapter Eight).

2. Remove the coolant reservoir cover (Chapter Ten).

3 Drain the brake system as described in this chapter.

4. Note how the brake hose is routed through the motorcycle. Make a drawing so the new hose can be

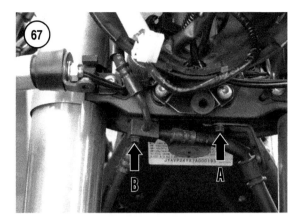

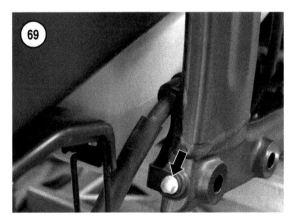

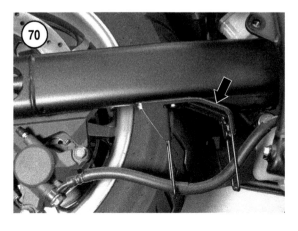

routed along the same path as the original hose or pipe.

5. Release any clamps or cable ties that secure the brake hose to the motorcycle. Note the location of all cable ties and holders.

6. Remove the rear brake master cylinder and reservoir as described in this chapter.

7. Disconnect each end of the hose being replaced. Once a hose is disconnected from a port or fitting, immediately seal the hose end in a plastic bad so brake fluid will not leak onto the motorcycle.

   a. Remove the banjo bolt and disconnect the brake hose from the rear caliper and master cylinder. Discard the copper washers installed on each side of the brake hose fitting.

   b. Disconnect the reservoir hose from the fitting on the master cylinder and on the reservoir.

8. If necessary, remove the brake hose guide bolt (**Figure 69**) and release the guide from the frame member.

9. Pull the brake hose from the brake hose guide (**Figure 70**) on the swing arm, and remove the hose.

10. Installation is the reverse of removal. Note the following:

   a. Compare the new and hold hoses. Make sure they are the same.

   b. If removed, reinstall the brake hose guide (**Figure 70**) and tighten the guide bolt to 7 N•m (62 in.-lb.).

   c. Route the new hose along the path noted during removal. Secure the hose to the motorcycle at the same points noted during removal.

   d. Clean the banjo bolts and hose ends to remove any contamination.

   e. Install a new copper washer onto each side of the hose fitting, and tighten the banjo bolt to 30 N•m (22 ft.-lb.).

   f. When connecting a brake hose to the rear caliper, make sure the neck of hose rests against the outboard side of the indexing post. When connecting the hose to the master cylinder, seat the hose neck against the bottom of the indexing post.

   g. Make sure the end of the reservoir hose securely engages the fitting at the reservoir and master cylinder.

   h. Refill the master cylinder and bleed the brakes as described in this chapter.

> *WARNING*
> *Before riding the motorcycle, confirm that the brake lights work and that the front and rear brakes operate properly.*

   i. Slowly test ride the motorcycle to confirm that the brakes are operating properly.

14

Table 1 BRAKE SPECIFICATIONS

Item	Specification mm (in.)	Service limit mm (in.)
Brake fluid	DOT 4	–
Front brake		
Brake pad thickness	6.0 (0.24)	0.8 (0.03)
Brake disc thickness	5.0 (0.20)	4.5 (0.18)
Brake disc outside diameter	298 (11.73)	–
Brake disc runout (measured 2 mm [0.08 in.] from disc outside diameter)	–	0.12 (0.0047)
Caliper cylinder bore inside diameter		
Upper bore	30.16 (1.19)	–
Lower bore	25.40 (1.00)	–
Master cylinder bore inside diameter	14.00 (0.55)	–
Brake lever free play (at lever end)	2.0-5.0 (0.08-0.20)	–
Rear brake		
Brake pad thickness	5.8 (0.23)	0.8 (0.03)
Brake disc thickness	6.0 (0.24)	5.5 (0.22)
Brake disc outside diameter	290.0 (11.73)	–
Brake disc runout (measured 1.5 mm [0.06 in.] from disc outside diameter)	–	0.15 (0.0059)
Caliper cylinder bore inside diameter	41.30 (1.63)	–
Master cylinder bore inside diameter	12.7 (0.50)	–

Table 2 BRAKE SYSTEM TORQUE SPECIFICATIONS

Item	N•m	in.-lb.	ft.-lb.
Bleed valve	6	53	–
Brake disc bolts*	23	–	17
Brake hose banjo bolt	30	–	22
Brake hose guide bolt			
Front*	10	89	–
Rear	7	62	–
Brake hose holder bolt	7	62	–
Brake pedal lever clamp bolt	7	62	–
Floorboard bracket bolts*	64	–	47
Front caliper bracket bolts	40	–	30
Front caliper bolts	27	–	20
Front brake hose union bolt*	10	89	–
Front brake lever bolt and nut	7	62	–
Front master cylinder clamp bolts*	10	89	–
Rear brake reservoir bolt*	7	62	–
Rear caliper bolts	27	–	20
Rear master cylinder bolts	23	–	17
Rear master cylinder bracket bolts	23	–	17
*Refer to text.			

BODY AND FRAME

Table 1 is at the end of this chapter.

BODY PANEL FASTENERS

Several types of fasteners are used to attach the various body panels to each other and to the frame. Note the type of fastener used before removing a panel. An improperly released fastener can damage a body panel.

Trim Clip

Quick release trim clips are used at various locations on different body panels. The plastic trim clips degenerates with heat, age and use. Installing a worn trim clip through the mounting hole(s) can be very difficult. Trim clips are inexpensive and should be replaced as necessary. Purchase at least a dozen if all of the body panels are going to be removed.

To remove a trim clip, push the center pin into the head with a Phillips screwdriver (A, **Figure 1**). This releases the inner lock so the trim clip can be withdrawn from the body panel (B, **Figure 1**).

To install a trim clip, push the center pin outward so it protrudes from the head, and insert the clip through the panels (C, **Figure 1**). Lock the trim clip by pushing the pin until it sits flush with the top of the head (D, **Figure 1**).

Quick Fastener Screw

The quarter-turn quick fastener screws (DZUS fasteners) are used mainly to secure one body panel to another. Use a Phillips screwdriver and turn the fastener 1/4-turn counterclockwise to release it from an adjacent panel. The screw will usually stay with the outer body panel as it is held in place with a plastic washer. This screw can be reused.

Flat Head Clip

To remove a flat head clip, insert a screwdriver under the head. Release the clip pawls by prying the head out of the clip (A, **Figure 2**), and remove the clip.

Install a flat head clip with the head protruding from the clip. Insert the clip into the panel, and press the head into the clip. This opens the pawls and locks the clip in place.

A worn flat head clip (B, **Figure 2**) can be difficult to install. These are relatively inexpensive and should be replaced as necessary.

Special Nut

A special nut (Tinnerman clip) is a U-shaped metal clip (**Figure 3**) that is pushed onto the edge of a body panel. It usually remains secured to the body panel during removal. If a special nut falls off, lightly crimp it together and push it back into place on the panel.

RIDER'S SEAT

Removal/Installation

Refer to **Figure 4**.

15

1. Securely support the motorcycle on a level surface.

2. Insert the key into the seat lock on the left side cover.

3. Turn the key counterclockwise, and lift the front of the seat until the seat tongue disengages from the lock on the seat bracket (A, **Figure 5**).

4. Pull the seat forward until the seat tang release from the rider's seat holder (A, **Figure 6**) on the fender bracket. Remove the seat from the motorcycle.

5. Installation is the reverse of removal.

   a. Slide the rider's seat rearward until its tang (A, **Figure 7**) engages the rider's seat holder (A, **Figure 6**).

   b. Press the seat down so the seat tongue (B, **Figure 7**) passes through the seat bracket (A, **Figure 5**) and engages the lock.

   c. Remove the key from the lock.

SEAT BRACKET

Removal/Installation

1. Remove the rider's seat and the left side cover as described in this chapter.

2. Remove the seat bracket bolts (B, **Figure 5**), and lift the seat bracket from the frame.

3. Installation is the reverse of removal. Tighten the seat bracket bolts (B, **Figure 5**) to 7 N•m (62 in.-lb.).

PASSENGER SEAT

Removal/Installation

Refer to **Figure 4**.

1. Remove the rider's seat as described in this chapter.

2. Remove the passenger seat bolts (B, **Figure 6**) from the front of the passenger seat.

3. Pull the seat forward until the seat tang release from the passenger seat holder (A, **Figure 8**) on the fender. Remove the seat from the motorcycle.

4. Installation is the reverse of removal.

   a. Slide the rider's seat rearward until its tang (**Figure 9**) engages the passenger seat holder on the fender (A, **Figure 8**).

   b. Secure the seat to the fender bracket (B, **Figure 8**) with the passenger seat bolts (B, **Figure 6**). Tighten the passenger seat bolts to 16 N•m (12 ft.-lb.).

SIDE COVERS

Removal/Installation

Refer to **Figure 4**.

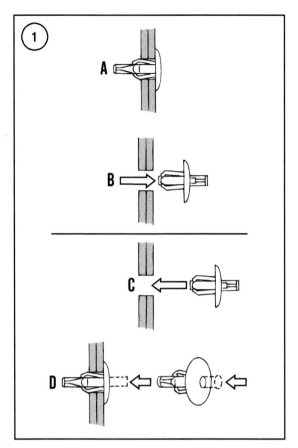

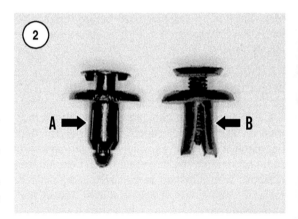

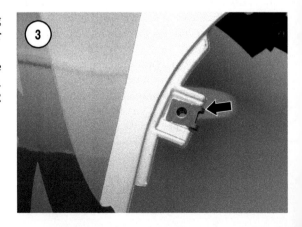

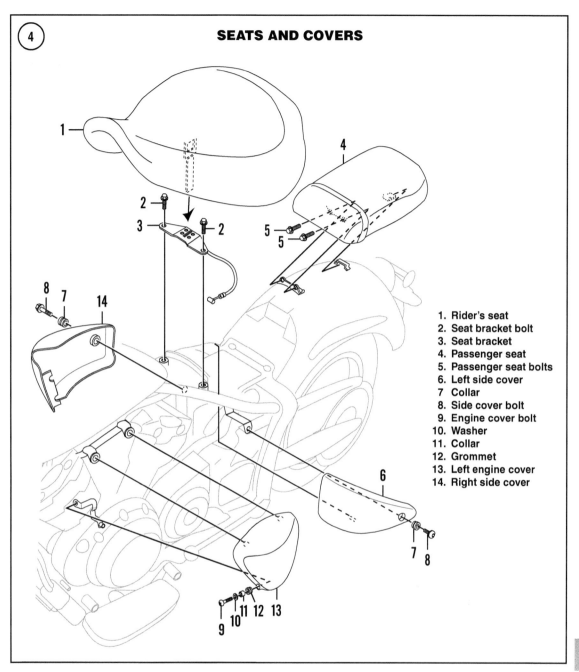

4 **SEATS AND COVERS**

1. Rider's seat
2. Seat bracket bolt
3. Seat bracket
4. Passenger seat
5. Passenger seat bolts
6. Left side cover
7 Collar
8. Side cover bolt
9. Engine cover bolt
10. Washer
11. Collar
12. Grommet
13. Left engine cover
14. Right side cover

15

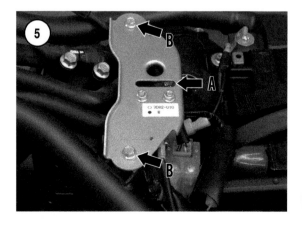

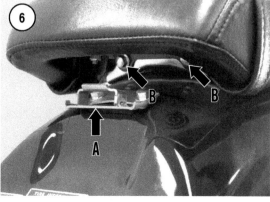

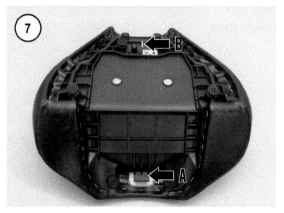

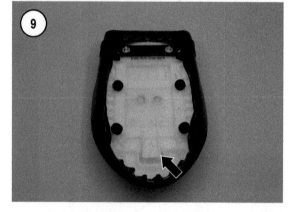

1. Remove the rider's seat as described in this chapter.

2. Remove the side cover bolt (**Figure 10**). Account for the collar installed with the bolt.

3. Slide the cover forward until the cover's forward edge disengages from the grommet(s) on the motorcycle.

4. When removing a left side cover, disengage the cable end from the seat release lever (**Figure 11**) inside the cover.

5. Remove the side cover.

6. Installation is the reverse of removal.

    a. When installing a left side cover, connect the cable end to the seat lock. Lubricate the cable end with lithium-soap grease.

    b. Slide the cover rearward until its forward edge engages the grommet(s) on the motorcycle.

    c. Tighten the side cover bolt to 7 N•m (62 in.-lb.).

LEFT ENGINE COVER

Removal/Installation

Refer to **Figure 4**.

1. Securely support the motorcycle on a level surface.

2. Remove the engine cover bolt (**Figure 12**) from the front of the cover. Account for the collar and washer installed with the bolt.

3. Pull the top of the cover outward until its posts disengage from the grommets on the cover bracket.

4. Installation is the reverse of removal.

    a. Make sure each post engages its grommet.

    b. Tighten the engine cover bolt to 4 N•m (35 in.-lb.).

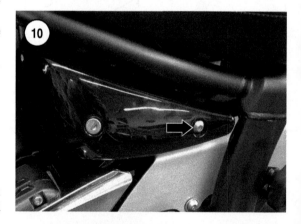

TOOL TRAY

Removal/Installation

1. Remove the rider's seat as described in this chapter.

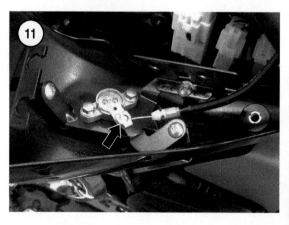

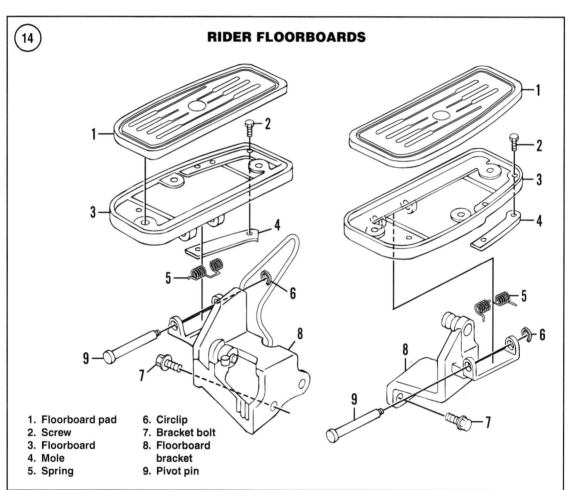

RIDER FLOORBOARDS

1. Floorboard pad
2. Screw
3. Floorboard
4. Mole
5. Spring
6. Circlip
7. Bracket bolt
8. Floorboard bracket
9. Pivot pin

2. Remove the battery cover from the motorcycle (Chapter Nine).

3. Release the forward end of the strap (A, **Figure 13**), and lift the tool kit (B) from the tool tray.

4. Lift to tool tray from the top of the battery. Note how the right side of the tray (C, **Figure 13**) engages the ECU.

5. Installation is the reverse of removal. Set the tool tray into place so its right side engages the ECU as noted during removal.

RIDER FLOORBOARD

Disassembly/Assembly

Refer to **Figure 14**.

1. Remove the brake pedal/footrest assembly (Chapter Fourteen).

2. Remove the shift pedal/footrest assembly (Chapter Seven).

3. Remove the circlip from the pivot pin.

4. Pull the pivot pin from the floorboard, and separate the floorboard from the bracket. Watch for the spring.
5. Installation is the reverse of removal. Pay attention to the following.
   a. Make sure the pin passes through the spring.
   b. The circlip must be completely seated in its groove on the pivot pin.

PASSENGER FOOTPEGS

Removal/Installation

Refer to **Figure 15**.
1. Remove the footpeg bracket bolts.
2. Lower the footpeg bracket from the frame.
3. If necessary, remove the footpeg by performing the following:
   a. Remove the nut from the footpeg pivot bolt.
   b. Pull the pivot bolt, and separate the footpeg from the bracket.
   c. Watch for the special washes, spacer, ball and compression spring.
4. Installation is the reverse of removal.
   a. Apply threadlocking compound to the threads of the footpeg bracket bolts.
   b. Tighten the footpeg bracket bolts to 23 N•m (17 ft.-lb.).

SIDESTAND

Removal/Installation

1. Securely support the motorcycle is on a level surface.
2. Remove the sidestand switch bolts, and release the sidestand switch (A, **Figure 16**) from the sidestand bracket.
3. Remove the sidestand bracket bolts (B, **Figure 16**), and lower the sidestand bracket from the frame.
4. Installation is the reverse of remove.
   a. Apply threadlocking compound to the sidestand bracket bolts, and tighten the bolts to 56 N•m (41 ft.-lb.).
   b. Tighten the sidestand switch bolts to 4 N•m (35 in.-lb.).

Disassembly/Assembly

Refer to **Figure 17**.
1. Raise the sidestand, and use locking pliers to disconnect the spring hook from the bracket boss.
2. Remove the self-locking nut from the pivot bolt.
3. Remove the pivot bolt and washer.
4. Separate the sidestand from the bracket. Account for the collar in the bracket boss.

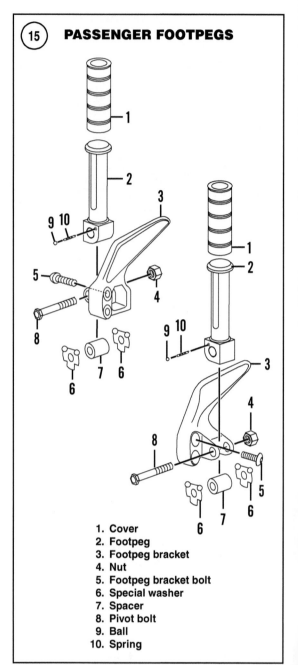

PASSENGER FOOTPEGS

1. Cover
2. Footpeg
3. Footpeg bracket
4. Nut
5. Footpeg bracket bolt
6. Special washer
7. Spacer
8. Pivot bolt
9. Ball
10. Spring

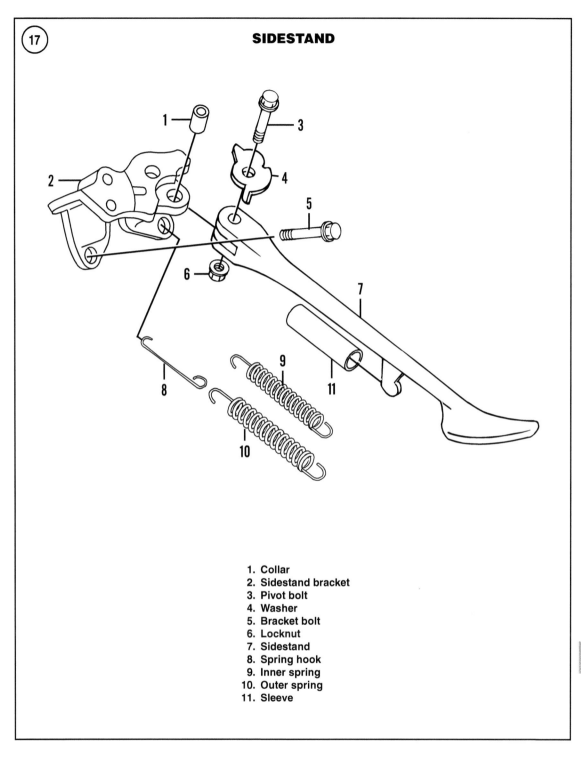

17   **SIDESTAND**

1. Collar
2. Sidestand bracket
3. Pivot bolt
4. Washer
5. Bracket bolt
6. Locknut
7. Sidestand
8. Spring hook
9. Inner spring
10. Outer spring
11. Sleeve

15

5. Assemble the sidestand by reversing the removal steps. Note the following:

   a. Apply a light coat of lithium-soap grease to the pivot surfaces of the mounting bracket and sidestand.

   b. Be sure the collar is in place in bracket boss.

   c. Install a new self-locking nut, and tighten the nut to the 56 N•m (41 ft.-lb.).

FRONT FENDER

Removal/Installation

Refer to **Figure 18**.

1. Remove the front wheel (Chapter Eleven).

2. Remove the front fender bolts (A, **Figure 19**) on each side, and lift the front fender from between the fork legs. The fender bolts also secure reflector/hose-

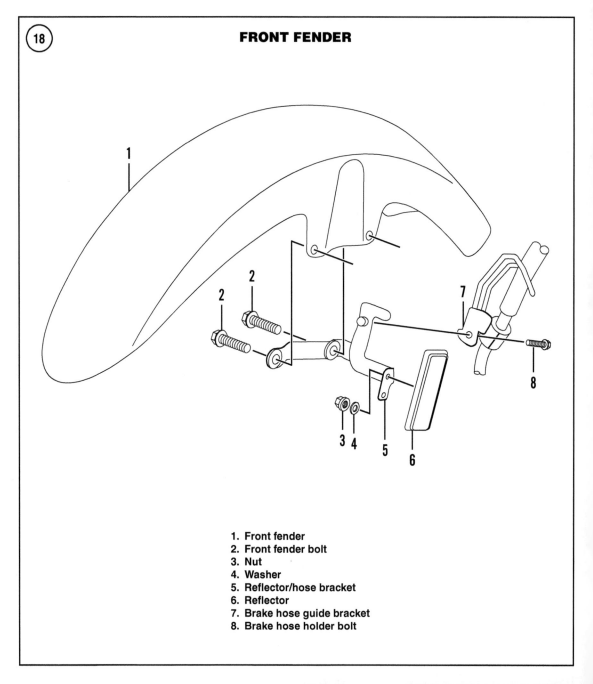

FRONT FENDER

1. Front fender
2. Front fender bolt
3. Nut
4. Washer
5. Reflector/hose bracket
6. Reflector
7. Brake hose guide bracket
8. Brake hose holder bolt

guide bracket (B, **Figure 19**) in place. Note how this bracket is positioned.

3. Installation is the reverse of removal.

   a. Position the reflector/hose-guide bracket (B, **Figure 19**) as noted during removal.

   b. Tighten the front fender bolts to 23 N•m (17 ft.-lb.).

REAR FENDER

Removal/Installation

Refer to **Figure 20**.

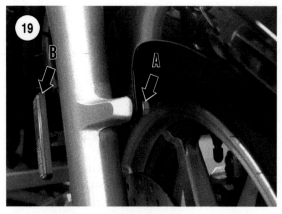

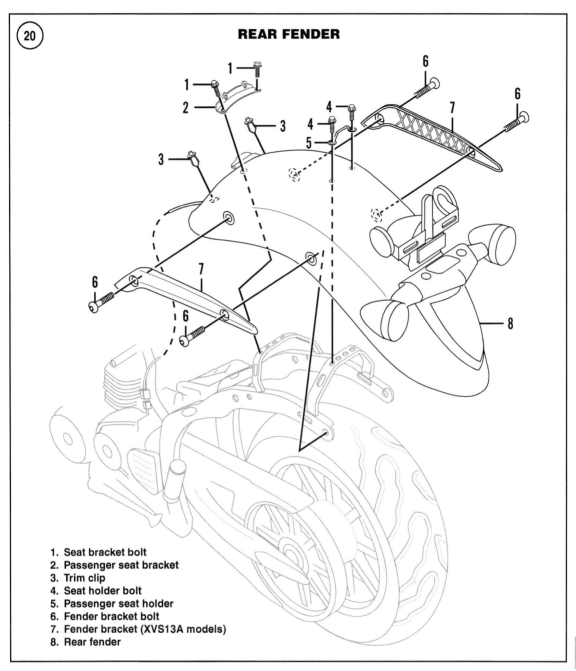

REAL FENDER — REAR FENDER

1. Seat bracket bolt
2. Passenger seat bracket
3. Trim clip
4. Seat holder bolt
5. Passenger seat holder
6. Fender bracket bolt
7. Fender bracket (XVS13A models)
8. Rear fender

15

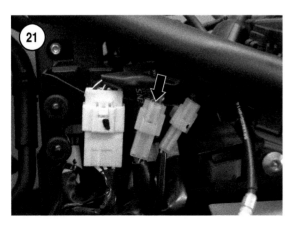

1. Remove both seats and the tool tray as described in this chapter.

2. Separate the halves of the taillight subharness connector (**Figure 21**).

3A. On XVS13CT models, remove the saddlebags and the saddlebag brackets as described in this chapter.

3B. On XVS13A models, remove the rear fender bracket bolts (A, **Figure 22**), and fender bracket (B) from one side. Repeat this step and remove the fender bracket from the other side.

4. Remove the trim clips (**Figure 23**), and release the fender from the front mudguard.

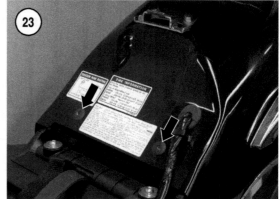

5. Remove the bolts, and lift the passenger seat bracket (B, **Figure 8**) and the passenger seat holder (A) from the fender.

6. Remove the fender from the frame.

7. Installation is the reverse of removal.

    a. Tighten the passenger seat holder bolts and the passenger seat bracket bolts to 16 N•m (12 ft.-lb.).

    b. Tighten the rear fender bracket bolts to 23 N•m (17 ft.-lb.).

MUDGUARD

1. Remove the rear fender as described in this chapter.

2. Remove the trim clip (**Figure 24**) from each side of the mudguard.

3. Remove the inner trim clips (**Figure 25**) and remove the mudguard.

4. Installation is the reverse of removal.

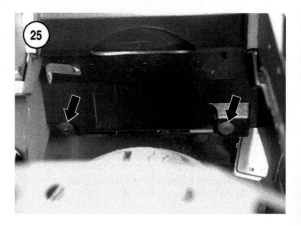

SADDLEBAGS AND BRACKETS (XVS13CT MODELS)

Removal/Installation

Refer to **Figure 26**.

1. Securely support the motorcycle on a level surface.

2. Remove the saddlebag bolts and washers that secure the bottom of the bag to the bracket. Account for the two grommets and collar installed in each mount.

3. Remove the saddlebag bolts and washers that secure the side of the bag to the bracket, and remove the saddlebag from its bracket. Account for the two grommets and collar in each mount.

4. Repeat Step 2 and Step 3 to remove the other saddlebag.

5. Remove the backrest bolts, and slide the backrest from each rear fender bracket.

6. Remove the passenger footpeg from each side as described in this chapter.

7. Remove the saddlebag plate bolts and remove the saddlebag plate from each side.

8. Remove the saddlebag bracket bolts and washers from one side. Remove the saddlebag bracket and the backrest bracket from that side.

9. Repeat Step 8 on the other side.

10. Installation is the reverse of removal.

    a. Tighten the saddlebag bracket bolts to 23 N•m (17 ft.-lb.).

    b. Tighten the saddlebag plate bolts to 23 N•m (17 ft.-lb.).

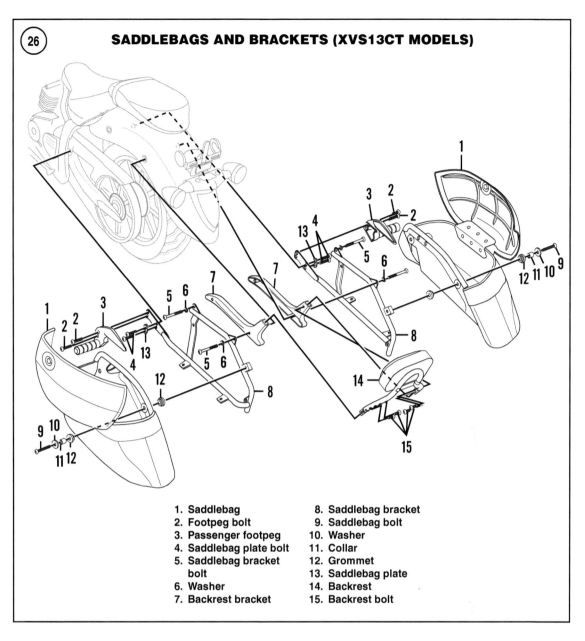

SADDLEBAGS AND BRACKETS (XVS13CT MODELS)

1. Saddlebag
2. Footpeg bolt
3. Passenger footpeg
4. Saddlebag plate bolt
5. Saddlebag bracket bolt
6. Washer
7. Backrest bracket
8. Saddlebag bracket
9. Saddlebag bolt
10. Washer
11. Collar
12. Grommet
13. Saddlebag plate
14. Backrest
15. Backrest bolt

c. Tighten the saddlebag bolts to 18 N•m (13 ft.-lb.). Make sure two grommets and a collar are installed at each saddlebag mount.

d. Tighten the backrest bolts to 23 N•m (17 ft.-lb.).

WINDSHIELD ASSEMBLY AND BRACKET (XVS13CT MODELS)

Removal/Installation

Refer to **Figure 27**.

1. Turn out the windshield assembly bolts from each side, and lift the windshield assembly from the windshield brackets.

2. Turn out the windshield bracket bolts and remove the bracket from one side.

3. Repeat Step 2 to remove the other windshield bracket.

4. Installation is the reverse of removal.

a. Apply threadlocking compound to the threads of the windshield bracket bolts.

b. Tighten the upper windshield bracket bolts to 48 N•m (35 ft.-lb.).

c. Tighten the lower windshield bracket bolts and the windshield assembly bolts to 23 N•m (17 ft.-lb.).

WINDSHIELD (XVS13CT MODELS)

Removal/Installation

Refer to **Figure 27**.

15

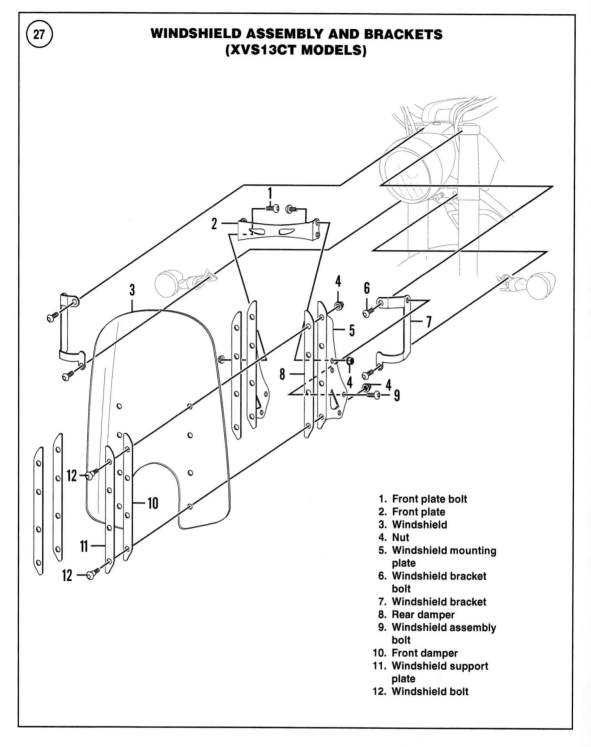

**WINDSHIELD ASSEMBLY AND BRACKETS
(XVS13CT MODELS)**

1. Front plate bolt
2. Front plate
3. Windshield
4. Nut
5. Windshield mounting plate
6. Windshield bracket bolt
7. Windshield bracket
8. Rear damper
9. Windshield assembly bolt
10. Front damper
11. Windshield support plate
12. Windshield bolt

1. Remove the nut from a windshield bolt, and remove the bolt.
2. Repeat Step 1 for the remaining windshield bolts on one side, and remove the support plate and front damper from that side.
3. Repeat Step 1 and Step 2 on the other side and remove the windshield. Account for the rear damper on each mounting plate.
4. Installation is the reverse of removal.

a. Install a rear damper, front damper and support plate on each side.

CAUTION
Do not overtighten the windshield nuts and bolts. The plastic windshield could be damaged.

b. Tighten each windshield nut securely.

Table 1 FRAME AND BODY TORQUE SPECIFICATIONS

Item	N•m	in.-lb.	ft.-lb.
Backrest bolts	23	–	17
Engine cover bolt	4	35	–
Front fender bolts	23	–	17
Passenger footpeg bracket bolts*	23	–	17
Passenger seat bracket bolts	16	–	12
Passenger seat holder bolts	16	–	12
Passenger seat bolts	16	–	12
Rear fender bracket bolts	23	–	17
Saddlebag bolts	18	–	13
Saddlebag bracket bolts	23	–	17
Saddlebag plate bolts	23	–	17
Seat bracket bolts	7	62	–
Side cover bolt	7	62	–
Sidestand bracket bolts*	56	–	41
Sidestand nut*	56	–	41
Sidestand switch bolts	4	35	–
Windshield assembly bolts	23	–	17
Windshield bracket bolts*			
Upper	48	–	35
Lower	23	–	17

*Refer to text.

15

INDEX

C

D

E

16

16

16

W

WIRING
DIAGRAMS

2007 MODELS

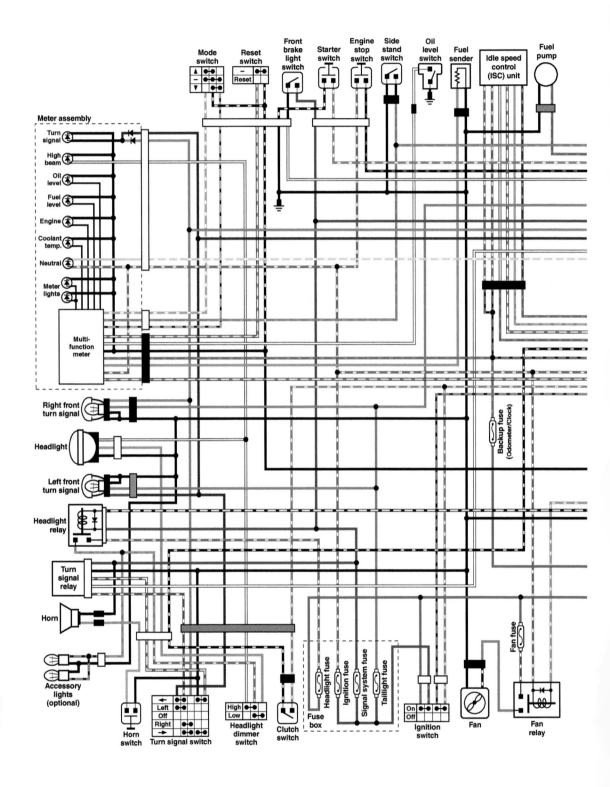

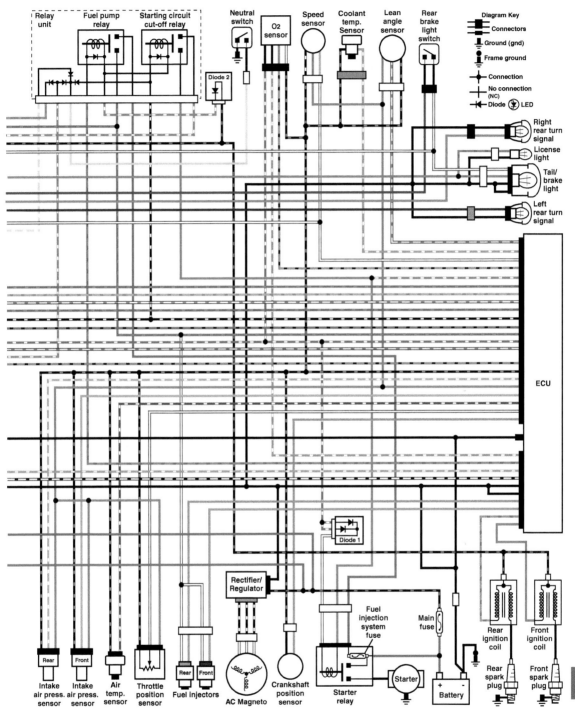

17

2008-2009 MODELS

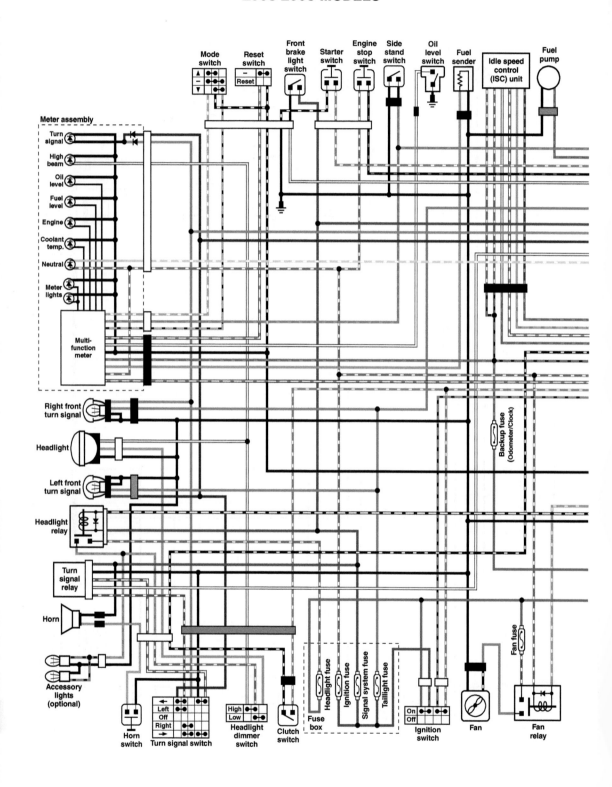

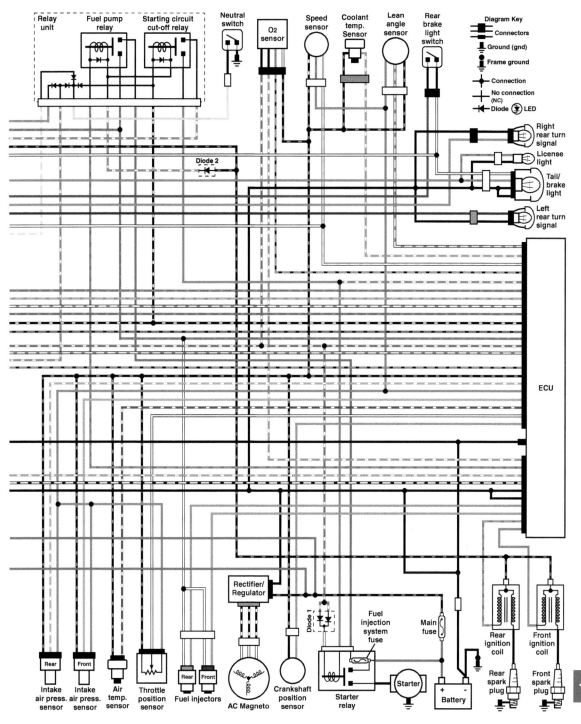

17

2010 MODELS

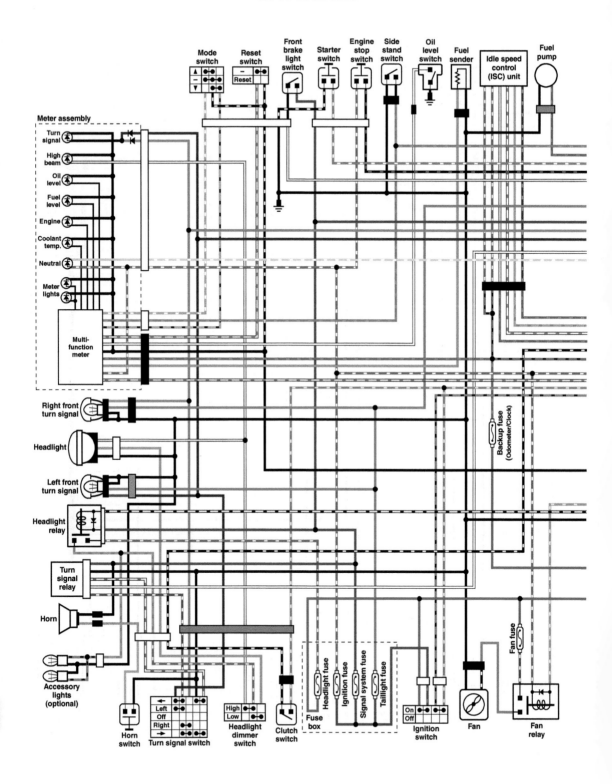

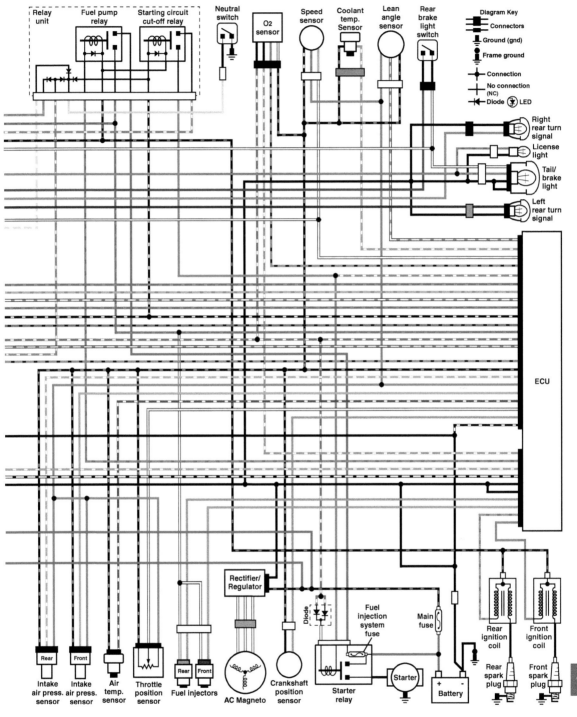

NOTES

NOTES

NOTES

NOTES

NOTES

MAINTENANCE LOG

Date	Miles	Type of Service

MAINTENANCE LOG

Date	Miles	Type of Service